I0884565

SEDITIONS

SUNY Series in Contemporary Continental Philosophy
Dennis J. Schmidt, editor

SEDITIONS

Heidegger and the Limit of Modernity

HERIBERT BOEDER

Translated,
Edited,
and with an Introduction by

MARCUS BRAINARD

State University of New York Press

Published by
State University of New York Press, Albany

Printed in the United States of America

For information, address State University of New York Press, State University Plaza, Albany, N.Y., 12246

Production by Marilyn P. Semerad
Marketing by Dana E. Yanulavich

Library of Congress Cataloging-in-Publication Data

Boeder, Heribert.
[Essays. English. Selections]
Seditions : Heidegger and the limit of modernity / Heribert Boeder ; translated, edited, and with an introduction by Marcus Brainard.
p. cm. — (SUNY series in contemporary continental philosophy)
Includes bibliographical references and indexes.
ISBN 0-7914-3531-8 (hc : alk. paper). — ISBN 0-7914-3532-6 (pb : alk. paper)
1. Heidegger, Martin, 1889–1976. 2. Philosophy. 3. Philosophy, Modern—29th century. I. Brainard, Marcus. II. Title.
III. Series.
B3279.H49B6313 1997
193–dc21 97-12835
CIP

10 9 8 7 6 5 4 3 2 1

Νηρέα δ' ἀψευδέα καὶ ἀληθέα γείνατο Πόντος,
πρεσβύτατον παίδων· αὐτὰρ καλέουσι γέροντα,
οὕνεκα νημερτής τε καὶ ἤπιος, οὐδὲ θεμίστων
λήθεται, ἀλλὰ δίκαια καὶ ἤπια δήνεα οἶδεν·

(But Pontos sired as the oldest of his children, Nereus, who neither distorts nor conceals anything; they call him 'the fatherly one' because he misleads no one and is gentle, nor does he ever lose sight of decrees, but always keeps appointed right and lenient options in view.)

– Hesiod, *Theogony* 233 ff.

CONTENTS

EDITOR'S INTRODUCTION

Seditions. By whom? And against which authority? Not by Heidegger, not against modernity, as the subtitle of this volume might lead one to believe. But by Heribert Boeder, and yet not against Heidegger and the modernity whose limit he marks but rather against contemporary thought and its Heidegger, its modernity, and, ultimately, its philosophy. And the divisive issue? First and foremost, difference. It is its radical attention to difference that decisively separates Boeder's thought from the contemporary discussion, which is enthralled by difference while, paradoxically enough, allowing it to wither perilously to mere similarity.

Already Plato saw that similarity poses the greatest danger to thinking: "whoever seeks to avoid deception must always and more than anything be on guard against similarities. For they are a very slippery sort of thing" (*Sophist* 231A 6 ff.). Kant, in turn, pinpointed the effect of such deception in expressing his concern about a tendency of his "syncretistic age, when a certain shallow and dishonest system of coalition between contradictory principles is devised because it is more acceptable to a public which is satisfied to know a little about everything and at bottom (*im ganzen*) nothing."[1] Since difference is the element of knowledge, the privileging of similarity has to result in the latter's expunction. And yet if, as Aristotle maintains, "[e]very intellectual teaching and every learning proceeds from a knowledge which was provided in advance" (*APo.* 71^{a}1), then it becomes clear in what way the privileging of similarity poses the greatest danger to thinking: it leaves the latter groundless and thus paralyzed. Since this danger manifests itself most forcibly today in the public's praise of difference, in its pluralistic mentality—for, as will be seen, what it calls 'difference' proves to be just similarity in disguise—the most pressing question has to be: how is this danger to be guarded against? By insisting not only in errancy but even more so in difference. And this is just what Boeder's thought does. Yet how does this set it apart from the aforementioned praise? Insofar as it focuses on that difference which requires a decision, one made on the ground of knowledge and thus following upon the acknowledgment of its necessary precedence over thinking, and in fact as the latter's very possibility.

The difference respected and at work here is not an indiscriminate distinguishing between possibilities, thus not just the generation of mere differences, which are then conjoined in endless series, but rather a distinguishing centered on the disjunction, on the either/or. In this regard the decision called for marks a transformation of what was formerly the judgment: on the basis of knowledge in the sense of what has already been decided, of what has been accomplished, it effects the exclusion of one option in favor of another, and in fact as that which is better—more precisely: the best. Since Boeder attends to thought alone, it is one thought that is excluded in favor of another, but only insofar as it makes a difference in the whole (*im Ganzen*), that is to say: all the difference. Hence, the difference honored here is not arbitrarily exclusive—as its basis in knowledge already indicates—but is made always and only with respect to the whole, whose "everything" is restricted to its integral parts, and in fact in view of constructing it as a totality. Only when a thought does not contribute to the establishment of the whole is it not taken into account. That this emphasis has to strike the public as seditious is already evident in the abhorrence the mere mention of exclusion arouses today; such has to run counter to the desire of a public living under the spell of *différance*. Nevertheless, the difference of chief concern here is ultimately and eminently that in which "everyone necessarily has an interest,"[2] namely, the difference harbored in the knowledge of the destiny of man as it has been voiced in the configurations of wisdom of our history: his destiny to distinguish himself from himself. The recovery of the knowledge of this destiny is Boeder's task. It alone grants the difference operative and of concern here its justification, its significance, and its urgency.

The sense of difference crucial to Boeder's thought gains further determinacy in the consideration of the three principial methodological moments of his undertaking in which it comes to bear—in the ἐποχή, the totality, and the ratio—as well as of the three totalities explicated by means of them—history, world, and speech. In what follows we shall outline in turn the significance of each of these clusters of "fundamental words" to his undertaking.

EPOCHÉ. The enabling moment of Boeder's thought is the ἐποχή. Although it is thematized only later, it nevertheless informs his thought from the very beginning, namely, in his pursuit of the intention to learn, whereby his understanding of intellectual learning rests on the deceptively simple distinction between what is to be learned and what one already knows. And this is bound up with the insight that learning is possible only to the extent that one listens to one who has knowledge. Hence, the attention to what is to be learned, to what one does not know, was seen to require reticence on the part of whomever wishes to learn, which is to say that one must initially cease to assert oneself, one's own concerns, and instead turn in openness and stillness to what is to be learned. Such reticence with respect to knowledge is the central feature of the ἐποχή operative in the thought presented in this volume.

Although Boeder's ἐποχή receives its originary impetus from Heidegger's, which itself is a transformation of the Husserlian ἐποχή, the talk in the foregoing of a knowledge that has precedence over thinking already indicates a crucial point of divergence from Heidegger and, furthermore, should make one hesitate to want to integrate Boeder into the phenomenological tradition, especially as his primary concern lies not at all with phenomena but only with thought as it is purified of all phenomenality. While it is true that for both Boeder and Husserl the performance of the ἐποχή brings about a modification of thinking and while neither allows this modification to give rise to the neutrality that paralyzes thinking and thereby renders it impotent, they part radically with regard to the character and end of the intended modification. On the one hand, Husserl's ἐποχή is purely instrumental; its methodical function is to open up the field of research proper to phenomenology, namely, pure consciousness, which is to provide an absolute foundation for knowledge. This ἐποχή can be employed or not—turned on or off, so to speak—at the will of the phenomenologist in order to effect the shift between the natural and the phenomenological attitudes. The ἐποχή excludes, or brackets, the thesis fundamental to the former attitude, namely, the "world-thesis," or the belief in the existence of the world, and thereby facilitates the move into the phenomenological attitude while also disclosing the desired field of research. If, however, the phenomenologist chooses to stop performing the ἐποχή, he then returns to the natural attitude and its world. By contrast, Boeder's ἐποχή plays no methodical role in the Husserlian sense, for it is rooted not in the foundational intention of an epistemology but in the aim to open a present for each thought that makes a difference. This ἐποχή cannot be turned on and off at will—hence there is no shift between attitudes. Rather, the thinking presented here always takes place, as it were, within it, under its influence. Furthermore, and most importantly, Boeder's ἐποχή does not target a thesis but instead "purifies" thinking of all idiosyncrasy, of all narcissism, which one might be tempted to impose upon what has been thought. The exclusion of narcissism yields the said reticence; such frees one to turn to the "*Sache selbst*" (thing itself) as it presents—that is, gives—itself.

Clearly such reticence was learned from Heidegger and in fact as *Gelassenheit* (releasement). However, whereas for Boeder it forms the starting point of thinking, for Heidegger it has a resultant character, coming to the fore only in the final phase of his thought: it itself is not Heidegger's ἐποχή but only the response to the latter. Here *Gelassenheit* follows upon his transformation of the exclusion proper to Husserl's ἐποχή, and in fact in the former's experience of the calamity marked by the "epoch"—a keeping-to-itself (*An-sich-halten*), a retention, even a withdrawal—of that which gives what is to be thought. It is his experience of "the mission (*Geschick*) of the withdrawal of the topic of thinking" that is decisive for his ἐποχή. And this is where Boeder parts with Heidegger, his teacher: instead of receiving its impulse from the latter's negative experience of what has been given, Boeder's thought is moved by the insight into the gift itself in the beginning of philosophy—an insight enabled only by a radicalization of this ἐποχή such that even Heidegger's thought was subjected to it; all thinking within the ἐποχή knows itself to be dependent upon the knower for the "gift," as it were, of the knowledge sought. This radicalization and the said insight necessitated the transformation of *Gelassenheit* into the distinguished sense of reticence operative in Boeder's thought. If for Heidegger *Gelassenheit* is a waiting upon that which withdraws itself from thinking, for Boeder it is the reverent (cf. αἰδώς) attention to what has been given, which entails a *Lassen* whereby one is "no longer determined to leave metaphysics to itself (*sich selbst überlassen*)"—which for Heidegger means leaving it behind—"but rather [is] in a position to leave it to its self and thus to let it be (*sein lassen*)."[3] *Lassen* in this sense at once brings about the liberation of metaphysical thinking from its continuum with technical thinking as posited by Heidegger and its detemporalization. Here, in keeping with the later Heidegger, the piety of thinking is no longer a questioning but rather a listening to what has been said (*das Gesagte*), though this has now taken on the distinguished sense of what is known (*das Gewußte*). It is precisely in Boeder's transformation of this piety into the acknowledgment of and attention to a preceding knowledge, of and to the gift that this knowledge represents, that the productivity of his thought becomes most apparent. It arises from decisions made in accordance with this gift and responds, as Boeder puts it, "logotectonically" to Heidegger's call for a "poetizing thinking" (*dichtendes Denken*).

TOTALITY. The elucidation of the gift here in question as well as of the productivity to which it gives rise is afforded only by way of Heidegger's question 'What is metaphysics?' and the decisive hint it gave to Boeder's undertaking. It directed his attention to metaphysics as a concluded whole, as a totality whose end was necessitated by its beginning. And yet his investigation of this totality revealed that Heidegger's account was errant: metaphysics proved to be not just a simple totality in the sense of the continuously increasing oblivion of that which gives what is to be thought, a totality whose end was marked by the decay of metaphysical into technical thinking.[4] And it no longer bore out

Heidegger's assertion that this thinking fell in a single epoch of the mission of the withdrawal of the topic of thinking. Furthermore, the topic of thinking was found to be not singular, i.e., not solely the Being of beings,[5] but different. Combined with the insight into the precedence of knowledge, these observations led Boeder to renew Heidegger's question, this time putting it to that metaphysics itself which was held to have come to an end. Its answer became evident as the result of Boeder's complete traversal of the whole of metaphysics, which showed itself to be a totality composed of three epochs, a state of affairs which accorded with the tripartite determination of the whole that metaphysics itself established for thought. Namely, in metaphysics the triad was esteemed as the simplest complete construct[6]—put abstractly: as possessing the unity of the syllogism and consisting of beginning, middle, and end, where the middle mediates the two extremes. A totality circumscribes "everything," though not everything in the usual sense of every single possibility. Rather, it comprises only the necessary parts, where their necessity is confirmed, as Aristotle put it with reference to drama, by the fact that they are "so closely connected that the transposal or withdrawal of any one of them will disjoin and dislocate the whole. For that which makes no perceptible difference by its presence or absence is no real part of the whole" (*Poetics*, 1451^{a}33 ff.). For Boeder a part makes a difference in the whole—that is, all the difference—only insofar as its presence necessarily contributes to the completion of that whole, helps totalize it, as it were; otherwise that part is not integral and thus makes no difference. This is the precise sense of difference on which Boeder's thought focuses; there is no room here for similarity, such as that thrived upon in the discussion of influences and effective histories, but only for rational positions, purified of all phenomenality, that are integral to a given totality.

Boeder has drawn the distinguished positions of each totality together into an architectonic, a topology—first of metaphysics, then of modernity, and now of contemporary thought. The logic employed in doing so is topological insofar as the aim is to differentiate the "complete" rational positions (the τόποι of the system) and then exhibit their relation to other such positions by arranging them in a "well-formed" architectonic—in the said totality. And yet, whereas Boeder's thought is guided by a systematic intention, i.e., to explicate the unity of a given totality, his work is by no means syncretistic, for the construction of a topology as he understands it hinges on the differences between its constituent parts. As will be seen, insofar as the history of philosophy is one of strife, of the crises of principles, there can be no facile reconciliation between divergent rational positions. Though any one type of reason does have three representatives in an epoch which are united by a common task (e.g., Kant, Fichte, and Hegel in the final epoch) and though that reason has counterparts in the other epochs (namely, Parmenides, Plato, and Aristotle in the first and Plotinus, Augustine, and Aquinas in the middle epochs), the differences between each position and each epoch are maintained—they are always guaranteed by the role the representative position plays in the fulfillment of an epochally-specific task and its determinative principle. The arrangement of these positions in an architectonic does not preclude difference but in fact preserves it by bringing the differences in the whole to determinacy.

This employment of the topology has obviously been learned neither from modernity nor from so-called postmodernity, which confounds thinking in terms of the totality with totalitarianism. Rather, it is metaphysics that has shown Boeder how to build logotectonically, to construct rational totalities—which were the sole subject of metaphysical thought. In his work, rationality is disclosed by way of interlocking wholes, where the "macrostructure" is given by the "logotectonic," which encapsulates the totalities of history, world, and speech. However, the actual key to the building central to Boeder's undertaking lies in the ratio (τόπος). It enables him to unlock the "microstructure" of the topology's constituent parts (its τόποι) and thereby to bring the talk of reason, rationality, and rational positions to determinacy.

RATIO. Contrary to trends in contemporary thought that are imbued with "a certain degree of misology, i.e., hatred of reason" (Kant, *GMS*, 395.33/11)—literally: hatred of the λόγος—Boeder's intention is to honor reason, both in its historical and mundane manifestations and in its present. Such talk already implies a distinction of reason, and in fact one that reason itself demands, for it has shown itself differently in metaphysics, in modernity, and in our present—despite the prevailing habit of viewing reason as somehow continuous, as having had a uniform character extending from some indeterminate "prehistoric" beginning of thought down to our present. Seen from our vantage point, on this side of the closure of metaphysics as well as of modernity, reason has indeed assumed a new actuality. But which? First, regarding its historical manifestations: in each epoch philosophical reason depended on the givenness of a divine reason for its actuality—even in its final epoch, in which the divinity was not a god but rather Nature (cf. *Sed*, 183).[7] In modernity, however, this principle, this ground, was expunged and thus the departedness of philosophical reason was sealed. As a result, reason could no longer be the faculty of principles but only the shadow of its former self, namely, thinking. The groundlessness of modern reason and its consequent indeterminacy has been deepened in so-called postmodernity, where reason is rejected because it is considered to be the source of dominance and terror (Lyotard). In light of these events, how could reason possibly attain actuality in our present? As strange as it may sound, by way of modernity's very rejection of philosophical reason: "Modernity requires and frees us to translate what has been regarded philosophically as 'reason' into a *ratio terminorum*" (11). By-passing the prevailing habit of confounding reason with thinking, the approach to reason operative here is one based on the acknowledgment first of the departedness of its historical manifestations and then of the fading of its modern transformations; reason regains its determinacy and thus its dignity via the attention to the difference it has made. In fact it was only the renewal of Heidegger's question 'What is metaphysics?' and the thematization of the totality it enabled that gave rise to this acknowledgment and, as a consequence, to the aforementioned translation. How so? In his investigation of the totality of metaphysics, the former science of reason, Boeder found it to be the history of the works of reason, of its philosophical accomplishments. Out of its groundlessness reason has regained its solidity as the *ratio terminorum* and thus has taken on a purely technical significance within the frame of the logotectonic: "Such a ratio, as it is realized in the work, is the only one we can experience and from which we can learn pure reason" (217). It is in this sense, then, that its present actuality is no mere legacy, but instead the result of both a recovery and a violent construction—for reason is not something that is already there waiting to be found, but must be elicited, demonstrated, or more precisely: built. In Boeder's thought it is the ratio that forms the basis of such building.

Here he has responded to Heidegger's call for a "poetizing thinking" (*dichtendes Denken*) first by transforming the sense of *Dichten* into a *Verdichten*, a compression, condensation. His is a poetizing in the sense of a building, and in fact of a refined logotectonic out of integral rational positions. Each of these positions is explicated as a ratio, a word whose usage capitalizes on its twofold sense: on the one hand, ratio as Latin for 'reason', and on the other, ratio as proportion. Due to the aforementioned translation reason is freed from its vague association with an innate human faculty and is now nothing but the ratio—"reason is a mere fiction at the point where it cannot realize itself in a basic and objective ratio" (146)—and rationality inheres in the practice of explicating it and its place within an architectonic built of such ratios but also in that architectonic itself and, by extension, in the logotectonic. The latter is an articulated totality, which is a three-tiered hierarchy of wholes. As for metaphysics, which, as will be seen, is paradigmatic for all of Boeder's building, it is a totality made up of three epochs, each of which consists of three types of reason. Each type manifests itself as a figure, which is the combination of three positions that are unified by a common task. As the smallest whole within this edifice, the ratio provides the means of laying out the structure of each position as well as making explicit how each fits together with its complementary positions into that figure. The ratio itself is a proportion built out of three terms, which derive from the dissolution of Heidegger's phrase 'the destiny of the topic of thinking' (*die Bestimmung der Sache des Denkens*).[8] The corresponding notation employed in the essays presented here is A (destiny),[9] B (topic), and C (thinking).[10] In the construction of a rational figure it is the term-sequence of its incipient ratio that is determinative of the complementary ratios in that figure. For instance, the first ratio in a figure of natural reason has the sequence C B A. Since the subsequent ratio always begins with the final term of the preceding ratio (and this holds for the construction of any figure within the logotectonic), the second ratio of natural reason has the form: A C B. Hence, the third ratio is written B A C.[11] This figure will be taken up again below in more detail and so in connection with the other types of reason constitutive of the totality of history; for now, at issue is simply the specification of the sequence of the terms as well as how the respective ratios fit together into a figure.

The exhibition of a thought as a whole composed of these three terms is said to be a "simplification" of thought (cf., e.g., 150-151), and yet it is a simplification not because it makes a thought easier to grasp or more immediately comprehensible, and so "does not claim to possess any didactic value" (162). Rather, it is as a condensation of that thought into its principal moments. But is Boeder's work not reductive, does the thought thus "condensed" not lose its richness, its "multifariousness," by way of its explication as a ratio? No. The usual sense of reduction implies that something has been left out. And yet insofar as the thought (as a ratio) is a *whole*, insofar as its unity has been demonstrated by means of the interconnection of its terms, there can be no talk of anything having been left out—for the ratio includes *everything* essential to its construction. This condensation has the chief benefit of making the completeness of a given figure perspicuous, and by extension that of an epoch and of the totality in question. And yet while it does enable one to note differences between rational positions more readily, it is not the last word on the characterization of a thought. Already given the repetition of rational sequences within other figures of, say, natural reason in other epochs but also within other types of reason, more information is needed in order to distinguish one ratio from another with the same sequence: for instance, the epochal principle or lack thereof to which the thought is subject, and the latter's corresponding task. These and other features will be taken up in what follows.

While the aim of the foregoing was to sketch the main methodological moments of Boeder's thought as well as to fix the sense of difference crucial to it, the specific productivity of his work—and hence the difference it makes—is to be seen most clearly in the doing itself, that is, in his explication of the three totalities of history, world, and speech. They themselves form in turn a whole—the logotectonic—the completion of which is the aim of Boeder's entire undertaking. It is on account of this that the present volume is divided as it is; in this way it may be said to give a cross section of his thought to date.

Though they often differ with respect to the totality thematized, the essays collected here are unified principally by the fact that Heidegger's thought is the chief concern or the starting point of each. He remains, to be sure, the mediating figure in Boeder's work, the one who instigated his "seditious" turn to the totalities of thought—beginning with the explication of history and then of the world and ultimately transgressing the latter's limit (and thus parting with Heidegger's thought) into the present of speech—and his consequent demonstration of their rationality in the form of the logotectonic. It is to Heidegger's achievement that Boeder's building responds, even though such building was dismissed by his teacher due to its "technical" character. Oddly enough, it is just the translation of technical reason—that is, logotectonic reason—operative in these essays that has managed to open up a present for the totalities of history, world, and speech, a present which Heidegger, though able to sense the significance of each, was unable to appreciate sufficiently.[12] And yet, as will be seen, wherever Boeder does engage in a critique of Heidegger's thought (which is most pronounced in the first four essays in the first section), such is motivated not by a desire to correct some "error" or to outdo him, but rather by the necessity of disclosing differences that Heidegger's account had to cover over in his effort to clarify and fulfill his own task. Such a critique is not just negative but fruitful, which is most conspicuous in the threefold benefit of the said disclosure: the limits of Heidegger's thought as determined by its task are discerned, philosophical thought is allowed to appear in its proper light, and the present task of thinking comes into view. On the other hand, one would err in reducing Boeder's repeated reference to Heidegger, explicit or implicit, to the mere dependence of a student upon his teacher; rather, such reference finds its justification solely in Heidegger's position within modernity, where he marks its limit, one that points to a new present for thinking. And the latter's task? Such gains determinacy only by way of Boeder's explication of the aforementioned totalities, each of which will be addressed in turn in what follows.

HISTORY.[13] This is the first totality Boeder encountered and explicated, and it has remained decisive—literally: *maßgeblich*—for his thought, in all his building. The turn to the totality was not motivated by some predilection on

Boeder's part but was instead a response to a directive that metaphysics itself gave to his thought. As noted above, he became aware of history—initially approached as metaphysics—as a totality only upon renewing Heidegger's question 'What is metaphysics?' Given the reticence so central to Boeder's guiding intention to learn and his thought in general, the scrutiny required by such a questioning would have been out of place were it not for a discrepancy he first perceived between Heidegger's experience of ἀ-λήθεια, of truth as unconcealment, and its significance in early Greek thinking. Heidegger's experience of its privative sense led him to assert the originariness of concealment and thus to see its primary instance in φύσις, which he held to be the site of a simultaneous "double-pivoting" between "an emergence into appearance and a self-concealment" (5). It is on account of this that he placed emphasis on the concealment proper to κρύπτεσθαι, citing Heraclitus's phrase φύσις κρύπτεσθαι φιλεῖ (Nature tends to conceal itself) as the first expression of ἀλήθεια in philosophy. Here he finds reason to believe that metaphysics, from its very beginning and continuously thereafter until its decay into technical thinking, is the history of oblivion, wherein the proper topic of thinking is increasingly forgotten. This manifests itself most intensely in his experience of the mission of the withdrawal of that topic, of the Being of beings. And yet, while disputing neither the legitimacy of such assertions given Heidegger's task nor the centrality of concealment to the proper understanding of ἀλήθεια, the early Greek usage of this word made Boeder aware of its originary basis in knowledge rather than in phenomena. Namely, he noted that concealment was fundamental to ἀλήθεια not as the κρύπτεσθαι of a φύσις but rather as the "positive" λήθειν (to deceive someone) as it bears upon knowledge. On the basis of this discovery Boeder was impelled to reevaluate the meaning of ἀλήθεια and in fact in its usage *prior* to the beginning of Heidegger's history of oblivion: in Greek epic poetry (cf. his "The Early Greek Usage of the Words *Logos* and *Aletheia*"). There he found that the transitive sense of λήθειν was the key to the originary understanding of ἀλήθεια. The deception indicated by this word manifests itself as the possibility of denying someone participation in a certain knowledge or of "pulling the wool over someone's eyes"—and is always expressed in a λόγος. Hence, one who wishes to know is dependent upon another who already knows and who may deceive him regarding the desired knowledge—in this respect there is an originary inequity regarding knowledge. Furthermore, the knower is in a position to decide whether and what the one seeking knowledge is entitled to know. Here and for the whole of Boeder's undertaking the fundamental insight is that ἀλήθεια is a feature of knowledge and hence of reason and that it has its element in the λόγος—not in φύσις. The insight into the gift determinative of Boeder's thought has its roots precisely in the disclosure of this originary state of affairs.

It is this insight, namely, into the gift of knowledge, as opposed to the experience of withdrawal, that motivated Boeder's reticent reappraisal of Heidegger's account of the first beginning of thought over against the other beginning. Boeder put the question 'What is metaphysics?' to metaphysics itself and, in keeping with the results of the said investigation of ἀλήθεια, found that metaphysics was not the history of oblivion but of reason, of knowledge, a history that Boeder later elaborates in his *Topology of Metaphysics*. The first two pieces in the present volume represent integral steps on the way to that elaboration.

"Why 'Being of Beings'?" is an investigation of the first two epochs of metaphysics in light of Heidegger's assertion that metaphysics has always had but one topic of thinking, the Being of beings. The significance of this essay lies, on the one hand, in Boeder's having shown that Heidegger's question of Being remains Heidegger's and is not, despite the latter's claims, the fundamental question of metaphysics. But the other, and initially more significant, achievement here is the demonstration of the fact that there is not just one topic of thinking, not just one concern of reason. This is shown most forcefully by his analysis of Aristotelian thought, where the topic is found to be not the Being of beings but being *qua* being. For Plotinus, on the other hand, the topic proves to be the two hypostases, spirit and soul. It becomes evident that not only the topic of thinking differs for these two positions but also the principles of the two epochs in which each is situated, such that, generally speaking, for the first epoch the principle is *justice* and for the middle epoch, *grace*. (Likewise, the principle of the final epoch is *freedom*; cf., e.g., p. 88 below.) Also noteworthy is that Boeder here makes strides towards the determination of the name 'metaphysics' by distinguishing First Philosophy from other manifestations of philosophy, e.g., that of the Stoics; he thereby calls into question the legitimacy of using the name 'metaphysics' in referring to the "whole" of philosophy, for it promotes the leveling of differences within the tradition. Here too it has become clear to Boeder that there is not just one uniform and continuous history of philosophy but a differentiated one, whose strata are made up of the different types of reason found in what is usually called 'metaphysics'. This insight impelled him to seek to articulate a differentiated history of reason.

In "The Difference Inherent in the 'Other Beginning'," Boeder takes his insight into the difference of reason one step further and for the first time lays out the architectonic of the whole of philosophy—taken "in the unity [not: uniformity] of a singular history"—and demonstrates the distinct tasks of the figures of natural and conceptual reason, respectively, in each of the three epochs of philosophy. Here his concern is to make perspicuous the distinction of reason *from* itself, or of First Philosophy from its other, a concern that also guides the construction of the *Topology*. In fact, the distinction of reason *within* itself (i.e., between natural and mundane reason) comes into view only after Boeder has taken up the totality of the world, i.e., of modernity as he articulates it in *The Rational Architectonic of Modernity*. His inquiry in this essay focuses exclusively on these two types of reason since his initial aim is to show that, contrary to Heidegger's reading, there was not just one type of reason unified by one topic and that the ground of their distinction lay in a difference in the task each type seeks to fulfill. (Another reason for not including mundane reason in the architectonic in this phase of his thought was that prior to the *Rational Architectonic* Boeder did not see this third kind of reason within metaphysics; his view was obstructed by the fact that he was still caught up in the horizon of Heideggerian thought. Thus, to begin with, he distinguished metaphysical from mundane reason in the same way that he distinguished the totality of history from that of the world. As will be seen, Boeder later came to distinguish the modern transformation of "historical" mundane reason and thereby was able to accord the latter its proper place in metaphysics.) In the architectonic sketched in this essay the positions of each epoch are divided into two figures: those of natural reason (c, b, a) and conceptual reason (A, B, C). Unlike the other, later essays in this volume the articulation of these ratios takes only philosophy into account; this changes when in working out his *Topology* Boeder hits upon the necessary relation of philosophy to a preceding wisdom. Hence, though he speaks of conceptual reason, the notion of conception remains indeterminate, and at best related to Hegel's concept. It is only with the insight into the necessary relation of philosophy to wisdom, into the dependence of the former upon the latter, that 'conception' gains its proper sense: the sheltering of the truth of a configuration of wisdom (σοφία)—namely, the knowledge of the Muses, of the Christian doctrine, and finally of the civil consciousness—in a logic and thereby investing it with the persuasiveness truth always needs in order to win anyone over. At this stage of Boeder's thought, the aforementioned figures always retain the same structure from epoch to epoch, which now holds only of the figures of wisdom, for it is in fact related only to itself. All of this building is carried out in the interest of establishing the uniqueness of the philosophy issuing from the first beginning as distinct from Heidegger's thought of the other beginning, a distinction that reveals the gulf between the totalities of history and the world.

As noted above, the fruitfulness of Boeder's critique of Heidegger is most conspicuous in its opening up a present for each of the totalities of concern here. To achieve this the continuum that Heidegger projected from technical thinking back into metaphysical thinking first has to be torn asunder; such is brought about insofar as the differences specific to and determinative of the totalities of history, world, and speech are made explicit. This intention has informed the critical dimension of Boeder's work from the "The Early Greek Usage of the Words *Logos* and *Aletheia*" to "Why 'Being of Beings'?" down to the more recent "Privilege of Presence?" In the latter he takes up another of Heidegger's fundamental assertions, namely, that metaphysics always understood Being as 'presence' (*Anwesenheit*) and its sense as 'being-present' (*Anwesen*). Here Boeder looks to the whole of metaphysics as well as to pre-philosophical sources for testimony regarding the alleged privilege of presence. Heidegger's assertion relies on the presumed phenomenal or "physical" basis of presence, whereas Boeder shows that in and before philosophy it is first and foremost a feature of reason. This becomes quite clear in the consideration of the Greek παρεῖναι (*Anwesen*): he shows that the presence it denotes is less the Being of an appearance than that of the intellect attending to it, which is confirmed by Heraclitus's use of the term: "'To be present' means 'to attend to and to understand something', thus 'presence of mind'. Only with reference to such attention is something in turn present and not just there or apparent" (84). Hence, its originary sense is bound up with reason (λόγος and νοῦς) and only secondarily with an appearance (φανερόν) and its φύσις, and this remains the basic sense of 'presence' throughout the variegated course of metaphysics. Further corroboration of this is provided by the nature of ἀλήθεια, "which is restricted to φάσις, to rendering something present in speech, because this something is out of view and thus inaccessible to attention. In order to know it, one has to rely on the willingness of a witness to communicate his knowledge. The witness is the one who was present and therefore knows" (84 f.). There is nothing "physical" here about the presence of significance to philosophical thought and its predecessor. In showing that Heidegger's claim is a projection necessitated by his own task and that it remains restricted to the latter, it becomes clear that the history in question is that of reason alone.

This is a first answer to the question 'What is metaphysics?' But the definitive answer results from "the distinction of reason," which is carried out by sharpening that question to 'What is philosophy?' Heidegger also raised this question,[14] turning to the name φιλοσοφία in order to elucidate the topic of the "first beginning" of thinking. It is in Heraclitus that he finds his answer, namely, that it is the love of τὸ σοφόν, which Heidegger shows in the end to be the Being of beings.[15] Boeder has shown that this answer is not borne out by metaphysics but has its rightful place in the horizon of Heideggerian thought. Instead he finds metaphysics' answer in the literal sense of 'philosophy', as the love of wisdom, which harbors the knowledge of man's destiny to distinguish himself from himself. This love manifests itself as the conceptual devotion, as it were, of φιλο-σοφία to a given σοφία, a devotion that conceptual reason demonstrates in its conception of that wisdom by effecting the distinction of reason. Metaphysics or philo-sophy proves to be just the accomplished works of this type of reason and so can be reduced to neither ontology nor theology nor henology.

In history reason is of three distinct types, each being determined precisely by the character of its relation to an epochal configuration of wisdom; in fact it is the strife between these types of reason over one of these configurations and its bequest that manifests itself in each epoch as a crisis of principles, on the basis of which alone the distinction of reason becomes possible. In the inaugural phase of each epoch *natural* reason comes first; its incipient ratio begins with thinking and is followed by the topic and then the destinal term—its notation reads C B A and marks an inversion of the incipient ratio of wisdom (A B C). It should be noted that its "naturalness" does not consist in the fact that it is "everyday," "innate," or "originary," but rather in its concern with thinking, which in the first epoch, e.g., discerns the distinction between a phenomenon and its Natures (φύσεις). Its first representatives make up the figure of physiology (Thales, Anaximenes, Xenophanes). By contrast, *mundane* reason is chiefly concerned with its topic, which in the first epoch is the κόσμος: not the world but the order of appearances. Its first representatives make up the figure of cosmology (Anaximander, Pythagoras, Heraclitus), the first ratio of which reads B A C.[16] Both of these types of reason have a negative relation to the given configuration of wisdom—which is why its destinal term is rendered as 'governing principle'—and seek to replace the rejected wisdom with one of their own. However, they differ regarding the aim of the wisdom they seek to establish: whereas mundane reason seeks to replace wisdom with its own productive distinction of man, one that, e.g., urges man to cultivate the "dry" soul in place of the "wet" soul (Heraclitus), or that he distinguish himself as a political being from his natural state (Hobbes), natural reason does not propose such a distinction but instead lays emphasis on the finitude of human understanding and the importance of man's being satisfied with how he is (cf. Xenophanes)—and it is just this satisfaction that indicates the pertinent sense of the epithet 'natural' for this type of reason. The distinction between natural and mundane reason marks reason's distinction *within* itself. The distinction of reason is completed, however, in its distinction *from* itself, which is effected by *conceptual* reason in its rejection of the previous two, whereby it purifies itself. This rejection is motivated by its positive, sheltering relation to the configurations of wisdom. Each figure of conceptual reason, which in the first epoch is made up of Parmenides', Plato's, and Aristotle's ratios, is carried by the destinal term, that is, by the destinal principle, so that its opening ratio is written as A C B. In each instance these positions "make all the difference" due to their rational sequences but also due to their contribution to the completion of a figure and thereby of an epoch and finally of the totality of history.[17]

Such completion marks "an end with distinction," both in the sense of differentiation and of dignity. The nature of this end sets it apart from the end of metaphysics as it was grasped by Hegel and by Heidegger: it neither results upon the complete development of the concept, whereby philosophy becomes equal to its idea, nor is it the decay of metaphysical into technical thinking. But neither does anyone put an end to it, as Dilthey asserts of historical consciousness. Rather, as Boeder makes clear, metaphysics ends upon the fulfillment of the epochal tasks set for it by wisdom; it departs in the certainty: "it is accomplished." Such becomes apparent only by way of that transformation of thinking which is made possible only by leaving metaphysics to its self, by acknowledging its departure and thus its abysmal difference from modern and also contemporary thought. Only by doing so is each of the three totalities of concern here granted its own present. In the attention to its departure, to its difference, it should already be clear that Boeder's undertaking is no mere attempt to resuscitate metaphysics, and certainly not to representiate it, but rather to make perspicuous and thus to honor what philosophy has been, that is, what it has accomplished. It is in view of its accomplishments, and especially of its supreme accomplishment in bringing about its end, that philo-sophy established the totality of history as the standard for all subsequent thinking, judgment, and thus building.

WORLD. With the end of metaphysics, with the closure of history, a caesura is drawn, a cut that opens a unique present for a new totality, namely, that of the world. This is the world of modernity. Not of the modern era (*Neuzeit*), but of a modernity (*Moderne*) completely severed from its history, which continues to have its present as the "underworld" of this world. A new kind of reason asserts itself here which marks a necessary impoverishment of its philo-sophical predecessor. Such was necessitated by the prevailing lack of a destiny (*Bestimmungslosigkeit*) in modernity, a lack resulting from the absence of all wisdom once philo-sophy carried it off with it in making its departure. Typically enough, the crisis experienced by modern reason in the aftermath of this departure and wisdom's consequent absence, manifested itself not in the acknowledgment of these events but rather in the outright rejection of philosophical reason, an act which effectively amounted to its asserting itself against a specter, though this had to seem otherwise to modern reason, whose task it was to establish the world as a totality separate from that of its history. A sign of the modern impoverishment of reason is to be seen in its replacement of "the proper subjects of reason"—totalities which Kant identified as "the transcendental ideas . . . of the immortality of the soul, the createdness of the universe, and the existence of God" (135)—with totalities of its own. Here modern reason testifies to its resolute worldliness by concentrating on totalities that are "exclusively determined by human existence," and not by reason. The new totalities—which Boeder has shown to be history, world, and speech[18]—"betray a reason which cannot be solely occupied with itself"—in contrast to metaphysical reason, and it is this inability that makes its impoverishment most conspicuous—"inasmuch as it is bound to deny these totalities an originary rationality. What is, or what is given"—that is, Being—"appears to be not only different from thinking as such but also prior to it. The idea, however, was not only the manifestation of what is but also of what is insofar as it is to be, it being what is reasonable." The privileging of Being, of what is, over what is insofar as it is to be, is in fact a privileging of Being over Being in the sense of being-accomplished, which, as noted above, was the result of conceptual reason's fulfillment of its destiny (how it is to be), the knowledge of which was bequeathed to it by a configuration of wisdom. Modernity's necessary rejection of the idea, then, proves to be the simultaneous rejection of the accomplishments of reason and of the wisdom which inspired them. In this way the principial character of reason is expunged, leaving modernity with just thinking, and in fact one that is always only secondary to Being. As a consequence, in modernity the gift, or bequest, that makes all the difference is transferred from the realm of reason to that of Being.

But which modernity is this? That which Boeder has laid out in *The Rational Architectonic of Modernity*, which he now sees to span from Dilthey's ratio by way of Schlick's down to Heidegger's. Its explication as an architectonic became possible only upon the acknowledgment of the end of modernity—a state of affairs implicit in the label under which contemporary thought stands: 'postmodernity'. And yet Boeder's modernity is clearly at odds with the one to which this 'post' refers, especially as contemporary thought tends to assume that it is continuous, extending roughly from Descartes to Heidegger. Its modernity is in essence the modern era, whose project has gone on and on until it somehow reached its "end" recently—though even after its demise it still seems to be present in our discourse. The lack of differentiation operative in the assumption of such a continuum becomes evident upon the exhibition of the *closedness* of history—not just *that* it has come to an end but rather *how* it has done so, namely, in showing *what* it has accomplished. The endowment of this end with such determinacy is one of Boeder's main achievements with regard to history. And it is on the basis of this achievement that he was able to turn to a modernity wrested from the said continuum and to grant it its dignity. This becomes visible upon the explication of its own end and thus its peculiar unity.

"Reason in Modern Thought" contains the results of Boeder's first efforts following the *Topology* to account for the whole of modernity logotectonically. However, although the majority of its fundamental traits are already in place here, the present its reason is accorded has not yet been fully sundered from that of metaphysics, nor from the present in which Boeder's own thought is situated. On the one hand, the worldliness of the mundane reason thematized in this essay has not yet been distinguished from the historicity of its predecessor, that is to say, it has not yet been shown that and how "modern" mundane reason has its own dignity while also being a transformation of "historical" mundane reason.[19] This is due to the fact that the latter has not yet been discerned in its own right, and for two reasons: first, because Boeder's approach to history was mediated by modernity, because he viewed its history through the lens, as it were, of modern mundane reason, he was initially blind to the existence of a kindred reason in history; second, this was intensified by the prominence given to natural reason in and prior to the *Topology*, a type of reason whose negativity temporarily eclipsed that specific to historical mundane reason—for prior to the explication of the distinction of reason within itself, the differences in the shared agonistic stance of natural and mundane reason towards conceptual reason remained closed to Boeder, and hence historical mundane reason initially was not discerned. On the other hand, in this essay Boeder has not yet fully recognized that his thought addresses modernity from the "outside" instead of from the "inside"; this is confirmed, e.g., by both its original title—"Reason in Present Thought"—and his reference to "our reason" as "mundane."[20] As in the case of the totality of history, the unavoidability of engaging the totality of the world solely from the outside becomes visible only upon the full acknowledgment of its closedness as a totality, a state of affairs which is expressed in Boeder's *Rational Architectonic*.—It should be noted that the point of these remarks (and this holds for all such remarks throughout this introduction) is not to bring "mistakes" to the reader's attention but rather to make clear which revisions Boeder's thought has undergone in the course of the unfolding and fulfillment of his own task. There are, after all, no mistakes in thinking, but only in historial scholarship, which thrives upon "correctness" without seeing that the conditions of "adequacy" implied in that notion are set by the task intrinsic to the thought and never by an extrinsic source, such as a community of experts. Each stage of an intellectual (*denkerisch*) undertaking must be accorded its own right in view of both the "sub"-task aimed at at the time and its contribution to the fulfillment of the larger task, which orients the entire undertaking.—All things considered, the achievement of this essay in view of Boeder's task is to be seen precisely in his construction of the architectonic of modernity and in fact as a closed whole; its construction hinges on the distinction of modern reason, which in this essay is taken in general as "mundane" as opposed to "metaphysical" reason. It is just the distinction of modern reason that has enabled both the disclosure of an historical mundane reason and thereby the aforementioned distinction of reason within itself—between natural and mundane reason in history—and the discernment of its modern counterpart in its uniqueness. Such ultimately led to the refinement of the architectonics of history and the world while also opening up a view to our present.

As decisions are always made here only in view of what has already been decided, the decisions Boeder has made in constructing the architectonic of modernity were based on the precedent set by metaphysics; it has provided him with the standards by which to build. Accordingly the acknowledgment of the end of modernity led him to expect a unified whole, one whose end marks the conclusion of its beginning by way of its middle. And yet although, in keeping with the foregoing determination of the whole, it too has a tripartite structure, the totality of the world differs from that of its history in that it comprises not three epochs but rather three sense-explicative dimensions, namely, the sense-explication: of the interpreted life, of the sciences, and of the productive nature of man.[21] Each of these names a figure of modern reason, each of which is made up of three rational positions, or ratios: hermeneutic (Dilthey, Husserl, Wittgenstein), technical (Frege, Schlick, Kuhn), and temporal or apocalyptic (Marx, Nietzsche, Heidegger) reason, respectively. These are ordered such that hermeneutic reason occupies the periphery of modernity, whereas apocalyptic reason, its core; technical reason mediates between these extremes. The construction of this totality already makes visible a key difference between it and its antecedent: the totality of the world marks an abridgment of the totality of history, a state of affairs deriving from the aforementioned impoverishment of the historical manifestation of reason. Hence, whereas history consists of three epochs, each of which is made up of three different figures of reason which are subject to the principle specific to that epoch, the world may be said to have only one epoch, which is made up of three dimensions, each of which, as noted, is but one figure of reason. Furthermore, unlike the rational figures constitutive of an historical epoch, these dimensions are unified not by an epochal principle but first and foremost by their negative relationship to metaphysics, which is evident precisely in their rejection of the latter and its epochal principles. However, despite modernity's negation of metaphysics, despite the cut separating the world and its history, modernity is unable to sever itself completely from metaphysics, to rid itself, as it were, of its provenance, for metaphysics continues to be the ground of the former's possibility. This is underscored by Boeder's disclosure of the positive relationship obtaining between the reason of both totalities: each type of modern reason is found to correspond to a type of metaphysical reason and in fact as the translation of the latter: hermeneutic translates conceptual reason; technical, natural reason; and apocalyptic, mundane reason.[22] These correspondences are visible with regard to the rational sequences within each figure and are thus important for the explication of the totality of the world, for the ordering of its dimensions and their constitutive ratios, as well as for the refinement of the totality of history, but the modernity of modern reason is to be seen in its difference from philo-sophical reason, a difference that derives in each instance from the absence of wisdom.

Hermeneutic reason gains its peripheral and thus inaugural position in the world as a result of its simulative relation to conceptual reason. The way in which it is a simulation becomes clear in two respects. First it aspires to the rank of First Philosophy, claiming to outdo its predecessor. However, while it asserts its priority on account of its intention to establish a new foundation for thinking, and especially for the sciences, by disclosing the origin of knowledge, it finds this origin not in reason but in human life—more precisely: in the pre-rational, doxic data of lived experience. Already this has to preclude any attempt to reduce hermeneutic reason to a mere continuation of conceptual reason. Yet the inappropriateness of such a reduction becomes most obvious in light of the second point of simulation: conception. Since it has no wisdom to conceive due to the aforementioned absence, the "conception" proper to hermeneutic reason cannot be that of the knowledge of a destiny; it conceives nothing rational but only the doxic data of human life. It is solely on the basis of such conception that reason plays any role in this sense-explication.[23]

Technical reason rejects the claim of metaphysics to the rank of science, let alone First Science. This already indicates that it, by its own testimony, is to be distinguished from what Heidegger terms 'technical thinking'. Technical reason neither marks the decline of metaphysical thinking nor does it stand in a continuum with the latter—Boeder's elaboration of the distinction of metaphysical reason has quashed Heidegger's assumption of the uniformity of reason and thereby torn the said continuum. It is only on this side of the end of metaphysics and within the world that technical reason comes onto the scene, and only as a result of the distinction of modern reason here in question that it has become determinate. Like natural reason, technical reason is concerned primarily with thinking and secondarily with Nature, and yet not with a Nature that is always already there, at hand, "in itself"—here "a φύσις that conceals itself no longer has any sense whatsoever" (190 f.). Rather, for this type of reason Nature is nothing but a scientific construct. In fact this Nature, and thus the world of concern to this type of reason, is thoroughly artificial, having been instrumentalized in the interest of furthering research. The chief aim of technical reason is the continual production of knowledge, of information, as well as of new technologies in order to guarantee such productivity.

Apocalyptic and mundane reason both have a negative relation to philosophical—i.e., conceptual—reason and seek to establish their own wisdom. However, mundane reason differs from its modern counterpart in that it contests philo-sophical reason due to the latter's positive relation to wisdom, for mundane reason itself rejects and seeks to replace that wisdom with one of its own. By contrast, apocalyptic reason has no wisdom to reject and thus can only reject the claim of that reason which gave the configurations of wisdom sanctuary, as it were—namely, conceptual reason. (It is the latter that is first and foremost the metaphysics against which modern thought as a whole is pitted.) Regarding their establishment of a wisdom, the decisive difference between these two manifestations of mundane reason rests on the presence of a preceding wisdom: historical mundane reason seeks to replace a present wisdom whereas apocalyptic reason responds to the absence of what was formerly wisdom by seeking to fill a need with its own wisdom, and even this is done only by way of postponement, that is, by calling for the *future* distinction of man from himself.

While these types of modern reason are unified in their rejection of metaphysics as well as in their privileging of Being over thinking, each of them "keeps to itself" in a way reminiscent of philo-sophical reason. The ratios constitutive of a sense-explication do share a task, just as did the members of each figure of reason in history, but that is all that links them to one another, strictly speaking. Otherwise, the ratios integral to the architectonic of modernity exert no essential influence upon one another. In fact each ratio may be said to be self-contained insofar as the transgression of the "boundaries" separating the ratios, but also the sense-explications, is ruled out—just as it is impossible for any modern ratio to be affected by a ratio constitutive of history. And yet the structural integrity of this architectonic would seem to be called into question by Heidegger's well-known encounter with Dilthey's thought, where the latter is held to have exerted an influence upon the former, a semblance apparently supported by Heidegger himself in *Being and Time*. It is precisely the dubiousness of the influence implied in the attention to such a conjunction of positions—the slipperiness of the 'and'—that Boeder exhibits in "Dilthey 'and' Heidegger: On the Historicity of Man." Here he shows that the assertion of such a conjunction gains its strength from the emphasis on similarities; the consequent vagueness ultimately paralyzes thinking insofar as the difference each thought makes, which inheres in their respective achievements, is covered over by the 'and'. Boeder by-passes such vagueness by focusing on the ratios of each position, where it is not the conjunction so much as the exclusive disjunction, not similarity so much as difference, that is crucial to the discernment of the achievements of each. Nevertheless, his rational approach does allow for the ascertainment of relationships between such positions. In the case of Dilthey and Heidegger, each of whom has his abode in a different sense-explication, they turn out to have but one point of convergence: "They come into contact, strictly speaking, in none of the terms of this proportion [of the 'destiny of the topic of thinking'] but rather in the historicity which in the former as well as in the latter case belongs to the determinacy of the topic: in Dilthey, the historicity of man in the history of his social reality, thus a reality brought about by man himself; in Heidegger, the historicity of the man who becomes cognizant of the said withdrawal and of the history of its beginning" (157). Both the differences and the points of convergence between the two remain hidden so long as one focuses on influences and thus similarities. In this case it is particularly tempting to do just that since Heidegger did indeed begin within the horizon of Dilthey's (and Husserl's) thought, namely, within the sense-explication of the interpreted life. However, he came into his own only upon descending into the core dimension of modernity, which he shares with Marx and Nietzsche: the sense-explication of the productive nature of man (cf. 154). It is within this neighborhood that his thought becomes pivotal for the demarcation of modernity.

As Boeder makes clear in "The Limit of Modernity and Heidegger's 'Legacy'," in many ways the central essay in the present volume, the limit marking the end of modernity becomes visible by way of neither its sense-explication of the interpreted life nor that of the sciences, but only by way of its core sense-explication. Whereas the former two draw out only the limit separating the world and its history, the latter sense-explication focuses principally on the limit to come—which Boeder shows to be the limit separating the totalities of the world and speech. This limit is heralded in Marx's, Nietzsche's, and Heidegger's projections of man's future distinction from himself, projections that were motivated by their experience of the expropriation of man—of his power, his will, and his knowledge, respectively—effected in history. Actually what they experience as expropriation is the aforementioned absence of wisdom. It is in response to the oppressiveness thereof that apocalyptic reason creates its own wisdom, thereby preserving the trace of the former configurations of wisdom: it gives voice to a new thought of man's distinction from himself, from his expropriated nature, which is to manifest itself in the communist society (Marx), the overman (Nietzsche), and the mortal (Heidegger) (cf. 193).[24] Unlike the distinctions envisioned in the former configurations, however, the present for the distinction projected by apocalyptic reason was failing—a present which, in the unity of what has been (*das Gewesene*) and what is present (*das Gegenwärtige*), sank into the hitherto (*das Bisherige*) as it was distinguished simply from what is to come (*das Künftige*)—and thus had to be postponed, pushed into the future. This lack of a present had to be felt due to the fact that apocalyptic reason considered the possibility of the requisite distinction to issue not from reason but from Being alone. The temporal character of the thought of Marx, Nietzsche, and Heidegger derives from just this dependence of reason upon Being for its distinction. They wait upon the future of a distinction whose advent they will never see—this is the barrier their thought runs up against (ibid.).

Of the ratios constitutive of the figure of apocalyptic reason, however, it is Heidegger's and his alone that opens Boeder's view to a future which simultaneously marks the end of modernity and is our present. The first index of the pivotal role Heidegger plays in this regard is given by his place within the architectonic of modern reason; his thought has concluding significance in a threefold sense: in completing his own ratio, he also concludes both the figure of apocalyptic reason and modernity itself. And it is just this place that entitles him to speak for the whole of modernity, just as Hegel had a privileged place with regard to philo-sophy. In both cases all the moments of their respective totalities are to be found in their ratios. In Heidegger this is most conspicuous with respect to truth, whose traditional definition as *adaequatio rei et intellectus* is rejected by modernity in its entirety (195). Its first two dimensions are characterized by a, so to speak, "positive" experience of truth—even in rejecting its traditional definition—whereas the ratios of the final dimension reject it based on their experience of untruth, to which the privative sense of ἀλήθεια drew Heidegger's attention. It is the hint provided by this name that directed him from the *sense* of truth as thematized by all of modernity back to the originary *nature* of truth, asking not simply 'What is truth?' but 'How does truth nature?' His pursuit thereof set him on a path that led back to the first beginning of thinking: "Starting from 'agreement', Heidegger's recollection of the 'nature of truth' can speak for the whole of modernity. He alone deals with the renunciation of the 'common concept of truth' in a way that reaches 'de-structively' back to the beginning of philosophy. With respect to the true in the sense of the φύσις of what appears, there he takes up the sole hint in the fundamental trait of self-concealing. The turn into the beginning of thinking, however, first yields the attention to the sheltering sense of self-concealing, to granting, even in the desheltering determined by the nature of technicity, more precisely: in the desheltering of the withdrawal characteristic of desheltering" (196). Again, Heidegger's experience of the withdrawal of that which gives what is to be thought is determinative of his entire undertaking. It is here that he finds the answer to his question 'What is metaphysics?': it is the history of this withdrawal and even of the oblivion thereof. His experience of this withdrawal gave rise to his vision of an other beginning of thinking over against that first beginning, one to be established initially by overcoming metaphysics but ultimately by leaving it to itself. Thus the second—but in fact primary—index for the centrality of his thought in general is that he is the only one to have opened a view to metaphysics as a closed history, and in fact as that of philosophy, as the sole history of the occidental tradition, a view that became possible only upon his disclosure of the first and the other beginning. In pursuing the hint provided by ἀλήθεια, upon which his entire thought hinges and which proves to be his legacy, in seeking to ascertain the nature of truth, Heidegger at once drew out the closedness of history and pointed to the impending closure of modernity.

It is precisely in the "twilight of modernity" which Heidegger's thought represents that the impending extinguishment of the "light" of modern reason may be grasped. This light finally died out upon the closure of the totality of the world, which was brought about by the exhaustion of the tasks pursued by its reason.[25] As Boeder's discussion makes clear, Heidegger's *Contributions to Philosophy* are a "*monumentum*" to this limit and thus the end of modernity in that they call to mind his conclusive achievement as well as those leading up to his. And yet it is only after having taken up the directive given by Heidegger's legacy that Boeder came to see the passing and thus the "death" of modern reason, the proper sense of which could be fixed only in light of the prior explication of the "death" of metaphysical reason. We recall: this directive first led him to the insight that the originary basis of judgment and its truth lay not in φύσις but in knowledge and hence in reason; furthermore, this pointed the way to the explication of the "sheltering" proper to metaphysics, where conceptual reason was invested with the task of sheltering the truth of a configuration of wisdom in a logic, thereby granting it persuasiveness. It is by virtue of this accomplishment alone that the talk of the end, and thus the death, of metaphysics gained its determinacy and thus legitimacy. Such accomplishment is the characteristic action of conceptual reason, an action whose end is determined by what has already been decided, by the destiny that specifies "how it is to be" in contrast to "how it is." It is upon reaching this end that conceptual "reason can utter the word of passing away . . . , of the solely conceivable 'dying': it is accomplished." As the "dead," the rational positions constitutive of history came to inhabit the underworld of the world of modernity. And yet, since this purely rational sense of accomplishment and death remained closed to him, "Heidegger never found nor could find any reason to think of the 'dead' involved in 'being-towards-death'" (208). Rather, by privileging Being over thinking and thereby expunging the primacy of the judgment and thus of the τέλος, he undermined the former basis of action and unwittingly obscured what philo-sophical reason accomplished for dwelling (cf. 171). The death of concern to Heidegger was instead that determinative of man's distinction from himself, that by virtue of which alone he was to become the mortal in the world of the fourfold (cf. "Mortal of Which Death?" below). Thus, as Boeder shows in "Action or/and Dwelling," the sense of accomplishment in Heidegger radically parted with its decisive sense in metaphysics. If for him "the nature of action is accomplishment," then what is to be accomplished "is either no action or else the action of that thinking which brings the [correlation of Being and the nature of man, or Da-sein] to speech. To build speech as the house of Being, to take up residence in its ἦθος, is its sole action" (173). The bringing of this correlation to speech is an accomplishment that had to remain postponed and along with it the building of the house of Being which was to provide the mortal with his abode. What is more, the futurity of this ἦθος and all that it entailed had to render such a dwelling indeterminate—consequently, forever unattainable—but also had to deny modern reason the said word of dying, leaving it to exhaust itself. It is only after transgressing the limit of modernity that a determinate dwelling becomes visible and in fact one that is disclosed by a poetic thinking that builds with a view to a truly poetic dwelling. Only that thinking which is mindful of the dead and their accomplishments is capable of such dwelling.

SPEECH. On this side of the world of modernity present thought finds itself within the totality, or sphere, of speech. It is especially here that it becomes apparent to what extent the building thinking thematized in the foregoing has all along been concerned not with the mere systematization of "past" thought—it is no historial enterprise—but with the transformation of *present* thought. This was already implicit in Boeder's approach to the totalities of history and the world, namely, in his acknowledgment of the departedness of the reason proper to each. But it was only after explicating their respective architectonics, after ascertaining the sense of this departedness and thus the achievements of reason in each, that he was able to turn to present thought and thereby take the final steps towards the fulfillment of his task. Thus, while always keeping in view what has already been decided in the preceding totalities, Boeder's aim in this third and final phase of his undertaking is to construct the architectonic of the sphere of speech, in which his thought has its proper abode and in which dwelling stands to regain its former binding claim on thinking. This is to be achieved by attending to the question 'Who is speaking?' in a transformed sense, the answer to which is gained by following "the hints of that conceptual reason which is at last left in peace, back to the conceived configurations of wisdom—not in order to repeat what has already been accomplished, thus to restore the metaphysical logic, but rather in order to lay bare the architectonic of those configurations" (254), to exhibit their rationality. For: "Only that which is in itself rational was able to call forth a philosophical reason. The Who of the [speakers of wisdom] first gains its proper ground in the architectonic, in a structure built out of ratios"—and it is upon this ground that dwelling is to regain its determinacy. As will be seen, the complete explication of the totality in question here rests on a distinction of speech both within and from itself, which, as in the totalities of history and the world, manifests itself in the distinction of the reason proper to the totality's different dimensions.

The totality of speech opens with the closure of the world. Properly speaking, however, the necessary access to this totality as such is gained only by way of the aforementioned transgression of the limit of modernity.[26] Though, as in the case of the move from history into the world, such must be distinguished from a simple shift between periods in a temporal succession, as is indicated, e.g., by the prefix 'post' in 'postmodernity'. This name testifies to the prevailing habit of expressing in temporal terms the vague feeling that modernity has come to an end and that a subsequent period has begun; yet such a naturalization of thought relies on the analogy of the phases in the course of, say, a life and thereby conceals thought's decisive atemporal character. By contrast, at issue here is a move from one self-contained, *rational* totality to its neighbor. The thematization of such a move rests on the acknowledgment of purely rational tasks, their fulfillment, and their integration into an architectonic, in light of which Boeder says: "The limit of modernity is transgressed only insofar as modernity's characteristic rejection of [metaphysics] is conceived as a fulfilled task. That is to say, it completely articulated our world and separated it from its history" (198). However, it is first and foremost the detemporalization of reason that has made such acknowledgment, all subsequent building, and thus the transgression crucial to present thought possible.[27]

The demand for such detemporalization arose from the recognition that temporality represented an insuperable barrier for the core sense-explication of modernity, specifically, its focus on the futurity of man's distinction from himself. This became most conspicuous upon the closure of modernity and thus the fading of apocalyptic reason, at which point its projections of the said distinction were not only not realized but were also met with indifference. And yet at the limit of modernity Heidegger is unique among his neighbors in that his legacy contains a directive whose transformation showed Boeder the way through history into the world and beyond into the present of speech. This transformation hinges on the said detemporalization. We recall: the decisive insight arose from Boeder's scrutiny of the originary sense of ἀλήθεια; he discovered that, contrary to Heidegger's claim, the concealment proper to ἀλήθεια was not that of the κρύπτεσθαι of a φύσις (Nature) but rather that of λήθειν as it bears upon a possible participation in knowledge. Thus he came to see that, on the one hand, the element of truth is not φύσις but the λόγος (in this case: the grounded judgment) and that, on the other, one seeking participation in knowledge is dependent upon another who already knows, a dependence that rests on the acknowledgment of the authority of this knower. Both of these observations testified not to the "physical" but to the purely rational basis of thought. And this insight enabled the discharge of the temporality with which the core sense-explication had shackled reason—consequently the future loses its power over reason—but also of the "physicality" or phenomenality in which it was embedded by modernity's privileging of Being over thinking. Such a detemporalization marks a purification of reason akin to that effected by conceptual reason, where it distinguished itself from natural and mundane reason (cf. 197 f.). Here detemporalized, that is, logotectonic, reason "finds its way out of Nature not only as it is the Nature of what appears but, what is more, out of Nature as the history of self-concealing and thereby severs the history of occidental thought from just this Nature" (6). Freed from the modern constraints of Nature and temporality—especially from the core dimension's emphasis on the future as distinct from the hitherto—logotectonic reason has managed to reestablish the distinction between what has been (*das Gewesene*) and what is present (*das Gegenwärtige*) and has thereby gained access to the atemporal present of thought. This is not to say that detemporalization results in the attainment of some "eternal truths." Rather, it effects a modalization of thought such that the contingency of the said future is abandoned in favor of the necessity of what has been, and in fact as it is determinative of what is present. Its necessity lies in its perfection, and it is its testimony to the thought of perfection, of the fulfillment of "how it is to be," that provides the directive which is to orient present dwelling. This directive is in fact made visible in the configurations of wisdom. It is no commandment, no prohibition—such demands obedience but no thought. Rather, it is a provocation of thinking to attend to the distinction between "how it is not to be" and "how it is to be," a distinction that is to be realized in "how it is" insofar as it is the said atemporal present. In the interest of opening up just this present, Boeder undertook the explication of the totalities of history and the world and is currently engaged in eliciting the totality of speech. Because it is in just this present and in it alone that the speech of wisdom can regain its claim on thinking, because what has been can be properly accessed only after the discharge of the temporality of thought, Boeder says that "the limit of modernity is not at all to be transgressed into a postmodernity but rather into the present of 'detemporalized' reason" (198), that is, the present of and established by logotectonic reason alone as the present of speech.

Speech is in fact the salient concern of present thought—not language, for it has its proper place in history. And yet, as Boeder illustrates in "Reason's Interest in Language," there it does not receive the exclusive attention of a special branch of philosophy but only the marginal attention of reason, and then only insofar as it is the expression of thought, of the concept. In this connection conceptual reason aimed at "the delimitation of thought, what is more: of the concept. It required the latter's separation from names" (214), and in fact in order to safeguard knowledge from the threat of untruth (223). In sundering the concept from names, conceptual reason assured the purity and thus "safety" of thought. Apocalyptic reason also thematized language in response to untruth, but following modernity's dissolution of the concept the active sense of speech had to attain primacy. Of its modern thematizations it is particularly Heidegger's understanding of speech as an indicating (as φάσις) in the sense of letting a φύσις appear, that points the way to the sense of speech crucial to this final totality, namely, as it enables dwelling.

Like the totalities of history and the world, speech also has three dimensions, though, as in the world, each dimension is occupied solely by one type of reason: anarchic, structuralist, and logotectonic reason, respectively. It is in the first two dimensions that the integral positions of what is usually called 'postmodernity' are located. The first of these is "the dimension of submodernity," the prefix 'sub' indicating at once its simulative relation to the core sense-explication of modernity—where Merleau-Ponty simulates Marx; Foucault, Nietzsche; and Derrida, Heidegger—and that it "sinks below [that sense-explication's] level of being the trace of wisdom" (13). This sinking marks an impoverishment of reason reminiscent of modernity's impoverishment of metaphysical reason through its rejection of the principle (ἀρχή), though here it is intensified by the expunction of the futurity central to the modern projections of the distinction of man. Having grown numb to its lack of a destiny, anarchic reason no longer experiences the expropriation that moved apocalyptic reason to such projections; instead the overwhelming experience in submodernity is that of violence—above all, of the violence of man against man, or more precisely: of one body against an other body—this motivates its negativity towards modernity but especially towards metaphysics, in which it sees the source of dominance (ἀρχή) and terror. The concern of the submoderns, then, "is in fact no longer the—still hermeneutic—scission between sense and nonsense in what is spoken but rather the social emancipation from the largely unconscious force in the orders of discourse. Thus the contemporary critique of metaphysics also aims at unmasking not the nonsense in metaphysical propositions so much as the totalitarian character of its totalizing thinking" (247) and its logocentrism, which are held to be sedimented in all forms of social interaction and its institutions.

For the submoderns the favored emancipative strategy in this regard is the effecting of a slide into mere difference that is ultimately meant to destabilize the orders of discourse and the institutions which totalizing thinking has supposedly established, a strategy captured most succinctly in the name *différance*. It is directed first and foremost against unity as it is presupposed by the totality, a unity formerly promoted by the modern projections of the future man and the principles of metaphysics: "The decomposition of [these] is the decisive event in contemporary thought" (245). Its decisiveness lies precisely in the fact that it expunges not just the totality and its unity but also identity and the grounded judgment, and so everything that formerly provided thinking with a standard, with its ground. This yields the most extreme licentiousness of thinking, which consequently plunges into the measurelessness of unrestrained difference, into a horizon in which the sole principle, as it were, is desire—whose maximization is always sought, either by its unbridled satisfaction or the postponement thereof.[28] On account of this, as Boeder notes, submodernity's motto has to read: "originariness of difference." The said destabilization at once creates such difference and gives free reign to a body's desires. The consequent instability is precisely the element of the "permanent revolution," the securing of ever more justice, and the democracy longed for by the pluralistic mentality.

This "originary difference" is none based upon the identity proper to reason and guaranteeing unity, but has been absolutely sundered therefrom. Anarchic reason knows only "the identity of a What or of what is mere being, ultimately of what appears" (309). It is against this sense of identity that it pits its understanding of difference in the interest of emancipation. And the beneficiaries thereof? Those who were formerly referred to as 'subject', 'person', 'individual', 'self', 'ego': "The semblance of unity fades away for the pluralistic mentality, however, not only with respect to what is spoken"—i.e., not only with respect to the concept and, by extension, its principle—"but likewise with respect to the speaker" (246). Thus in view of the "death of man" resultant upon such fading, Foucault asserts that the alterity to be sought is not only that of being different from the others but especially from oneself: one has to change again and again through the constant recreation of oneself in the pursuit of self-actualization, a pursuit driven by desire. In fact it is the speaker as body that becomes the arena of difference in submodernity; this is attested by its anthropological interest, which itself marks a radical transformation of the core sense-explication's interest in man: on the one hand, man becomes the other—put most excessively: the Wholly Other—an other which manifests itself as the said body in a network of other bodies; while, on the other hand, sexual difference is held to be more originary than the former ontological difference. In the wake of submodernity's transference of the center from the subject to the other, and in fact as it is a perceived and sexualized body, the talk can no longer be of 'intersubjectivity' but rather of 'intercorporeality'. Here every other finds itself with the others, that is, sensitized to, in solidarity with, and, what is more, dependent upon them. It is a plurality of such others, of bodies, that currently populates the social landscape.

Submodern society is dominated by the pluralistic mentality, "which is buttressed by what is taken for granted: the agreement to differ openly not only in opinions but already in attitudes—which themselves are ever changing. To be excluded here are only those who break with the consensus concerning such openness" (242). The anonymous and ubiquitous They (*das Man*), which an other encounters always only as the others, cultivates this mentality and insures the desired openness. It is the openness of *différance*, which rests on a rejection of the exclusive disjunction in favor of the interminable conjunction (cf. Derrida, *FL*, 920/921 f.). *Différance* lives off of a distinguishing *ad infinitum* that refuses to make a decision, a definitive judgment; such is postponed indefinitely in the interest of subverting the violence held to have been done by totalizing thinking while itself doing violence to difference by leveling it, such that everything becomes equally valid (*gleich-gültig*), and thus forcing it to slide into similarity. Such distinguishing is based on the assumption of the necessity of constant change, which amounts to the continual production of differences. In reality, however, it disables all true production, namely, of knowledge, by abolishing its dependence upon what has already been decided and thus upon a preceding knowledge; at most, thinking under the spell of *différance* is productive of fictions, but as they make no claim to truth they can never be productive of knowledge. Since for this mentality there can be no just distinction of one individual from another—let alone from oneself—in accordance with "how it is to be," the individuality of every other turns out to be an individuality *en masse*, the homogeneity of which is underscored in movements with such slogans as: "We are different." The They of this We demands that the said openness be shielded from the threat of constraint and ultimately of totalitarianism. But as Boeder points out: "Totalitarian here is the notion that everything has to change—an everything, however, that in the social sphere can mean only: most things. Thus totalitarian thinking also remains caught up in everyday life: the pluralistic mentality in fact sees in it the evil of its own privation but is not able to understand itself as the mother of this invention" (*Sed*, 253). Wherever the grounded judgment has no place, wherever the choice between options that excludes one possibility in favor of another is barred, wherever identity is dissolved in favor of mere difference, of similarity, reason has to remain blind to the knowledge of the configurations of wisdom, that is, the destiny of man to distinguish himself from himself, and therefore is condemned to non-dwelling (cf. 197). The first dimension of the sphere of speech is stamped by such non-dwelling.

This also holds for the middle dimension of this sphere, though not because it is entirely indifferent to the configurations of wisdom as submodernity is, but because it is able to appreciate them only as "texts." Boeder has provisionally adopted the name 'postmodernity' for this dimension; although its complete explication is not presented here, certain of its key features may nevertheless be relayed. It is the place of structuralist, or linguistic, reason, which finds its exposition in pure linguistics (Jakobson), semiology (Barthes), and structural anthropology (Lévi-Strauss) in connection with psychoanalysis (Lacan). Structuralist reason translates hermeneutic reason and yet, while it also lays claim to the rank of First Science, it dispenses with its ties to philosophy since it considers itself to be prior to even the latter; what is more, it completely discards hermeneutic reason insofar as it does away with the latter's ground, namely, the doxic data of lived experience, leaving the speaker only as a component of communicative contexts. And it is just this approach to speech that confirms its kinship to the first dimension of this totality; yet despite their common ground in a speech that does not allow of dwelling, the difference between these first two dimensions is to be grasped as a distinction of speech within itself, namely, they part with regard to their respective understanding of the instrumentality of speech. Whereas the submoderns seek to alter communication and its regulative orders of discourse as sketched above, the postmoderns maintain, so to speak, a theoretical distance from them, seeking to disclose the functions of speech in that communication. Put differently: the difference is between the speech of violence and non-violence and that of pure communication. After the explication of these dimensions, only one remains, the explication of which will bring the distinction of speech from itself to determinacy.

The third and final dimension of speech, the one in which logotectonic reason and thus Boeder's thought is situated, has neither been fully explicated nor has it been named, though its contours may be sketched in light of the final four essays in this collection. Logotectonic reason marks a translation of technical reason. They are akin insofar as both are fully cognizant of the fact that they lack a topic of their own, yet they differ radically with regard to their technical character: unlike its predecessor, logotectonic reason is technical not by virtue of its concern, which for technical reason was the speech, world, and history of the sciences, but rather by virtue of the way in which it exhibits the history, world, and speech of what has been thought in their architectonics, namely, by means of a logic of ratios. This logic has been operative from the start in Boeder's construction of these architectonics. Speech differs from its antecedent totalities, however, in that it has not yet been concluded and, most importantly, is and remains "an open sphere": "Here history and world are only seemingly reduced to moments of speech, for it is not the totality of what the 'concept' has been. The sphere of the actuality of speech cannot be exhibited as a closed construct. It is precisely here that the antipathy of the submoderns to thinking in terms of totalities has its roots" (11). And yet, despite the prevailing desire that they continue in support of endless revolution and research, the dimensions of anarchic and structuralist reason just discussed have indeed come to an end, have literally played themselves out—a state of affairs confirmed by their complete explication in rational figures. The openness of this sphere cannot arise from these dimensions, then, but only from that of logotectonic reason. Yet this openness derives only accidentally from the current incompleteness of Boeder's explication of the sphere of speech, for while his thought is clearly still "in the making," it is most definitely intent upon reaching its end, its τέλος. Rather, the necessity of the said openness inheres in the way in which the logotectonic's constitutive totalities are connected with one another, where the pivotal point of contact lies between the final dimension of speech and the beginning of history. What this means becomes clearer in light of the τέλος towards which Boeder's thought is directed.

The teleology of his undertaking is determined by its task: to recover (*Herausretten*) that in which "everyone necessarily has an interest"—that is, the configurations of wisdom (σοφίαι) and their knowledge of the destiny of man—from the departedness of philo-sophy. This recovery is simultaneously a saving of these configurations from the danger of their falling into permanent oblivion, of their becoming forever closed to us, a danger that has steadily mounted as a result of their continuously decreasing audibility, which began in the totality of the world but has become most intense in the first two dimensions of speech. And yet it is the positive sense of recovery and saving that is determinative of this undertaking, a sense noted by Heidegger: "Saving (*Rettung*) not only snatches something from danger, but 'to save' actually means: to set something free into its own nature" (*BWD*, 144/150). Within the horizon of Boeder's thought this has to read: to set wisdom free into its own present and thereby grant it its dignity (cf. *Sed*, 294). This requires that we regain access to and thus "an ear for the configurations of wisdom of our tradition—for what they give to be thought" (293). But how? By attending to the destiny of the topic of thinking and so only mediately, which is to say, first by following the hint provided by conceptual reason in its conceptions of just those configurations; it distinguished itself from natural and mundane reason in response to the latter's bequest of the knowledge of man's destiny. It is just such conception that points to the answer to the question 'Who is speaking?' and thereby gives determinacy to the "oft-cited neighborhood of poetizing and thinking," the talk of which formerly veiled "the relation appealed to here between σοφία and φιλοσοφία" (252). The said configurations have been accorded the rank of σοφία not by Boeder on account of some predilection on his part but by the attention of conceptual reason to what they gave to be thought, namely, in its conception of just that wisdom. Thus it is the judgment of conceptual reason that has enabled the distinction of the works of wisdom from those of poetry, those of Schiller, e.g., from those of a Lessing or a Shakespeare, the former's thought having been conceived by Fichte. In gaining insight into wisdom's bequest to conceptual reason, Boeder was able to slip free of Heidegger's *Es gibt–Sein* and turn to the gift in the beginning of philosophy.

In the sphere of speech this calls not for another conceptual reason but rather for a reason "that distinguishes what is said from what is spoken, that understands what is said in the sense of a 'teaching'" that is "meant to be abided by—whether one accepts it or not"—and as such is constitutive of the space of dwelling. By effecting this distinction of speech from itself, logotectonic reason makes the directive or indicative speech of wisdom audible, sets it free into its present. This is a kind of speech that has to remain incomprehensible to the dimensions of sub- and postmodernity already due to their preoccupation with instrumental speech, but it is especially the renunciation required by what the σοφίαι give to be thought (cf. 278), namely, the directive which they each bring into view, that renders those dimensions deaf to the speech of wisdom. Its directive teaches that "to be man is a destiny for men which they fulfill only in their distinction from themselves and not just in their distinction from other animals" (293). The τέλος of each epochally distinguished teaching comes into view by way of the presentation of the knowledge: of the Muses in Homer, Hesiod, and Solon; of the Christian doctrine in the Synoptics, Paul, and John; and of the civil consciousness in Rousseau, Schiller, and Hölderlin—each configuration presents an autonomous vision of the distinguished man as hero, as saint, and as citizen, respectively.[29] Each of these visions has "a permanence that comes to bear only within human dwelling and, only on the basis of it, in ever individual words and deeds." It is just this recovery of the configurations of wisdom that is to by-pass Heidegger's postponement and regain the dwelling grounded upon the binding claim of the σοφίαι—for, as Boeder says of the New Testament, directive speech contains the message "not of a future dwelling but rather of one that has been and therefore is visible in all necessary determinacy" (291). It is precisely on account of their fundamental role in the establishment of the space of dwelling that these configurations are—to borrow Kant's phrase once again—necessarily of interest to everyone.

But if, as Heidegger asserts from his oppressive experience of the challenge of technicity, the mortals "still have to learn to dwell" (*BWD*, 156/161), then how? Not by attending to the thing, which, grasped entirely in terms of its naturing, gathers the world of the fourfold and, by granting thinking access to the latter, points to a future dwelling. So long as he could not see the singularity of his present, so long as he could regard technical thinking only as a continuation of metaphysical thinking, the thing's epochal significance for dwelling had to remain closed to Heidegger. In fact, in keeping with his task, he himself barred his access to this significance by privileging Being over thinking, that is, by focusing on the thing in its phenomenality as that which alone gives what is to be thought, and not on the thought—more precisely: the judgment—that guided the formation of the thing and installed it as a sign in the space of dwelling; and so he had to say: "the things have never yet at all been able to appear to thinking as things" (*D*, 163/171). But if dwelling is no longer to be learned in this way, then how? Boeder points to the answer in commenting on the foregoing remark: once detemporalized reason has torn the continuum between technical and metaphysical thinking, once it has fully explicated and thus duly honored the types of reason proper to the world and especially its history, it becomes clear that "the things"—including works of art—"have appeared to thinking indeed as things, have obviously taken on their historical determinacy *from thinking*, because they have been thought specifically with reference to a perfection that is proper to each thing. It is on account of this that they were destined to be beautiful. Our history is replete with examples of beauty, i.e., of things that testify to their destiny of perfection" (*Sed*, 180). The thinking determinative here is that of the "judgment of the concept," namely, that thinking which judges a thing in view of the extent to which it has fulfilled its destiny, has become equal to its concept, i.e., what it was destined to be. It is just this thinking that "has authoritatively molded the formation of the things in our history—embracing even the characteristic things of dwelling" and thus is the prerequisite of the dwelling in question. Consequently, in order to learn to dwell it is necessary to learn this way of thinking. But how? As Boeder notes, since the thought of perfection has its present not in the sphere of speech but alone in history, its recovery cannot be the goal here but rather the transformation of what was formerly the judgment, which requires the cultivation of the faculty of distinction. It is gained by learning to distinguish what is already distinct, that is, what has already been decided, what has been accomplished, from both history and the world (259)—and this proves to be Boeder's reason for having gone through their respective totalities, for having established the architectonics of what has been thought there. But this judgment can also be learned by that thinking which attends to the signs provided by the things of dwelling, things which in each instance testify to their having been thought and in fact with respect to their formation: "Only the purity of formation grants judgment an abode. Yet such is first and only grasped when thinking has learned what has been purely said, what has been purely thought, which has given what is to be thought, which has set reason itself on its way to the purity of formation" (262). In their beauty, in their purity, the things are signs of the aforementioned destiny of perfection, the standard of which was set for the "judgment of the concept" by the configurations of wisdom and their knowledge of man's destiny. This was determinative of the dwelling and the corresponding formation of its things which came to fruition in the Europe of our history. And it is here that one first encounters what is distinct; it is from this history that one can learn the thinking that makes all the difference, that makes our dwelling possible.

The intention to cultivate just this thinking, and thus logotectonic reason, has informed Boeder's undertaking from the outset, but such marks only the first leg of his odyssey, the stages of which have entailed the construction of the architectonics of history, the world, and now speech; in fact the final and decisive leg thereof consists in the recovery of the configurations of wisdom, the attainment of which will hail the completion of not only the third dimension of speech but also of its totality and ultimately of the logotectonic; such is decisive since "only with its completion does the traversal of these spheres provide the necessary testimony of its reason" (315), only thereby can it achieve its τέλος: the recovery of dwelling. This journey began with the explication of what has been thought in the totality of history, where philo-sophy's dependence upon the bequest of the configurations of wisdom was disclosed and in fact in view of the distinction of reason. However, with the accomplishment of its tasks philo-sophy made its departure and carried those configurations away with it, thereby inadvertently depriving dwelling of its ground. Nevertheless, the subsequent explication of the totality of the world, which in its negation of philo-sophical reason everywhere bore testimony to the absence of those configurations, showed that a trace of that wisdom had been preserved and in fact by modernity's core sense-explication in a wisdom of its own making, albeit one that allowed only of a future dwelling. Met in turn with excessive indifference, this last trace of wisdom has been expunged in the first two dimensions of speech, an event that has fortified the blindness to the thought that enables dwelling. And yet this history, as it were, of the enervation of wisdom's claim on thinking has its roots not in the world, not in speech, but already in history, and in fact in its beginning: it is natural reason's rejection of wisdom that has sown the seeds of this blindness—a deed which Boeder has accorded its merits. Thus it is surprising that it is in the third dimension of speech that wisdom stands to regain its binding claim on thinking; it is surprising that it is just its reason that is invested with the task of recovering the configurations of wisdom and in fact by excavating it from our concluded history, this reason which is a translation of technical reason, which itself is a translation of natural reason. But this is possible because logotectonic reason's relation to wisdom is characterized neither by the former's indifference nor by the latter's negativity, but by reverence. It is in this sense that all the building discussed in the foregoing proves to be logotectonic reason's palinode, as it were, undertaken so as to atone for natural reason's original negation of wisdom (cf. Plato, *Phaedr.* 243A f.), a palinode whose composition is dyadic in form: the edifice of what has been thought has been erected in order to raze the obstructions that induce the blindness to the "message" of the configurations of wisdom. The completion of the third dimension of speech—and it is here that the sense of its openness becomes determinate—is to be achieved through logotectonic reason's return to the configurations of wisdom, whereby they are to be set free into their present: "The present of each [configuration] is appreciated not in the acceptance and transformation of knowledge as it occurred in the conceptions of our history; rather, each reveals to us its present with what is thought in it. In order to bring out what is thought as that of reason, the thinking proper to logotectonic reason is needed" (*Sed*, 315). The said return hinges on a distinction of the beginning that abandons Heidegger's search for the "more incipient" beginning and instead focuses on the beginning that makes all the difference. Here the beginning of wisdom proves to be not just "more incipient" but rather *the* beginning; only its gift, its bequest of the knowledge of the destiny of man, makes the beginning of philosophy clearly thinkable. It is in coming full circle, as it were, that logotectonic reason intends to recover the configurations of wisdom, to set them free into their present, a present that is no longer bound up with that of conceptual reason but is that of speech. Insofar as the sphere of speech is completed by returning to the beginning of wisdom, speech may be said to be the ἦθος of dwelling. It is to be entered not by way of an ethical science but alone by way of the distinction of speech from itself, whereby it "is no longer simply the speech of wisdom but rather the speech of that which gives what is to be thought," that is, the said message of dwelling. This marks the final leg of logotectonic reason's odyssey.

ACKNOWLEDGMENTS. This volume has benefited from the generosity of so many people, a number of whom are due special mention here. First and foremost I should like to express my gratitude to Heribert Boeder, who has given so munificently of himself in the course of my work on this volume. He painstakingly went over each of the translations presented here, helping to improve them immensely, and spent hours discussing his thought with me, which contributed greatly to my ability to write the foregoing introduction. Gerald Meier gave me the initial impetus to undertake this project. I am grateful to Guido Heinrich, Arne Homann, and Sven Jürgensen for their insightful suggestions and comments on my introduction and for our discussions, as well as to Friederike-Andrea Dorner and Elisabeth Harth for patiently answering countless questions concerning the German language and for their unfailing intellectual support. My thanks also go to Dirk Effertz for his scrutiny of and invaluable comments on the majority of the translations included here and to Thomas Caplan for reading through this volume in its entirety and making many helpful suggestions. I am indebted to Pierre Adler for locating many of the English translations listed in the bibliography as well as for his suggested solutions to several of my translation quandaries, but also to Hans-Ulrich Lessing at the Dilthey-Forschungsstelle at the Ruhr-Universität Bochum for his assistance in locating the available English translations of Dilthey's work. At the State University of New York Press Marilyn Semerad was nothing but forthcoming in response to my many questions concerning the physical production of this volume. And finally, my thanks go to Dennis J. Schmidt, without whose support of and enthusiasm for this project the present volume would not have been possible.

M. B.
Osnabrück, February 1996

NOTES

1. Immanuel Kant, *Kritik der praktischen Vernunft, Akademie-Ausgabe* V (Berlin: de Gruyter, 1968), p. 24; *Critique of Practical Reason*, trans. Lewis White Beck (Indianapolis: Bobbs-Merrill, 1956), p. 23. [Except for certain texts cited in this introduction, all works cited and/or referred to in this volume are listed (along with their abbreviations, where relevant) on pp. 327-336 below. Clarification of the conventions followed in citation may be found on p. 327.]

2. Kant, *CPR*, B 867 note. Cf. also Martin Heidegger, *Gelassenheit* (Pfullingen: Neske, [10]1992), p. 11; *Discourse on Thinking*, trans. John M. Anderson and E. Hans Freund (New York: Harper & Row, 1966), p. 44: "was jeden Einzelnen von uns unmittelbar und unablässig in seinem Wesen angeht" (what concerns each one of us immediately and incessantly in his nature).

3. See p. 184 below. Hereinafter, all page references to the present volume stand alone in parentheses immediately following the relevant quotation unless another work is cited in the body of this introduction, in which case the first citation of the present volume following the said work is denoted by *Sed* with the relevant page reference. Furthermore, no page references are provided in those instances in which subsequent quotations fall on the same page as previously cited.

4. 'Whole' and 'totality' are not Heidegger's terms, of course, but Boeder's, which he in turn acquired from metaphysics. Nevertheless, these terms are implicit in Heidegger's question and his talk of the "epoch" of metaphysics.

5. In keeping with current conventions, throughout this volume *das Sein* has been rendered as 'Being' and *das Seiende* as 'being' or 'beings'. In those instances which might give rise to confusion, the German has been provided following the relevant term.

6. In *The Rational Architectonic of Modernity* (pp. 18-19) Boeder points to the precedent for his use of the triad, that is, its central role in metaphysical thought. As examples he cites both Aristotle (*de caelo* 268a11-13) and Kant (*Critique of Judgment*, 197 note), whose thought was, albeit for different reasons, structured in accordance with the tripartite determination of the whole. [Boeder's publications are listed on pp. 337-341 below. All titles referred to in the body of the text have been rendered in English. In those instances in which the texts referred to have not yet appeared in English translation, the English title is provided in brackets following the original German title in the publication list. This convention has also been followed regarding works listed in the general bibliography (pp. 327-336 below) which are referred to in the course of this volume but for which no English translation was found.]

7. Throughout this volume a distinction has been made between 'Nature', which renders *Natur*, and 'nature', which renders *Wesen*. Cf. the German-English Glossary below for other translations of *Wesen*.

8. Cf., e.g., Martin Heidegger, *Zur Frage nach der Bestimmung der Sache des Denkens* (St. Gallen: Erker, 1984), and "The End of Philosophy and the Task of Thinking." As Boeder notes, Heidegger thought this phrase only in its unity. What is more, he focused only on the simple relation of topic and thinking, whereby the destinal term was regarded as inseparable from the topic.

9. Divergences from the translation of *Bestimmung* as 'destiny'—not 'fate'—will be noted in the course of the discussion of the totalities explicated by Boeder. Cf. also the glossary entry for this term (pp. 319-320 below).

10. The only exception is found in "The Difference Inherent in the 'Other Beginning'," in which two types of reason (natural = c, b, a; conceptual = A, B, C) are articulated with a view to exhibiting how the key positions within each epoch fit together into an architectonic; the individual terms of each position are not emphasized.

11. As will be seen, three types of philosophical reason are constitutive of history, in which they are distinguished in view of the character of their relation to wisdom (cf. pp. xxii f.). In each epoch their figures are built as follows:

Natural reason:	Mundane reason:	Conceptual Reason:	Wisdom:
C B A	B A C	A C B	A B C
A C B	C B A	B A C	C A B
B A C	A C B	C B A	B C A

Since there are only three possible ratios of thought, seeming replications are to be found from one figure to the next. However, three points of distinction must be taken into account for their fundamental differences to be evident: first, the incipient ratio is determinative of the rational sequences of the subsequent ratios in the figure and, furthermore, its initial term proves to be the prevailing concern of the entire figure, a concern that is visible as its diagonal, so that above: for natural reason it is clearly thinking (C) that is pivotal; for mundane reason, the topic (B); and for conceptual reason, the destiny (A)—more precisely: the destinal principle. Second, the task unifying the three ratios in a figure distinguish a ratio in that figure from like-constructed ratios in the other figures. Finally, although the sequences sketched above are repeated from epoch to epoch, the principle of each epoch determines the task of its constitutive figures such that a figure of, e.g., conceptual reason in the first epoch must be distinguished from its kindred figures in the middle and final epochs. The figures presented above are translated in the totalities of the world and speech: natural into technical and finally into logotectonic reason; mundane into apocalyptic and then into anarchic reason; and conceptual into hermeneutic and then into structuralist reason. While the explication of the totalities of history and the world depended upon Boeder's preceding insight into the construction of the epochal configurations of wisdom, it is only in the third dimension of the totality of speech that wisdom is taken up in its own right. Its explication is Boeder's current task. (It should be borne in mind that this schematic presentation of reason does not exhaust his explication of what has been thought, but remains an external means of exhibiting the interconnection of the logotectonic's constitutive ratios as well as its completeness.)

12. *Gegenwart* is rendered throughout as 'present', unless otherwise noted, as distinguished from the Heideggerian reading of *Anwesenheit* (presence). The former is a feature of reason, whereas the latter is connected with a phenomenon and, ultimately, its φύσις. It is Boeder's non-physical reading of *Anwesenheit* that opens up a view to the originary sense of this term, namely, the presence of reason with something, i.e., its attention to something. Cf. in this connection the remarks on 'detemporalization', pp. xxxiv f., but also those on *Anwesen* in Boeder's "*Veritas seditiosa*," p. 7 and "Privilege of Presence?", pp. 81-90 below,

as well as in his *Ground and Present as the Aim of Early Greek Philosophical Inquiry*, pp. 224-231.

13. Throughout this volume 'history' (*Geschichte*) has been distinguished from 'historial scholarship' (*Historie*), just as 'historical' (*geschichtlich*) has been distinguished from 'historial' (*historisch*). The term *Historie* is connected to ἱστορεῖν (observation), which is concerned with phenomena. On Boeder's reading, however, *Geschichte* is not a discipline, not an endeavor, but solely a totality of reason, which has been purified of all phenomenality.

14. Cf. Martin Heidegger, *Was ist das – die Philosophie?* (Pfullingen: Neske, [10]1992); *What is Philosophy?*, trans. William Kluback and Jean T. Wilde (New York: Twayne, 1958).

15. For Boeder's account of the Heraclitean τὸ σοφόν, see "Dissensions," pp. 91-99 below.

16. In fact, in connection with the historical manifestation of mundane reason the epithet 'mundane' is not meant to imply that its concern lies with the world. Rather, its name derives from Boeder's distinction of modern reason within the totality of the world and thus is in effect a retrojection into the totality of history. This will be taken up again in the discussion of apocalyptic reason below (cf. p. xxviii).—It is worth noting here that apocalyptic or temporal reason is so named because of its projections of a future distinction of man from himself. The futurity of the advent of the distinguished man heralded therein is the source of the epithets 'apocalyptic' and 'temporal'.

17. Cf. note 11 above concerning the construction of the respective figures of these ratios.

18. It should be noted that the totalities of history, world, and speech were not explicitly thematized in modernity but are, as Boeder has shown, discernable in its works; modern reason would generally wish neither to call itself 'reason' in the metaphysical sense—and thus from the modern standpoint it is better to speak of 'thinking'—nor to lay claim to its translation of metaphysical reason. Nevertheless, Boeder has drawn out the rational character of modernity by way of the ratio, and it is on this basis that the talk can be of 'modern reason'—by extension, this will hold of the thinking proper to so-called postmodernity.

19. This lack of distinction may also be found in varying degrees in "Why 'Being of Beings'?", "The Difference Inherent in the 'Other Beginning'," and "An End with Distinction."

20. Since the present Boeder referred to at the time of writing the essay in question was that of modernity, or the totality of the world, and the present in which his own thought is situated is that proper to the sphere of speech, it was felt advisable to change the title to "Reason in Modern Thought" as well as all references to the present to 'modern' wherever modernity is meant in order to avoid confusing the reader. The order of the sense-explications of modernity was not changed, for doing so would have required that the entire essay be rewritten. Since the positions within modernity have been discussed in a way that differs from the other essays in this collection and since the order of the sense-explications is in this case of lesser importance, the essay was retained. See note 21A regarding the change in the order of the sense-explications of modernity.

21. (A) In working out the architectonic proper to the sphere of speech, Boeder has found it necessary to modify his original construction of the architectonic of modern reason, namely, by switching the positions of the first two sense-explicative dimensions; previously, technical and not hermeneutic reason was located on the periphery of modernity—this is in fact the structure maintained in "Reason in Modern Thought." The current order is reflected in all the other essays in this volume in which the architectonic of modernity is thematized. This change was necessitated by the fact that hermeneutic reason is a simulation of conceptual reason and thus must be "adjacent" to the latter. For Boeder's account of this revision, see pp. 12-13 below.

(B) 'Sense-explication' (*Besinnung*) has a threefold sense in Boeder's thought: the act of disclosing the architectonic of modern thought; a figure of modern reason; and an individual ratio in such a figure. This is, of course, to be distinguished from the proper Heideggerian sense of the term, which has been rendered as 'recollection' throughout this volume.

22. The global characterization of modern reason as 'mundane' becomes less prominent following upon the distinction of modern reason and the elaboration of its differentiated relations to metaphysical reason; 'mundane reason' has come to denote almost exclusively its historical manifestation.

It is important to bear in mind that the talk of modern reason's translation of metaphysical reason focuses on the correspondences between the rational sequences in the figures constitutive of each totality. This is not to be confounded with some presumed influence exerted on modern by metaphysical reason. Such is ruled out already by the autonomy of each ratio within its own figure and, in turn, its totality.

23. Given the dissolution of the principle in modernity on the one hand and wisdom's complete lack of significance for hermeneutic and technical reason on the other, the destinal term (*Bestimmung*) of their ratios is rendered as 'directing intention'.

24. Because apocalyptic reason harbors the trace of the knowledge proper to the configurations of wisdom, the destinal term is rendered as 'destiny' in its ratios.

25. Strictly speaking, with respect to modernity the talk can be only of the exhaustion of its task and not of its accomplishment since its reason knows no τέλος achievable in the present—due to the absence of wisdom, modern reason has no access to the thought of "how it is to be" except insofar as it remains postponed—but finds its finitude only in the distinguished sense of death.

26. The transgression in question here is not to be confused with that proper to submodern strategies of undermining occidental institutions. There a virulent irreverence prevails, whereas the transgression effected by Boeder arises precisely from the reverence mentioned at the outset in connection with the ἐποχή.

27. Synonyms for 'detemporalization' are 'dephenomenalization' and 'dephysicalization'. The former is preferred given the break with temporal, or apocalyptic, reason necessitated by such a purification of reason.

28. In the final analysis, for the ratios of anarchic reason, but also of structuralist reason, the destinal term is rendered as 'reigning impulse' given their expunction of the destiny, their rejection of the principles constitutive of metaphysics, and the principial character of desire, drive, and impulse for these types of reason.

29. In this volume the wisdom of only the first two epochs are treated at length. Homer is taken up in connection with Parmenides in "Access to the Wisdom of the First Epoch," whereas all three ratios of the wisdom of the middle epoch have been explicated in "The Present of Christian *sapientia* in the Sphere of Speech." As for the wisdom of the final epoch, thus far only Rousseau's ratio has been explicated (cf. "Rousseau or the Awakening of Self-Consciousness"); the remaining ratios have been touched upon elsewhere in connection with the conceptual reason of the final epoch; cf. Boeder's "Conceptual Reason in the Final Epoch of Metaphysics."

SOURCES

Regarding the previously published writings of Heribert Boeder gathered here, we extend our thanks to the original publishers and journals for their generous permission either to republish or to publish their English translations in the present volume.

1. "*Veritas seditiosa*" was written for this volume. It was first read at the outset of his lecture-course "Zur Rationalität des christlichen Wissens" (summer semester 1994).

2. "Why 'Being of Beings'?": "Weshalb 'Sein des Seienden'?" *Philosophisches Jahrbuch im Auftrag der Görres-Gesellschaft* 78 (1971), 111-133.

3. "The Difference Inherent in the 'Other Beginning'": "Das Verschiedene im 'anderen Anfang'," in: Ute Guzzoni, Bernhard Rang, and Ludwig Siep, eds., *Der Idealismus und seine Gegenwart. Festschrift für Werner Marx zum 65. Geburtstag* (Hamburg: Meiner, 1976), 3-35.

4. "Privilege of Presence?" is a revised version of an essay bearing the same name which was first read at "Potentiality and Presence," The Forty-Second Annual Meeting of the Metaphysical Society of America held at the Pennsylvania State University, State College, March 8-9, 1991. The essay was subsequently published in the *Graduate Faculty Philosophy Journal* 16:1 (1993), 75-84.

5. "Dissensions" is a revised version of an essay bearing the same name which first appeared in: Kenneth Maly and Parvas Emad, eds., *Heidegger on Heraclitus: A New Reading*, Studies in the History of Philosophy, volume 5 (Lewiston, NY: Edwin Mellen Press, 1986), 167-177.

6. "The Distinction of Reason" is a translation of "Die Unterscheidung der Vernunft," which was first read at "Aufgaben der Philosophie heute," Arbeitstagung des Fachbereichs Kultur- und Geowissenschaften (Universität Osnabrück) in Verbindung mit dem Institutio de Filosofia (Università degli Studi di Urbino), October 24-26, 1988 and subsequently published in *Osnabrücker Philosophische Schriften* (April 1989), 10-20.

7. "Which Thinking Makes All the Difference?" is a revised version of an essay read at "The Ancients and the Moderns: Paradigms in Philosophy," Hannah Arendt Memorial Symposium in Political Philosophy, March 6-7, 1991 at the New School for Social Research, New York. It appears here for the first time.

8. "An End with Distinction" is a revised version of an essay bearing the same name which first appeared in *Research in Phenomenology* 13 (1983), 149-158.

9. "Reason in Modern Thought" was first read at Duquesne University, Pittsburgh, on August 25, 1980 and subsequently published as "Reason in Present Thought" in *Research in Phenomenology* 11 (1981), 159-175. Published here is a slightly revised version of that essay.

10. "Dilthey 'and' Heidegger: On the Historicity of Man" is a translation of the revised text of "Dilthey 'und' Heidegger. Zur Geschichtlichkeit des Menschen," *Phänomenologische Forschung* 16 (1984), 161-177.

11. "Mortal of which Death?": "Sterbliche welchen Todes?" in: Walter Brüstle and Ludwig Siep, eds., *Sterblichkeitserfahrung und Ethikbegründung. Ein Kolloquium für Werner Marx* (Essen: Die blaue Eule, 1988), 38-48.

12. "Action or/and Dwelling," a translation of "Handeln oder/und Wohnen," was originally read in Italian under the title "Agire o/e Dimorare" at "Heidegger e la filosofia pratica," Polermo, November 23-25, 1989. Published here is a revision of the English translation, which first appeared in the *Graduate Faculty Philosophy Journal* 14:2/15:1 (1991), 47-59.

13. "The Limit of Modernity and Heidegger's 'Legacy'" is a translation of the revised text of "Die Grenze der Moderne und Heideggers 'Vermächtnis'," *Braunschweigische Wissenschaftliche Gesellschaft, Jahrbuch 1990* (Göttingen: Erich Goltze, 1991), 75-88.

14. "Twilight of Modernity": "Zwielicht der Moderne," *Philosophische Rundschau* 38:4 (1991), 275-285.

15. "On Reason's Interest in Language": "Vom Vernunft-Interesse an der Sprache," *Acta Institutionis Philosophiae et Aestheticae* 4 (Tokyo 1986), 45-56.

16. "The Dimension of Submodernity," a translation of "Die Dimension der Submoderne," was written for a forthcoming *Festschrift* for Aldo Masullo entitled *"Intersoggettività" – "Fondamento," "Paticità."* A slightly different version of this essay has recently appeared in German in *Abhandlungen der Braunschweigischen Wissenschaftlichen Gesellschaft* 46 (1995), 139-150. It appears for the first time in English in the present volume.

17. "Is Totalizing Thinking Totalitarian?" was first read under the title "Ist das totalisierende Denken totalitär?" at the Carl Friedrich von Siemens Foundation, Munich, on March 26, 1992 and subsequently published in English translation in the *Graduate Faculty Philosophy Journal* 17 (1994), 299-312. Published here is a revised version of that translation.

18. "Judge Contemporary Art?" is a translation of "Heutige Kunst beurteilen?" The essay is a revised version of one first read under the title "Wie begegnet die Philosophie der Kunst?" at "Kunst und Philosophie im Dialog," Vortragsveranstaltung der Industrie- und Handelskammer (IHK) Osnabrück-Emsland, May 4, 1993. It appears for the first time in the present volume.

19. "Europe and the Things of Dwelling" is a translation of "Europa und die Dinge des Wohnens," which was read at the symposium "Der Kulturkanal Arte," held by the Internationales Fernseh-Forum für Musik (Osnabrück/Zürich) on November 11, 1992. It appears for the first time in the present volume.

20. "The Present of Christian *sapientia* in the Sphere of Speech" is a translation of "Die Gegenwart der christlichen *sapientia* in der Sprach-Sphäre," which is an expanded version

of the final two hours of his lecture-course "Zur Rationalität des christlichen Wissens" (summer semester 1994). It appears for the first time in the present volume.

21. "Access to the Wisdom of the First Epoch" is a translation of "Zugang zur Weisheit der Ersten Epoche," which was first read within the frame of his lecture-course "Das frühgriechische Denken und der Anfang der Philosophie" (winter semester 1994-1995). It appears for the first time in the present volume.

SEDITIONS

VERITAS SEDITIOSA

Yes—a separation had to occur, one not sought after and hence avoiding the clamor of rebellion Erasmus had heard in Luther's *veritas seditiosa*. In total stillness with respect to Heidegger's accomplishment, the *sed* of a departure arose, one effected as a *seditio*—remote from the critical affectation predominant today, remote from its strained efforts at self-assertion. But our *seditio* is not merely not an overcoming of metaphysics, it is not even a recuperation from it; for another metaphysics has become apparent to us and incited the present demand for distinction, another metaphysics because an ἀλήθεια other than that of Heidegger's experience of withdrawal has been attended to.

A *sed* urges us to give it voice, effected as a *seditio*, awakened by that to which Heidegger always only alluded as "the most ancient of the ancient" (*das Älteste des Alten*). This most ancient no longer permits the expectation of an "other beginning"; rather, it awakens that which has long since been begun as σοφία, as it is ever more ancient than φιλοσοφία—in each epoch, it awakens the latter. Here "the most ancient of the ancient" comes to speech, this side of the history of philosophy, this side of the world of modernity as well: only now. In this present, however, realized only in a *seditio* by what has been thought in the former configurations of wisdom, realized in their deliverance from the violence of sub- and postmodern thought. How can this occurrence be understood?

In the midst of this world Husserl gave the appearance of having and being able to renew the *ordo philosophandi* in accordance with the Cartesian and Kantian models—grounded in the methodical stance generated by the "radical" ἐποχή. Its radicality dissolves into an illusion not only in Husserl's recollection of Descartes, an illusion whose truth is to be encountered in Heidegger's experience of withdrawal. It is only with the "expropriation" thought by the latter that the radical ἐποχή truly came into the world—on this side of all autocracy of an "attitude."

That experience, however, had to make a turn on this side of modernity—towards a radicalized "poverty" of thinking. This turn was no longer to be "experienced" with Heidegger but rather to be unfolded out of an expunction of all determinacy—precisely on account of this, solely *ordine* and yet not "speculatively." But then how? We answer—neglecting Plato and Heidegger's aversion—by way of a "story": Beckett's title can serve us here as a guiding word: "*Sans*." "Without." From the experience of our present it became a catchword for him. It is a word of endurance. How is that? We first ask: without what or whom? We answer: without either, and elaborate: to stand in the present of contemporary thought without joining in the debate, that is to say, with those who in this today, in its everyday, do the talking for philosophy. Thus 'without joining in the debate' means first of all: without allowing oneself to be dictated the themes of their discourse, without making a contribution to them.

One might think: what absurd obstinacy! Moreover: what vanity! Such character traits may have their causes but no reason (*Grund*). By contrast, the said 'without' most certainly has a reason, that is, the modest intention first of all to learn and only to learn, namely, to learn thinking from what has been thought in philosophy, more precisely, this and only this: to attend to the destiny of the topic of thinking (*die Bestimmung der Sache des Denkens*)—to that which gives what is to be thought. Whoever is "expert" in these matters will easily note here: already this intention has been learned and in fact from that thinker who expressly raised the question 'What is called thinking?' This from the experience: "What is most thought-provoking in our thought-provoking age is that we do not yet think" (*WD*, 3/5 f.). A word from Heidegger—my teacher.

In all the talk while learning, there was no participation in his topic and thus none in the fulfillment of his task. Who would have participated, for instance, in the unfolding of Hegel's system? Perhaps after the manner of a "scientific community," where participation in research is indeed taken for granted? This is certainly how one learns "to do science," but is thinking also to be learned in this way—precisely that thinking which Heidegger asserted is still lacking?

In the philosophy business the prevailing opinion is that in learning, all that matters is engaging in critique. But this is only the flip side of a learning that misunderstands itself as repetition. Such alternatives suppress what is aimed at in learning to think from what has already been thought: to exercise reticence with respect to those thoughts which, in the sense-explication of our world and in the philosophy of its history, have made all the difference—with respect to the thoughts that have, judged in light of the history of science, broken free of the matrices of "ordinary science," that were able and had to assert a new paradigm. The applicability of this model to philosophy lives, however, on the fiction that there too a kind of "ordinary science" persists in the continuum of technical progress.

This fiction is not without cause. It lies in an age-old habit, namely, in that of drawing the philosophical distinction between what appears and its Nature (φύσις). Although the ground of such distinction has disappeared along with the philosophy of our history, the conviction still prevails that one need only attend to what appears, to "phenomena," as is done in the so-called positive sciences, in order then to inquire—somehow "philosophically"—into its "Nature." The illusion of such philosophical inquiry manifests itself, however, in the violence of what appears in asserting its "regional" character—while its "specific" character has long since disappeared. Though the philosophy business makes a virtue out of the calamity of reason's no longer having a subject appropriate to it—for such would have to be a totality. This is manifest in the assurance that the thinking proper to the science of pure reason, or so-called metaphysics, was totalitarian.

Phenomena and their description are to guarantee first of all the immediate comprehensibility and thus accessibility of philosophy. This illusion—and it became an illusion as soon as the relation between the phenomenon and its Nature became groundless in modernity (the progression of modern art is already instructive in this regard)—this illusion was, of course, also promoted by Heidegger insofar as he offered time and again a phenomenal introduction to his thought, which then seems even less comprehensible. On the other hand, it was precisely he who gave a decisive turn to the traditional relation between what appears and φύσις insofar as he understood the latter as a truth to which it is essential that it conceal itself. Precisely this is a turn, however, away from the Nature which was regarded as the essence of what appears to the Nature which, as self-concealing, determined the history of occidental thought. Once again: not the Nature of this or that, nor even the Nature of the All or what is first with respect to everything, but rather φύσις as it is the event of a concealment and in fact one that has come to be historical in occidental thought.

An earth-shattering occurrence already becomes apparent here: that which all philosophical science of this history sustained was the difference and thus the relation between Nature, or essence, and what appears. At the limit of modernity Heidegger slips completely free of this relation while remaining caught up in its first side, namely, φύσις as the event of concealment in truth as it is understood by the Greeks, namely, in unconcealment. It is precisely on account of this that his relation to philosophy as phenomenology literally remains shady. In the end Heidegger's thought no longer deals with phenomena but rather with an event of concealment that destines thinking to forget its proper topic—spoken in Heidegger's darkness: thinking turns to what appears, to what is present, to what is, even to the Being of beings—both with reference to its universality and also to its divinity—but by way of this turn forgets precisely Being itself.

No light penetrates the darkness of Heidegger's thought so long as reference continues to be made to the double-pivoting of a φύσις that is simultaneously an emergence into appearance and a self-concealment. This reference fades insofar as thinking finds its way out of Nature not only as it is the Nature of what appears but, what is more, out of Nature as the history of self-concealing and thereby severs the history of occidental thought from just this Nature. This was our point of departure from Heideggerian thought.

In order to clarify just what occurred with our turn, it is now necessary to elucidate how it came about.

Heidegger already taught the attention not to phenomena so much as to what has been thought—this being for the entire philosophy business, and especially for its contemporary manifestation, an abomination of, shall we say, inbreeding. But how did Heidegger attend to what has been thought? With the decisive qualification that it belongs to a history of oblivion and even to what remains unthought—precisely in this respect, one unbridgeably severed from the likewise historical, since it is missive, commemoration. If he sought out what has been thought in its strength and abstained from all manner of critical belittlement, then by no means only so as to take advantage of some opportunity to place himself on its ground; for his place remained the turning (*Kehre*) of the said oblivion into the noticing of just that oblivion and the history of concealment. This could only mean: to tarry in the presence of the mission of this history as it was present for him in the concealment proper to the "truth" or neg-ligence characteristic of technical thinking. It is precisely on account of this truth that what is said in the name ἀλήθεια, in truth as unconcealedness, for him becomes the legacy of his thought. As indicated above, it was only in taking our point of departure from this legacy that our turn could begin. But that means at the same time: in view of the usual notion which Heidegger read, as it were, as a bastion of forgetful thinking—namely, the locus of truth is judgment. The scrutiny of this notion, however, was ultimately referred by Heidegger's rejection of it no longer merely to the beginning of Greek thinking but rather—due to the oblivion of the hint in the name ἀλήθεια, or unconcealedness, an oblivion which started already in that beginning—to what has been spoken pre-incipiently and thus to the pre-philosophical ἔπος of the Greeks. It was precisely here that it became necessary to hear from what has been spoken, what has been said concerning λόγος and ἀλήθεια (cf. my "The Early Greek Usage of the Words *Logos* and *Aletheia*"). What was to be heard there—once again, beyond the ἀλήθεια which for Heidegger remained bound up with φύσις?

'Αλήθεια has its place in the relations dominant in letting someone know something—where one is dependent upon the knowledge of another and at the same time is faced with the possibility that he who was questioned will prevent a participation in knowledge. Here knowledge is based on testimony, on an attention to (*Anwesenheit bei*) something. Contrary to Heidegger's habit of representing being-present (*Anwesen*) with reference to appearing and this in turn with reference to an emerging to which a self-concealing is simultaneously essential, Homer has it be understood: the key to the sense of being-present lies not in being-present as it is held to be a modification of appearing but rather in one's attention to (*Anwesen bei*) something, in one's regard of (*Achten auf*) something or someone.

The denial of participation in knowledge by means of an immediate deception or by eloquently pulling the wool over someone's eyes is met by a discernment on the part of reason as the sole superior adversary. It is not as if it could replace the testimony of eye and ear. Rather, its discernment is related only to the said denial, to the attempt to deceive. As for what presence is as an activity of reason, such is understood precisely with respect to this limit, to an incipient negativity. This state of affairs is of elementary significance for the comprehension of philosophy as the science of reason. It stands or falls with the said limit, whose actuality continues to be the distinction between "how it is" and "how it is not"—thus the delimitation of "being." Just this is attested insofar as ἀλήθεια, or what is called 'truth', has its element in the λόγος, in its critical nature. It is only via this λόγος that a truth can be safeguarded against deception. The pre-philosophical understanding of ἀλήθεια proves to be a bequest for its status in early Greek philosophy.

Just how fundamental the privative character of ἀλήθεια is to such letting-know is manifest in the earliest philosophy, namely, in pre-Parmenidean physiology and cosmology—astonishingly enough, precisely in the fact that there is no talk of it whatsoever. For letting-know has no significance for their respective constitutions since their knowledge radically severs itself from all hearsay, instead being grounded, on the one hand, on one's own presence with what appears and, on the other hand, on the presence of the latter as the κόσμος of everything. This is in turn present with him who understands the λόγος of the ἁρμονίη of this κόσμος because he has attained reason from the latter and by no means from a plurality of appearances.

Only with Parmenides' dismissal of both forms of presence does ἀλήθεια turn up in philosophy. How so? In fact, renewed as the topic which a goddess lets one know, but with the decisive difference that what is given to be known does not depend on the attention of a "Muse," that is, an attention to everything; rather, such shows the ground of its truth within itself. To take on the corresponding reason in pure reflection—precisely this task faces the listener in this case and thus he has to produce the knowledge in question as his own.

Why recall all of this? Because it is just in this regard that our departure from Heidegger's view of what he called 'the first beginning of thinking' occurred. Yet this separation was by no means carried out by thinking Heidegger's thought "further," but rather by subjecting it to an ἐποχή, by stepping out of the field of resistance which he himself generated to the investigation just recalled and in fact in his reliance on the self-concealing inherent in the nature of truth, a nature that was held to have been constitutive of the history of occidental thought. It was only this detachment from this last point of bondage to the φύσις which conceals itself in what appears that opened up our view to the history of philosophy in light of the rational works constitutive of it and no longer to the "theory of the Being of beings" attributed to it.

Precisely this view asserted of occidental thought that it privileged thinking over Being as it is that of beings. It took up the demand to think "Being itself" as the destiny which has priority over thinking. It seemed to have remained what had everywhere gone unthought in that history. In our transformed stance towards that history, however, Parmenides already revealed: thinking is in fact to be urged to bring its topic, namely, "how it is," to the determinacy of "being"; this, however, in keeping with the prior standard of the difference between "how it is to be" and "how it is not to be," namely, according to the standard set by Θέμις and Δίκη, or the directive provided by what has always already been established. It is precisely on account of this that the thinking which is freed of all observation of appearances takes on the fundamental trait of acknowledging "principles" (cf. my *Ground and Present as the Aim of Early Greek Philosophical Inquiry*). The determination of thinking is perfectly perspicuous here and lacks any of the obscurity characteristic of the "mission" of history as it is thought by Heidegger.

The complete traversal of the history of metaphysics (cf. my *Topology of Metaphysics*) revealed: it possesses a historicity which is grounded in the acknowledgment of principles; for these are epochally distinguished and thus the corresponding acknowledgment is as well. What calls forth the said differences? It is just this question that resulted in our complete departure from Heidegger's "history of Being." Its originary "there is–Being" (*es gibt–Sein*) was transformed into an incipient "it gives," a gift that is given as knowledge and in fact as an epochally distinguished bequest of σοφία to φιλο-σοφία. The latter is always offered a knowledge concerning man's destiny to distinguish himself not only from other animals but, prior to that, from himself. Yet that which—unlike, for instance, in the teachings of Buddha—in our tradition, and only in it, called forth a philosophical reason is precisely that state of affairs already touched on in the aforementioned elucidation of ἀλήθεια: it has its abode in λόγος and thus in the latter's πειθώ, or persuasiveness—opposed to the possibility of deception.

Each epoch of philosophy begins with a negative stance of thinking towards the respective wisdom as a type of knowledge for which just this wisdom cannot offer any guarantee. Only the self-assertion of reason contrary to the wisdom which it itself does not furnish makes possible reason's distinction from itself, its purification into perfect self-activity in a positive relation to the knowledge that has been given and thus in the conception of its truth within the bounds of a logic that it itself furnishes.

It already follows from this shifting stance: there has never been a one-tracked history of philosophy but always a history distinguished within itself—said in view of Heidegger: never the one "epoch" of metaphysics, that is to say: the keeping-to-itself of Being itself in a growing oblivion of that which properly gives what is to be thought. This, as it were, "physical" view of the history of thought had to be abandoned, though we held fast to what Heidegger saw as the task of thinking in a transformed sense. Yet in each epoch of philosophical thinking, the task proved to be: to conceive the truth of a configuration of wisdom—namely, the knowledge of the Muses, of the Christian doctrine, and finally of the civil consciousness. It then became clear precisely in view of this: an epoch of the said history is concluded wherever precisely this task is accomplished as a common endeavor. This history of philosophy is neither completed insofar as philosophy becomes equal to its concept nor does it fall into ruins insofar as metaphysical thinking abandons itself to technical thinking. It is concluded as a tripartite architectonic of that which is epochally accomplished. It is just this then that grants the departedness of architectonic reason, which according to its epochal principles is constructive reason, its sense, namely, that of an accomplished task.

The topic of thinking is at present no longer what Hegel called 'physical and spiritual Nature', no longer those totalities of pure reason which Kant had represented in the dialectic of pure reason, but rather a history, a world, and a speech which are separated from all "Nature." This insight initiated the sense-explication of modernity—to be sure, one inconceivable to modernity itself (cf. my *The Rational Architectonic of Modernity*). Only the notion of a closed history freed our view for the other notion of an equally closed world of the sense-explication, which explicates itself as that of modernity in singular significance and in fact with the pervasive severance of our world from its history. The clarification of the characteristic architectonic of this sense-explication was the second stretch of the course of our undertaking. What did it contribute to the clarification of our task?

As the explicated world, ours was initially distinguished into three dimensions, for the sense-explication proper to it is first directed to the sciences, which are no longer grounded philosophically—to their speech (Frege), world (Schlick), and history (Kuhn)—then to the sense-construct of the life lived through (*erlebt*)—in its history (Dilthey), world (Husserl), and speech (Wittgenstein)—finally, to the other future over against our world as it is first historically determined (Marx), then mundanely (Nietzsche), finally linguistically (Heidegger).

In this final dimension the sense-explication has the peculiarity of severing itself expressly from philosophy and in fact in favor of the thought of man's distinction from himself. Thus, each time a trail is left here by what the configurations of wisdom once brought into view. Such a view of the distinguished man, however, is failing for the core sense-explication of modernity. It remains referred to a future before which it pauses. Unlike the muddle-headed advocates of utopias.

The distinction of the said sense-explicative dimensions of our world reflected on its history and brought the following to light: the reason that in each instance takes a negative stance towards a configuration of wisdom, towards its givenness, is distinguished within itself. Taking its point of departure from the determinacy of thinking—in the case of the first epoch, as observation (ἱστορίη) in accordance with the difference between what appears and its "Natures"—it is "natural" reason; taking its point of departure from the determinacy of the topic—again in the case of early Greek philosophy: as the κόσμος of the totality of what appears—it is "mundane" reason. Distinguished from both of these incipient types of reason, purified of both into the conception of the truth of a type of wisdom, it is "conceptual" reason.

The sense-explication of modernity translates "natural" into "technical" reason (Frege, Schlick, Kuhn), "mundane" into "apocalyptic" reason (Marx, Nietzsche, Heidegger), but "conceptual" into "hermeneutic" reason (Dilthey, Husserl, Wittgenstein). Here it should be noted: the selection of authors is guided entirely by the difference that their respective thoughts make within the framework of intellectual tasks. This selection completely disregards an estimation in view of their effect on the public.

Yet can there still be any talk of types of reason within the sphere of modernity? Does this talk not relapse into the assumption of a faculty of human reason? The introduction of a reason proper to philosophy and its history has freed itself from this assumption, a reason introduced with its early Greek beginning in the negative stance of thought towards the knowledge of the Muses as something given. The common ground relating the latter and philosophical knowledge lay, however, in the presence claimed by both sides. Yet Heidegger contested the "privilege of presence" in the thinking of our tradition—not least due to the priority he had to give the future; and it is on account of this that he in turn had to radically temporalize the sense of "Being."

It might now seem—and this semblance has also become operative in present thought—that Heidegger asserts a priority of absence (*Abwesen*) over presence (*Anwesen*). Yet this is an oblique view, namely, one still attached to the so-called "question of Being." This question had its sense only on the basis of the question concerning the nature of truth. It hit upon the precedence, due to its originariness, of concealedness over unconcealedness. It is not presence and absence that make all the difference there, thus also not "Being," but rather the disclosure of a remoteness to the things of the future world and the growing propinquity to them—to let them become of concern instead of being present. In a concern that takes on the significance of the future. If, in the epochs of its conception, reason has been the "faculty of principles" (Kant), there can no longer be any talk of it with regard to the sense-explications of modernity, for it is by no means present in the latter as that philosophical reason which is called forth by a configuration of wisdom—neither in negative nor in positive significance. Modernity requires and frees us to translate what has been regarded philosophically as "reason" into a *ratio terminorum*. Into which? Precisely into that ratio which Heidegger was able to understand only in the unity of the phrase 'the destiny of the topic of thinking' since it is involved in the "event of the appropriation" of Being (itself) and thinking. With its dissolution into its three terms, this phrase allowed for a "building," for that "tectonic" thinking which discloses the sphere of history as well as that of the world in their architectonics.

But even if the latter is, if not a closed, then at least a complete construct, the ἐποχή inherited from modernity, and thus the reticence with respect to what has already been thought, is to be intensified. The ἐποχή thereby enables us to become aware of our own place: the sphere of speech—as it is to be appreciated neither intrahistorically nor intramundanely. Here history and world are only seemingly reduced to moments of speech, for it is not the totality of what the "concept" has been. The sphere of the actuality of speech cannot be exhibited as a closed construct. It is precisely here that the antipathy of the submoderns to thinking in terms of totalities has its roots.

But how can this sphere be at all determined as such? Indeed, no longer as such but rather by way of its distinction as an open sphere. In what way?

We recall: prior to all wisdom, man distinguished the genus 'living being' within itself, namely, into man and the other animals. Only the configurations of wisdom show how man is capable of distinguishing himself from himself, namely, as hero, as saint, as citizen. In the history of philosophy, however, it is reason which distinguishes itself both within—into natural and mundane reason—and from itself, and in fact as conceptual reason. That which was correspondingly distinguished in the world of modernity was the sense proper to each sense-explication. And thus we talk only loosely of technical and apocalyptic and furthermore of hermeneutic reason. These stand only seemingly for a distinction of reason from itself. An observation of some consequence. To what extent?

What becomes of this bequest of distinctions within the sphere of speech as it harbors the tasks of present thought? To begin with, its first horizon drew our attention to the fact that the rational architectonic of modernity as just sketched was not properly structured inasmuch as its periphery had been misinterpreted. Namely, we have come to see that the periphery is occupied not by technical but rather by hermeneutic reason. Why? The periphery is the place of the encounter of what in the sphere of history has been the innermost type of reason—namely, the said conception—since it distinguished a given epoch. Hermeneutic reason can only simulate—to be sure, not: imitate—this reason. What is given to hermeneutic conception is no longer the truth of a given wisdom but rather the truth of a Being which is lived through, which is dispersed immediately into a multiplicity of phenomena. We recall here only Husserl's "principle of all principles": whereas, e.g., the Aristotelian principle of non-contradiction let reason stay with itself, with the state of affairs as a rational one; in the Husserlian principle, in question is something that primarily has to be given in a perception and thus is extrinsic to thinking, to reflection. Every phenomenon "of an originarily giving intuition" stands for this principle, which, unlike the Aristotelian principle, hasn't the character of an axiom, hasn't the character of a truth to be acknowledged in the actuality of reason, more precisely: of the λόγος. The Husserlian principle is an assertion that has its truth in the will and in fact in the will to truth, to phenomenological science. Wittgenstein pushes this mentality to its extreme, a mentality which says: description, not explanation, is the task, and it explicitly excludes the concept as such.

To understand a bequest which is originarily, since it is in itself, nothing thought: here it becomes apparent in what way this hermeneutic intention is different from a conception of a bequest, which is precisely the eminent sense of something thought, something known, since it is not just known how it is but, prior to that, how it is to be and how is not to be—thus it knows the difference the "law" makes.

The first sense-explicative dimension of modernity is, as was said above, a simulation of conceptual reason, for there is no wisdom in this world that would allow of conception. The dimension of technical reason, however, moves from its previous peripheral into the intermediate position of the sense-explicative architectonic of modernity and thus—and this is important—into the immediate neighborhood with, as well as opposition to, apocalyptic reason. Each rejects the other—especially regarding the future and thus the present of man within the sphere of modernity.

The occasion for this revision of the sense-explicative architectonic of modernity arose from our observation that in contemporary thought the core sense-explication of modernity is simulated—Marx by Merleau-Ponty, Nietzsche by Foucault, Heidegger by Derrida. What occurs there? Whereas the former in each case left the trail of the said σοφία with its demand for man's distinction from himself and, precisely on account of this, abandoned philosophy, the simulative way of thinking proper to submodernity turns against this demand for an other future of man and therefore is able to slip into the guise of philosophy—into the externality of a guise since the attempt is made to abandon philosophy philosophically. Precisely because this attempt depends on the core sense-explication of modernity and simultaneously sinks below its level of being the trace of wisdom, we speak in this regard of the formation of the dimension of "submodernity."

What characterizes its way of thinking? It is an-archic, and this not only in the modern sense of the rejection of all principles of conceptual reason but, what is more, of their modern translation into something that asserts "dominance," that is held to assert the unity of a world. Here 'anarchy' does not mean that this thinking relinquishes all regulation, that it abandons itself to arbitrariness. No, it is—as they say these days—externally regulated and in fact by that "outside" constituted by the so-called others. It is precisely on account of this that Derrida speaks of a "responsible anarchy." Here thinking knows itself to be bound to answer to the others, to their alterity and ultimately to the alterity of the "Wholly Other." They are others, however, no longer in the sense of an ego as a *res cogitans*, no longer even of an ego that enters into intersubjectivity, but rather of an ego of intercorporeality—as Merleau-Ponty terms it. Thus the responsibility in question here is that for the other as he is encountered *in corpore*. This will have to be further developed on the appropriate occasion (see, for now, "The Dimension of Submodernity," pp. 227-239 below).

Here we can direct only an orienting glance at the totality of the sphere of speech—a totality not closed but rather one distinguishing the horizons of thinking.

We recall briefly: in the history of philosophy, reason distinguished itself within itself—as natural and mundane reason—and then from itself as conceptual reason. In the world of the sense-explication, sense distinguished itself within itself, and in fact according to its hermeneutic and technical understanding, and then from both according to its apocalyptic understanding. Now as far as speech—let us say: responding—is concerned, it distinguishes itself within itself insofar as it forms on the one hand the said anarchic horizon of thinking, but on the other that of linguistic operations. In the latter, the hermeneutic sense-explication's contribution to the articulation of the world is abolished and transferred to the sciences, which are no longer even the simulation of philosophy, sciences which we characterize as structuralist: first, pure linguistics (Jakobson); second, semiology (Barthes); third, the theory of subhistoric and submundane linguistic structures, namely, structural anthropology (Lévi-Strauss) and psychoanalysis (Lacan). If 'subhistoric' is said here instead of the usual 'prehistoric', then because the structures disclosed there remain present no less than do the submundane structures of the "unconscious."

The distinction of thinking from itself within the history of philosophy was borne by conceptual reason; within the world of the sense-explication, by its apocalyptic type. How are matters now with this distinction within the sphere of speech proper to present thought? In view of modernity, only one sense-explication remains to be transformed and in fact that of technical reason. But how on earth could a descendent of just this type of reason take upon itself the task of distinguishing reason from itself? In which determinacy does it even come into view here? In precisely the one that accepted thinking in the transformation of Heidegger's legacy, namely, his understanding of ἀλήθεια. In its formation of history and world into closed constructs, it already proved to be—spoken with Heidegger—a building thinking, though as "logotectonic" it dismisses his thinking. Specifically in the translation of what for him remained "poetizing." It is exactly this logotectonic thinking just invoked that is in the process of arranging precisely that horizon of speech which requires a distinction of thinking from itself. Only as such does it serve the aim of all wisdom. That is, dwelling and its ἦθος. The contemporary establishment of an ethics-market and the most diverse supplying of it has noticed this somehow, but disguises what is characteristic of dwelling by projecting a continuum extending from conventional moral philosophy to a theory of action. Here, at the great expense of acumen, trivialities are offered which are readily accessible to common sense.

What dwelling is, how action is subordinate to it, have been brought into view by the configurations of wisdom of our tradition, and precisely this was appreciated in a certain way in their conceptions—we recall here only the inaugural manifestations of conceptual reason in each epoch: neither Parmenides nor Plotinus nor Kant takes his point of departure from action, that is, from giving preference; each stresses the precedence of something that is not at one's disposal. The modern attempts that took shape in the projections of an other dwelling of man are no less instructive, despite their having foundered. Such foundering points most insistently to what the philosophy of conceptual reason has known: the truth of a wisdom, namely, of the knowledge of dwelling prior to all habits, has to be one already given. It cannot be fabricated or established by a consensus of a majority of provisional opinions. For, strangely enough, dwelling is—unlike the patterns of human behavior—highly uncommon since, for it, man's distinction from himself is imperative. It is precisely on account of this that the speech of the type of knowledge in question is in fact in an eminent sense an inhabited (*gewohnt*), but not a common (*gewöhnlich*), speech. It cannot be appreciated as what is spoken but only as what has been said, and this in the exceptional sense that the listener abides by what is said to him. Therefore, in his case the aforementioned distinction begins with one of listening itself. The New Testament says it well: whoever has ears with which to listen—that is to say: for whom listening is not an immediate but rather a mediated, namely, an expressly given and thus distinguished, listening.

Logotectonic thinking is focused on this distinction. Learning this distinction is the first task of reason where its history, namely, that of philosophy, has been dismissed not only with the articulation of our world but also where the limit of this modernity has been transgressed into the horizons of thinking constituting the sphere of speech. Its first horizon elicits the simulation of the core sense-explication of modernity and lets thinking loose into the said anarchy. The other horizon is that of the linguistic reason just sketched. Both horizons melt into the sole place that present thought demands: *hic Rhodus, hic saltus*. Which leap is called for? Once again: to man's distinction from himself and in fact with reticence regarding the configurations of wisdom which no longer presently address anyone as they did in their respective epochs; no longer, as in modernity, as projections of an other future of the other man; but rather as those that have been. Here the positions of thought regarding a knowledge of the destiny of man which thinking itself does not furnish is completed in the sense of that completeness of that knowledge which was proper to the Muses, to the Homeric seer who knows, namely, how it actually is, how it will be, how it is before.

For us such knowledge of a concluding whole cannot be that of philosophy as it has been First Science. After its passing and the fading of its modern adversary, all that remains of that knowledge is the accomplished vision of man's distinction from himself, as it was brought into view in the configurations of wisdom of our tradition.

"Without"—we began with this contemporary code word. The familiarity of what it addresses, however, does not yet offer the distinct knowledge of our present. For such, a distinction even in the experience of this "without," of the *sed* of the aforementioned *seditio*, is required. A distinction that is itself to be further distinguished: that of speech both within and from itself.

HISTORY

WHY "BEING OF BEINGS"?

The "question of Being"—it is Heidegger's question, and it remains his, not least due to the twofold answer that precedes it: on the one hand, the question of Being is the unifying question of all metaphysics—namely, the question concerning the Being of beings (*Sein des Seienden*)—on the other, it was never raised by this metaphysics—namely, as the question concerning the truth of Being. After, in all of metaphysics, the question of Being remained caught up in the turn towards beings, what has been forgotten therein is to be inquired into in the future: "What is Being? It is Itself. Future thinking must learn to experience and to say it" (*BH*, 328/210).

This question of Being—it has stood there already for a long, an astonishingly long time as a challenge. Still a challenge of "future thinking." Of which future? It is determined in accordance with the cited bifurcation in the sense of the question of Being. Yet why is it not entirely a question of the present and a demand on present thinking? Is not everything to be experienced and said time and again now? Must not a demand on future thinking make one hesitate? Hesitation given the assumption that for a "thinker," future thinking and it alone is what is absolutely inviolable. Or could it not be moved most decisively by the determination of what it must learn?

Or is what is repulsive about metaphysical thinking only gathered in the present? One is reminded here of the repeated projections of the "philosophy of the future" (Feuerbach, etc.), which obviously coincide with the rejection of the entire metaphysical tradition—however different these attempts may be. Such a rejection—it is, as I have shown in "The Natural Consciousness," peculiar to the kind of dominance proper to the principle of the philosophy of the modern era—can meet this tradition as a whole, however, only after Hegel grasped it in the unity of a singular history. And what remains of this history and its unity "beyond" his concept?

After Heidegger also elucidated the name 'metaphysics' in a way that promotes the rejection of the knowledge thus characterized, this name has everywhere become a scarecrow for thought today. Considered precisely—and in fact in view of the metaphysical positions in question—it proves to be a cenotaph.

Yet the talk here need not be of the inconsequentiality of this name insofar as one instead keeps to what "metaphysics" expressly presents in its history as its topic. Concerning this, it is said in "What Is Metaphysics?": "It means beings as a whole and speaks of Being. It names Being and means the being *qua* the being. From its beginning to its end, the stating proper to metaphysics moves strangely in a persistent confusion of beings and Being" (*RGM,* 365/211).

Obviously of concern here is not the mere occurrence of the word 'to be' (*sein*) in philosophical texts, nor a description of the meaning and manifold use of this word, and finally not even the logical analysis of 'is' and its modalities. Rather, at issue is the question concerning the Being of beings as the "guiding question of philosophy" (*N* I, 90/67 f.) and thus a topic that philosophy brings to speech everywhere and explicitly as its topic. It is precisely to what is explicitly said there that we shall attend in what follows.

I

Why "Being of beings"? How does philosophy come to consider the "Being of beings"—in such a way that the contrast of Being with beings is essential to the exhibition of its own knowledge? But does it ever come to this? Does it not necessarily begin as a consideration of the Being of beings? Heidegger knows: even if the transmission may be uncertain, already Anaximander had to talk about beings and regarded their Being. In Parmenides no doubt seems possible, it is explicitly said here; Heidegger repeatedly cited this as the purest expression of that which is most worthy of thought in the whole of our philosophical tradition: "It is, namely, Being." And Plato? Need there still be any question here—in view of the "struggle with the giants for Being"? Prototypical for all metaphysics, however, is Aristotle's question and in fact with the phrase 'the being *qua* the being' (*das Seiende als das Seiende*), which denotes its topic; Heidegger's insertion of the second 'the' (*das*) supports his view that that Being must be meant here which makes every being a being.

And yet—the history of First Philosophy, the crisis of its principles, makes one ask in response: Is that so? Is that said? It is not so. It is not said. Without entering into ancient philosophy (cf. instead my "The Origin of 'Dialectic' and the Theory of 'Being'" and "On Plato's Proper Topic"), we shall only scrutinize the evidence in Aristotle, since it remains of immediate importance for the further answer of the question raised at the outset.

"There is a science that views being *qua* being and what occurs in it with regard to itself" (*Metaph.* 1003a21). This science is First Philosophy—the first over against the other sciences, in particular over against second philosophy, which considers a being that is in motion and that has that motion's ground within itself.

To consider being only insofar as it is a being—one usually hears therein the proper task of "ontology." That this name first appears towards the end of the sixteenth century is less odd than that it also arises *de facto* from the way of thinking proper to school-philosophy, remains limited to this, and is rejected everywhere when it comes into contact with the protagonists of the philosophy of the modern era.

Now is it an inconsequential accident that Aristotle does not name his theory of being *qua* being 'ontology'? Hardly, since he gave this theory a specific name. For him it is the "theological" science (1026^{a}19)—theological in the twofold sense that it is first of all proper to a god and that it treats of what is divine (983^{a}5).

To what extent now does this science consider being *qua* being (1026^{a}31)? Does it perhaps consider at one time one and then the other—on the one hand, being; on the other, the divine? Is First Philosophy divided into ontology and theology? However one may determine the coherence of what is thus distinguished insofar as one is, following Heidegger, on the look-out for a unified origin of the "onto-theological" character of metaphysics—the fact remains: "metaphysics represents the beingness of beings in a twofold manner: on the one hand, the whole of beings as such in the sense of their most general traits . . . ; at the same time, however, the whole of beings as such in the sense of the highest and thus divine being . . ." (*RGM*, 373/217).

It must be stressed here: Aristotle does not himself set forth any such bifurcation in the topic or the mode of inquiry proper to First Philosophy. On the contrary: he attends persistently and expressly to its uniformity (*Metaph.* 1003^{b}13; cf. *APo.* 87^{a}38). Such does not in fact exclude the possibility that the bifurcation of his theory remained concealed from him, but in any case it leads one to separate Heidegger's interpretation from what is said and makes one hesitate in the face of the common contrast between an "ontology" and Aristotle's "theological science."

Which place would an ontology have in the system of the Aristotelian sciences? It would certainly be sought among the "theoretical" sciences, in mathematics and physics. But could it be at all regarded as a science of its own if it treats of "the whole of beings as such in the sense of their most general traits"? And does theology perhaps also represent the "beingness" of beings? It would indeed be mere representing, such as this ontology is, were it to pursue a universal such as "beingness."

Aristotle has us understand: First Philosophy fixes being as such in its gaze "with respect to the whole" (*Metaph.* 1003^{a}23, 1005^{a}33); the universality addressed in this phrase has its sense only on the basis of the character of the principle and ground proper to the being with which theology deals; it is First Philosophy insofar as it treats of the first, and only on account of this does it treat of being as such in view of the whole; for the primary being is the first not only insofar as there is nothing "prior" to it but also insofar as it is the first with respect to every other (1026ᵃ29).

Aristotle knows no ontology, that is to say, no science that concerns itself with the "most general traits" of beings. He is resolute: if First Philosophy could not be theology, it would have to be "physics" (1026ᵃ27). There is no place for an ontology here, whereas obviously nothing prevents school-philosophy, indifferent to this theology and physics, from representing beings as such according to their most general traits. Such representation indeed becomes a science only when it practices linguistic analysis, when it describes and compares the philosophical and everyday uses of the words 'to be' and 'is'.

The internal structure of Aristotle's three theoretical sciences already reveals that they cannot be supplemented by an additional one—to say nothing of a fundamental ontology for all three. In what is obviously an ascending order, Aristotle names: mathematics, physics, theology. And he makes this order comprehensible on the basis of the constitution of the beings themselves in question. Here two and only two moments along with their respective opposites are decisive; from them the completeness of the organization of the theoretical sciences may be inferred.

The first possible connection of the decisive determinations of being as such would be this: not there separately (*gesondert da*) and only in transition. But things of this kind are not at all mentioned since they lie, like that which is "accidental," outside of the scope of any science. The first level of theory is mathematics; it treats of a being which—in a qualified way—is likewise not there separately and yet is "unmoved"; in this way it fulfills what is demanded of the subject of a theoretical science: this subject is "of necessity" because its "principles" or grounds cannot be otherwise; they always remain equal to themselves.

But the mathematical sciences grasp being *qua* being only with respect to something "accidental," which it abstracts and isolates from a being (1003ᵃ25; cf. *Ph.* 193ᵇ34). That which is not merely "in thought" but is there separately by itself and is at the same time in motion by itself, such is the topic of "physics." And the topic of theology is such that it is there separately and thereby not merely "in thought" (193ᵇ34), but by its very nature is unmoved.

The theory of being *qua* being achieves completeness via the various possibilities of ascribing or denying separate presence and transition to a being. Yet these two respects determine not only the organization of the theoretical sciences; in accordance with them, the hierarchy is also determined. It obviously is directed towards a first that is there separately and that lacks any kind of transition.

If one does not take these two determinations to be obvious or somehow derived from the "phenomena," one must ask: why is the first characterized by just these? Why is it just these two respects that in their shifting connection deliver the outline of the entire theory of being?

Here it must be asked: how does Aristotle at all come to regard being *qua* being as the topic of the first theoretical science? Because he, in the philosophical tradition—he sees it this way himself—questions concerning the first principles and causes of beings—in short: concerning the first of beings. But why: of beings? Would this perhaps be the same as: of things or the phenomena or whatever one might name among that which is immediately available? Was this house or this shrub readily, i.e., without philosophical decision, a "being" for Aristotle?

To be able to speak of this house or of this shrub as "beings" required a lengthy discussion and this precisely because philosophy had never spoken imprecisely of beings but instead with complete determinacy; and due to this determinacy, the compatibility of the talk about beings with something like this house and this shrub had to be scrutinized and demonstrated.

Philosophy had talked all the more definitely in that it found occasion to talk of beings for the first time in the critique of its earliest themes—of the All and its first. Parmenides showed: that which is to be intuited is solely being, namely, the separateness of "how it is" and "how it is not." On the only passable "path of inquiry," on the path of "how it is," he contests the compatibility of the older theme with being and summarizes that which differentiates as follows: "Μοῖρα has bound it [*sc.* being] to be whole and motionless" (B 8.35).

The history of the consequences of this word need not be repeated here (cf. my "Parmenides and the Decline of Cosmological Knowledge"). Nor is this the place to unfold the intrinsic connection of these two determinations with that former theme of philosophy. For here they are only to be set in relation to the Aristotelian theory of being *qua* being.

But how is 'being there separately' explained in contrast to 'being whole'? In post-Parmenidean philosophy, being is reinterpreted as the "All"; and the component parts of this All are also regarded in turn as "beings" insofar as these parts are in themselves uniform, indistinguishable, and retain in everything that comes to be and passes away the identity of their character; thus understood, each being is a something, constantly separated from every other by way of the definition of what it is.

With that which remains equal to itself and separated from another, which likewise remains equal to itself and uniform within itself—such as, e.g., Empedocles' "elements"—that which is proper to the Aristotelian definition is not yet fulfilled. The passage through so-called sophistry and dialectics, the exposition of its significance for a "human wisdom," its pertinence to a λόγος, and its relation to the difference between opinion and knowledge, remains essential to the theory of being.

Something is there separately not just because it is addressable on its own; it must also be there primarily, namely, not only being there because it inheres in another, occurs along with something else. One has to be able to say of it and to see: it is there without having to refer to anything else.

The Aristotelian theory of being—and that means the theoretical sciences—is divided and ordered in view of a first being, which as the first is characterized by the fact that it is there for itself and is immovable. Now why should one address this first as the Being of beings when of concern here is obviously a certain being? Its determinations show that Aristotelian First Philosophy, namely, theology, remains bound up with the Parmenidean theory of being.

And yet: the latter theory did not take itself to be theology; the latter being was no first over against another; it was unique. It could not by any means be reconciled with that which does not fulfill, not even in part, its determination to be whole or uniform and motionless. There was no place here for sciences, regardless of which kind, for any consideration of the "prior" (grounds and causes) or the first; and so a theory of being "*qua* being" was also unnecessary. But does just this Aristotelian phrase not give occasion to talk of the "Being" of beings?

How does this phrase come about in the history of the theory of being? Only a brief retrospect is possible here. The decisive blow to the Parmenidean theory of being does not come from the attempts to save the older theory of the "All" but rather from so-called sophistry. In what way? Parmenides had rejected traditional knowledge as the "opinions of the mortals" insofar as he not only showed its incompatibility with the character of insight but also exposed the insecure ground of its previous status.

Protagoras objects to this that for man the "truth" of opinions alone is of importance and this especially with regard to what, according to his character, the topic of the opinion is: the estimations which guide human action. Here knowledge does not simply conflict with ignorance but rather better with poorer knowledge; its superiority is proven by the persuasiveness with which it is exhibited. "How it is," or "being," is that which persuades in the conflict of opinions.

The sophistic blow to the Eleatic theory of being is completed, however, only in the proof that the same fate befalls it as does the opinions in Zeno's dialectic. Gorgias shows how this theory is itself nothing but an opinion and, what is more, an indefensible one, lacking persuasiveness. The critique is here carried out, in keeping with the Eleatic manner, purely on the strength of the λόγος and expressly regarding its character; for the argument leads from the impossibility of being itself via the impossibility of the insight into being to the impossibility of making being clear in discourse.

In its uniqueness over against the multiplicity making up the topic of opinion, being now appears to be just as meaningless as the insight into it appears to be empty and inconsequential. How does a theory of being arise here once again? In the recollection of the sophistic art of refuting convictions—convicting them of contradiction—and generating convictions—raising the possibly true to the probable and the most probable, for instance, by way of "mythical" depiction. This recollection keeps to opinion as that which can be influenced and generated; it sticks to the cognitive character of the corresponding art, to its causation, to the verification of the knowledge in the work.

Plato's division of "being" into visible and invisible being issues from the division of persuasiveness which he developed in view of the sophistic art: persuading on the basis of expert knowledge and persuading without knowledge. It is not as if Plato wanted to reject "human wisdom" as Parmenides did. Of concern to him is rather to set opinion in relation to knowledge, on the basis of which opinion can attest its correctness.

There is no new theory of being that could treat only of "the" being. Now being is essentially related to the difference between opinion and "science" and thereby to the intention to mediate them. Moreover, in his later work Plato's theory is a "human wisdom" whose aim is to impart to life the determination of the Good—Plato wants the *Timaeus* to be understood as a link between the *Republic* and the *Critias*.

The connection between opinion and knowledge originarily attested by the "arts" demands a division of being into being "somehow" and being "truly." This requires a discussion of the Eleatic thesis of the incompatibility of being and non-being, with the result that even non-being "is" and in fact in its relation to being; it "is" as the other over against that which continually remains equal to itself, and it is more or less close to the latter—in a descending order along which the mediation of insight moves.

The causal connection between the topic of opinion and the topic of insight or knowledge, compels not only the aforementioned division of being but also the differentiated addressability of the being which is "in truth"—already due to the shifting viewpoint of estimations that assert themselves in opinions and can even conflict with one another. Precisely because the being that is in truth has to be distinguished according to the particular "what" of opinions—they judge about courage or propriety or utility or such things—

Plato cannot see the first with respect to this multifarious "what" in the fact that it is a being; the one and absolutely uniform first has to lie "beyond" being. And it is to be addressed as the "Good" because the rationale sought here is not merely supposed to make it intelligible as to why a certain something is as it is, but rather: why it is good that it is as it is—a rationale that is in turn even intelligible to itself. For that which is to be judged is to have or is to issue from knowledge.

Integral to the development of this question is Plato's insertion of the theory of being into an exposition of the first, of a principle to which (as the "One") as well as to being, an other belongs, namely, "the undelimitable dyad." That these principles can be interpreted neither each on its own nor with one another as the "Being" of beings hardly requires any further discussion.

But how are matters now with being "*qua* being" in Aristotelian First Philosophy? The expression '*qua* being' obviously recalls the fact that other sciences, that all sciences, are also concerned with beings. Why 'sciences'? Certainly Plato also knew a kind of knowledge that is different according to its "what" and furthermore differentiated according to its "precision." But is the multiplicity already that of the sciences?

As Aristotle depicts them the sciences are characterized not only by their region of beings but also by their beginning with grounds and causes that can no longer be derived from higher ones. Each science treats its own γένος of beings, but since being itself and the One are not of generic universality, neither can there be only one science.

Fundamental to this insight is the separation of "dialectic" from science and in fact through the segregation of the justification of an opinion from scientific justification, from proof. The analysis of "logic" proper to science puts an end to the "experimenting" (*Metaph.* $1004^{b}25$) characteristic of the dialectical mediation of knowledge and opinion. The logic of opinions is developed as a "topic," the ground being pulled out from under sophistic argumentation; it is no longer a threat to the theory of being, nor to the sciences.

The Aristotelian determination of science opens up the possibility of completely freeing the "what" of being from its link to the estimations characteristic of opinions in order to search for being in the total multiplicity of that which is determined in terms of this question, of that which is addressed by it. In each instance this addressing meets a universal of greater or lesser universality; closed kinships or lines of beings become manifest—closed according to their adherence to certain principles which cannot be further reduced. That which can be regarded as a principle, however, is predetermined by the character of science as such.

Now has the relation to the "Good," to the estimations in human action, also vanished along with the unbinding of knowledge from its essential relation to human opinions? By no means—and this is of importance for the character of First Philosophy. In what way?

We start with the Aristotelian system of the sciences: completely in accordance with the character of science itself, they are organized according to the differentiated adherence of the "principle" to being. If it has the principle within itself, then the corresponding knowledge is "theoretical"; if it takes its start from that knowledge which is proper to a different being, more precisely: to man, then the corresponding knowledge is either "poietic"—provided that its topic obtains a presence which is independent of the producer—or it is "practical" insofar as one prefers a certain action for oneself ($1025^{b}21$). Seen in terms of the adherence of the principle to being, the topic of the practical sciences has the lowest rank.

However: seen as a possibility of human action, theoretical science also becomes thematic in the region of the science of action, and in fact with the exposition of the question concerning which kind of action—seen in terms of the whole of human life—is to be given preference. If theory here proves to be most preferable, then not due to that universal preference of its topic, namely, a preference that justifies only the precedence of theory as science over the political and practical sciences. Of concern here is rather theory as human activity, and the preference of it is justified only by way of the estimation of theory as an activity that is likewise divine. As such, however, it is verified only by way of a science that is related to something that by its nature is "much more divine" than man ($1141^{a}34$).

The preferability of theory over other orientations of human life depends on the possibility of a theology, of a theoretical science of the "γένος that is to be esteemed as the highest" among those beings which have the principle, the ground of their presence, within themselves ($1026^{a}21$; cf. $983^{a}5$). Aristotelian theology completes the Platonic theory of the Good in that it provides the latter with the security of a theoretical science. Even this provenance hardly suggests that Aristotle wants First Philosophy to be understood as ontology.

But it is nevertheless incontestable that the consideration of being *qua* being is proper to precisely this theology. Once again: why '*qua* being'? One sees immediately that a contrast with the consideration of being in the sense of mathematics and physics is intended here. They consider beings not under the scope of the two determinations that belong to them—as was said—from the standpoint of the incipient theory of being. With respect to these determinations, mathematical being becomes, so to speak, a secondary concern for Aristotle—

all the more so once he deprived it of its mediating significance (Plato) and in fact with the liberation of the "what" of beings indicated above.

The "physical" sciences share with theology the consideration of being insofar as it is there separately in its particular "what." The former sciences distinguish themselves from theology because they consider being insofar as it is in motion; to consider it *qua* being means accordingly: insofar as by its nature it is motionless. But whether it is in motion or not, such also makes a difference for the way in which it is there separately.

If one understands Aristotelian First Philosophy as ontology, then it indeed remains a supplement to "physics," and this is then also already "ontological." This mixture was promoted not least by later rational theology in that it—we mention here only Thomas's *Summa contra gentiles*—took up, especially in its proofs of the existence of God, Aristotle's extensive reflections at the conclusion of his *Physics*, which led to a moving Unmoved. Thus the impression arises that there would be a transition from this science to theology, especially as the same "proof," so it seems, is repeated (*Metaph.* XII), even if in an abbreviated form, in what is usually characterized as Aristotelian theology. That Aristotle does not talk of "god" in his treatment of the moving Unmoved in the *Physics* does not seem to have warranted attention.

Here it has to be remarked: Aristotelian First Philosophy is not theology because god would be its subject; 'divine' and 'god' appear therein "predicatively" and in fact in the course of the consideration of being *qua* being, which is, to be sure, oriented from the start—from the character of the science—towards a first—not towards the Being of beings in the sense of the most general traits of beings but rather towards a determinate being that is just as determinate as, or rather in truth: which is even more determinate than, the being considered by the "physical" sciences. In what way?

Being *qua* being—here to be taken into consideration is everything that is addressed "as being" (*als seiend*). Insofar as such consideration is scientific, already within this multifarious addressing of beings it has to be at once intent upon bringing out a kind of first to which the others addressed "as being" refer—namely, the "what" in the state of affairs which is expounded in each instance.

A science, however, has to state not only what, for it, is the first with which it deals—here, among everything that is addressed "as being," the essence—but likewise what is regarded by it as already acknowledged in advance of any treatment of the topic—the so-called axioms (*APo.* $72^{a}14$; *Metaph.* $1005^{a}19$). Prior to the treatment of being *qua* being, here such is nothing but the so-called principle of non-contradiction. This first rules out what is impossible to address "as being"; it is what is acknowledged in advance in all addressing of something "as being": the state of affairs that exhibits the form of the state of affairs (cf. my "The Principle of Non-Contradiction or the State of Affairs as State of Affairs"); it should be noted: of concern here is a first that itself "is," that is the case and necessarily so; only as this first is it a universal, though not an abstract-universal—and thereby related only to a discourse that is to let something be known, to expound "how it is," openly and not only allusively.

Entering into the treatment of being *qua* being, the independence and the status of this science with respect to all the others must first be indicated. In order to do so, one has to know what that means: 'all the others'; they must be presented in the completeness of their order. As for how—this was already discussed.

To consider being *qua* being—here nothing is said of something other than "simply": it is. The provenance of the fourfold of being, according to which it can be addressed here, remains dark if one assumes that Aristotle has derived them from the "phenomena." The fact of the fourfold already suggests a twofold distinction; thus being in the sense of accidental being is also coordinated with the opposition of the true and the false; this opposition is "the other over against" the former (1026ᵃ34); both are extrinsic to being insofar as it has to be there separately; for both "are" only in relation to it—on the one hand, to that being with which something determinate has come together or not; on the other, to that being with which something determinate is brought together or from which it is kept apart in thought.

In both senses, being falls outside of the region of the theory of being *qua* being. It is excluded by the character of science itself and its rationale (1027ᵇ 33). Now the distinction of being in the sense of the categories and of the scission in accordance with the possible and the actual, remains "adjacent" to these modes of being. The theory of being deals with both of these modes of being and with them alone.

An account of this need not and cannot possibly be sketched in the present context. In keeping with our the guiding intention, only one thing is important here: to emphasize that the investigation of being *qua* being belongs to First Philosophy, which considers a first that is there separately and is immovable. Aristotle himself recalls this repeatedly in the course of his account. Nor in this context is his concern with the most general traits of beings as such.

How is the being considered by First Philosophy there separately? First of all it may be expected: in a way other than is the being considered by physics. This being is also there separately but—and such is shown by the causation of its motion, its generation and changing—as that which is "synthesized." The independence of First Philosophy as a theology depends upon the demonstration of a being that is not only there separately but thereby is also there as something simple. It is precisely the latter that Aristotle seeks to determine via the clarification of what the unifying moment is in the synthesized.

And what is meant when the being considered by First Philosophy is held to be an immovable being? Here it is in fact obvious that it has to be different from the being considered by physics; yet it is precisely on account of this that it is no help to take one's bearings from motion and its kinds as physics presents them; rather, the denial of motion here has to refer expressly to being *qua* being, to its difference from non-being, to a "motion" that is the transition to being—with respect to something that is or can become something determinate.

The independence with which the theory of being *qua* being develops both characteristics of the first being is fully manifest in the conclusion of their treatment, namely, where being is seen in a new sense of the true, which is to say: in its opposition not to the false but rather to ignorance, to a lack of insight (1051^{a}34). This section, with which the treatment of being *qua* being within theology ends, is no mere appendage to the exposition of the only two ways of talking about being, ways which are of importance to First Philosophy. Rather, this section draws the two together into one. But why is it this being in the sense of the true?

It should first of all be emphasized: in the rejection of the difference between the true and the false from the field of the science of being *qua* being, this step was already announced and thus its place is expressly premeditated; obviously it was not possible or at any rate not feasible prior to the clarification of the proper sense in which the first being is there separately—as a simple essence—and is immovable—as something totally and necessarily actual (1072^{a}31)—to enter into the specific sense according to which it is something true.

The determination of being as the true can and must be taken up once again after the investigation of "synthetic" being and its unity has clarified the sense in which the talk can be of a "simple" being. Thus the difference between the true and the false is also extensively unfolded in terms of being-synthetic in order then to make the transition to the non-synthetic or the simple. Here the exteriority of the true which—opposed to the false—lies in the conjoining and separating understanding, falls to the side. And the actuality of the simple proves to be insight itself. The originariness of being-present (*Anwesen*) as the immediate attention (*Dabei-Sein*) to what is simply and actually there, is manifest here.

The theory of being *qua* being leads to the actuality which is the insight into the simple and to a non-being which is accordingly nothing but a lack of insight. In this way it accomplishes all that is required for the cognition of the character of the first being. It aimed precisely at this and not at an abstraction of the most general traits of beings as such.

The theory of being *qua* being does not lead from beings to their Being, for it is and remains occupied with the This, with the being that is immediately there. This immediacy is attained not only at the point where a being emerges as the actuality of "touching" in insight; the consideration also begins with what is immediately there, only it is another immediacy, namely, the one familiar to us "earlier": that of sense perception. The being to which the investigation attends is not characterized as a "phenomenon" but rather as one sensorily perceptible and thus in view of our immediate relation to the being. There is no such immediacy—at least for Aristotle—to a or the "Being" but only to a determinate being. Within this immediacy to the latter, the question as to "whether there is such" has no sense (1041^{a}15).

In the addressing of what is immediately there for sense perception, Aristotle discloses a perception that is proper to reason; he leads the latter to the conviction of its possible independence. In this connection, however, it still remains open as to what Aristotle also left open in his introduction of First Philosophy as theology: is there an essence here that is there separately and is immovable, and this essentially means: is there an essence here that attends to itself as something that is purely rational? This question is not to be confounded with the other, "whether God is"—as it is raised for rational theology in Anselm and Thomas Aquinas. That which Aristotle first leaves open here is decided concerning the progressive clarification of what such an essence is destined to be.

In the course of its question concerning first grounds and causes, First Philosophy has to develop first of all in the treatment of being *qua* being those determinations according to which a being proves to be in itself a first, in order then to show how an essence (whose entire actuality is the activity of the insight into the simple) is the first or the ground over against all other essences. Only as this ground does it become a determinate This for us.

Over against all other essences—the 'all' is restricted here to the being considered in the *Physics* since it has the privilege of being there separately and of having the ground of its transitory appearance within itself. But if the multifarious grounds of this being cannot be reduced to a ground of supreme universality—and such a universal could not be a determinate This anyway—then how can the talk be of a first in view of this 'all'?

It obviously must be ruled out that it gives subsistence or imparts the determinacy of its specific kind to any- and everything. Rather, it has to refer to that motion which keeps natural causation itself going; and that is the most perfect motion, namely, the continual rotation of the heavens. But how does the first give rise to motion here? Certainly not after the manner of natural causes.

The first of First Philosophy can found nothing but that which it itself is: the attention to the simple, which it itself is—to it as the best. Why 'the best'? Whence the Good? Whence the estimating? Rationally attending to something, or put briefly: insight, is an action. That is, it displays the character of the action of preferring the one over the other. Wherever reason is not servile, wherever it is free to attend to something (*bei etwas dabei sein*) or not, to the one instead of to something else, there it shows what it prefers. Insight ultimately prefers itself over non-insight; it prefers the true in the sense mentioned above. An essence is perfectly happy that is continually free to attend to itself and has to stay with itself as the best among all others. That reason which is "separate" and "immovable" in this way is most fittingly called 'divine' and 'god'; by virtue of his character, he sets the yearning of every other reason into motion, and this moving is visible for Aristotle in the course of the stars.

Is the "Being of beings" presented here? Is the question concerning it the guiding question of metaphysics? Aristotelian First Philosophy is not guided by this question. And what is his position with regard to the fundamental question of metaphysics if it reads: 'Why are there beings at all rather than nothing?' Which sense could this question have in Aristotle? Does that ground which he acknowledges to be god provide the answer to such a question? How would it be comprehensible for him that everything, and most of all the perfect being, could also not be? How—if it is a being possessing the determinacy which Aristotle developed?

II

But now First Philosophy has indeed spoken of the Being of beings. It likewise knows what Heidegger characterizes as the guiding question as well as what he characterizes as the fundamental question of metaphysics. And how did First Philosophy come to this? This was the question already raised at the outset but which required an elucidation in view of Heidegger's answer to the question 'What is metaphysics?' in order to be able to show, namely, that and why First Philosophy comes to talk of the 'Being of beings' only after Aristotle.

This occurs in the phase that essentially remains determined by the Plotinian version of the principle. In this phase, that interpretation of Aristotelian First Philosophy also appears according to which it is ontology on the one hand, theology on the other. Even if this interpretation is established in the course of "natural theology," in particular by the structure of Suarez's *Metaphysical Disputations*, Thomas Aquinas nevertheless reveals a corresponding tendency.

In his commentary on Aristotle's *Metaphysics*, he remarks: "the same science is that of the first being and the *ens commune*."[1] Being *qua* being—here it is *ens commune* and this is even the proper topic of this science, even if with a certain qualification: "Although the *subiectum* of this science is the *ens commune*, in sum it is spoken of in terms of those [beings] which are separate from matter and according to Being and reason."[2] In order to understand the shift which becomes apparent in this context, one has to take into account the fact that so-called metaphysics can no longer be First Philosophy here, since it can no longer be theology proper after this rank has been transferred to the *Sacra doctrina*. Metaphysics in fact still has to be "theological," although its *subiectum* is the *ens commune*; for "being, insofar as it is being, has as its cause precisely God."[3] But the treatment of God as cause here has a restricted sense with respect to its treatment in theology proper, which "considers precisely divine things with respect to themselves as the subject of a science."[4] The treatment of the *principium subiecti* of metaphysics is entrusted to theology.

Here Aristotelian First Philosophy is pushed in the direction of an "ontology," after in this context the first rank is granted to a theology for which "God" has essentially no predicative significance, for which he is instead *subiectum*. He can be such only in a science that is based on the expression, on the revelation, of his own knowledge and thereby on his own appearance. Even if this appearance is not that of a natural thing, it in any case allows for the talk of him as the determinate God, who he is by virtue of his incarnation.

Since this thought does not confine itself to the exegesis of scripture, since it rather takes on the form of a doctrine and further of a science, it turns out that Thomasian theology—although derived through the revelation from God's knowledge—has to begin with the question as to whether God is (cf. my "The 'Five Paths' and the Principle of Thomasian Theology"). That the question does not have the same sense in this context as it does in Aristotelian theology and hence cannot be answered in the same way, starting from the theory of being *qua* being, was already indicated above.

Nor is this god the "principle" as is the Aristotelian god; rather, he is the creator and in the sense of creating "the universal cause of the whole of Being";[5] he is the principle in such a way that he brings forth beings "along with all their principles,"[6] and one of these principles is Being. However, he not only brings forth the Being of beings; he himself is also Being. Here it seems that what Heidegger said about the complete confounding of Being and beings in metaphysics is confirmed. Yet this only seems to be the case.

God is Being itself—for Thomas this is a proposition of revealed divine knowledge; it is based on the name which God gave himself when Moses asked him who he is: *Ego sum qui sum* (I am who I am). This revelation already dominates the Augustinian exegesis of beings; we refer here in particular to his commentary on Psalm 101 (cf. S. II, c. 10).

God is *ipsum esse subsistens* (precisely Being that subsists). The Being here addressed is to be separated from Being in the sense of the *principium formale*, which along with the *essentia* is constitutive of every created being. God is Being in the manner of an hypostasis, of an independent nature.

As one of the two "formal principles" of beings, Being is that whereby something is ("*quo est*") in contrast to the fact that it is a being ("*quod ens est*"). Time and again the attempt has been made to trace this distinction back to Aristotle, a distinction which later was developed into that between *existentia* and *essentia*. Such attempts conceal what is decisive here, namely, the difference in principle. They are characteristic of the standpoint of an "ontology" that is indifferent to the first of First Philosophy and its crises.

That Thomasian determination of the two formal principles of beings addresses the latter obviously in terms of their causation. Thus this determination by no means repeats the Aristotelian distinction between a "first" and a "second" essence. Rather, the viewpoint decisive for the Thomasian determination is creation; seen in terms of it, Being is on the one hand the created *principium formale* of beings, from spirit to matter—and is thereby, in view of creation itself, separated from every *essentia* as the preceding idea in the creator's knowledge—on the other hand, however, the Being of this creator himself. And this is not a difference between "sides" of the same coin but rather the one and the other Being are radically separated in the sense of the scission between what is of this world and what transcends it.

It is precisely this scission that carries the sole wavering with it which can be observed here: no confounding of Being and beings but rather a confusion is to be seen in the talk of God as Being itself—this because his intelligibility remains problematic due to his transcendence: he can be known only as the cause of what is of this world; by contrast, "neither a Catholic nor a pagan knows the nature itself of God as it is in itself."[7] If, however, Duns Scotus demands that Being be removed from this principal scission, that it be understood "*univoce*" (univocally), then his treatment is open to an ontology for which it is an abstract-universal over against beings.

Deus est ipsum esse subsistens—the addition of '*subsistens*' contrasts it with a Being that is *inhaerens*. To talk of an *inhaerere* of Being has no sense in Aristotle, although it does in Thomas insofar as every being "has" its Being and this because it is given to it. Again, it should be clear how the talk of Being as a *principium formale* of beings is to be grasped completely in terms of the doctrine of creation. This also ought to make one hesitate to want to find a Being of beings in Aristotle.

III

It was already remarked: the principle of that phase of First Philosophy in which Thomas Aquinas also has his place, found its decisive version through

Plotinus. However consequential the translation of the Plotinian One into the god who is his own Being may be—in principle it changes nothing. When Thomas says, for instance: "that which has Being and is not Being is being by participation,"[8] then this is almost a literal translation of the second thesis of Proclus's *Elements of Theology*—transposing the One into Being. The common basis is the thought of participation, of the having of the One, or of Being, without thus being Being oneself. In this manner the question as to how philosophy comes to treat of the "Being of beings" is pointed on its way.

Concerning the guiding thread of the return to Plotinus, we choose a thesis from the *Liber de causis*—a work on which Thomas commented in his late years in conjunction with the writing of the *Summa Theologiae*.

First a preliminary recollection: with reference to the doctrine of creation it is said in the treatise *De potentia Dei*: "The first effect, however, is Being itself, which is presupposed for all other effects, and it itself does not presuppose any other effect";[9] and further: "namely, it is the most common first effect and is more intimate than all other effects."[10]

The corresponding thesis of the *Liber de causis* (4) reads: "the first of created things is Being, and nothing else is created prior to this."[11] In his exegesis Thomas recalls Dionysius Areopagita, and the chapter "On Beings" in *De divinis nominibus* indeed offers an extensive exposition of the same thought. Even if Thomas was hindered by his dominant intention to relate Dionysius to Proclus, he nevertheless recognized that the *Liber de causis* descends immediately from Proclus's *Elements of Theology*.

The thesis (138) from that work on which Thomas draws reads as follows in the translation he used: "Of all that participates in the divine property and is deified, the first and highest is being."[12] The agreement of the theses becomes apparent, of course, only in light of the reason that Proclus provides. Without entering into this here, we emphasize only the difference between the two: the *Liber de causis* talks of "created things" and of "Being"; by contrast, Proclus talks only of participating essences and the being as first among them.

If Thomas speaks of Being as the first effect of the creator, it should also be heard that this creator himself is Being and in fact his own, proper only to himself. If the author, or at least the translator, of the *Liber de causis* likewise speaks of Being as that which is first created, then he is thinking here of a creator who is the non-being-, since he is the "hyper-being-," One and Good. If Proclus says of the being that it is the first and the highest, then it is not such among that which is created but rather among all that which is determined by its participation in the divinity. Its participation is in fact not characterized by a *creatio ex nihilo* but rather by a procession out of nothing, where here the thought is not of what is totally null and void but rather of the One that transcends all beings.

What does all of this mean? Which principal decision contrary to Greek philosophy is effective here? At the beginning of the second treatise of the Fifth Ennead, Plotinus asks: how is the procession of everything out of the One compatible with the simplicity of this One? "Now, because nothing was in it, therefore everything is out of it." A surprising justification, as is the one immediately following it: "and so that beings are, it itself is therefore not being."

Previously the talk was of the simple One, whose simplicity was expressly underscored by the hint that no doubling or bifurcation whatsoever of anything and according to some aspect appears in the One. Thus, that everything is in it, is ruled out; everything must be outside of it. But how? As expression and degradation of the One, namely, as the unity of a multiplicity and with a view to what is first different from it: as the unity, as the identity of something twofold.

Yet in this way the 'therefore' is understood only with regard to the 'what' but not yet with regard to the 'is'. The ensuing justification refers to just this: the One is itself not a being, so that beings are; these could not be, in other words, if the One were to be whose simplicity were to let everything sink into indistinguishability. The One is only as something different from itself—as the unity of an other over against itself.

The question remains: how do beings in their multiplicity proceed out of the simple One? This is "itself not a being, but the One is the progenitor of beings." And the assertion follows this, from which—mediated by Proclus—the aforementioned thesis of the *Liber de causis* stems; namely, Plotinus continues: "and this generation is the first one."

The procession of everything out of the One is more precisely: "something like" a generation—this characterization is to be taken as a hint, and yet the artificiality of the chosen expression reveals that a metaphor is not seized upon here at random. Rather, it expresses an operation and thus prepares for the transition to the notion of creation, as is shown by the ensuing justification of generation: "since the One is perfect because it seeks nothing, has nothing, lacks nothing, its, so to speak, overflow"—literally: its flowing-out-above—"and its superabundance have created other things."

A production has its motive in the function that that which has been brought forth has for the one who brings it forth. Such a ground falls to the side in view of the perfection of the One: it seeks nothing because it can lack nothing; and it lacks nothing because it can have nothing; and it has nothing because it cannot be; and it is not because it is the One, without thereby being "something." Having is incompatible with the simplicity of the first, for having would have to be thought as participation, but all participation has only its beginning and end in the first.

If Plotinus sees in the procession of everything primarily "something like" a generation, then he separates it from production on the basis of knowledge, as was familiar from the *Timaeus*; if he then further speaks of a making, then he revokes the notion, bound up with generation, of a homogeneity between progenitor and what is generated.

And now to the reason for creation: the overflow of the One. It is less a reason than it is a hint regarding the groundlessness of this occurrence. The overflow of the One is totally incomprehensible and the sign of its being beyond all insight.

Qua being, being is what has come to be. "What has come to be, however, has been turned towards the One and has been fulfilled and came to gaze upon [the One], and as such it is spirit. And its standstill with respect to [the One] has created the beings; the vision of it, however, the spirit." Instead of as 'reason', νοῦς is here rendered as 'spirit' in order to express that of concern in this connection is a type of reason that "is" not as such but rather has "Being."

In the abridgment carried out in the foregoing, all of this is initially nothing more than a disconcerting story. Only it should be clear that the fundamental traits of the later doctrine of the "Being" of beings, traits resulting from the creation of everything by the transcendent first, can be traced back to Plotinus—even if the kind of creation is essentially modified in the *Doctrina Christiana* such that of concern there is a production on the basis of knowledge and will and power. And it should also be clear that Plotinus does not merely supply some changes to Aristotelian theology but in principle parted with the latter.

He also knew this and made it clear, and in fact in his extensive debate with the decisive determination of the Aristotelian principle as the actuality of insight and with the principle's attending-to-its-self as the best (V. 1. 9. 8; V. 1. 4. 16; V. 3. 8. 35; V. 9. 7. 8). If one has understood this debate, then one will reservedly judge Plotinus's frequent appeal to Plato, more precisely: in view of the character of the new principle. As well as his recollection of Parmenides, to whom, namely, he ascribes the thought of an identity of cognition and Being.

In its transcendence the Plotinian principle is abysmally separated from the principle of a science as Aristotle had determined it, and thus the corresponding theory also cannot display any construction in keeping with Aristotelian First Science. If Plotinus's thought moves essentially in hinting, it is certainly no less rigorous than Aristotle's on account of this; nor is it—as one often hears regarding Plotinus's successors, especially in certain of Meister Eckhart's expressions—"bold," bolder than the Greeks. His hinting saying has to be "bold" in contradiction and in the impossible because it talks in principle of something whose consequences also rule out immediate addressability.

Yet how do things look in Plotinus regarding "Being"? To this point the talk was only of "the being"—of the fact that as being it is what has come to be, a becoming that has been brought to a standstill, a procession out of the principle; and further: that this standstill is bound up with a reversion to the origin and that, in this reversion to what has come to be, a view is attained which being turns into spirit.

Being (*Seiendes*) and spirit are the same—having come to be out of the first and having reverted to it. This same is what is first created and it is the first over against everything else down to non-being, first within the order which arises in the imparting of the One to the multiplicity. Spirit is therefore not only the first, it is also every being. The question concerning the "Being" of beings will thus most appropriately regard the character of spirit—particularly as Plotinus developed it in the treatises constituting the Fifth Ennead; here, especially the third is considered in connection with the account of the emergence of spirit (ch. 11 ff.).

As such, being has to be instituted. As that which has been instituted there, it is determined only in the reversion to its origin. This reversion is self-knowledge, becomes such in being freed from the many externals in terms of which the yearning for the simple cannot be fulfilled; that which in each instance is addressed proves in the addressing itself to be already many, namely, what is differentiable.

Self-knowledge is a having-gone-into-oneself. Only in the interior is that which has been brought to a standstill, "being" (*seiend*; V. 5. 5. 18), and only there has spirit become actual out of a mere capacity, active in the determination of what it is—it is visible to itself as something determinate.

From the fact that Plotinian self-knowledge is essentially the experience of a split, it becomes clear that this self-knowledge—although the same in name—is in principle something other than the self-insight of the Aristotelian first. It is also precisely on account of this that Plotinus, unlike Aristotle, does not turn to "all men" insofar as the yearning for knowledge is proper to them, but rather to the individual who is prepared to go into himself.

Which split? Here it is not so much to be thought that in self-knowledge the knowing and the known and knowledge itself are distinguishable—a "many"—but rather that their unity is one that has been "seized" upon in the stride towards the simple; it was only this that compelled one to go into himself in the first place. Spirit "has" its unity only after it has received it, after it has found it. In finding itself, spirit becomes aware of the fact that it was previously only a "yearning" and an unstamped aspect—in his exposition of the "*repraesentatio*," Suarez will still talk of the fact that the faculty of insight is "informed" by its object.

Whenever spirit is fulfilled in the activity of self-knowledge, it is already split within itself (V. 3. 10. 45; cf. V. 3. 11. 13, where δεδιχάσμενος is to be read). Thus self-knowledge is as the knowledge of unity, of the sameness of the knowing and the known, more originarily: knowledge of the split—'more originarily' in view of the precedence of that yearning for unity and thus for determinacy. Yet this comes from a lack, a "need" (V. 3. 15. 10), which confronts spirit with its difference from the principle, at the same time with the principle's transcendence of the activity of spirit.

What is first elicited by the One was the being, and this meant first of all: something brought to a standstill (V. 1. 4. 21). Plotinus explains: it comes to a standstill due to its yearning for the One, from which it does not want to further distance itself. The standstill means the reversion of the first being to its origin and in fact in the quest for its own unity and thus determinacy. It proves to be that of the spirit that knows itself. It knows what it is in that it knows how the Being of the being which it is, is determined; essential to spirit is: having-been-given. In self-knowledge the deception about beings as independent is dissolved for spirit. As such, beings are given in the whole and in the first, the givens of something that gives, which has to transcend all knowledge. "And just as much as spirit has from that [first principle], it may know both what has given and of what that [first principle] is capable. Experiencing and knowing this, in this way spirit will also know itself. For it itself is one of the givens, what is more: it itself is everything that is given" (V. 3. 7. 3).

It is just in self-knowledge—spirit "is" not its "self," it "has" its unity only by virtue of its participation in the One—that for it above all the notion of its own independence dissolves. It experiences itself as a This and thereby something determinate only because it came to be out of the yearning for the origin which let it come to be, which gives it "Being." It is only on account of this giving that "Being" is different from "beings"—and in fact on account of the thing and its first, thus not merely in the sense of logical analysis as Aristotle presents it in *On Interpretation*.

In terms of simplicity, self-knowledge does not go beyond the assertion: "I am that" (V. 3. 10. 35)—in Aristotle, such talk makes no sense; it makes sense only where the individual first must come to this self-intuition—or simply "I am a being" (V. 3. 13. 24)—and such makes sense only insofar as the 'am', as 'to be', can be separated from the ego, from the self-knowing ego, and considered as a "that," as the determinate actuality of consideration itself in which spirit ceases to be mere capacity.

"There is" (*Es gibt*) only what has been given, and, along with the giving, the 'to be' is what first came to be; it is the standing still of the overflowing—it no longer wants to proceed and comes to a standstill in the turn inward (V. 5. 5. 16)—but it is only a being where it is also a determinate something, and it is such only in the self-knowledge of spirit. "It is a being"—this is so only after "what it is" has been determined (V. 3. 15. 13). Here it should be clear: the separation of Being and beings is prompted by a theory for which beings as such are in principle givens.

The question concerning the origin of the given—it is initially the question concerning the simple "self" of self-knowledge—presses beyond the givenness of beings back to the giving of Being and to what gives. It gives (*Es gibt*) a Being that it neither has nor is. Through the giving itself or through expression, that which it gives here is something totally different from what gives.

That which gives is different from its gift to the extent that Being cannot be given to beings only once and then remain entrusted to them; rather, Being must be given continually so long as beings are to be "saved" (V. 3. 15. 12), to be kept from the relapse into the indeterminacy of a nothingness—a thought that, with the thesis of the necessary "*concursus*" of the creator, entered into the doctrine of creation found in the *Sacra doctrina*. Here the principle's transcendence finds expression in Being itself.

As far as its transcendence of knowledge is concerned, such is expressed in the ground that is to be thought for giving: it occurs "in friendliness" (IV. 8. 6. 21) or unfoundable benevolence. Unless one wants to take the following as the ultimate foundation: it is better that not everything remains concealed; it is better that the Good deshelters itself in everything, communicates itself (IV. 8. 6. 1). In this estimating, which accompanies the consideration of beings with respect to their Being, the following question has its sense: 'Why are there beings rather than nothing?', of which Heidegger says it is the "fundamental question" of metaphysics.

Being is to be distinguished from beings in view of the transcendence of its principle and the way in which it grounds everything. In keeping with this specific way, Being and, along with it, beings are divided into three strata: first the Being of "full" determinacy, or insight, as it is proper to self-knowledge; then the Being of lesser determinacy, or life, as it is characterized by self-movement; and finally "mere" Being, which is not further determined—of a rock, for instance.

On each level of this gradation, by way of which the One is transmitted to each individual, Being is "real" (*sachhaltig*); it includes things of corresponding determinacy. It is precisely on account of this that later philosophy can speak of a more-or-less of "reality" within the span extending from the self-knowing spirit to the inanimate body.

Here it should be noted: the transcendence of the Plotinian principle not only sets a being over against itself; non-being, which is matter, also shares worldliness with beings. In this regard, this principle attains a "totality" of dominance which is foreign to the Aristotelian principle. The former's scope extends not only to that which can be the topic of theoretical science. For it is not the presence of the topic demanded by knowledge itself but rather its occurrence, in whatever mode, that has its ground only in the transcendent first. If this first is then seen as a god to whom, in addition to the power over everything—power is also the Plotinian principle—a preceding knowledge of everything is also proper, a knowledge that corresponds to his "artificial" creating, then the *liberum arbitrium* has to become problematic. And this more radically than in the Stoic tradition.

"Being is fulfilled, however, when it takes on the character of knowledge and life" (V. 6. 6. 20), when it shows itself in this determinacy. Being is all the more fulfilled the more clearly it is the trace of an "interior" and of the One itself (V. 5. 5. 13), which gives the "superfluous" Being, by way of the latter's reticence, with the unity of a determinate something, of a something of determinate reality (*Sachhaltigkeit*). Mere Being or the occurrence of something is the last and weakest trace of the origin since in this trace that and how all Being is given becomes least of all conceivable. It is only a mediate trace which first must lead to the interior of life and of knowledge before the transcendence of that which gives everything is acknowledged in self-knowledge.

The importance that the referential character of Being and its stratified order has for Plotinus is manifest not least in his extensive discussion of the Peripatetic and Stoic doctrines of the categories (in the first three treatises of the Sixth Ennead). There he turns at once against an exposition of the categories without regard to the aforementioned distinctions of Being and thus of beings. He resists a consideration "in general," which remains indifferent to the principle and the descending order of its giving.

The decided segregation of the One and the Good from every "something" and thus also from everything that is addressable and knowable—incidentally, Plotinus was quite familiar with the contradictions entailed therein (cf., e.g., V. 3. 14)—calls to mind the roll of the "something" in Stoic "dialectic." There, something over against beings was regarded as a *genus magis principale* (Seneca, *epist.* 58; *SVF* II, 329). This testifies first of all to the orientation towards the abstract-universal customary in school-philosophy. And yet a more precise account is required here.

The something includes everything in itself, being and non-being, and this obviously not in the manner of a principle but rather with the universality of thinking. This universal something is all the more indeterminate insofar as it does not restrict itself to what is determined as being or non-being but rather is aimed at the potential determination: whatever can be said, whatever can be signified: the "thing" as it is taken by the understanding (*SVF* II, 166); and this thing is non-being. With reference to which being? To the body—in Plotinian terms: to "mere" being. This being is one that occurs "externally" over against the interior of an understanding that judges the phantasmata in view of their truth and that means with respect to their correspondence to something occurring externally.

And what does this mean for the characterization of a being? It is a body; this means not only: it is something of a certain size occupying a certain position, but prior to that: it is something that can be met "externally," that is, it has to be met insofar as it has caused an impression internally. Now that which has an effect from the outside is distinguished from that which is internally grasped, from a determinate something insofar as the former "has" Being in addition to its determinacy or, speaking with Seneca: has *substantia*.

With respect to this having of Being, the foreignness of the Stoic doctrine to the Aristotelian theory of being *qua* being is obvious. Here the horizon proper to "Greek" philosophy, its orientation towards presence for the proof of knowledge, is left behind. The Plotinian principle appears within a horizon that first becomes apparent in the determination of the being as just presented: it refers to an All that corresponds to this being—even and exactly in the abolition of the independence of everything that is and, most of all, merely is: namely, bodies.

And finally how are matters with the characterization of the principle that itself gives Being—that it is above all Nature and beyond all addressability? How can this characterization be justified? In what does it have its strength? This question leads beyond the theme of the present investigation. We note only this much: this would be the place to attend to the break with "Greek" philosophy, starting from the Stoically determined proof of knowledge, in particular from the role of the "assent" of the understanding and the conditions for "thinking something with assent" (*credere*).

How did philosophy come to treat of the "Being of beings"? This question has yet another side: how did philosophy come to leave the Being of beings behind? An answer precedes this question as well—and in fact the philosophy of the modern era has given it. If one listens to what it has said, if one attends to what has been done from Descartes to Hegel, then what Heidegger means by the phrase 'Being of beings' turns into another question.

What appears under the name 'ontology' in the modern era should make it easier to abstain from seeing First Philosophy in it. Such an abstinence may also aid in denying the name 'metaphysics' the right to say something about First Philosophy—about what it has been, or better: has done.

NOTES

1. Aquinas, *Commentary on Aristotle's Metaphysics*, 6, 1: *eadem est scientia primi entis et entis communis.*

2. Ibid., *praefatio*: *Quamvis autem subiectum huius scientiae sit ens commune, dicitur tamen tota de his quae sunt separata a materia secundum esse et rationem.*

3. Ibid., 6, 3: *ens inquantum est ens habet causam ipsum Deum.*

4. Aquinas, *Commentary on the "De Trinitate" of Boethius*, 5, 4: *ipsas res divinas considerat propter seipsas, ut subiectum scientiae.*

5. Aquinas, *S. Th.* I, 45, 4, 2: *causa universalis totius esse.*

6. Ibid.: *simul cum omnibus suis principiis.*

7. Ibid., I, 13, 10, 5: *ipsam naturam Dei prout in se est, neque catholicus neque paganus cognoscit.*

8. Ibid., I, 3, 4: *quod habet esse et non est esse est ens per participationem.*

9. Aquinas, *De potentia Dei*, qu. 3 a. 4: *primus autem effectus est ipsum esse quod omnibus aliis effectibus praesupponitur et ipsum non praesupponit aliquem alium effectum.*

10. Ibid.: *ipsum enim est communissimus effectus primus et intimior omnibus aliis effectibus.*

11. *Liber de causis*, 4, p. 26: *prima rerum creatarum est* esse *et non est ante ipsam creatum aliud.*

12. Proclus, *Elements of Theology*, 138: *Omnium participantium divina proprietate et deificatorum primum est et supremum ens.*

THE DIFFERENCE INHERENT IN THE "OTHER BEGINNING"

Reason and World: Between Tradition and the Other Beginning—with this title Werner Marx characterizes the "dilemma" which thoroughly motivates his reflections: one side is the truth of metaphysics brought to perfect determinacy, a truth which has lost its persuasiveness; while the other side is the conviction that philosophy needs an other beginning, but one that still lacks in determinacy and thus in perspicacity.

One might want to pass over this with the facile objection: is this anything more than the open admission of an indecisiveness on the part of contemporary philosophy? Now—does this careless question have any idea of what is being talked about?

I

The sides of the dilemma: the first side, the tradition, is likewise that of reason. Insofar as reason owes its determinacy to no other knowledge than that of metaphysics, the tradition is to be taken as the history of reason. Though not as it is the scattered and even distracting stuff of concern to the historians of philosophy, but rather in the sole and thus gathering relation to an "other beginning"—this understood, following Heidegger, as the beginning of a thinking, of the other over against metaphysical thinking.

As a whole the latter comes into view not due to the completeness of its development—such would hold of metaphysical knowledge—but rather by virtue of the relation of the other thinking to metaphysical thinking. Its beginning is not merely an other but rather the other due to the oppositional, exclusive character of this relation. It is first and only in stepping back from this relation—thus in view of *Heidegger and the Tradition*—that the said dilemma sets in.

This stepping back has no intention of accommodating the need for "objectivity" and historical "justice" with respect to the tradition; such a need does in fact call for satisfaction, but it is not philosophy's. Those who need this take

Heidegger to be an interpreter of the tradition, contrary to whose judgment about this or that philosophy something more probable may be proposed. Here at play is the consideration of whether he was driven to reject metaphysical thinking perhaps by an erroneous interpretation of the thought of ancient philosophers.

That the other beginning is in any way held to have to be related to metaphysics or to be the beginning of an other thinking—the violence of this truism causes the distinctions within "secularized" philosophy to become blurred and leaves one in the dark as to how the other beginning can be determined only in the sequence of the Marxian and Nietzschean counterthoughts, to be the beginning of the other thinking over against metaphysical thinking.

II

In stepping back from Heidegger's relation to the tradition, a dilemma appears—though only when the first of the relata is to be held onto just as firmly as the other: the dilemma sets in only when the other beginning is acknowledged to be needed, if not seen clearly to be necessary. And the first side? What makes a move in view of this side against the repulsive relation? Perhaps this or that sympathy or predilection for ancient philosophy which biases and informs one's judgment?

Or is thinking compelled for the first time in view of the relation of the other beginning to metaphysics to suppose that the latter might have something to offer the former?

But what then? Perhaps the exemplar of a fundamental and systematic thinking that yields a knowledge possessing thoroughly elaborated determinacy and decisiveness? Yet what is knowledge without the persuasiveness with which truth wins one over? But whom or what, if not just that reason whose determination causes it to be opposed to the "world" of the other beginning?

Not merely opposed; rather, that reason which is essentially metaphysical resists this world, denies it a present. How could that in which Heidegger saw "the most obstinate adversary of thinking" (*NW*, 247/11) be able and permitted to be occasion for stepping back from the repulsive relation to the tradition? Would that not mean: siding with it and relinquishing along with the other beginning the difference between the two in its entirety? The said dilemma would then be spurious and only a muffling of the fuss about the "destruction of reason." Perhaps it is not altogether clear of which reason. Thus we shall briefly take up its metaphysical determination along with the requisite distinctions.

III

To begin with, it should be stressed: unlike the thinking claimed in the other beginning, the thinking characteristic of reason is inherent in knowledge and ultimately in science, with respect to which reason is the "faculty of principles." It is no pregiven faculty but rather one produced by and for "theory."

Which determinacy installs this faculty's thinking in knowledge? One gladly takes one's bearings from language: knowledge is a having-seen. But such does not yet touch on knowledge as scientific—just as little as the talk of the "seeing" characteristic of reason reveals the rationality of knowledge.

I. To see and thus to know what is there: what appears, what is manifest, what is present. However, insofar as what is there to be known and thus is to be seen, is "everything" that is there but which never lies *in toto* before one's eyes, something unifying must be seen in what appears in many places and at many times. Should such a view prove to be true, that which unifies must allow of being shown and in fact as a first that is visible as a first both in its distinguishing and in its unifying—not excogitated in the course of a genealogy.

c) The first appears as the first side of the first difference of everything that appears, a difference which is determined to be an opposition. The first is what is originary in the latter insofar as it segregates the other side from itself. But the first is likewise and prior to that the whole of this distinguishing relation in that it, different from the opposites and thus from what appears, is manifest as their balance, even if only temporarily. It appears and is manifest recurrently.

b) Yet the first appears and is manifest constantly when it is determined with respect to the knowledge of it. This knowledge is different from the usual variety; it does not stand in an exclusive but rather in a transitional relation to the latter. Accordingly the first is the One, which is manifest (because it is compatible with its opposite) in what appears—in the whole as in the parts—as a proportional balance. It is the κόσμος which prompts the distinction of knowledge, the purification of seeing, the cultivation of knowing, and the delimitation of the soul. The first does not appear but is manifest in what appears as its life.

a) The first, or the One, appears and does not appear, is manifest and is not manifest, is initially segregated from everything and as such is with everything in the manner of the balancing knowledge and in this sense is something constantly present. Here all differentiation is completely formed into the determinacy of the opposition: the One is not only the first side in contrast to everything that appears, not only the balancing proportion of the opposites, but is in its balancing, in the κόσμος of change, itself oppositionally determined. To acknowledge this means: to have reason, not only a soul.

A. And what does it mean: to be reason? No longer: to be attentive to or present with the One, which is itself present, but rather to be in the One as that which alone is true. Along with what appears, this also excludes from presence the opposition between the One's being-manifest and its concealing of itself, reducing the opposition to the simple and necessary separateness of "how it is" and "how it is not." The activity of reason is at home in the critical character of "being," here seizing upon its determination in order to carry out the latter henceforth in the manner of self-determination. Having turned back into the departedness of the knowledge of the One, insight is won over by truth itself and, in the balance with that which is necessarily true, is therefore unshakable in acknowledgment—unlike opinions, which are not opposed to truth but rather extrinsic to it due to their contradictoriness.

Inasmuch as the balance of the first with respect to everything has passed over to the determination of pure insight, inasmuch as insight has its ground in the critical character of "being," the present has become that of theory.

B. Even if insight is absolutely different from opinions, its ground remains related to them, for the contradictoriness of all that is extrinsic to being can be resolved; by way of their justification, opinions can be related to insight, for they are already—although differently from that which is truly justified—related to the ground of insight, are compatible with that ground. The ground of their distinction is, namely, something which remains the same with itself, ultimately the simplicity of the One. But such is likewise the ground of their relation; namely, inasmuch as the latter occurs variously in everything that is the topic of opinions, moreover, inasmuch as it, even in distracting, urges one to attend to the true, to bind every decision to the true, which has already been decided upon, the ground is the Good itself in supreme universality.

C. In the cut that sets the self-determination of reason free, justice, or the "equality of the mission" of oppositional appearances, has returned to the simple mission which installs the being that makes all the difference for truth, in perfect equality with itself. Insight is "in" being and is there the relation to the necessity of difference, a necessity by virtue of which insight is determined by its destinal principle. This principle is that which, in a second step, takes on the determinacy of the Good in order, in a third step, to achieve equality with the actuality of insight—in such a way that the destinal principle of insight not only becomes visible in its universal determinacy but also is there as an individual characterized by precisely this determinacy. It sees itself as the best and is thus exposed to its own regard: in its destinal principle it sees its face. Such is perfect θεωρία.

Here the destinal principle has become perspicuous for insight in such a way that in the former it sees the motive for remaining with itself. Only in this way is reason known as something having its own actuality. If reason was initially sheltered as insight in its destinal principle, then with the perfect perspicacity of this principle, it is finally sheltered within itself. Its action is balanced where it no longer attends to this principle as something determinate which is related to it but rather itself fulfills that determinate something's determinacy.

II. In the reason which has been unfolded into perfect identity with its governing principle, nothing but reason itself is there for it, and it attends only to itself. But insofar as everything that is not reason itself is related to it as the first, an imbalance enters onto the scene, one that entrusts reason to a governing principle it fulfills no longer in the unfolding of identity but rather of difference. (c) This reason knows, is first related to, something given which is extrinsic to it in order to reach from this "dogmatic" start via (b) a skeptical phase—the "agreement" of knowledge with the thing, an agreement which itself is still extrinsic—(a) the "gnostic" result that this reason itself is something extrinsic in the sense of what has been exteriorized.

A. Its proper self-determination begins once more with a cut insofar as it determines itself to be the totality of all that is extrinsic. How is that? Everything is the exteriorization of an origin which is absolutely different from it. Absolutely, that is, with respect to pure distinguishing, to the difference between the undifferentiated and the differentiated. The latter is different from its origin: Being—differentiated within itself: beings or the totality of the determinacies which distinguish the things—converted to its origin: "reason" as the being having the richest determinacy and the first in the imparting of the unity to the levels poorer in determinacy.

The activity of this reason of difference is not so much insight as it is recollection—which is not to be confounded with retention. Just as Being as exteriorization is a procession, so too is thinking an inversion—not merely to an attending-to-itself but rather to a transcending-of-itself—a return to the origin for which reason, knowing that it has been given, strives as its ground. In the second movement of self-determination, reason keeps to this ground as that for which it strives. Its theory is "speculation."

B. Its second step also lets the transcendent One emerge in appealing determinacy and in fact in the revelation of its self. Such is, however, a "word" that in its existence is both repulsive and attractive—such that the reason which is essentially singularized and "psychic" has to distinguish itself in its own givenness: it is the reason that is either "natural" and expressly obfuscated or illuminated by the light of revelation. The one as well as the other concerns it as an alien predetermination. In this way the difference governing the entire second movement reaches its extreme.

Nevertheless—it is precisely in this respect that the first side of the difference, namely, the undifferentiated, takes on, so to speak, reason, though in such a way that rationality remains a predicate that never exhaustively expresses the activity of its subject. This already because reason as such gives nothing. It is, however, giving in the sense of the revelation that yields the Trinitarian differentiation in what is essentially undifferentiated. And it is only with respect to the giving of revelation, of this determinate ground of return and recollection, that the giving of the origin becomes a creation of everything on the basis of knowledge, will, and power.

Natural reason does not know that it is neither within nor with itself; it deceives itself with its conviction that it is independent.

C. Yet the third step shows: the illusion of independence is no mere illusion; for the light of revelation lights the way only for that recollection which is already cognition, is illuminated by the "natural light"—all the more so as the latter arises from the same ground. The assent to what is revealed is not merely compatible with that which can be cognized by natural reason but rather has in this cognition the presupposition yielded by that which itself is self-revealing: Nature as created. With respect to revelation itself, this reason asserts itself as the "natural" form of doctrine and science, or as the "order" of their exhibition. In this way the cognizing proper to natural reason is the labor which both testifies to the former's independence and yields its shelteredness in revealed knowledge. That is, it begins its exhibition in that which itself is self-revealing insofar as the latter is there for it—demonstrable by virtue of its own light. On account of this, reason's striving for this essence or its attention (*Dabeisein*) to such as that which is absolutely different becomes perspicuous to it on the basis of the natural determinacy of such striving. Thus it is within and with itself—also according to the standard of difference.

III. However, if this is considered as difference in the light of this sole reason, for the latter it shows an inequity, so to speak, an injustice: as natural, reason attains a certainty in natural theology which it lacks in natural philosophy or natural science and thus in its own realm. It turns from the difference of the transcendent first to the contradiction in its natural character.

This contradiction finds its preliminary development insofar as (c) natural reason projects Nature as an object not only extrinsic to it but also determined in opposition to reason itself. So reason remains that of consciousness, even if that which the object "in itself" and thus in truth is, passes from that which allows the object to be determined as extrinsic, over to (b) the uniform substance of the intrinsic and extrinsic and further to (a) the intrinsic and itself intelligible ground of every individual object.

A. Only the progressive determination of consciousness to become self-consciousness yields the cut with which the third movement of self-determining reason begins. It cuts off the consideration of what the (natural) object is in or within itself, in the certainty that natural reason itself is within itself as its ground and in fact such that its natural character is in this respect no longer a finitizing determination.

For: reason discloses the Being which is contained in its own nature. As such it is not a being-given but rather a being-posited, with its nature posited as true. As long as it represents itself in something given, it is in a totality which is an other over against it—be it the soul, the world, or God. And how is it within itself? What is this nature? Such can have its determinacy only by virtue of reason's activity, by virtue of its positing something as true. And how is this in turn determined? How is it explicated?

The reason which, on the basis of its natural character, is essentially representational reason, deals as such with that which is inherent in it and in fact in the sense that such ultimately lies completely within its power; furthermore, reason can will that it be true and therefore is itself firstly the giver of what is there to be known.

The nature of reason—reason has to be in its nature, and its Being, that is to say: the activity just determined, has to issue from its nature—is the representation or idea of a non-representable "totality," though one that is necessarily to be presupposed by it, a totality that is an absolute. But since the reason in this absolute is spontaneously active, is free will, the "representation" of its nature is the idea of freedom. Such is the concept whose complete development is the activity of reason; as determinate reason, it is distinguished: this praxis is unfolded into moral and theoretical reason as the other over against undifferentiatedly free or absolute positing.

And conditioned positing? It shows that and how this reason is only that of self-consciousness: precisely as theoretical reason and thus in the present proper to it, it is the other reason since it is related to a conceiving (on the part of the understanding) which is different from it, a conceiving which is in turn dependent upon a representation different from itself, namely, an intuition that in turn depends upon something non-representational: upon a kind of material and thus upon something given.

Reason is joined together with sensuousness via the understanding but only due to the distinction of conceiving, which as something connected with the understanding is conditioned by an impetus given to its activity. In this way reason is reminded of its natural character and is conscious of itself as the reason of a being which is also a sensuous being. This determines its activity to be syllogistic. In which sense?

Reason is certain of its absolutely free nature. But how does it verify its certainty if it itself cannot give what is to be known without reference to something else? If the entire present of theory is restricted to the field of Nature in which conceiving is in fact independent but not free? How can what is there possibly be the existence of its nature or of that which ought to be in the sense of self-legislation?

Reason can only will that its nature be there, and it has to will this existence as a consequence and exteriorization of its nature. However, this consequence cannot only not appear for it immediately; rather, its entire theory rules out the knowledge and thus the verification of such a consequence insofar as the existent nature of reason, or spirit, cannot be an object of experience. Not only does the nature of reason, that is, freedom, have to be joined together expressly with its existence; what is more, the middle term of the syllogism has to be Nature, and such is not an impossible middle term only when it is determined in such a way that it is not considered to be the Nature of things-in-themselves but rather of appearances.

Theory yields no other truth regarding the certainty of being-free except this: freedom is not impossible. It is precisely this that is the sufficient reason (*Grund*) for the self-consciousness of reason (*Vernunft*): it is free to acknowledge itself as free reason, to claim freedom as its nature, to be active in the manner of self-legislation.

B. Such would be ruled out if the entire theory proper to this reason were the knowledge of Nature and not, prior to that, the knowledge of this knowledge with the distinction of the object into the thing-in-itself and the appearance. This knowledge is itself an act of freedom. And it is with this act that the second step in the third movement of reason is concerned. It shows: the ground in which reason as its own ground cannot only not include another Being as its activity; rather, this Being is all of reality. This requires the proof of the fact that nothing is given which would not be posited by reason.

The material of intuition given in sensation is nothing but the impetus with which reason determines itself to be a representational activity or to restrict itself with respect to something other than itself. But such is possible only insofar as the nature of reason, that is, freedom, takes on the determinacy of its Being, or activity—in fact not representing but rather positing—visible in the idea of freedom that has been developed into a judgment, namely, that which expresses the first certainty about positing: the positing of what is undifferentiated—without opposition, the positing with no object.

Did this reason, which came to reason out of self-consciousness, expunge the recollection of the natural character of its light? No doubt in the sense of that middle term of the syllogism which Nature was—its first term was the method as cognized. But here also the nature of reason has to be expressly joined in its theory with the existence of that nature. Here the joining knowledge is the self-developing consciousness of the system of the originary activities of spirit.

In the system of the laws of science, consciousness appears as the completely developed certainty about the nature of reason. But as for how it as representationally active, as theoretical, reason is inherent in this nature, the exposition of this has to recall the natural character of the light of reason insofar as the difference between 'to be' and 'ought' is constantly renewed in representation and in fact in the representation of the ideal which presses for ever greater determinacy.

The reason which turns back into its equality with its ground—it started out as sensuous and thus representational reason—is spirit. With respect to the latter, the activity (as an ideal that in each instance appeals) of the absolute ground is determined to be striving. It acts with respect to itself as the incessant demand for the equality of that which reason realizes by way of representation with the absolute ground of precisely this representation.

The spirit of praxis, or of the contradiction between being-determined and determining, is the middle term of that syllogism which joins "Nature" as the furnished presupposition together with the "logical," which was determined on the basis of the certainty of freedom to be the absolute activity of the ground of reason.

C. From here the third step is already assigned its task: to determine the "logical" itself to be the middle term of the syllogism insofar as reason attains equality with its ground as an attention-to-itself as well as a being-within-itself. But this only insofar as it becomes obvious: the ground is not the ground of reason but rather: reason is the reason of the ground. Yet this amounts to reason's dissolution as a form of consciousness and thus of the representation of objects, even if its object be only the longed-for absolute, which reason knows to be its ground.

For striving as the absolute activity of the ground, an activity related to representing, the object (*Gegenstand*) had already had the meaning of resistance (*Widerstand*). On the basis of the transformed determination of the relation between reason and ground—of their equality in the sense of the reciprocity of their absolute actuality—the resistance proves to be that solely of the representational activity in general or of "natural consciousness."

In advance of the ensuing investigation, it must be emphasized: not the rejection but only the history of the exhaustion of the experience of resistant consciousness discloses in its result what it opposes: absolute knowledge.

In the endlessness of scattered sensuous representation and in the infinity of the representation concentrated on its ground, the concept penetrates this sensuous representation and links these extremes together in the proof that the appearing contents of representational thinking are finite and can be exhausted.

Freed absolute knowledge realizes, determines itself in a twofold sphere: that which is concerned only with the middle term of the said syllogism, that is, in the sphere of the pure concept—put concretely: of the absolute idea—and, on the basis of the latter, in the sphere which is that of the philosophical sciences—put concretely: of the idea of philosophy.

Reason is within itself as its own ground into which it has returned—from representing into conceiving. Reason attends to itself to the extent that it has turned back into the beatific vision of the accomplished formation of the system of science as the system of known actuality. Namely, it penetrated the totality of Nature, of physical as well as spiritual Nature, in such a way that in the completed labor of determination, it verified the certainty that it is all of reality and thus of determinacy as well.

The movement through the first and the other spheres of the truth of completed theory is summed up in the well-known distich:

> Whatever is rational, that is actual,
> and whatever is actual, that is rational.

Science was able to verify: not only that freedom is not impossible, not only that freedom is possible, but that actuality itself is free because it has been conceived.

Is that itself still a resistant thought? At any rate, it was the most offensive. In it modernity seems to have collided with reason.

IV

For the mass of the tone-setting remarks on metaphysics, that impetus was transformed long ago into the conviction: here the incredibility of all metaphysics is to be felt immediately. Accordingly the foregoing distinction and development of its reason only allows the reply: so what? It is a view without consequence because it lacks all content, for such has to be sought by philosophy with respect to the world and its changeability. Or should one object, following self-knowing reason, that 'world' "in general expresses the formless totality of the manifold" (Hegel, *GW* 11, 352.27/511), and further that changeability is only the most extrinsic among the determinations of that objectivity which is extrinsic and seemingly indifferent to the concept (*GW* 12, 176 f./757-759)?

With respect to the world, the said dilemma between tradition and the other beginning is of no concern, but only the diverse problems which the changeability of the world brings with it; the first of them is the interpretation of the changes that have already occurred, for the world itself must prove to have changed, to be no longer metaphysical. With the assumption that metaphysics also has interpreted the world—though guided by the "presumptuousness" of a philosophy that understood itself to be an end-in-itself.

To what end an other beginning? Has the world not already begun differently since the end of metaphysics? What sense would the study of the tradition have if not to show the entire extent of the changes that have occurred and the changeability of the world which is left to man's discretion? There one is concerned about the future of mankind, participates in today's events, and asks wherever possible: what is to be done? For one is in good company with his concerns.

By contrast it may seem: in the said dilemma, philosophy is still concerned only with itself. Indeed—even when the *cornutus* of tradition and the other beginning reveals the unity of philosophy only on the skull.

V

What was the offense in the most offensive thought of metaphysics? Basically that reason itself gives itself everything there is to be known and along with the latter is sheltered in the system of science. Here is the "adversary of thinking"; "for centuries"—thus in the modern era—it has been "glorified reason"; it seemed to lay claim to and to attain glory, to which formerly was attributed the other light, the *lumen gloriae*, over against the natural light. And to whom did that seem to be the case? To him for whom the glory was failing and along with it the shelteredness of everything that is his own—to man and his advocates.

A semblance that has its ground. In order learn which ground, let us listen in on a "conversation" in which Heidegger—author of the aforementioned judgment passed on reason—found himself with Hegel—author of the most offensive thought of precisely that reason. It is only in terms of the topic of thinking that what that adversary is up to, can be seen.

In terms of the "topic of thinking"? What was mentioned above announces itself immediately in the form of a reservation: the topic of metaphysics was essentially a topic of knowledge and of science and only on account of that, a topic of thinking. Already in its first crisis and with its true beginning (Parmenides), metaphysics expressly cut this thinking off from the commemoration and presaging of memory and only thereby set the self-determination of reason on its way.

Is that to say: Heidegger was mistaken from the start regarding Hegel's topic because he was mistaken about that of metaphysics? By no means. How could one hold a conversation with the deceased when at issue is a topic which is not even there as a differentiated one? How could it be there for Heidegger if not in the present of the other beginning? Only the destiny and the distinction of the topic of his thinking draws the topic of metaphysics into the sole present of philosophy—not as an historially pregiven object of former, possibly actualizable interests but rather as a topic that the thinking of the other beginning ultimately requires for the distinction of its own topic.

Heidegger's "conversation" does not fall among those natural attempts whereby "one" enters into a discussion with Hegel or some other metaphysical position; such attempts only succeed in introducing—as far as the essentially present philosophy is concerned—the topic of metaphysics within idle talk. And what then remains of the aforementioned reservation? As such it is awaiting its dissolution.

VI

What is the topic of thinking for metaphysics and, along with it, for Hegel? The Being of beings. Heidegger knows that the requisite distinction requires a more determinate account, as the title of the conversation announces: "The Onto-theo-logical Constitution of Metaphysics." Feuerbach already emphasized what is offensive in metaphysics with the name 'onto-theology' without, however, getting to the bottom of its "constitution" and thus of the bifurcation addressed here.

The topic of metaphysics is being as such in general and in the highest (*ID*, 49/58). The unity of this twofold, the Being of beings, remained "forgotten" in the determination of being as such. Metaphysical thinking turned away from the origin of its topic. Correspondingly in the reversion (*Umkehr*) inherent in the other beginning, Being is the nearest "unthought from which what has been thought receives its naturing space (*Wesensraum*). But what has already been thought prepares what has not yet been thought, which enters ever anew into its overflow" (38/48)—in the overflow of the source from which what is unthought issues without being able to escape its origin.

As onto-theo-logy, metaphysics itself prepares the topic, that which is "controversial," for memory: Being in the "difference between Being and beings" (40/50). This difference is the naturing space "in which" what has already been thought is there and which a "topology" (*Erörterung*) still has to disclose—in the reversion from the oblivion of the difference via its incipient veiling to concealment as the "source of this entire thinking," the source which "alone establishes and prepares for it the area of its abode" (ibid.)—'for it'; one would like to say: for inhabited thinking.

From this sketch it is already striking: the reversion of thinking reverts to its Wherein (*Worinnen*). The oblivion of its topic is contained in an incipient veiling and this in turn in the originary concealment. Accordingly the return is foreshadowed in nothing other than the "nature of truth." Like Being with respect to beings as such, so too with respect to truth, unconcealedness is that which is nearest to what is unthought. Accordingly, thinking no longer contemplates the true ground of the true and thus of knowledge but is instead concerned with the origin of truth in that which it is not: about the arising of unconcealedness out of concealment, thus out of its other with respect to which it itself is actually the other.

Such gives rise to the question concerning the relation to the first over against this other and concerning the ground that itself is this relation: ground of the difference between Being and beings. However, Heidegger does not allow himself to be led astray on this count; he remains in the counter-turn of a thinking severed from Being, a relation that makes him attend, as the "unconcealedness" already did, to the incipient name of difference; for he experienced: the first in the difference—which is earlier according to its topic—between Being and beings as such is "originary differing" (*Austrag*): the unity of the self-manifestation of Being and of the appearance of beings as such:

"Being makes its way over (that), over-comes deshelteringly (that) which makes its advent as something of itself unconcealed only by such over-coming (*Überkommnis*). Advent means: to shelter itself in unconcealedness: being thus sheltered, to come near and be there: to be a being.

"Being manifests itself as the desheltering over-coming. Beings as such appear in the manner of the advent which shelters itself in unconcealedness" (56/64 f.).

VII

At this point one will hardly be able to contain himself in his indignation at incomprehensible discourses and—to put it mildly—will regard the limit of what can be reasonably expected of others to have been exceeded. Even if the quoted passage were to be returned to its context, to the train of thought of the essay, that feeling would be inevitable. For there has been no lack of it, and how often it has already been voiced.

The complaint about the incomprehensibility of this or that philosophy is an ancient practice, and one would need only to recall Fichte's terse answer in the "Preliminary Recollection" to his *First Introduction to the Doctrine of Science*, were Heidegger's language not in fact different from that of metaphysics.

The strangeness of discourse cannot possess the offensiveness of an affectation when one has an ear for how Heidegger's thought is gathered and, when necessary, deliberately strange, provided that the thought of the difference between Being and beings makes a difference in the topic of thinking and so of discourse as well.

Yet as far as the limit of what can be reasonably demanded of philosophy is concerned, the sensitivity for that limit would instead need to be fostered on this side of the thought gathered—contrary to the diffusion of scholarship and of dabbling in the topic of other sciences.

The complete distraction of thought is expressed in the mode of drivel. Such is not the same as the thoughtlessness of idle talk, since unlike the latter it attacks speech itself; it is no accident that it makes use of, of all things, a scientific terminology aimed at univocity and degrades just this terminology to sham words which are merely brandished about. But even there, speech is still "communicative," it finds its recipients. Thus the "comprehensible" is distributed to all sorts of the understanding.

VIII

The resentment concerning the incomprehensibility of the quoted passage, however, need not remain occupied with this sentiment; it can turn to what is said in an attempt to translate it into what is already familiar. Here of help is historial scholarship. And what can it yield here for explanation where metaphysics is held to have nothing to say? Even when a certain uneasiness prevails regarding the boundary drawn for pre-metaphysical thinking—before Plato or before Parmenides or before Anaximander?—: what comes to mind here for comparison are the beginnings of Hesiod's *Theogony*, whose "first and foremost" is Χάος: the opening. And it would not be difficult to trace 'over-coming' and 'advent' back to the narrative of the *Theogony*. For philosophy, explanation of that kind proves to be an evasion in the face of the necessary demand of thought: to be clear here and now about what is said.

It is already on account of this that Heidegger emphasizes: the turn to the origin of metaphysics is no "historial return to the earliest thinkers of occidental philosophy"; for in truth "the step back out of metaphysics into the nature of metaphysics, viewed from the present and drawn from our insight into the present, is the step back out of technology and the technological description and interpretation of the age, into the nature of modern technicity, which remains to be thought" (*ID*, 42/52).

The present—such is no changeable or interchangeable point of view, no horizon which is itself faceless. Its face is marked by modern technicity. This becomes conspicuous and therefore makes it easy to overlook the fact that this face belongs to the present proper to "theory" and thus to the insight (*Einblick*) that is affected by a nature that remains to be thought, finds itself in distress, and so knows itself to attend to the topic of thinking (cf. 31/42). It is only this insight that is struck by how the description and interpretation of the age is itself still technical in the sense of a "technology" which, of course, is not to be sought out in the system of the technical disciplines but rather in the surrounding haze of decayed art, religion, and philosophy—these being understood as types of metaphysical knowledge. It is precisely for that reason that Heidegger also speaks of technology as the "metaphysics of the atomic age" (42/52).

The popular descriptions and interpretations of the age, the interpretations of the changed and changing world, indeed make various kinds of distress felt insofar as they profess to be occupied with something in itself obscure. In this connection they are unseeing, they engender the illusion of the distinction of themselves from what they interpret, through the critique of the various manifestations of technicity. But such critique is merely the requisite fuel for further changes in an already changed world.

What Heidegger knows as the technological description and interpretation of the age, both of which are themselves technological, provide themselves with the semblance of thoroughness and the permission to prognosticate through historial reversions and associations. They lack the uniformity of a singular return and thus in their plurality they remain just as obscure as the world that is represented in terms of its most striking changes.

With his "step back out of metaphysics" Heidegger's thought also and eminently remains in the present. Wherever it seems incomprehensible, it becomes no more comprehensible but rather confused by recourse to thoughts which historial scholarship finds in the past or has posited as being there.

IX

The world is the formless totality of the manifold. It shows the unity of a form, namely, of a face, only in the present proper to theory. "Technology" is found in the world, is caught up in it; therefore, for technology the world cannot take on the determinacy of an "essence" and thus of thought. Insofar as it describes and interprets the world, it attempts to expunge ever more the latter's foreignness—in an endless progression, because it is confronted time and again with new changes.

Although "technology" as such takes modern technicity to be what stamps the contemporary world, this remains a formless and faceless totality for it, since it understands technicity itself as the manifold of that human know-how which has brought about the changes conspicuous today and which constitutes a totality only insofar as it teaches one to regard everything in terms of its changeability and workability.

In the present proper to theory, this technicity would be visible as an "essence"—'would be' due to the reservation yet to be developed that this essence would then no longer be determined to be that of technicity, because it has to be "speculative." Yet technological thinking not only resists speculation but also posits it as something negligible, with respect to which it ought to behave merely indifferently. Yet this is obviously not easy, for even when this thinking regards as negligible the difference that the thought of Nature makes, it can nevertheless assert itself as an undifferentiated thinking only in a *regressus ad infinitum*; namely, on the one hand, it is obsessed with the concern that man remain the master of his technicity or rather become such; on the other, it allows for a corresponding, dominant knowledge only as a "pluralistic" ethics, which itself is technically grounded (23/34).

It is only the question concerning the nature of technicity that destines Heidegger to raise the question concerning the difference between Being and beings, taking the question concerning the origin of the onto-theo-logical constitution of metaphysics as his point of departure. Only the answer to the latter question does not merely set technology aside but rather reveals it as an undifferentiated thinking which arises from the collapse of the onto-theological bifurcation of metaphysics.

Its lack of differentiation provides the sole impetus to take up the question concerning the nature of technicity as the question concerning the nature of truth with respect to oblivion, to turn to truth as unconcealedness, to emphasize the relation to concealedness inherent in it, and so to go back to the totality of the differentiated concealment.

"The difference between Being and beings, as the distinction between over-coming and advent, is the desheltering-sheltering originary differing of both" (57/65). This is the totality of the difference as difference: both the being-apart and the being-towards-one-another (*Aus- und Zueinander*) of the differing sides as well as the being-apart of the "Between" "in" which these sides are "drawn towards one another." In short: the being-apart of the being-apart-from- and being-towards-one-another is "originary differing."

It is not the first "Whence" but rather the first "Wherein" that is the first of originary differing, the first "it gives" (*es gibt*). The dif-ference (*Unter-Schied*) is no thing and thus no causation (*Ur-Sache*) whence there is the Between; it gives the latter itself as its self. On account of this, the dif-ference is also itself what is differentiated in the Between. This should be noted so that no thought of it may exceed the present, the sole present of the nature of technicity.

"In originary differing prevails the clearing." But because this prevailing is to be thought dif-ferently, Heidegger continues: "of what closes off"; and because the clearing—or the "open" and finally the "free" (*EP*, 72/65)—is the one proper to what closes off, hence the addition: "self-veiling." Thought differently, originary differing is what closes off the open or the clearing; thought with differentiation, it holds of what closes off: it veils itself; thought uniformly, the differentiated is the clearing of what closes off.

For originary thinking, the present of originary differing is a coming (*Kommen*) that is unfolded into the "desheltering over-coming" (of Being) and "the advent which is sheltered in the unconcealedness" (of beings as such). This coming, however, is itself dif-ferent, namely, regarding the other in the sense of what is failing. It is the other of the other beginning. Namely, that which refers to the coming which is itself dif-ferent, is the failing as it, in the coincidence or collapse of the onto-theological bifurcation of metaphysics, becomes the impetus for thinking.

X

The "other" metaphysics, or "technology," is subject to the failing dif-ference. The question concerning the nature of technicity directs our attention to the First Metaphysics in order to learn to what extent originary differing "remains everywhere concealed as originary differing and thus forgotten in an oblivion which withdraws from even itself" (*ID*, 60/68). This withdrawal is unfolded into a history. How does it begin?

It is not the Parmenidean beginning that captures Heidegger's attention but rather that stamping of Being which he knows as the Heraclitian λόγος. Namely, it is to be regarded as the start of ontotheo-logy because here the difference of the coming as such, so to speak, bypasses attentiveness; this dif-ference is there as "that which allows whatever makes its advent to lie before us" and "collection," but passes into the reciprocity of "ground," the dif-ference being unstable within itself.

The fleetingness of its "clearing" is manifest in the fact that the other side of "collection" already appears as bifurcated within itself: "grounding everything in the universal and founding everything on the singular"—this being understood "in the sense of the highest (Zeus)" (61/69). From this follows: the difference between Being and beings as such veils itself in the difference of this other. Here that first, namely, the "desheltering over-coming," passes over to the other side within the other of the "advent"—in such a way that the over-coming itself becomes a What of the advent, of what makes its advent, is present, is a being, and in fact becomes the highest being, because its desheltering determines itself to be a founding and finally a causation by this being.

The god who "enters into philosophy" in this way has nothing in which he shelters himself in making his advent. He seems to have already made his advent—not even that; he is always already there and seems to be sheltered within himself. And along with him, First Metaphysics, until it is said "God is dead" and, in the collapse of the difference that he made, the Other Metaphysics establishes undifferentiated thinking and suppresses the difference of the nature of technicity.

Yet the result of the oblivion, which withdraws from even itself, emerges not only in the conviction that God is dead, but prior to that in the completely developed reciprocity of over-coming and making its advent, where they appear "in one another in reflection." In the reflexive "orbiting of Being and beings around one another," originary differing reaches the extreme of metaphysical difference (62/69).

The clearing was that of what closes off. Its closedness is the light of the "reason glorified for centuries" which—after it had completely denaturalized its light—on the one hand knows the rational as the actual and the actual as the rational, while on the other it feels that it has descended from and is dependent upon an origin that is alien to it. This feeling is convinced that reason, contrary to the origin's sole actuality, engendered and established in vain the illusion of being not only a thing possessing its own and supreme actuality, not only the cause of a world different from itself, but the reason of what alone is actual.

XI

The start and end of metaphysics reveal: that which closes off the clearing veils itself, denies the thought of it, and oblivion even withdraws itself expressly into technological thinking, which represses the dif-ference even in the form of the onto-theo-logical bifurcation. Its metaphysics says: whatever is failing has failed to make its advent because it cannot be; for along with methodical attention and reflection, even the possibility of forgetting is essentially excluded.

The other metaphysics over against this first, says: that which is failing—the death of God proves it—need not be; it is not needed; it is superfluous and therefore harmful; what the world leaves to be desired, the critique of existent conditions yields.

In keeping with its intention, however, technological thinking remains metaphysical; for it considers its world not only as the given horizon of productive human activity but also as a horizon projected from out of this activity itself; it is precisely on account of this that the world changes, corresponding to the changes in man's power, will, and knowledge.

Technological metaphysics does indeed situate the onto-theo-logical bifurcation in the past, but it holds all the more resolutely to the "logical." To object to the former that logic has "not fallen from the sky" does not resolve anything because there is no knowledge which could be more indifferent to its provenance than is logic. Viewed with respect to the world, however, it is logic which stems from technicity and not technicity from logic. It is precisely on account of this that logic is essentially that of the reciprocity which, beyond the metaphysical logic of ground, has its beginning in the "equation."

The thinking that has escaped onto-theo-logy holds to the "logical" only because it is techno-logical. And only because of this is the "logical" manifest in the world of technicity itself. How and to whom? Not to technology but rather only to the thinking that questions concerning the nature of technicity and, on the basis of the said nature of truth, knows technology itself to be a result of the history of an oblivion which withdraws from even itself.

The start of this history shows: not the λόγος but rather the "logical" of metaphysics is one-sided: the other side of "assembling," which attracts the first side of "letting-be-present," or over-coming, towards itself in such a way that it, within itself twofold, inaugurates the reciprocal relation of the ground and develops perfectly to the point of the aforementioned orbiting of Being and beings around one another.

Accordingly the logical still has to show itself in the world of technological thinking in the determinacy of assembling and thus of the advent which desheltering includes as its other. Heidegger saw: the whole of gathering appears in the manner of amassing (*Raffen*); amassing brings together without looking beyond the formless totality of the manifold. The determining, i.e., desheltering, within such assembling is manifest in the manner of positing, of a positing which is transitive and which comes over to whatever makes its advent.

The world of technological thinking is by its nature the "sy-stem" (*Gestell*); it is the ultimate determination of the logical proper to onto-theo-logy in the latter's restriction to the secularized logical. Its one-sidedness is expressly disguised for and by the metaphysics which has come to lack differentiation, namely, technology. The failing difference pervades this thinking only as uneasiness about man's remaining or becoming master in his technical world. This is intensified into the care for man's remaining or becoming man. Such indicates: the nature of the essentially human technicity is itself nothing human (cf. "The Question Concerning Technicity").

That ultimate one-sidedness of the logical dawns only on the questioning concerning the nature of technicity. Insofar as the failing of the difference is manifest to commemoration and presaging as the dif-ferent coming of "originary differing," the other world is formed within the nature of technicity itself into the horizon of technology. It takes on form and face from what collects, which is neither a divine nor a human logic, but the "thing" which has never made its advent. It collects and determines, it distinguishes what the world is, namely, its world (cf. "The Thing").

The world of the "sy-stem" is not one and the same with the world of the "thing" and is one and the same with it. This is the final contradiction generated—but by what? Perhaps the third movement of self-determining reason? But then did it not come to rest with its perfect fulfillment? Does the logical middle of the completed syllogism allow for a further determination?

Does the "logical" of onto-theo-logy also appear in any way, then, in the determinacy which the world took on for "secularized philosophy"? But then this—although no onto-theo-logy—would certainly not be the same as "technology" since it would be oddly related not only to the world but also to the present proper to theory.

XII

The "logical" of onto-theo-logy itself is determined perfectly in nothing but the development of the idea. We recall here only the two moments of its determination:

"Insofar as it has truly attained its reality, the concept is this absolute judgment whose subject as the self-relating negative unity distinguishes itself from its objectivity and which is the being-in-and-for-itself of the Same but which is essentially related through itself to [objectivity]—thus is end-in-itself and drive" (Hegel, *GW* 12, 176.21/758). End-in-itself—the objectivity permeated by the end has its being-in-and-for-itself, or its developed truth, in the relation of the distinguishing-exclusive unity of the subjective concept to itself. Drive—this concept is related by itself to its objectivity, which is distinct from the subject in order to sublate the separation lying in this difference; it is the drive for unification (177/759).

End-in-itself and drive are the moments of the subject in the absolute judgment, which is the idea. With respect to this subject, objectivity is in turn explicated as that of being-posited—according to both existence and form, it is permeated by the subject—and objectivity as such—thus it is what is external to the concept: "the side of finitude, changeability, and appearance"—that is, being different from something differently determined, the becoming-different of what is the Same, and the being-differently of the Same in the sense of the difference between appearance and actuality. Here the path of the "decline" of the externality which is indifferent to the concept and its relating is already delineated. Its sequence can first be derived from the decline of natural consciousness, because it acts as if it is indifferent to and independent of the element of the pure concept, "absolute knowledge," and negates the latter in this way.

End-in-itself and drive—are these to be regarded as moments of the idea of the world, to be sure an idea which has not yet been absolutely determined?

Marx sees them in the "capital" that permeates the totality of the relations of production, that subjects human power—that of those who work—as manpower, and expunges the manifold determinacy of products as an "indifferent being-apart" in that it includes them as wares in the circulation of its self-preservation through the production of surplus value.

Nietzsche sees those moments in the "morality" which permeated the totality of the relations of dominance, which subjects the human will—that of the value-positing creators—in the quest for ideals that disavow their thetic character, in this manner enfeebles the end-positing will, levels the hierarchy of its centers of dominance in order finally to carry the mendacity of morality to extremes with the socialist society and the morality of a "social" conscience.

And technicity? It has permeated all relations of care, subjected human thinking in each "inaugurating" action, and reduces every thought that takes offense at it, to the business of a critique which serves to intensify its effectiveness. It especially monopolizes man's "world-forming" activities with the comprehensive demand: everything must become different—different in the sense of the comparative 'better'; only in this way is it immediately clear.

In the cited characters—capital, morality, technicity—end-in-itself and drive no longer appear as the moments of the subject of the idea but rather as "secularized." The logical of the former onto-theo-logy is seen, namely, in the world as the latter's form and in fact as a form that confronts form-giving man as an alien power and thus violently, thereby subjecting his power, his will, and his knowledge. If thinking is the nature of man, then he experiences here in each instance that non-identity which Feuerbach had demanded as that of thinking and Being, as that of his nature with what is. The correlation of thinking and Being becomes apparent to him on the basis of this foreignness.

Those characters or persons or masks of the logical do not arise as something alien that, say, makes one curious, but rather as something alien that dominates—completely penetrating the whole of human relations. Completely, because it does so in such a way that dominance in general is suffered only as heteronomy.

XIII

Here the question imposes itself: how is the logical of onto-theo-logy related to the acknowledgment of dominance? Heidegger saw: the self-veiling originary differing and the oblivion of the desheltering over-coming, or of Being, leaves the desheltering to the discretion of a first ground which—itself a being—is determined to be the first cause. As such, reason forced an acknowledgment that went as far as its glorification.

And what does the movement of the self-determining reason just presented yield for that question? It came to light in the foregoing: the reason which finds itself in its ground keeps in each instance to itself with its self-determination, where it does not merely attend to this ground, to it as that which is primarily there, but rather where it views that which is primarily—and even if only naturally—there as itself and thus itself is the true topic. Where reason attends to itself—it also does so where it attains the acknowledgment of its natural light in the "doctrinal," and in this sense "mathematical," exhibition of revealed knowledge—there it has fulfilled its destiny. Here is in each instance the place where one addresses the metaphysical acknowledgment of dominance and its lord.

It is not good when there are many different lords; there should be one lord. This word from Homer is cited by Aristotle at the conclusion of his "theological science," or First Philosophy, which itself appears as a dominant type of knowledge since it deals with the lord, with the first, with the highest principle. The onto-theological bifurcation here retreats into the unity of First Philosophy; yet it is meaningful to talk of it as the one "theology" only in the retreat itself. Once again, it depends on the differences and their conjunction if at issue is the determination of the lord and his dominance, if at issue are the epochal principles in the form of the true topic.

Aristotelian First Science starts with the exposition of the state of affairs as such and grasps it in turn in the principal state of affairs which is known as the "principle of non-contradiction" (cf. my "The Principle of Non-Contradiction or the State of Affairs as State of Affairs"). The intermediate reflection defines the reality of a thing as one that is present insofar as it extracts from that which is first for us—since it is there for the senses—that which is there for pure—since it is simple—insight and can only be true. The third movement determines the actuality of this insight itself to be a true thing in this sense and in fact on the basis of all that which is not only there for the senses but also has the ground of its transitory appearance within itself. In light of this, the true thing, which is active reason, proves to be the moving Unmoved, the first ground, the lord of the order and beauty of appearances.

Thomas's *Sacra doctrina* begins with a state of affairs which announces difference in its simplicity as the fundamental trait of the principle of the middle epoch: I am who I am. The doctrine translates this by and for natural reason into the proven state of affairs and principle: God is. Its execution is the distinguishing between what he is not and what he is. Once again, the true thing and, along with it the character of the Lord, is determined only in the third reflection following this first one: namely, where God, as himself different, having become a rational creature, even man, finally proves to be the judge of all rational creatures in order to bring about the just order of the justified through the distinction of the world. With respect to the life of the sole just judge, which itself shows the way, the intermediate reflection elucidates the general movement of the rational creature to God in the manifold of comportment determined by Nature and grace.

And Hegel's one science? In its intermediate movement it is that of logic. From this we gather the universal mode of dominance proper to the principle of the modern era: the pure concept becomes "subject" where it has "subjected" its moments, Being and essence, and has proved to be their absolute ground (*GW* 12, 24/591); here it has subjected nothing but that which is its own. This subjection is the acknowledgment of the ground that has become perspicuous to itself. It is precisely on account of this that the first part of science yields the subjection of representation to the concept, or the apagogical demonstration of absolute knowledge, the possibility of which natural consciousness, blind to the Nature of its representational thinking, has excluded. Beyond the logic, the immediacy of the absolute idea is developed via physical and spiritual Nature into the idea of philosophy. It is the true thing, which has subjected every determinacy, which has taken the latter in its own development back into itself. In this way, having achieved equality with its idea, philosophy, that is, science, is lord. It rules as that which conjoins insofar as the system of science has both posited and sublated the exclusive relation between the rational and the actual.

XIV

The exposition of the logical itself yielded the final acknowledgment and justification of dominance; namely, it proves that and how, with the lord of metaphysics, heteronomy is completely excluded. The topic of its knowledge is obviously one other than that of caring thinking; a whole determined differently than it, is the world of man, the horizon of his activity. Yet this remains a poor account as long as it is not elucidated as to why all dominance is suffered as heteronomy and why that which is alien in it takes on the determinacy of the said characters of the logical.

We recall: unlike the occasional environment, the world of human action is a horizon that has been projected in this action itself. To the thinking that deals expressly with this horizon, the world shows a face; thinking sees a form in it: capital, morality, technicity—in each instance a form that does not allow man to attend to himself, a mask (*persona*) that disguises his nature from him, or that "in" which he has to be. It does not allow him to catch sight of the social character of production, of the playful character of life, of that indigenous flourishing of speech.

If one surveys the sequence of those forms and their formations, then the progressive separation from the critique of existent conditions is manifest in the way in which it is characteristic of "technology"; the "critique of political economy" already is to be separated from such critique. Yet only the question concerning the "nature" of technicity completes the separation. In what way? Unlike technicity itself, this nature, especially as the one inquired into, permits of no critique of itself, for it is there only as an expunction of all determinacy: the condensed estrangement proper to the heteronomy of the said forms of the world. Whereas these spread only fear and urge their overcoming, that nature engenders an anxiety which is not to be overcome but rather adopted.

"Technological" description and interpretation as well as the corresponding critique are moved by a concern with what this thinking considers itself to have dealt with insofar as it emphasizes the changeability of the world, since, for thinking, it is a horizon that has been projected by man himself. But wherever an alien lord of man is seen in the world along with one of those forms, the representation of the changeability of the world is reduced to the thought that the overcoming of the fear of that lord—he rules only in such fear—concerns the necessary result of a history, a result which itself compels a change in the whole (Marx) or makes such possible (Nietzsche) or not impossible (Heidegger), according to the different determinacy of the forms of the world.

And what about anxiety? How can an expunction of all determinacy give rise to anxiety? Insofar as it remains related to a determinate form of the world: it is the nature of technicity and, in the latter, that of both morality and capital. Related to fear. Nevertheless an expunction of all determinacy: a nature not viewed but rather inquired into, and it remains so insofar as it prevails as anxiety.

Anxiety cannot be overcome. It is expressly to be adopted. Insofar as thinking casts off its anxiety in the face of anxiety, it becomes released (*gelassen*). In this way it does not repress the anxiety but only transcends the anxiety in the face of itself: the anxiety in the face of the thinking that characterizes "technology."

Released thinking imagines another world for the nature of technicity. This world, however, is only seemingly the other over against the form of the world of technicity. Namely, if this world is the nature of technicity, it can only be the first over against the other world of technicity. Nevertheless—insofar as this nature is that of technicity, insofar as it remains related to the latter, it holds: what prevails is this form of the world, and this nature prevails as anxiety. But from this it follows: it prevails as an expunction of all determinacy insofar as it is not perspicuous within itself. And why not?

The nature of technicity is the topic of a questioning, not a criticizing, thinking. Nevertheless, questioning thinking cannot dispense with critique, for it is thrown time and again back to the totality of determinacy, a totality from which it takes its point of departure: technicity as the form of the world. Questioning remains bound to technicity—not in the feeling of this nature as being failing but rather with the imagining of what is failing in the nature, of what has been failing. Yet this is nothing but the "thing" and, in fact, in the truth with which it is or "things." The thing things—this does not express an identity, a relation, but rather a simplicity that transcends thinking: Being as that which is absolutely different from thinking but which nevertheless has the form of thought, namely, of the logical, for the thing is what it is as assembling. The thinging thing is the logical as the nature of technicity, which is absolutely non-perspicuous within itself and nevertheless to be inquired into.

The thing assembles the world—one different from that which has its form in technicity. How is it different? Technicity is a type of knowledge which serves man and which is developed by him alone. Seen as a form of the world, his servitude passes over into dominance, which is possible only when something is manifest in the world which is alien to him. Inquired into as such, that which is alien gives rise to the assumption: the nature of technicity is itself nothing human. Unlike in the case of capital or of morality, such an assumption can no longer be "scientifically" dissolved and dismissed as "mystification," for here it springs from a form of the world which itself is a type, and even the properly human type, of knowledge.

Here thought takes the turn: if the world is that of the thing and the thing is not that of man, then man is to be viewed as the man of the assembling proper to the thing. But in which determination? No longer as an animal that has reason but rather as one of those assembled by and distinguished with respect to the thing which constitute the world of the thing. The thing is in that which is distinguished and thus determined as earth and heaven. As a thing, however, it does not attend to something. Yet something attends to it which in turn does not attend to itself but alone is subject to the death with respect to which the attendant is distinguished into the mortals and the immortals.

The world of the thing is that of a bifurcated standing-apart—determined over against the world of the "sy-stem," or undifferentiated challenging, over against the world of "calculative" thinking and inferring, or of a thinking on the basis of the equation of everything, an equation which knows no middle term. But those distinguished within that "fourfold" also lack a middle term; they have the assembling middle term outside of themselves in the thing. The thinking of the other beginning turns expressly against "mediating" thinking, against the mediation of relations, against the contradiction which returns to the relation of the ground. Does it also fall into the anxiety in the face of thinking? Or does this view itself fall into the anxiety in the face of what has been thought? A strange way of talking, but one which least of all can and wishes to presume that Heidegger was frightened of what has been thought in metaphysics. What would there be to be feared there? The fear would bypass anxiety.

XV

Shouldn't the question be allowed: what is the ground of that expunction of all determinacy in which Heidegger installed the world of the thing? Such was possible only in the course of the question concerning the nature of technicity. This question in turn remains dependent on the fact that the form of technicity is projected into the world. Where does the impulse come from in the first place to project one of the said forms into the world and thus to subject the totality to critique?

Metaphysical reason was determined by the present proper to theory. To see a face—such meant for reason in each of its epochs: to return to the point where it is perspicuous to itself in its total determination. The "seeing" proper to this reason was speculative. Such does not hold of that seeing which projects a form into the world of man. Each time, this form breaks the unity of the present insofar as its face is seen in repulsive determinacy. It is precisely on account of this that thought is subject to the demand that it be "practical."

Where the form itself appears as a type of knowledge, namely, as technicity, thinking in fact transcends it with the question concerning the nature of technicity, though without attaining the present proper to theory and thus the attention-to-itself (*Bei-sich-Sein*) proper to its reason. On the contrary: the world of the thing once again eliminates, and this time even in its "nature," speculative thought; it confirms—in a word—that the latter is outside-of-itself (*Außer-sich-Sein*).

This intensifies the question: does the expunction of all determinacy, an expunction which still and only prevails in the sense of a "fundamental mood," namely, of anxiety, have a ground?

Where should one turn in the attempt to answer this question when not to the "logical" in the said characters or forms of the world? But that means: to metaphysics. To which? To precisely the one which perfectly elaborated the logical as well as the speculative and which previously appeared only as the most offensive type of all metaphysics. Faced with the latter, the question must once again be raised: does the offense point to a resistance in speculative thought itself? For the well-known rejection of metaphysics and the thesis of its end proves to be a crisis in the acknowledgment of the principle of the modern era.

We shall seek it out where it appears in completed determinacy, namely, in the system of systems, in which it becomes obvious that philosophy has become equal to its idea and in this sense has fulfilled its destiny.

The system of systems becomes evident in the result of Hegel's *Encyclopaedia of the Philosophical Sciences* as the concluding movement of science which develops the idea in its existence or as the true topic: the system of syllogistic reason whose parts derive their determinacy from the pertinent conjoining *medius terminus*. In the third syllogism, such is "self-knowing reason." With the retrospect on the whole of cultivated knowledge, conceiving determines itself to be such reason and its intuition.

We recall briefly: in the sphere of the logic itself, the absolute idea is merely "formal," nothing but the method. So that this method be that of truth, the content of cognition has to be derived from it. "The method itself expands through this moment into a system" (*GW* 12, 249.9/838). The requisite content is first of all none other than the method's absolute beginning: "the simple relation to itself, which is Being. But it is"—in the result of the logic—"also fulfilled Being, the self-conceiving concept, Being as the concrete, likewise absolutely intensive totality" (252.31/842)—absolutely intensive or real as that totality which Nature is. Thus: "as the final result, truth," initially only "pure, also comes to be the beginning of another sphere and science." As a determinate truth, however, such is necessarily distinguished: the idea "divides itself primally" (*sich urteilen*; *GW* 20, § 577) into "physical and psychic Nature"; it is the former as an immediately posited totality, the latter as one which turns back into itself.

The idea of philosophy is self-knowing reason in its essentially syllogistic activity and in fact in that syllogism in which it itself appears as the middle term. Only here is the entire actuality of the concept revealed, i.e., to distinguish itself within itself and thus to determine itself only through itself.

The concept's distinguishing of itself within itself is—where the concept is not only the "adequate" concept and thus the idea, but where the idea has developed its existence into that of philosophy—the idea which primally divides itself into its manifestations. These are themselves syllogisms which also are determined by their middle terms. The first is that of Nature, or the side of the immediacy of the absolute idea, while the other is spirit, or the returning movement of mediating conceiving.

Self-knowing reason is split into spirit and Nature and in each instance yields by way of these as the middle terms of a syllogism a specific system. The idea of philosophy, however, is that syllogism of this reason which primally divides itself into both of the other syllogisms and which yields the system of rational syllogisms. Viewed with respect to the sequence of their occurrence, they are the manifestations of that middle term; viewed with respect to their completed type, their manifestation or revelation. According to the first side, difference appears in what has been split: Nature and spirit; according to the other side, however, it reveals itself as the movement of distinguishing and thus determining, in short: of conceiving, because it is the movement of the idea.

In that principle which is the fundamental relation of the system of systems, the sense of dominance and "subjection," which is proper to the "subject" of the idea, is now also manifest. The syllogism that is the idea of philosophy leaves no doubt: nothing alien is subsumed here because Nature and spirit are, according to their determinacy, derivative; neither is a first. The idea which is concrete as philosophy is a "subject" in such a way that it subjects—as the Kantian idea of freedom already suggests—only itself and is subjected only to itself.

Nature and spirit are differentiated totalities, neither of which can set itself up as the sole totality—with the suppression of the other by each—only because these mutually excluding totalities are conjoined as moments of the self-distinguishing concept. As such, however, they relinquish the determinacy they have as these manifestations to the determinacy of the idea, which reveals itself in distinguishing. The idea is no alien lord over against that which it subjects but rather has expunged the latter's indifference to it, or the unrelatedness of objectivity as such to thinking.

Contrary to the widespread maligning of the "system" as the violation of the individual by the universal, contrary to this maligning with which thinking itself testifies to its having become undifferentiated, it should be noted: the method which has been expanded into a system is intent exactly upon saving the differences of the true as the differences of the conceptual determination and in fact in such a way that philosophy, according to its idea, allows nothing to make its advent, nothing to enter into itself, that is not known as something different in the rigorous sequence of clear conceiving. But because that which is different itself has to be developed into the truth of what is contradictory, the activity of reason is condensed into the disjunctive syllogism.

Such is really no longer a syllogism: "For the middle term, which is posited in it as the totality of the concept, itself contains the two extremes in their complete determinacy. The extremes, as distinct from this middle term, are only as a positedness to which a proper determinacy over against the middle term can no longer be ascribed" (*GW* 12, 124.30/702). "The difference between that which mediates and that which is mediated has been dropped. That which is mediated is itself an essential moment of that which mediates it, and each moment appears as the totality of what is mediated." From this it follows: "the form of the syllogism, which consists in the difference between the middle term and its extremes, has sublated itself" (125/703).

Accordingly the idea of philosophy reveals: Nature and spirit relinquish their proper determinacy in their conjunction via the middle term of the logical, for "they possess [such determinacy] only insofar as they have not yet gone back into their unity" (11.23/577). Into which unity? The logical? Where it itself no longer occurs as an extreme term of a syllogism but rather as its middle term, this characterization is inadequate. Where the logical takes the two totalities of the real as moments back into itself, it is "the knowing concept" (*Enz.*, § 477). It is real "as the universal knowledge that stays immediately with itself in its determinacy" and in doing so is "self-knowing reason." Here this reason is no type of consciousness but rather the result of science and its idea. Now could the said anxiety have its ground in this speculative reason? Does something happen then in the immediate staying-with-itself (*Bei-sich-Bleiben*) proper to knowledge?

XVI

In the end philosophy grasps is own concept—that is to say: it retrospects only on its knowledge (§ 473) and thereby sees that and how the logical proved itself in light of its concrete content (§ 474). The usual hasty objection reads: it has not proved itself. To whom did it not? To man, and anxiety still calls to mind this answer, for anxiety can indeed be man's alone. The question concerning the nature of technicity has us understand, of course: this nature is nothing human.

Here the comment presents itself: that speculative reason is also nothing human and is dropped with Feuerbach's transition from "theology" to "anthropology"—to say nothing of speculation's having become "incredible." Nor was man unknown to speculation, although it knew quite well to distinguish man's expressions from what consciousness knows, and showed him his nature and his position where natural consciousness expressly established itself as the adversary of absolute knowledge (Hegel, *GW* 9, 304/341 f.).

Yet just that sequence of the forms projected into the human world allows that "anthropology" to be regarded only as a sign and not as an explanation. The anxiety which arises with the nature of these forms, its expunction of all determinacy, instead leads back to something whose occurrence has its ground in the idea of philosophy itself.

What could that be? A transition? That is the illusion in which Feuerbach's rejection of onto-theology in favor of "anthropology" arises, whereby the latter poses as the former's necessary result. But as already indicated, the illusion of this transition in the sequence of the forms of the world clearly fades. In fact each of these is represented as the necessary result of a history; yet the transition from its present into man's other future appears necessary only in the first position (Marx), for Nietzsche only as possible, for Heidegger as not impossible, and each time as a "radical change"—finally within itself without any transition but "presumably all of a sudden."

What does the philosophy that has grasped its own concept, that has become equal to its idea, say to this?

Hegel comments on the result of the *Science of Logic*, in particular on the immediacy of the absolute idea, which Nature is: "But this determination is not something that has come to be and a transition, as . . . the subjective concept in its"—yielded by the disjunctive syllogism—"totality becomes objectivity and, as subjective end, comes to be life" (*GW* 12, 253/843). And further: "The pure idea, in which the determinacy or the reality of the concept itself is elevated to the concept, is rather absolute liberation for which there is no longer any immediate determination that is not both posited and the concept; thus in this freedom, no transition takes place; simple Being, which the idea determines itself to be, remains perfectly perspicuous for [the idea] and is the concept which stays with itself in its determination." This has to hold all the more for the idea of philosophy since for it the concept's staying-with-itself is also perspicuous in its distinguishing manifestation. The immediacy of the Being of "Nature" is here taken back into that immediacy with which philosophy retrospects on its own knowledge and only on it. Hegel had allowed the present proper to this retrospect to be exhibited by another retrospect in that he concludes with a quotation taken from Aristotelian theology.

How could he do that? He knows his insight to be bound up with Aristotle's by virtue of a singular development. From this it follows: from its "oriental" appearance onward, the history of philosophy is subject to the sole determination of the idea with which it finally attains equality. There can be no transition of speculation beyond that. Though it is not the historial approach to philosophy which proves this, since it remains only an extrinsic representation of the movement of science, which in its beginning has taken the dark and confused thought of the Orient back into the clarity and distinctness of Being as that "immediate" which is "indeterminate," and thus into the concept. Even the whole of "religion" has gone back into the latter, a religion which began as that of the natural light, which is nothing given, no light from light, but rather which arises out of its night. A transition inherent in the certainly true reality, which is the realized idea of philosophy, remains ruled out.

How are matters then with the development which was asserted for the forms projected into the human world? Are they perhaps indifferent to the idea of philosophy? What do they say? As science, metaphysics is dead; in its secularized appearances, it possesses a stifling liveliness. No—stifling is what is dead.

We recall only Marx here: the capital by which the worker as machine is faced is "dead labor which dominates and sucks dry the living manpower" (*MEW* 23, 446/423)—dead because it is "past labor." "It is only the dominance of amassed, past, objectified labor over immediate, living labor that turns the amassed labor into capital." "Capital does not consist in the fact that amassed labor serves living labor as a means for new production. It consists in the fact that living labor serves as the means whereby amassed labor maintains and multiplies its exchange value" (*MEW* 6, 409/36).

The moments of the idea, end-in-itself and drive, have become the moments of what is dead, which is projected into the world of man as its historically resultant form. The dominance of what is dead is likewise manifest both in the result of morality: in nihilism, insofar as it paralyzes with general purposelessness the volition of the creators; as well as in the result of technicity: in "errancy," in which thinking solidifies into the lack of differentiation.

"To hold fast to what is dead, that is what requires the greatest strength" (Hegel, *GW* 9, 27.26/19). Heidegger held fast to it in the question concerning the nature of technicity. This question turns from the dominance of what is dead towards death itself in order to distinguish it as what shelters from what displaces reason. Yet it also holds of this return: it remains bound to view "nature" as that of technicity. This prevents one from seeing what death shelters and even the question concerning the What. Death remains the "shrine of nothingness."

Undifferentiated thinking—it is that which is idea-less—can regard the dominance of what is dead, as it is viewed by Marx and Nietzsche and Heidegger, as only an exaggeration that, with the dissolution of that which remains a "metaphor" for it, has to prove to be empty talk. But this thinking contradicts itself by its concern.

Death is the death of man, as is anxiety. In the question concerning the nature of technicity, the latter as well as the former refers to something that is not human. Now this question can be elaborated only as the question concerning the nature of metaphysics. How could this nature be different from the idea of philosophy?

To say: metaphysics is dead; or even only: it has come to an end; or even more feebly: it is past; must indeed be regarded as metaphorical talk that conceals the fact that it knows not what it is talking about. 'Metaphysics is dead' can only mean: it is departed—rendered different (*verschieden*) not from this or that, and thus not relatively, but rather absolutely, namely, in the sense of "departing" (*Verscheiden*). And which role would this have with regard to the idea of philosophy?

Here it must be expressly emphasized: questioning in this way is permissible only for the accomplished, at least the self-accomplishing, progressive determination of the human world as the forms projected into it. This movement is a return of the different thinking, of the non-philosophy which finally awakens from its difference to the present proper to theory, not shedding its difference thereby but rather bringing it to determinacy. What does this mean?

XVII

First this question: why is it possible to elaborate the question concerning the nature of technicity only as that concerning the nature of metaphysics? The form that is projected into the human world is each time an offensive face that as such demands the total change of the world and therefore of man. This demand reduces the present to a critical point which no longer lets the past but only the future be separated from the present; the past is, strictly speaking, no longer the past but rather something offensive that, as an historical result, has completely penetrated the present. What is there to be known for caring thinking is solely this result and its history, for only with respect to it is thought assured of catching sight in the present of that which is necessarily and universally "how it is."

The history of human power is that of the relations of production; the history of the will of the producers shows the history of metaphysics no longer merely as an accompanying ideology but rather as a movement that itself intervenes in life in a corrupting manner. The history of those volitional beings who discover, who deshelter and thus intervene with violence in the existent conditions (cf. Heidegger, *Introduction to Metaphysics*), refers to a "mission" of originary concealment, a mission that can be delimited as a totality of the dominant knowledge and on the basis of the historical present only as metaphysics, and can be unfolded into a "missive" sequence of the "coinage of Being" (*ID*, 60/68).

The understanding takes offense at the fact that this sequence reveals no necessity; but it may not do so since it has progressed in such a way that the turn of the present into the completely other future is no longer viewed as at all compulsory but rather as not impossible. This paradoxical progression indeed points to something unthought to which the question concerning the nature of technicity corresponds and which the question concerning the nature of metaphysics takes up. The span of its history up to its end in Nietzsche is held to show simply which difference the beginning makes as the beginning of an oblivion that withdraws from even itself.

Which beginning? The Greek one? So it seems. And one has to have taken this semblance seriously, one has to have let oneself be guided by it down to the beginning which knowingly makes all the difference: the idea of philosophy in its fulfillment. But how? Such can never be immediately gathered but rather only by means of the suffering proper to the thought of Marx, Nietzsche, and Heidegger, since it alone leads to that which is to be viewed as the entire difference: death and, basically, philosophy's departedness in accordance with its idea.

The return from the semblance of the first beginning in the Greeks has taught, however, what a principle of epochal determinacy is, and reveals: that departedness as a difference from itself is thinkable solely on the basis of the principle which determines the modern era.

The method that has been expanded into a perfect system can know itself only as the sole principle in an historical sense. This confirms not only Hegel's history of philosophy but, prior to this, the history of consciousness itself, in particular the movement of its "religion," which, in the outline of the modern era's progressive determination of the light of natural reason, includes the forms of the ancient world in order to arrange these as prior and subordinate to conceptual science. The history of substantial or objective thought returns to that of subjective or free thought.

It is only when the historical beginning of philosophy is no longer taken up in a dark Orient but rather takes on the determinacy of the first beginning in the Greeks, and in fact from out of the other beginning, that the history of metaphysics loses its externality to the thought of the topic itself, that this thought appears in that semblance which it itself is to dissolve. The dissolution shows: Heidegger's return into the ground of metaphysics is a return into the ground of the principle of its modern era, the principle which had suppressed the question concerning its "advent" with the demonstration of its provenance all the more so as it had to assert that its development is its history only in extrinsic significance. Such left no doubt: our sole "land," our sole ground and fundament, is the spirit of the modern era.

Insofar as the idea of philosophy has proved in its perfect realization that Nature itself as appearance is the manifestation of the first of the moments of the concept, reason returns as no longer natural; it is no longer a type of consciousness where it, retrospecting on its knowledge, knows itself. In this science it has expunged every trace of the fact that it has been given and thus the uniqueness of the principle of the modern era is completely assured—down to the crisis that becomes understandable through this principle but which cannot be visible to the reason proper to it.

This principle's difference from the older, likewise epochal, principles emerges only by way of its absolute departedness, as it is asserted by non-philosophy with its "basis"-theories or the proof of the givenness of reason, which excludes its speculative character because such excludes the present proper to theory—and yet it also indicates with the "faces" of the historical present.

In the movement of non-philosophy, the principle of the modern era is not rejected, despite all offenses; it is by no means deprived of the persuasiveness of what is principally true. The outcry against "speculation" or the melancholy at one's inability to engage in it should not interfere in the needful movement with which the principle of the modern era—the principle that "needs" human being since it departs from itself and thus from speculative reason's attention to itself—expunges its uniqueness.

XVIII

The ground of the expunction of all determinacy with respect to which anxiety taken on as anxiety understands itself and in which the world of the other logical, of the other assembling, namely, of the thing, is imagined, the ground of this nothingness is the departedness of metaphysics, of its perfectly realized idea. In this way death has taken on determinacy. And which treasure does the "shrine of nothingness" keep safe?

The assembling of the principles of philosophy.

But then are they not those of metaphysics? Does the Same perhaps return? The principles of "physical and spiritual Nature"? Matters are not so easy with the departedness of the principle of the modern era, which certainly with good reason appeared as the sole idea of philosophy, of the perfect system of science.

Philosophy has departed from itself, from itself as the theory of principles, which metaphysics was. It continues to be the theory of principles but not meta-physics. The "logical" has—having gotten free of "physics"—turned. Whereto?

The different philosophy does not reject metaphysics but rather addresses its gift, takes it on. It does not, of course, take on its epochal principles in the determinacy of the topic that is firstly true but rather in that determinacy which shows the crisis of its truth. It is only in their crises that the principles are of equal rank. It is on account of this that the topic of the resurrected First Philosophy is: the crisis of the principles.

XIX

From released thinking Heidegger expected a "new steadfastness" (*neue Bodenständigkeit*). How is it to be determined? According the "old" steadfastness of the "country path"? Was it such as the essentially rural one? Was it such only in the lee of the withdrawal accompanying the departedness of the principle of the modern era and even reaching into the beginning of that era? The fundament of the country path in the vicinity of church and castle provided support only by virtue of the older principle.

The fundament is that which is given which the principle of the modern era accommodates by virtue of its departedness. The fundament is this principle's ground only in its unity with the older principle, which is distinguished within itself and is therefore determined. The "piety" that attends to what is currently "transmitted" in the tradition turns to this unity.

The question concerning the nature of technicity allowed Heidegger to see the "piety of thinking" in questioning. The answer to which the indeterminate character of precisely this nature is brought, lets the haze of "techno-logical" questioning, of the placing-in-question that lacks both place and fundament, dissipate.

Out of the anxiety of the "other beginning," a thought-worthy vision encourages this answer: "I have seen the wicked exultant, towering like a cedar of Lebanon. When next I *passed* he was gone; I searched for him and he was nowhere to be found" (Psalm 37: *Vidi impium superexaltatum, et elevatum sicut cedros Libani. Et* transivi *et ecce non erat; et quaesivi eum et non inventus est locus eius*).

PRIVILEGE OF PRESENCE?

The only one who has asked the question 'What is metaphysics?'; the only one who, by the scope and way of his thought within the sphere of modernity, was urged to raise this question; the only one who has thought of metaphysics not as having a history but as being the singular history of the Occident; has repeatedly asserted—and who has contested this?—: metaphysics is the theory of the Being of beings, and this Being is continuously understood therein as *Anwesenheit*. The sense of Being in the tradition of occidental thought is *Anwesen*. And this not only favors presence among the tenses of speech but even obscures the temporality of Being and consequently its historicity.

These assertions have a well-defined right within the bounds of modernity—a right that elicits the projection of technical reason back into the history of natural reason, back into what seems to be the beginning of metaphysics, seen as the turning point at which the prospect of the other beginning of thinking opens. To be more precise in view of the legacy Heidegger left behind: the turning point which can be envisioned only by way of the hint provided by the name ἀλήθεια. This legacy is the legitimate father of errancy, of errant reason. And yet Heidegger has produced quite a flock of illegitimate children who make little more than impotent mistakes. Incapable of insisting in errancy, they pursue their own idiosyncratic vagaries—this without renewing the incessant question of a thought oppressed by the presence, not by the remnants, of metaphysical thinking and speaking. Theirs is the task of unmasking bits of metaphysics, taking for granted Heidegger's answer, which precedes his question 'What is metaphysics?' as an experience. Heidegger's thought is, so to speak, engulfed in metaphysics because it is the history of our world. He always envisions it as a totality and cannot approach bits and pieces of it—contrary to the practices of the learned flock, which cherishes a memory of Plato or of Hegel, a memory of Kant or of Husserl, only to find that Heidegger is right in asserting the privilege of presence within the occidental tradition. But this is like having "a memory in Chicago and a memory in New Orleans" (Louis

Armstrong), perhaps more innocent, though no less obnoxious for students who are plagued—as Heidegger rightly observes in his *Contributions to Philosophy*—by the predilections of philosophy professors.

Heidegger experiences metaphysics as an oppressive intramundane totality, one increasingly so due to the mounting sediments of its major tenets, which therefore had to be grasped de-structively. His experience of this totality, the "mission" of the ἔσχατον, has been confused with general statements about metaphysics which can be verified only in piecemeal fashion (cf. the Vienna Circle).

The privilege of presence. Indeed, Heidegger intends to break it. Why and how? In the *Contributions* he says: with the preeminence of presence it has been "decided that in that which is most obvious lies concealed the strangest decision" (*GA* 65, 460)—more appropriately translated: the κρίσις ἀτοπώτατος. Here we see that Heidegger's assertion is linked to his experience of ἀλήθεια. And any critique of this assertion must meet him on that ground. There we have met him (cf. my "The Early Greek Usage of the Words *Logos* and *Aletheia*"), and the Greek notion of ἀλήθεια has induced us to contest the projection that metaphysics is in its totality the theory of the Being of beings. We have denied this even in the case of Aristotle (cf. "Why 'Being of Beings'?", pp. 19-43 above). We have denied that Being is to be understood there *in toto* as *Anwesen*. And this denial is no piecemeal refutation but is instead necessitated by—as Plato's *Parmenides* says—a διέξοδος διὰ πάντων: a passage through all, not only traversing the entire field of metaphysics but also establishing this as an historic totality different from the Heideggerian one, for it is completely severed from that continuity which ends in a way of thinking determined by technicity.

But what about the common ground of the hint inherited from ἀλήθεια? In a renewed scrutiny (cf. my *Topology of Metaphysics*), it was seen to point to νοῦς, to reason, and this called for the consideration of the ἀρχαί, which in turn led to the epochal distinctions of the said history and finally to the distinction of reason itself.

On the basis of this knowledge, we now approach the notorious assumption of the privilege of presence. First let us assume that 'presence' is a proper translation of *Anwesenheit*, which is a proper translation of παρουσία. How is it that the sense of Being should be *Anwesen*, παρεῖναι? Added to this is Heidegger's assumption that *Anwesen* is akin to φαίνεσθαι, which in turn refers to φύσις understood as the primary instance of ἀλήθεια.

Let's come to terms now with our terms. The Greek view of these matters first of all demands the remedy of this confusion. Which one? That of φαίνεσθαι and παρεῖναι. This is particularly grave, for it obscures the elementary fact that παρεῖναι is only secondarily the Being of that which comes into view but primarily the Being of the viewing itself in the sense of attention, which the early Greeks also specify as λόγος in the sense of taking something into consideration or of giving thought to it. This is fundamental for the early Greek understanding of παρεῖναι as obviously differing from the φαίνεσθαι of this or that.

To repeat the results of a previous investigation into the distinction of Being as γενέσθαι, φαίνεσθαι, and παρεῖναι: being in the originary sense is understood as γενέσθαι, which does not necessarily imply a temporal sequence (cf. my *Ground and Present as the Aim of Early Greek Philosophical Inquiry*, pp. 220 ff.). Consider Hesiod: first of all, Χάος γένετο. Its Da-sein does not imply παρεῖναι, nor is such implied in the γένεσις of its children. They are there either as the realms of darkness under and over the earth or as the realm of light, whether steady (αἰθήρ) or transient (ἡμέρα), and the offspring of Night "are" in the sense of overcoming, engulfing, or gripping; Ἔρις (Strife) is not there in the sense of παρεῖναι, nor is her child Λήθη (Oblivion)—they happen, they occur.

And what is the Being of Γαῖα (Earth) and of Ἔρως? Neither is to be reduced to a common Being with Χάος. This is the first lesson to be learned from the *Theogony*. Common to them is only γενέσθαι as such but not a common mode of εἶναι. In what way "is" Earth? In always being the infallible seat of everything that is, in the sense of being sat upon or—as we used to say—of "existing." Πάντα "are" there in the sense of occupying a seat, which in later theory is seen as a τόπος. They take place. Thus Οὐρανός (Heaven) is the seat of the gods. Such is obviously not the case for Χάος and Ἔρως. These and Earth are there in fundamentally different ways, and it would be absurd for a Greek to state of them: πάρεστι, or to assert their presence. They are because γένοντο: they came to be there. Only Earth and her Heaven—to repeat: her—have this distinction: they offer a seat to everything either here or there. In a closed sphere, Heaven is there to give shelter to everything (ἵνα περὶ πάντα καλύπτοι). As far as these πάντα are concerned, it must be noted that none of the passing γενόμενα are considered—death, yes, but not dying. Nevertheless, subordination appears, resulting from subjection in the realms of Zeus and his brothers.

After having put everything in its place, after the complete establishment of the "seats" of everything, we now ask: what about φαίνεσθαι? Its kinship to φάος (light) is indisputable. Φαίνειν means 'to bring to light' or 'to come to light', most of all 'to come to the light of day, which offers visibility'. With the change of night and day, φαίνεσθαι is transitory—finally with reference to the cycle of the year and in that sense to time only. This cycle depends on the perpetual motion of the heavens. It not only involves disappearance or passing away, such as that of a flower, e.g., of the φαινίς (anemone), but also a temporary concealment (κρύπτεσθαι), even of the shining stars themselves—including the sun. Neither φαίνεσθαι nor κρύπτεσθαι ever affect πάντα, a totality, but only an indefinite multitude of single φανερά (appearances) that are already there, that have already, so to speak, taken place. And even simple saying, understood as φάσις, refers to the alternative of concealing an ἔπος in one's heart. It must be assumed that there is already something in its place, be it concealed or brought to light, something different from the terrestrial and celestial γενόμενα, which first of all offer a place.

Time and again Heidegger pointed to the Heraclitian dictum φύσις κρύπτεσθαι φιλεῖ (Nature tends to conceal itself) because he saw in this the earliest and virtually only instance of ἀλήθεια in its originary meaning. But to begin with, it should be noted that φύσις here means 'Nature' neither in a universal nor in a general sense. Rather, it belongs to a φανερόν (appearance) and tends to conceal itself in the latter. For φύσις is always that of contrary predicates, such as dry and wet, and thus of appearances that seem to exclude one another.

But now to the main point: φύσις is not an, let alone the most originary, instance of ἀλήθεια, for there is a fundamental difference between κρύπτειν and λήθειν. And this leads us to the precise understanding of παρεῖναι, or *adesse*, which becomes particularly obvious in the proverb παρέοντας ἀπεῖναι (being present, they are absent), which Heraclitus quotes in speaking of the ἀξύνετοι (the uncomprehending), that is, of those who are present and yet absent. And this implies a lack of νοῦς and of the attention it devotes to something. 'To be present' means 'to attend to and to understand something', thus 'presence of mind'. Only with reference to such attention is something in turn present and not just there or apparent. Turning once again to Heraclitus (B 72): those who are absent "differ from the λόγος with which they converse most continuously; that which they meet daily, appears (φαίνεται) alien to them." It is not present to them because they themselves remain absent due to a lack of attention to the λόγος, the ratio of the opposed Natures in that which is visible and actually seen.

It is only after Xenophanes and Heraclitus that we enter the proper field of ἀλήθεια in philosophy. This notion derives from a positive λήθειν in its primary transitive sense. Such concealment affects one who is in turn attentive to something, who wants to know it, but who is frustrated in his attempt by someone else, by someone who gives heed to the fact that he should not know it. This is the horizon of the early Greek sense of ἀλήθεια, which is restricted to φάσις, to rendering something present in speech, because this something is out of view and thus inaccessible to attention. In order to know it, one has to rely on the willingness of a witness to communicate his knowledge. The witness is the one who was present and therefore knows. This is exactly how Homer understands the state of the Muses, whom he has to approach because "we" mortals know nothing, but depend on hearsay. They know everything, he points out, because they are present. To be present is in itself a privilege with respect to the intention to gain knowledge. It insists on the distinction between being present oneself and having heard from someone else (cf. *Odyssey* VIII, 491 ff.). Ἀλήθεια is demanded, given, or refused, where participation in knowledge is sought. When such a refusal is impossible—and such is the case in both physiology and cosmology—the demand for ἀλήθεια makes no sense and is thus absent from the testimonies of pre-Parmenidean philosophy. Such relies on either an ἱστορεῖν (to observe) or a ξυνιέναι (to comprehend "how it is"). These are essentially open to anyone who gives heed and is attentive, who achieves presence of mind. This implies that one gives oneself a λόγος independently of anyone else's λόγος.

If it makes any sense to say that knowledge is privileged over against ignorance, then its precondition—namely, presence in the observation of phenomena and in the comprehension of the difference between "how they appear" and "how they are"—is necessarily privileged. But not all philosophical knowledge is based on such presence either in ἱστορίη or in ξύνεσις. This is particularly obvious in view of the Parmenidean ἀλήθεια and the ἐόν (being) it implies.

To speak of a theory of being prior to Parmenides is totally unwarranted. Thus, we arrive now at the main historical instance in which the Heideggerian tenet that Being is understood as presence must be scrutinized and clarified. In what sense is the Parmenidean ἐόν present? Obviously not in the sense demanded for either observation or comprehension, since thinking is directed on its proper way beyond any attention to phenomena. Subject to the pure presence of θέμις, of that which is established *a priori*, thinking is bound to convince itself of an ἀλήθεια that is no longer denied by someone's λήθειν but is instead neglected by the λήθεσθαι of mortal reason. It is characteristic of this reason that it regards being and not-being as both the Same and not the Same. It vacillates. The revelation of the steady heart of truth destines thinking to the steady attention to the difference between what is to be and what is not to be. Set on the path of "how it is," it becomes aware of the ἐόν, of that which is purely within the bounds of necessity. Being (*Seiendes*) has, so to speak, taken place within θέμις (that which is originarily established). There it is.

But it has no appearance whatsoever. And what about its *Anwesenheit*, its presence? Thinking here gives its attention only to the decision concerning the impossible (the contradictory) and the necessary (the identical). Thus, the path of "how it is" opens to the movement of πειθώ alone. It persuades itself of the ἀλήθεια not in observing the ἐόν but in observing the signs set for its way, the way of primary logic. What then? Does the ἐόν lack presence? It has no presence of its own but only within the bounds of necessity. There it has its identity, which is fundamentally different from that of the δοκοῦντα (the stuff of opinion). The identity proper to pure reason is being the same within the same, that is, within the bounds of necessity (B 8.29). The identity supposed by opinion is being the same as oneself and not the same as something else (B 8.57). Only the latter is considered by Heidegger in his "Identity and Difference," though with reference to Plato (*ID*, 14/27).

The insight into that primary identity stems from the attention to being as being-accomplished, as a fulfilled destiny. There is no presence but that of what has been accomplished. And thinking meets it because it moves on a path leading exactly to the goal of such presence. What sense does it make to speak of the privilege of what is necessary over against what is impossible? Is there a privilege of what is necessary over against what is just real? But the ἐόν cannot be merely real and that is the stumbling block of its modern interpreters—including Heidegger, who tried to dwell here on a seeming vacillation between Being and beings.

To repeat: thinking is set on the path of πειθώ concerning an ἀλήθεια which it has to accept. It accepts, i.e., conceives, the truth of what is to be by attaining the insight into Being in the sense of being-accomplished. As for Being, self-contradiction is excluded; as for thinking, the *progressus ad infinitum*.

Now let us take just a glimpse at the Platonic transformation of the Parmenidean beginning: first of all, Being is distinguished not in order to include but rather to relate that which has the appearance of an accomplishment—in particular, the experience of virtues—to that which is truly accomplished, namely, the ideas. The former participates in the presence of the latter and thus elicits an ἔρως for what has been accomplished. The erotic and thus intense intention transcends in turn the horizon of the senses and enters the noetic realm. Secondly the multitude of the truly accomplished beings depends on the principal unity of the ἀγαθόν, which is beyond the οὐσία, that is, the presence of the ideas themselves. And lastly the corresponding thought assumes the logic of dialectic.

Finally to Aristotle: first of all he transforms dialectic into science. Secondly this science attains the presence of being, starting with the ὄν as λεγόμενον, accordingly with the basic formula: 'this subsists in that in a certain respect'. This formula gains its proper content when something definite in its presence is pointed out and the latter is distinguished, it being either potential or accomplished (ἐντελεχεία ὄν). And finally the determination of what has been principally accomplished is ascertained. The first god attends to himself alone, his intellectual activity being the highest accomplishment. This final phase of Greek thought clearly emphasizes the priority of the presence which is that of the mind itself, which is completely different from φαίνεσθαι, from any appearance. If there is a privilege of presence here, then it is that of θεωρία alone. With the middle epoch of philosophy and its emphasis on the *veritas facta*, not only *visa*, the situation radically changes.

This is already obvious in the metaphysics of Plotinus. Its principle excludes both the presence of reason and of being. Both derive from the primary One, to which not only being but even an indeterminate something is denied. Prior to the presence of spirit is here the presence of being in the primary sense of being-given. This givenness reflects on spirit in that it is constituted only by the *conversio* of being to its giver. *Conversio* is prior to intention. It acknowledges the givenness of being and of its own activity by χάρις, by grace. Thinking is primarily acknowledgment, and thus the givenness of the only beings in Plotinus—namely, spirit and soul—is characterized as ὑφίστασθαι. This implies subordination to the primary One.

In Augustine the acknowledgment of the givenness of Being appears firstly in the relation of the soul to its creator and then principally with the Trinitarian substance. Father and Son give themselves to one another, this communication becoming explicit in the spirit of love, or rather *dilectio*, which is the *donum*, the gift par excellence. This Trinity is approached only through him who has given himself to mankind. In this case, divine substance is transformed by *subiectio*. This opens the way of thinking determined by humility.

Thomas Aquinas abandons this type of thinking insofar as he establishes it first of all as a methodical *traditio* of the *Sacra doctrina*. The active acknowledgment of the givenness of Being is that of the rational creature which is attested by its motion into God, whose grace gives perfection to Nature. Finally the principally practical importance of the givenness of Being is asserted in the way given by Christ to follow the *veritas facta*, accentuating this gift in the manifold grace deriving from it.

While the primary sense of Being in the middle epoch of philosophy is being-given, that of the final epoch is being-posited—this because of its basic poietic character. Such has to be the case insofar as it accords with the principle of freedom understood as self-determination. The Kantian moral law is not something of immediate presence, not something given by a divine legislator, but rather something posited by autonomous reason. Here the term of thinking is centered on both its self-subjection to this law and the defense of its purity. The knowledge of natural objects is made subservient firstly to the recognition of freedom as a fact, finally to the duty of the good will to produce and realize its proper object, namely, the highest good in the world.

Time and again Heidegger pointed out that *Anwesenheit* is translated by Kant—as already by Descartes—into the objectivity of objects. And yet Heidegger's claim totally obscures the express motive of Kantian thought, which already in its theoretical intention is principally concerned with the "salvation of freedom." This motive does not demand an interpretation of the objectivity of objects but rather the distinction between the object as thing-in-itself and as appearance. Only the horizon of freedom and its corresponding positing enables us to understand how the production of scientific truth tends to maximize the formative capacities in objectivation and to minimize that which is given, reducing it to the material of sensation. This clearly brings out the fundamental distinction between the actuality of an object and its reality.

In Fichtean thinking, even that residue of givenness is integrated into Being, which is determined as the originary acts of the human mind: positing, contra-positing, and co-positing. The reflection on these acts illuminates the moral law and its positing as a result of the freedom in reflection. It demands that the ego be ego, that it strive for the ideal of absolute identity.

Whereas Fichtean thinking is primarily determined by a striving which radically transforms the mode of thinking, Hegelian thinking in its principal form overcomes the reflection of a consciousness and the striving of its will. It is determinative by progressively distinguishing the pure concept within itself. The prime mover in all conceptual positing is negativity. As for the sequence of determinations in the Hegelian concept, it becomes quite absurd to presuppose a Being of beings, let alone Being as *Anwesen*, the latter in turn being understood as the objectivity of objects. How could one claim *Anwesenheit* for the absolute idea, for its moments of Nature and negativity? We are faced here with the truth as it emerges only through its complete production in the mode of self-determination, starting with the Being (*Sein*) that is equal to the nothingness (*Nichts*) within the first and most abstract concept, that of becoming (*Werden*). In this beginning of Hegelian logic not even Fichte's preconscious acts are accepted as given.

Now to return to Heidegger's position within the sphere of modernity, which we have shown to be severed from the history of metaphysics (cf. my *The Rational Architectonic of Modernity*). He never completely shed the hermeneutic provenance of his thought, instead admitting its continuity with the thought of both of its phenomenological predecessors, Dilthey and Husserl. Heidegger stuck to the principle of all principles concerning the presence of phenomena in consciousness, though only insofar as such implies the strict demand for experience. Taking as his point of departure Being as it is presupposed in Husserlian First Philosophy, Heidegger insists on the seeming phenomenality of Aristotelian being; this gave him the most important historical foothold for asking: what is metaphysics? He assumes that the theory of being *qua* being amounted to an inquiry into the Being of beings, and he even asserted that the generality of this *Leitfrage* (guiding question) covers the span of thought from Anaximander down to Nietzsche. However, just as Aristotle denied a γένος of being, so we deny a γένος in the sense of that question's generality. We have come to deny the hermeneutic assumption that the history of metaphysics is a sequence of interpretations of the Being of beings.

Yet we have to acknowledge Heidegger's transformation of hermeneutics in his abandonment of the question concerning the sense of Being in favor of the experience of its truth. The recourse to the privative sense of ἀλήθεια gave rise to the articulation of an experience engaged by a prior untruth or concealment. It is here that we find our true motive for rejecting the privilege of presence. The basic experience of concealment in the ἔσχατον of metaphysics, that is, in its destiny, must allow for the future of the other beginning of thinking over against metaphysical thinking and, what is more, for the future of the other world, which the realm of technicity excludes. Heidegger harkens from the experience of metaphysical oblivion back to the ἐποχή in the destiny of its world, where even the question concerning the Being of beings is quashed in favor of the technical system of beings alone. Here the traditional privilege of presence is doomed to the calamitous privilege of the challenge (*Stellen*).

Is there an εὐπορία to be recognized which meets the extreme ἀπορία in the Heideggerian "mission" of history? The latter is understood as a gift, or present, in the giving of which the giver is reticent, reserves himself, remains concealed. The experience of a truth that is denied evolves within modernity as an experience of the expropriation of man—in Marx, of his productive power; in Nietzsche, of his productive will; and in Heidegger, of his productive knowledge. How so? Such expropriation refers to an appropriation of Being and thinking, one which the occidental tradition developed in the reverse and even perverse sequence of thinking and Being, that is, with thinking in the determinative position. And so it appears that the latter has established the privilege of presence: thinking has privileged itself—so it seems.

There is indeed such a determinative sequence to be seen in the first metaphysical positions of each epoch, that is, in those of Parmenides, Plotinus, and Kant, respectively. But if we come to distinguish the simple ratio, or *Sachverhalt*, of Being and thinking from its full, that is, mediated, form by including the destinal principle, then it becomes clear in each of the cases mentioned that thinking itself—although determinative for its corresponding topic—is in turn preceded by a certain destinal principle: θέμις as present in ἀλήθεια; the ineffable One as present in its beauty (καλλονή); freedom as present in the moral law.

But what renders such precedence possible? The fact that φιλο-σοφία is preceded by a σοφία. Metaphysics has never installed truth but only the logic which properly conceived it. We need only recall Hegel's insistence on the distinction between truth and *Gewißheit* (certainty), or rather between truth and the science of logic. Metaphysical, or conceptual, reason has privileged presence only insofar as it has itself been privileged by the present of its destiny. Such privilege was offered by the epochally distinguished types of σοφία—the presence of Parmenides' ἀλήθεια referring to Homer's δίκη μοίρας; the presence of Plotinus's beauty of the primary One referring to John's non-relational union of the divine Father and Son; the presence of Kant's moral principle referring to Rousseau's freedom of humanity. In each instance the originary "there is," or rather the "it gives" (*es gibt*), for philosophy is a present offered by a σοφία whose truth was to be conceived.

With all due respect to the moderns, we ourselves feel privileged by the insight: no future.

DISSENSIONS

Something on the dark side again? Why? Speaking of Heidegger and Heraclitus—or of Heidegger on Heraclitus—the latter's darkness appears to have faded in the light of historial research, whereas the former's darkness still persists, in spite of the attempts at translating his thought into a "plain and familiar language," or rather into the familiar discourse and "average" understanding of philosophical "problems." At first sight Heidegger's lectures and essays on Heraclitus have regenerated his notorious darkness. But at second glance it turns out to be a non-notorious, unnoticed darkness that evokes the strange question: who is speaking? Who is speaking when Heraclitus joins those who listen not to him but to the λόγος (B 50)? This leaves those who habitually listen only to one another in the dark, in their own darkness. The darkness appears to be intensified—bordering on the absurd—when Heidegger finds himself no longer in a position to listen to the λόγος but bound to listen to the speech that speaks. What could be more repulsive than the darkness of an experience that expropriates the common speaker of the speech in his familiar discourse?

What does this suggest? Never mind the language, but mind your speech to the point where it is no longer yours—to the point where listening before speaking is imperative. This indicates a sense-explicative dimension that is different from the one in which the assertion is made: language cannot be private. A thinker cannot disown his language, but he must disown his speech, asking himself: who is speaking? Here a darkness prevails that is other than the darkness in Heraclitus's listening to the λόγος. We assume that when Heidegger turns to Heraclitus, he revives the latter's darkness in order to elucidate his own—listening to the speech that itself speaks.

The difference between λόγος and speech already indicates that Heidegger is able to draw a hint from Heraclitus only on the basis of the recognition of their fundamental dissension over who the speaker is. He must not bridge the gap. It has burst upon him in Nietzsche's experience that God is dead—that all gods are dead. But how does this affect the λόγος? Did it not engage Heidegger's attention insofar as it was pre-metaphysical? As for its involvement in "onto-theological" thinking, Heidegger concedes to it only the benefit of ambiguity.

I

What then is the Heraclitean λόγος?

1. To start with an apparently trivial reply, there were λόγοι other than his own; and he heard some, perhaps most, of them (B 108). They are akin to his own discourse insofar as they also lead the listener through everything (B 1), from what appears first down to what comes last—and that is man. In the end he gives the λόγος (apparently his own account of everything) and teaches the others his knowledge. Why should they listen? Hesiod (B 57), for instance, made known the "measures" of everything and the establishment of justice in the world, the measures of distribution as they are also to rule human affairs. But the Heraclitean account no longer follows the pattern established in the *Theogony*. Like Anaximander and Pythagoras, he sees the κόσμος in the distribution of everything established by the conflicting φύσεις of that which is not only generated but which also appears and disappears. In Anaximandrian thought, the even distribution of opposing Natures, and thus the κόσμος itself, is transitory. In Pythagorean thought, only their mixtures are transitory, while the harmony of the differing Natures remains stable. Heraclitus points out, however, that harmony involves a λόγος in the sense of a relation, which is the only stability that guarantees the continuity of the κόσμος; the measures of distribution remain balanced (B 31).

The measures of what appears are grounded in the relation of its opposing Natures. These tend to be hidden (B 123), both in their difference and in their identity. What is seemingly obvious often detracts from the underlying Natures and their λόγος. The Heraclitean account thrives not on "collection" but rather on discernment—analyzing everything with reference to its Nature and thus establishing "how it keeps" its truth. And this means: "how it relates." Discerning everything in this manner, the Heraclitean account claims to be an ἐὼν λόγος—a saying of "how it is" (B 1). Heraclitus says that the accounts of other men do not have such adequacy. But why did they remain inadequate?

Obviously the Anaximandrian account of the κόσμος—only secondarily of the "world"—was concerned with the difference, with the opposition and conflict and thus the relation, between the constitutive Natures: not things but rather their truth as it is stated in the predicates 'is wet' and 'is dry'.

Pythagoras too explored the relations of opposites implied in the harmony of the κόσμος. So why did this cosmology not attain the λόγος that "is"? Heraclitus replies that they did not understand the primary relation: the difference of the One from All—ἕν – πάντα (B 108). They lacked in the utmost discrimination because in their attention to the φύσεις they were restricted to the observation of what appears. And that primary relation is a harmony which is never apparent (B 54).

What is the relation between the One and All? The opposition of the One and the Many is commonplace in post-Parmenidean thought, but there is no mention of it in the extant work of Heraclitus. He refers to the "many" only as men who, due to their opinions, have dissociated themselves from the common λόγος (B 17).

But was that relation not addressed in the Pythagorean distinction between the soul and the body? Restricted to the One and All, the harmonizing soul is in the parts of the body, it contains them. Thus the soul's departure from the body could only mean: transition to another body.

Heraclitus attains the λόγος ("how it is") inasmuch as he grasps the opposition in the relation as such: the One is not only implied in All—collecting the Many—but at the same time different or apart from All. It is the Same that assumes different states and in doing so makes the transition from All to the One and from the One to All (B 10). Finally, transition itself claims to be its own opposite state inasmuch as it rests in the simultaneity of the exchange (B 84). Heraclitus alone accounted for this relation. Such is the ground of the κόσμος, of both its transitory and its stable harmony.

The constantly recurring exchange of night and day, winter and summer, war and peace, satiety and hunger (B 67), tends to expunge the simultaneity of the opposing states in the realm of the different Natures and thus in the relation 'One–All'.

In summary the earliest philosophy was not concerned with "Nature" understood as a totality—not even with "beings" and things—but with the discernment of appearances and their Natures, with what is "just" in the relations of these Natures.

2. Anaximander noticed that it is only the ἄπειρος φύσις that encompasses every state of the appearances (φανερά) and allows for conflicting Natures within itself—those that are productive of a transitory κόσμος. Pythagoras learned that it is the soul whose Nature is interminable breath, that harmonizes the different Natures of bodies and embraces them all. Heraclitus, however, understands that it is the λόγος that "is" which grants both transition and stability in the harmony of all Natures, in their harmonious exchange and distribution.

There is no point in relating One and All while the former is only implied—obviously—in the latter. It is the withdrawal (B 122) of the One from All that inaugurates their relation. And this makes all the difference for the consideration of the λόγος as such.

The One differs—being integrated with the Many in All and simultaneously apart from All, having departed from it (B 108). The One sustains a life of its own. It is not only related to All but by its partition is the ground of this very relation, of the primary λόγος. In its differing states, the One alone is the governing principle of the relation 'One–All'. Having ceded everything and thus any form of appearance, what is it then? Heraclitus calls it: the σοφόν.

The One establishes the λόγος in differing from itself (B 51). In this regard it is the σοφόν—something similar to the essentially predicative φύσεις. This "truth" of the One, however, has no opposite with which it could be exchanged; it thus indicates the singularity of the "pre-logical" One: ἓν τὸ σοφὸν μοῦνον (B 32). And why σοφόν? The One in All is fire; the One detached from All relates to these as that comprehension (γνώμη) that steers every transition and controls every exchange in All (B 41).

The σοφόν is the governing principle of everything. Its comprehending Nature points secondarily to the executor of this governing principle: Zeus (B 31). The fire that is appropriate to him—lightning (B 64)—lends the necessary force to justice (B 94), primarily safeguarding the measures of fire itself (B 30), the proportion of its differing states (B 31). Justice, the content of the σοφόν, would be pointless without the reference of the One to All; and this reference is established only through the knowledge and force of Zeus. Left to itself, everything is hybrid; therefore, the measures must be enforced. Does this mean that Heraclitus slips into "onto-theology"? To repeat: the use of force is inevitable in the establishment of justice—as already Solon pointed out. There is no κόσμος but for the enforcement of the σοφόν by one who is himself involved in All. But one is needed who is not only part of it—like fire—but who understands the One that has departed from it, and thus understands what it means to be different from oneself—or rather: to be departed from oneself, apparently "dead."

It is the predicate, the Nature, or "truth" that appoints its appropriate subject. The governing principle, being the σοφόν, evokes its representative: the σοφός of the dominant force: Zeus. He knows the One that differs from All—inaccessible to human knowledge because of its divinity, or accomplishment (B 78). This does not penetrate the silence of the One but depends entirely upon its λόγος. Only a god may know in himself the simultaneously differing states of All (B 67). This knowledge qualifies him to know the said governing principle.

3. The difference between the divine and the human state of mind is the result of a "war" (B 53), of a clash of judgment concerning justice. Men would not know of it but for the experience of their own injustice (B 23). For the god, All is beautiful, good, and just (B 102), because his All is defined as the κόσμος. Men alone are engaged in ἀκοσμία (disorder), their state of mind being characterized by the "many." Only they are negligent of the common governing principle and consequently of the common λόγος. They distinguish themselves by a way of thinking that is δοκεῖν (to assume; B 17). Their privation of the common λόγος suggests to each of them a private κόσμος (B 2), which is just one's own world and no κόσμος at all. Their lack of γνώμη must not be confused with an opposing state. They have no power to resist the workings of the κόσμος; even in their sleep—though it is most private—they are obliged to cooperate with its process (B 75).

Δοκεῖν is the way of thinking that has unwittingly and without force deprived itself of the common λόγος (B 72). But why? A man's way of thinking is determined by his soul; and this is generated from water, the opposite or "death" of fire (B 36), and thus detrimental to a thought of guidance (B 117). On the other hand, there is a λόγος in the soul which is without bounds (B 45), because it extends in its experience to the opposite of its origin and thus tends to grow (B 115) with comprehension. But this clashes with the "wet" aspirations or "fumes" (B 12) of its origin. Insight is acquired only in the experience with the opposite fire and thus with their common λόγος (B 114). In the final analysis, this is the λόγος of the One and All as it speaks to intelligent experience within the κόσμος of All.

But again, what makes all the difference for the realization of one's listening (in the ὁμολεγεῖν) is one's distinction of oneself: differing from oneself in establishing the "dry soul" (B 118). This implies the "death" of the originary soul. Those who have achieved this "living the death of mortals" (B 62) are the heroes of immortal fame (B 29) and the gods—victorious in the battle that reveals the difference between gods and men (B 50). No wonder that the Many do not understand the Nature of gods and heroes (B 5); only these have knowingly accepted the governing principle of All, which is the One that differs from itself insofar as it is the σοφόν.

II

Governing principle—reality—attention. The ratio of these terms in the work of Heraclitus yielded the following sequence: reality is the λόγος of All. Its governing principle is the σοφόν. The "philo-sophical" attention to it accords with the λόγος of "One–All" (B 50). How does this compare with Heidegger's exposition of that λόγος (*GA* 55, 373)? Strictly speaking, not at all; for Heidegger is concerned with another topic. One could say that Heidegger dealt with the collective character of λόγος—taking into account the selection that goes with it but not its discretion and the corresponding discernment. Where would this leave us? Does the foregoing sketch make any difference for the exigencies of contemporary thought? It appears to remain utterly indifferent to such exigencies.

When Heidegger turned to Heraclitus, he had the end and thus the beginning of metaphysics in mind (225)—having transformed the Nietzschean experience that God is dead. Shall we escape this with the assertion that only the god of Christian morality is dead—keeping in the back of our minds a substitute for the Augustinian and Pauline god? That will not do in view of the modernity of modern thought and its dis-appointment. Even if the gods of Heraclitus and his Zeus could not die, they certainly have vanished out of sight.

But faith and the thinking inherent in it were not Heidegger's primary concern. What gave rise to Heidegger's attention to Heraclitus was the destiny of his own "ratio"—indicated to him in the Greek name ἀλήθεια. And his only treatise under this title was again devoted to Heraclitus—having previously established the priority of ἀλήθεια over the λόγος (378). The dissension of Heidegger and Heraclitus over the latter's tenets is grounded in what Heidegger regards as destiny in Heraclitus. And thus Heidegger's assessment of Heraclitean thought is basically incorrigible. A destiny is not to be corrected. What are the consequences?

Showing his primary concern, Heidegger concentrates on Heraclitus's question concerning ἀλήθεια: "That which never sets, how could anyone deny it a share in a certain knowledge?" (B 16). Heidegger's translation differs from this one (*GA* 55, 109). First of all, he does not consider the transitive use of λήθειν (to deceive someone; to deny someone a share in a certain knowledge). Shall we say he neglected it? It said nothing to him.

What is the position of Heraclitus himself? That which never sets—it must be prior to the fire which appears as the sun, and be at the same time related to it; it must involve the directive that guards the sun's course, the measures of its rising and setting. The sun is known to see everything on its course; but that which never sets surpasses it—not only seeing everything but also knowing everything, even by its non-apparent Nature. How could anyone not only hide from it, as the Nature of anything tends to do, but positively deceive it, as only men are wont to do? This is what λήθειν tries to achieve, restricting the range of someone else's knowledge.

If that which never sets is the governing principle, why would anyone want to deceive it? And in terms of what? Obviously not in terms of one's appearance—as if hiding from the sun. What one has in mind can only be his soul, and more to the point: its Nature, or the depths of its λόγος, the relation of the "dry" that opposes the originary "wet." And how does this λόγος of the soul become manifest? In the predominance of either knowledge or opinion. Opinion draws opinion into common delusion. And those who benefit from it for their reputation are keen on defending and preserving it, expunging the λόγος that "is"; but these deceptive machinations will be brought to justice (B 28) and cannot deceive, and thereby hamper, the execution of the common governing principle—the σοφόν, which never sets. Failing to grasp its λόγος, men only deceive themselves (B 1).

This is the line of thought suggested by the extant passages of the Heraclitean λόγος. There is no testimony—in spite of B 112—of any preoccupation with the ἀλήθεια which is Heidegger's primary concern. But why then does he turn to Heraclitus in the first place? What he is after is not ἀλήθεια so much as its origin as indicated to him in the "positive"—over against the privative—derivative, named λήθη (oblivion).

Again Heidegger suppresses the dependence of ἀλήθεια on the sense of the middle voice of λανθάνεσθαι. Why should he suppress it? For the very same reason that made him restrict its sense to κρύπτειν—in accordance with his prevailing thought of an originary concealment in what is called 'truth'. Heidegger is bound to avoid the originary reference of ἀλήθεια to intelligence. All modernity is bound to deny in some way or other the antecedence of thinking with regard to Being—whatever that may be. Yet there is good evidence that metaphysics never held what modernity denies.

Is the suggestion here that there has been a mistake? That would be silly. Moreover, such an opinion would avoid the issue of modern thought. Its exposition is out of place here (cf., e.g., "Reason in Modern Thought" and "The Limit of Modernity and Heidegger's 'Legacy'," pp. 133-148 and 183-198 below, respectively, and *The Rational Architectonic of Modernity*). Instead, let us take a final glimpse at ἀλήθεια as it becomes a central issue for philosophy in Parmenides.

III

On closer examination the Parmenidean inquiry did not dwell on the sense of ἀλήθεια but explained it only in terms of the ἐόν: being. Why? Its destinal principle appears first of all and immediately in the discernment of the only paths of inquiry, singling out the path of persuasion as the only one productive of insight, at once emphasizing the reference of ἀλήθεια to insight. This requires the discernment of "how it is" and "how it is not." The former path leads to the insight that resembles the knowledge of the essentially predicative φύσεις in cosmology. In the end, "how it is" is nothing but the fulfillment of the destiny.

What this means for insight and for the inquiry by means of the pure λόγος, is indicated at the outset in the revelation that Parmenides receives. It is spoken to him in what the mortals can only see as the "House of the Night," the terminal of the "bad destiny," which death is. Parmenides must have been familiar with a poem concerning a descent into Hades which already saw it as the place of a fatal τρίοδος (forked path) for the departed. Both Plato's *Gorgias* (524A) and Virgil's *Aeneid* (VI 540) refer to a tradition that understands the parting of the paths in the sense of a judgment passed on the soul: one leading to the accomplished life on the Isles of the Blessed, the other to its opposite in the emptiness of Tartaros. Virgil extols the poet from whom this revelation apparently originated: Museaus (cf. *D-K* I, 2[67]).

The "knowledgeable man"—Parmenides—deserves and finds the fulfillment of theory in the realm of the unobservable being, which is destined to be "how it is to be," the only way that convinces and leads to insight, to its enjoyment of "being accomplished."

Again Heidegger points out the destiny, but only with reference to the inauguration of that history which metaphysics or "onto-theology" is. No trace remains of the serene enjoyment that pervades the theory of the fulfilled destiny, the accomplishment of its realization. For him, what Hegel called the "judgment of the concept" (*GW* 12, 84/657) has vanished: the judgment 'this is good', and even more: 'this is perfect', is accomplished. That is the content of the Parmenidean ἀλήθεια and only thus is it unfolded in terms of "being" (ἐόν)—not at all because "being" somehow became questionable. The destiny is that of "being" only insofar as the predicate 'is accomplished' evolves for the λόγος, detached from all appearances, as the only "Nature" or truth in which insight has its proper place. The "heart" of truth (of "how it is") is the clarity of "how it is to be" (of the fulfilled destiny). Only as such is it patent and clear—a message that Aeschylus and Sophocles also will convey.

With the ἐόν determined as it is to be, the ἀλήθεια has a content that is utterly different from the content of δόξαι. There is no longer an ἀλήθεια and thus no longer a γνώμη concerning the appearance of the differing "Natures." With the rejection of the δόξαι, the possible reference to such Natures—which were the content of the Heraclitean λόγος—is also abolished.

But how is it that Parmenides deserved the disclosure of that destiny? The dominant concern of the "knowledgeable man" in the observation of the apparent κόσμος of what appears, of the harmony of its Natures, was exactly the destiny of the mortals as indicated by Θέμις and her Δίκη. They made him enter the realm of the unobservable, proper to them, as the only place for the disclosure of the content of "the" ἀλήθεια and the content of the δόξαι, which are the fictions of mortals.

In his position—within the framework of modernity—Heidegger was barred from those considerations. The scope of his endeavor was determined by the destiny of his own thought, which suggested to him something entirely different in the ἀλήθεια—not the ἐόν but rather the λήθη. Such is the withdrawal of the *Befugnis* (authorization; *GA* 13, 224) of what Parmenides knew as Θέμις. The esteem for Heidegger's ensuing concern with both the beginning of metaphysics and "Da-sein" is certainly more to the point than the habitual corrections of or elaborations on his venture into Parmenidean and Heraclitean thought. To meet him there requires a demanding effort, for one is confronted with the question: what has led him here? This is even more significant when one sees the ease with which Heidegger's place is missed, when one assumes that, in turning to Heraclitus or Parmenides, he wandered off into the distant past. He stayed with his present—circumscribed by the exigencies of modern thought. Here alone is the place of dissension. *Hic Rhodus, hic saltus.* But beware of "Nature": *natura non facit saltus.*

THE DISTINCTION OF REASON

These days there is no lack of talk about 'reason' and 'rationality', at least not in the world of papers; but also in other respects the demand peculiar to the Enlightenment—"Be rational"—has survived Hegel's critique, as has morality. And as for rationality in the technically determined circumstances of life, the appeal to it always finds, despite every critique of technicity, a sympathetic ear. Unconcerned about the indeterminacy of the reason claimed. Yet as is well-known, the clarity of the use of a word is independent of the concept of a thing. The concept continues to be relied upon just as little as is the former pure science of reason—First Philosophy, or metaphysics.

That the descendants of the pure science of reason neither can nor wish to be its heirs nowhere becomes as clear as in their sensitivity to the Kantian phrase: "Pure reason is indeed occupied with nothing but itself and also can have no other vocation" (*CPR*, B 708). This sensitivity has as its flip side the susceptibility to the factual or imaginary pressure of public opinion for justification. One is only too familiar with philosophy's readiness—asked for or not—to offer to the public's pressing practical problems, when not rational solutions, then at least approaches to rational discussion—ultimately a discussion led rationally. Indeed, for ages philosophy seems to have had its sole indisputable actuality in such discussion; in it philosophy is perpetuated—even when it offers no scientific progress. Let us counter this discussion, which has been scheduled to infinity, with Plato's χαίρειν ἐᾶν—that is to say: let it have its fun, provided that it is such.

As for reason as it was formerly conceived, today the critique of it is alive primarily in the so-called non-philosophy of the French submoderns. They aim concretely at the former *differentia specifica* of man—this with respect to those modern sciences of man's language, life, and work in which the *animal rationale* reached an understanding of itself. It seems: with the notoriousness of his communal, psychological, and linguistic patterns of behavior, time is running out for this interest. Especially due to the opening up of the border regions of the ζῷον λόγον ἔχον's self-conception by structural anthropology and psychoanalysis. Here it seems about time that the philosophy handed down to us be overcome as logocentric.

This conviction capitalizes on Heidegger's attempt to overcome metaphysics, but also on Nietzsche's critique of Christian faith as well as on Marx's critique of political economy. But what separates the submoderns from these moderns on their common ground of non-philosophy? The former have extinguished the expectation—which moved Marx, Nietzsche, and Heidegger—of man's future distinction from himself since the latter seem to the submoderns to have harbored the embers of the old reason, which was disposed to totalitarianism. Here is our Rhodes, *hic saltus.* Here we are given the signal to leap, for in the history of philosophy the distinction of reason had in each instance as its bequest the thought of man's distinction from himself. We shall briefly elucidate this here and in fact—as far as that bequest is concerned—starting with the aforementioned moderns.

The experience determinative for them is in each instance that of an expropriation in the productive nature of man. The respective sense-explications express a sequence that recalls the former *operationes Dei*: namely, power, will, knowledge. The world—which is constituted by human power, the will in this power, and the knowledge in this will—reaches distinction in the present as an historical present.

The history in question is first of all—seen with Marx—that of human power as it is realized in material production. Driven by anomalies in the relation between retarding forms of society and progressive modes of production. They reach their extreme where the capitalistic mode of production has separated the producer-class from the possession of the means of production and thus has reduced its productive power to the ware 'manpower'. This state of affairs has to be revolutionized such that the means of the socially productive men come into their control and regulation. The idea of this revolution at the end of all prior history awaits a transformation of the whole of humanity—or of the genus.

Nietzsche brings forth particularity in its universality—and in fact with the discernment not of human power so much as of its will and in fact in anticipation of the transhuman masters of the earth. But how are they even possible once the will required for them has degenerated into the history of Christian and ultimately socialist morality? The nihilism which emerges in the historical present—which is to say: the devaluation of the highest traditional values—announces a shattering crisis: the will is alienated from what it initially desires, namely, its self—as a consequence of its subjection to the divine will, finally to the social will. A revaluation of the previous measures of value requires the breeding of a man who overcomes above all himself, pity for others and moreover for himself, and achieves his segregation from the previous man in his distinction from himself—in a boundless affirmation of life which also affirms the return of the last man, of the disgust at his self-sufficiency.

In Heideggerian thought, the modern distinction of man from himself ultimately goes beyond both its generic and its specific determinacy and attains singular determinacy. What singularizes man or not is his relation to his death. Which death becomes the determinative ground here? Not the one that snatches man and the other animals from life but rather the one that belongs to the Being of the There, or of the openness, in which he exists mundanely, historically, and linguistically. This other, never necessary, but rather possible death refers to the nothingness of every being, to the originary concealing in every revealing of "how it is." The recollection of this originary dimension of truth in the sense of "unconcealment" already vanished from metaphysical thinking; for technical thinking, such has become absolutely inaccessible. As the theory of being in general and in the highest, metaphysics had already repressed that other death. Moreover, technical thinking expunges the trace by which death characterized the Being of beings.

Heidegger's expectation of a not impossible distinction of man from himself is based only on the unveiling of that oblivion as such, or of the withholding in the former nature of truth. This expectation concretizes the said distinction in three respects: firstly as the distinction of the world of things from that of the ego-subject; secondly as the distinction of the history of the other thinking over against metaphysical and technical thinking; thirdly as the distinction of the speech that grants man a dwelling, from the language of information.

Three phases become apparent in which the core sense-explicative dimension of modernity sought man's distinction from himself—concentrated on history, world, and speech, on these three no longer as "natural" totalities but rather as totalities constituted by and for man. Even if not as such totalities, it is nevertheless precisely these themes that always lay claim to the reason of modernity—be it in the sense-explication of the interpreted life or in that of the sciences (cf. "The Limit of Modernity and Heidegger's 'Legacy'," pp. 183-198 below and *The Rational Architectonic of Modernity*).

In each of the three positions just sketched, philosophy is abandoned. On the other hand, each renews the thought of man's distinction from himself and thereby recalls precisely those configurations of wisdom which have been bequeathed to philosophy. Furthermore, each focuses its attention on another epoch of the history of our world: Marx, on the modern era; Nietzsche, on its middle epoch; Heidegger, on the age of the Greek beginning. As departed from the world of modernity, in this reversal a completed history becomes apparent. It allows for no extension into the old Orient—unlike the Hegelian history of the world and of philosophy. The totality, being made up of three epochs, each consisting of its own configuration of wisdom and consequently its own philosophy, is no longer based on the singular development of the pure concept (cf. my *Topology of Metaphysics*).

Yet even if the distinction of man from himself is attended to, must not the configurations of Oriental wisdom also come into view? Let us touch upon its most radical manifestation, namely, the teachings of Buddha. What could be more demanding with respect to the said distinction than precisely those discourses which present the so-called four noble truths? Those concerning suffering, the generation of suffering, the redemption from it, and finally the path that leads to redemption. Being as he is, man suffers variously, and it is precisely at such suffering that his distinction from himself aims here.

Greed appears as the root of all suffering—firstly greed for existence; then for individual existence; finally for exclusive individuality. It is awakened solely by that which cannot disappear of its own accord—namely, by the ignorance about the generation and corruption of what may become the object of greed.

It is precisely on account of this that man's distinction from himself is sought in the dissolution of individuality and thus of the drive for self-preservation. The corresponding redemption is concerned with passion, hatred, and deception. What is called nirvana, or fading, has its sense only as the nothingness of these three, by no means as the aforementioned nothingness of the beings of our tradition. His distinction of himself in the detachment from singularizing passion, hatred, and deception, is completed in the dissolution of the individual as such. By contrast, the configurations of wisdom in our history lay claim to man as an individual *animal rationale*, which is historical exactly in the crises of his rationality. As crises of a σοφία, in each instance they will call forth the φιλοσοφία of an epoch and stamp its reason. They are crises of the persuasiveness, the credibility, the certainty of precisely that truth which establishes such a configuration of wisdom as one that is rational in itself.

The first epoch of our history has its σοφία in the works of Homer, Hesiod, and Solon. As for the distinction of man from himself, it concerns him not as a mere individual but rather as such according to his status in the realm of justice. Here each is subject to the directives of his "share"—be it in life span, in reputation, in what is available to him. The share implies firmly established limits, and the latter become present especially where they are controversial. Then the decision concerning that to which each is entitled, is made in the assembly or by the judging king or according to the law. These decisions possess an aspect of rationality insofar as they seem grounded and executed on the basis of the insight of the father of the gods and men, more precisely: on the basis of his "firm reason." Wisdom, which is dependent upon the message of the Muses, is devoted to this reason.

The crisis of the persuasiveness of this wisdom comes to fruition in its rejection by a knowledge based on the rational knowledge of man alone. With this rejection, philosophy begins and in this beginning, the first distinction of reason occurs; for the rejection of the knowledge based on the message of the Muses, is itself a differentiated rejection.

On the one hand, reason is articulated with respect to thinking; on the other, with respect to its topic. In the first instance, observation (ἱστορεῖν)—more precisely: the discernment of truth, or φύσις, from appearance—itself determines the topic appropriate to it, namely, everything that is present to it as becoming; finally, it is cognizant of the interpretative character of all knowledge and of the task of an endlessly improving search for the more probable; thus in the progression from Thales via Anaximenes to Xenophanes.

The other type of reason over against this one does not merely reject the former wisdom but rather meets it in the same topic, namely, the realm of justice, though this type of reason no longer sees this topic in what has been done but rather in what has appeared without human agency—persuasive in its κόσμος (Anaximander), in the latter's ἁρμονίη (Pythagoras), in the λόγος of this ἁρμονίη (Heraclitus). On the basis of the latter, the ἤθη possible for man are distinguished—the habit of the sensible and that of the non-sensible. Here at issue once more is man's distinction from himself.

The distinction of reason is completed, however, first by way of its own distinction from itself, namely, into two types: natural reason in the aforementioned physiology and mundane reason in the aforementioned cosmology. The third type of reason is articulated neither with respect to thinking nor to the topic but rather with respect to the destinal principle, and it is precisely therein that it encounters the construction of the configuration of wisdom itself. Furthermore: it conceives the destiny that holds sway in the latter, shelters it in a logic appropriate to it, offers it its persuasiveness. It is precisely therein that what is called metaphysics begins.

Conceptual reason is concentrated in its self-articulation on the destinal principle. To take it as his point of departure meant for Parmenides: he had to be brought into the House of the Night, which the mortals are able to understand only as the realm of death. There thinking is set on a τρίοδος, on a forked path—similar to the one known from Hades; for the court there sent those who acted in accordance with "how it is to be" to Elysium, the others, who acted in accordance with "how it is not to be," into the dark reaches of Tartaros.

The knowledge of the Muses enables one to distinguish how it is to be from how it is not to be—the determination that lies in the share allotted to each, a share of fixed limitedness. Immediately related to thinking, the decided separateness of the paths of "how it is" and "how it is not"—more precisely: of the necessarily and of the impossibly true—emerges from this knowledge of the μοῖρα. Its destiny to take only the first path is made known to thinking as θέμις, or what has been established, though its topic is not known to it. Thinking must itself bring its topic to determinacy on the path of "how it is" and in fact solely with the persuasiveness of logical argumentation. In accordance with the path, the topic is "being," and due to the way in which thinking imparts its destiny to "being," it is that which is always already "complete" or perfect.

The thought of being as that which is perfect is conditioned by the purity of reason. It is pure not only due to the independence of its activity from sense data but even more so by the abolition of its instrumental status in questions of action, thus of its "dialectical" use in keeping with the question: what follows when I do this or that, or not?

Reason is pure only by way of the purification which is required of it in its focus on the destinal principle. It is pure on the basis of its distinction from itself, from its natural as well as from its mundane types. It is pure only in the fulfillment of a conceptual task set by a pregiven wisdom. Where none is given, no metaphysics arises. This state of affairs is veiled only scantily by the continuation of its so-called problems in the humdrum of the schools, which makes no difference for the world.

The core sense-explicative dimension of modernity impels us to attend to the epochal differences in the distinction of reason. Similar to the first, the middle epoch of our history begins with a doubled rational figure—in both cases with a dogmatic, then a skeptical, and finally a gnostic phase. However, neither of the first phases follows the wisdom of the New Testament but rather precedes it; only the gnostic types of natural and mundane reason accompany this wisdom. Nevertheless, all of them stand in an exclusive relation to the knowledge of the New Testament, although they immediately exclude only the metaphysics of the first epoch. Thus with Chrysippus on the one hand, with Epicurus on the other.

Again in the case of mundane reason—especially in its concluding hermetic form—the thought of a distinction of man from himself comes to the fore. This in obvious kinship with the corresponding demands of the New Testament.

But beyond this, how is a distinction of reason from itself achieved here? Plotinian metaphysics overcomes Gnosticism as much in its hermeneutic as in its hermetic forms. This insofar as its reason encounters the destiny in Christian knowledge; such is not merely "God" but rather his glory; for only in the latter is he present—as for the knowledge of the Muses, the said share is present in the directive. Essential to each destiny is its own present. But noteworthy in the Plotinian destinal principle, that is, in the beauty of the absolutely simple One and Good, is this: it transforms the unity, as thought by John, of the Son of God with the Father and those who are his in love; for this unity is not to be thought relationally, not as a relationship between substances, and thus remains something ineffable in the sense of the categorial tradition. On the other hand, the Plotinian conception is the most radical negation of Christian knowledge, namely, insofar as the ineffable One excludes not only the possibility of the divine word, but even more that of its incarnation.

The Plotinian distinction of reason from itself remains incomplete. It achieves only its self-relinquishment to a first which is neither reason within itself nor accessible to the latter's insight. It is Augustine who first completes it insofar as he discloses the substantial unity of the divine Trinity in view of the *subiectio* of its word—this in the conception of the destiny as understood by Paul, namely, of the paradoxical glory of the Crucified, thus of he who died in shame. Augustinian thought does not start with this destinal principle, however, but rather with the topic, which is the relation between the soul and God—unfolded into the mirroring of the divine Trinity in, spoken with Augustine, the "spiritual mind." It is only with respect to this topic that the destinal principle is disclosed as the incarnate word of what is in itself ineffable—audible not in discourse so much as in that word's doing of truth; it is on account of this that he became man and not merely spirit or soul in his subjection to himself. In him the substantial God becomes "subject." Thinking subjects itself to him in turn with a faith that seeks its perspicacity and thus its credibility in reason—a reason as different from its natural as from its mundane types. It in no way relinquishes itself but instead expects its perfection in the *visio beatifica*.

One is mistaken with respect to the *amor sapientiae* of the middle epoch if one understands it merely as a continuation of the philosophical θεωρία of the first epoch, thus if one blurs the epochal difference of the prevailing configuration of wisdom—the difference between "knowing the truth" and "doing the truth." And then what is specific in the knowledge of the final epoch also remains concealed: that truth wants to be produced. From its poorest to its richest determinacy. Methodically.

The consideration of the epochally distinguished traits of thinking comes to bear, of course, only when the triad of θεωρία, πρᾶξις, and ποίησις is removed from its foundational context in Aristotle. Only then can it become clear how the foundational sequence πρᾶξις, ποίησις, θεωρία holds in the middle epoch, while the sequence ποίησις, θεωρία, πρᾶξις holds in the final epoch.

The principal significance of these sequences first becomes visible in connection with the instrument of method with which a reason that is at first still thought as given produces itself as the actuality of consciousness—this once again in the unfolding of the figures of natural and of mundane reason, the former inaugurated by Descartes, the latter by Hobbes. The debate between them is an example of the reciprocal occlusion of their respective types of philosophy to one another due to the difference between the tasks which engage their respective types of reason.

In fact the inaugural phase of the final epoch, concluded with Leibniz and Berkeley, already reveals the principal significance of freedom in that epoch. In the determinacy peculiar to it, however, it first comes into view in the corresponding configuration of wisdom coined by Rousseau, Schiller, and Hölderlin. Again, of concern is man's distinction from himself. We recall here the *Social Contract*: man has to distinguish himself from himself in order to become a citizen (*CS*, I, 7), specifically: through the realization of civil liberty (I, 8). Such requires firstly the transformation of human nature; secondly the transformation of the individual into a member of the civic body; thirdly an alteration of the constitution of man with violence; and finally the replacement of physical with moral existence.

Regarding the latter, Kant sees in reason the faculty "by which man distinguishes himself from all other things, indeed from himself, insofar as he is affected by objects" (*GMS*, 452.7/69). These are his own words in the *Foundation of the Metaphysics of Morals*. It is precisely this reason that man not only has, but is—as moral subject, as rational being or spirit. But as in Plotinus, the distinction of reason from itself also remains incomplete here since the rational being cannot know his freedom but can only presuppose it. It also remains incomplete in Fichtean thought due to the unattainability of the ideal for that ego which realizes its freedom.

The accomplished distinction of reason from itself in the conception of the wisdom in question, more precisely: of its destiny, that is, the freedom of the "divine man in us" (Kant), is first to be regarded as the freedom of that personality which the absolute idea is as the result of Hegelian logic. Moral as well as religious reason remained a form of the consciousness which insists upon its finitude. The *Phenomenology of Spirit* shows that and how the reason of consciousness has to direct itself into its ground (*sich zugrunde richten*). As distinguished from the latter type, reason is the movement of the pure concept. Moreover, this concept is pure of that intuition which Fichte had asserted to be intellectual intuition.

Only in the methodical and systematic determination of the pure concept through its distinction within itself, only in the absolute self-determination thus understood, does the destinal principle as freedom become one that is known; and with respect to the reality of the philosophical sciences it proves finally to be the freedom of philosophy. As a conceiving theory of physical and spiritual Nature, it has become equal to its idea. Its end-in-itself is fulfilled, its drive satisfied. With the accomplishment of its task, the metaphysics of the final epoch has passed away. On the other hand, what do the belated gestures of overcoming or even the picking at the bones of metaphysics within the sense-explications of modernity mean?

Now in view of these sense-explications, does the distinction of reason still have a present? Such is attested by the different sense-explicative dimensions of modernity, each of which unfolds into its own completeness—in view of the history, world, and speech of the interpreted life; in view of the speech, world, and history of the sciences; in view of these three as they are proper to productive human being (cf. *The Rational Architectonic of Modernity*).

Of course: since there is no wisdom here whose destiny would urge reason to conception, reason's distinction from itself is also not attained. Yet how would reason have reached the point of thinking the closedness of that world which was articulated in the said architectonic of the sense-explications of modernity in singular significance? In its peripheral dimension Dilthey, Husserl, and Wittgenstein conceived the doxical products of human life. Yet this life knows no distinction of man from himself. This bequest for the distinction of reason from itself falls within modernity only in the expectation held by Marx, Nietzsche, and Heidegger. The non-philosophy of submodernity has sought liberation from its future, has even introduced the talk of a new *sapientia*. But it has not found its way into that present in which the much-discussed question 'Who is speaking?' could have been directed to what is rational in those configurations of wisdom, configurations which had formerly called forth the conceptual reason of metaphysics.

The distinction proper to that reason remained dependent upon the bequest of natural reason. It is precisely this bequest, however, that has been disposed of in the modern transformation of that reason into technical reason. Instead, there remains the bequest of mundane reason. Yet to elucidate this falls in the exposition of the transformation which the nature of truth underwent within modernity. More on this elsewhere (cf. "The Limit of Modernity and Heidegger's 'Legacy'," pp. 183-198 below). To end on a dry note.

WHICH THINKING MAKES ALL THE DIFFERENCE?

The traditional distinction—already medieval—between the ancients and the moderns referred to a quarrel between both sides over common topics which proceeded according to common standards of evaluation. The ancients, or traditionalists, were challenged by the moderns with a view to superiority. Such would make no sense without the recognition of a common horizon. There was no dissension over the common world, no rejection of its traditional exposition, no denial of the possible coexistence of the conflicting sides, but only a claim to superiority on the part of the moderns so as to provoke the ancients and their established ways or procedures—be they in logic, devotion, or whatever else. The quarrel of the moderns with the ancients remained all the more of relative importance as it was obvious that—as La Bruyère already remarked—we moderns will be the ancients in due course, certainly after a few centuries.

This awareness of continuous historial change was not, however, shared by Descartes, nor by Kant. They did not engage in the famous quarrel of the moderns with the ancients, did not claim a relative superiority, but insisted that their thinking made all the difference—a difference so radical that they saw no need to establish themselves as moderns. They insisted on a fresh beginning of thought—not merely transforming its previous fundaments but instead establishing them for the first time, while respecting the continuity in logic. A radical beginning for which ratio? We take this to be an ambiguous question—asking for both the type of reason which made such a claim and the ground of this reason's self-esteem.

Before we pursue this question, however, let us reflect for a moment on our position in so-called postmodernity. If this name refers to a modernity which we consider to be a *singulare tantum*, then it reflects an embarrassment, one that indicates an outright inability to reject the claim to singularity intrinsic to the sphere of that modernity.

It is impossible for the postmoderns to throw off the yoke of modernity because they feast on its labors. To that extent they are the "submoderns." In what way? First of all the periphery of the modern world was established by those within modernity who claimed the inheritance of First Philosophy and instituted the realm of hermeneutic reason. Here we encounter Dilthey, Husserl, and Wittgenstein with regard to the history, world, and speech of life, the latter being characterized by its objectivations in structures of sense and meaning, in "doxical data." Attached to this stratum we find once again the academic modifications of what hermeneutic reason achieved. The submoderns, however, flourish mainly with respect to the Husserlian position. Though they establish their abode with reference not to thinking and its prior directing intention in Husserl's theory so much as to the topic, i.e., the "*Sachen selbst*," that is, to the phenomena within consciousness. Here is the decisive point: the submoderns abandon the transcendental ego and its objectivating performances—which are hinged on intentionality and sense. Accordingly the corresponding thinking is abandoned, i.e., the modes of belief and their thetic productions—these being the necessary presuppositions for the activity of a reason whose only function is to scrutinize the fulfillment or non-fulfillment of sense enacted by the noemata within the stream of conscious life. The rejection of the transcendental ego entails the rejection of the reason evoked by its productions; prior to this, such entails the elimination of the belief in that reason to which Husserl appealed time and again—and quite desperately in his final period. It must be emphasized that such a belief in reason is totally alien to the metaphysical tradition; rather, it is a radically modern tenet, just as is that of the co-originariness of reason and unreason. The submodern suspicions turned against reason arise in response to the demand to "believe" in reason. This indicates the topological proximity of Husserl's position to Nietzsche's and its revaluation of faith.

Next comes the attention given to the sciences—their speech, world, and history within modernity. Each of the corresponding thrusts—due to Frege, Schlick, and Kuhn, respectively—has its consequential waves within the academic humdrum. Yet in the case of the submoderns it is primarily Kuhn, his view of the progress of scientific research and its technicity, who offers them an abode—with regard not to "puzzle-solving" thinking as determined by its dominant matrices or paradigms so much as to what is the matter in the sense of the prevailing problematic situations, to the topics that present themselves in the course of ordinary research. The submodern beneficiaries of what currently matters in science thrive on the ensuing problems for society-at-large; they respond with technical reason to so-called ethical problems that are posed by the scientific production of knowledge in various fields, such as in genetics.

The third and central dimension of modernity is constituted by a thought that no longer simulates the former First Science but has instead resolutely abandoned it. That feat we owe to Marx, Nietzsche, and Heidegger—although even today the academic concern finds itself unable either to acknowledge this or to resist the attempt to integrate these thinkers into the continual tradition of the endless evolution and involution of so-called philosophical problems. Praise be to Foucault's honesty in considering his own thought to be non-philosophy!

The degrading descent of the submoderns from this concern with human productivity in view of its history, world, and speech, is primarily attached to the Marxian position. Yet again they abandon the destiny which in Marxian thought is denoted by capital as determined by auto-finality and the impetus to unite with labor—the "subject" (cf. Hegel's "idea") of the production process being related to an objectivity in the sense of the productive power of the workers. Here the corresponding thinking established itself as science in the sense of a critique of political economy. Such is of no interest to the submoderns. Instead, they cling to the Marxian analysis of the immediately given social reality, while reinterpreting its powers of economic expropriation as the powers of sub-economic alienation in the field of linguistic structures, ones that by their established rules violate the exhibitions of individual life, the expressions of its desires. Thus, emancipation became the revolutionary cry, the compulsory fetish of the wares of the Marxian critique appearing as the superficies of the compulsions that emanate from the rules of communication, which in turn emanate from the so-called establishment dominating a society. Sub-economic force, or, as Foucault puts it, violence: such is the central issue for the submoderns, who have abandoned their initial Marxism. "Unmask the compulsive orders of discourse": this program has been pursued by leaving behind the topics of the Marxian underground for those of Nietzsche and finally of Heidegger—no longer restricted to politics but with the widened scope of questioning morality and ultimately of deconstructing metaphysics—the last disguise and stronghold of the compulsory, totalitarian rules of language and thus of thinking.

Whereto have we strayed? Is the quarrel between the ancients and the moderns, is the thinking that makes all the difference, lost from view? In the submoderns we meet a way of thinking that is not only unfit for such a difference but even strangles the very possibility of such. How so?

In each of the cases proposed, the destinal term in Heidegger's phrase '*die Bestimmung der Sache des Denkens*' (the destiny of the topic of thinking) is expunged. The immediate impact of the submodern positions on society is due to the curtailment of the ratio—the relation between the *Sache* (topic), that is, the matter of contest, and critical thinking—by eliminating the middle term of both, which is the destiny—whether as the transcendental ego bestowing sense on its objects (there is no transcendental ego where the ἐποχή is impossible) or as the paradigm (there are no paradigms to direct an ethical research) or as the destiny of capital (the disappearance of this notion, which reflects the Hegelian idea, has only recently been confirmed by Derrida's play of associations on the word *caput* in *The Other Heading*). The thinking that makes no difference—apart from its idiosyncrasies—has successfully obfuscated its irrelevance by radically interpreting its *Sache* (that which is at stake, is contested) as an interpretation. This folly, however, is not in itself irrelevant; it must be praised, for it approaches speech as a sphere of its own, distinct from our world and distinct from the latter's history.

The difference of speech from its intramundane and its intrahistorical manifestations has not yet been elaborated and established. Therefore, we turn back to the difference that the thinking of modernity achieved in severing our world from the latter's history—the world as understood by way of the sense-explication first of the elementary doxical data, then of the sciences, and finally of the productive nature of man (the expropriation of his power, his will, and his knowledge). What in this last domain is reflected upon as history refers exactly to these modes of creative operation—in the end, with Heidegger projecting the expropriative history of metaphysics.

The positions that are constitutive of modernity and differentiate its world give testimony to a thinking that makes all the difference. To be found there are differences obviously more abysmal than those effected by new paradigms in the history of the sciences. Why?

The philosophy of the schools has always known paradigms or matrices and a corresponding ordinary teaching, but only in our time has such led to the fictional notion of philosophical research modelled on the example set by the sciences and the communities of experts. Those following this fiction have difficulties—to say the least—in establishing common tenets, let alone in determining the actual state of research in a specific field. Ordinary science, yes—but what about ordinary philosophy? Is this a rhetorical question? If so, then we would rather leave it alone. But can we? We can so long as we concentrate on a thinking that makes all the difference and not just on modifications of doctrine, provided that the *placita philosophorum* can reach the level essential to knowledge.

Turning to the examples set in the history of metaphysics with an eye for a thinking that makes all the difference, it is first of all necessary to abandon

Heidegger's fiction that there is a sole topic of metaphysical thinking, namely, the Being of beings, and that the history of metaphysics is accordingly to be seen as a sequence of interpretations of this Being of beings and of the corresponding ways of thinking itself. Instead of rehearsing the legitimacy of the Heideggerian projection and its limits, we shall take a short cut, now approaching history not as that of metaphysical thinking but as that of philosophical knowledge. In its edifices we encounter a thinking that makes all the difference and we shall now observe how it does so. We shall find that the difference of thinking inheres in a difference of reason. There has never been just one reason but always differing types. Why? The answer, strange though it sounds, is: because of philo-sophy as such. This assertion is not only strange but dark. In order to clarify it we ask: which then are the different types of reason?

It is obvious that we no longer talk of reason as supposed in talk of the *animal rationale*—neither the adventitious reason of Aristotle nor the created *lumen naturale* of Thomas Aquinas nor the reason as a mode of consciousness in its Hegelian formation, transformed finally into the pure concept, into absolute spirit.

We shall speak here of the ratios which are constitutive both of the history of philosophy and the world of modern concern—ratios that are established in terms of "the destiny of the topic of thinking."

Turning to that history: which is the first ratio of these terms? It starts with the thinking inherent in a new type of knowledge: ἱστορίη (observation). This determines the corresponding reality. Observable are the appearances of heaven and earth. Those of the latter are characterized by generation. This in turn is subject to a determinative φύσις that manifests itself as being prior to earth: the aquatic Nature. The ratio establishing the sequences of those three terms is the first manifestation of natural reason. As such, making all the difference to pre-philosophical thinking and its σοφία, namely, that of the Muses.

The point here is that the observational character of Thalesian thinking determines the totality that falls within its scope: all that appears is πάντα τὰ φανερά—contrary to the still prevailing opinion that philosophy somehow started with a spontaneous interest in what we, and not the early Greek thinkers, are used to calling 'Nature'.

Is the Thalesian ratio a paradigm? Not for its rational sequence. For with the next step we see a shift in its terms. Anaximenes transforms the resulting term of the Thalesian ratio into a φύσις that precedes observation: psychic Nature. What originarily determines thinking and the corresponding totality is air or mist. Here thinking has to be characterized as διαγνῶναι (knowing asunder)—namely, knowing the differences that constitute a totality of appearances within the extremes of varying density according to a controversial tendency in their Natures.

In this ratio, thinking is predetermined while determining its topic. There is one more step to take in order to accomplish the first figure of natural reason. The Xenophanean ratio accepts as immediately given the reality which grows out of earth and water and which moves in the heavens—it is strictly limited to appearances, having no regard for hidden Natures. What appears on the earth are mixtures not of diverse Natures but rather of primary appearances, such as earth and water. Appearance, however, is strictly denied to the divine force that moves the totality of appearances; this entails an onslaught on the manifold visualization of the traditional gods. The elimination of their appearance gives access to the second term: the determinative divinity. It moves everything by its perfect faculties of observation. It is present without appearance. This leads to the determination of the final term: thinking as specifically human observation. In contrast to the divine, it never attains τὸ σαφές (perspicacity) but only approaches it in endless progress. Human knowledge deriving from ἱστορίη remains δόκος (the assumption of what is probable).

This is the result of the first development of natural reason. Its figures in the middle epoch of philosophy—attached to the names of Chrysippus, Carneades, and Numenius—and in the final epoch—here we have Descartes, Spinoza, and Leibniz—exhibit the same pattern. A sequence of paradigms only—if putting it this way makes any sense—despite an always possible though negligible ordinary philosophy.

Philosophical reason is never of one type only. Thus its natural type is accompanied by another, and one only; this is its mundane type, which becomes explicit for the first time in the thought of Anaximander, Pythagoras, and Heraclitus. Instead of this figure, however, we shall present its analogue in the inauguration of the middle epoch of philosophy.

The Epicurean ratio opens—as is characteristic of mundane reason—with the *Sache* as its first term. Its primary motive in this instance is the opposition of pain and enjoyment as present in affections and desires. Already here the shift from the theoretical bias of the first epoch—recall Anaximander's κόσμος φανερῶν (the order of appearances)—to the practical bias in the philosophy of the middle epoch becomes obvious; and this is more fundamental than a shift of paradigms. The governing principle following upon Epicurus's topic is the ἀπονία (non-encumbrance) of the body and the ἀταραξία (non-disturbance) of the soul. And finally the consequent term of thinking is the activity of φρόνησις (deliberation) and its practical inferences, attaining the status of a firm belief in φυσιολογία.

The second ratio established by Aenesidemus shatters this dogmatic belief in thinking by initiating a "search without assumption" (ζήτησις ἀδόξαστος). As a consequence the corresponding topic is what appears to me alone and may even be obvious to me without any recognition of external facts. And finally: the determinative goal of "skeptical guidance" is the "calm of the soul."

The third, that is, the gnostic stage in this figure of mundane reason—exemplified by the "Poimandrus"—rejects from the very outset the possibility of attaining such a goal by human effort. Instead, the governing principle is a divine operation. It provokes the corresponding thinking and determines its vocation to be "thanks-giving," this with respect to a topic that is the other world of pure light as opposed to the world of darkness; the latter must be explained and this is offered by the apostasy of an individual light that generated mankind as such and, prior to the latter, the prison-world of the soul. This distinction of the world is the resulting topic of the fully developed mundane reason of this epoch. It is again transformed by Hobbes, Locke, and Berkeley in the inaugural phase of the final epoch of philosophy.

Here we shall consider only the third and final type of reason in that epoch. Its appearance results from the distinction of metaphysical—or, strictly speaking, conceptual—reason from both natural and mundane reason. This distinction means that the respective figure no longer turns on the term of either thinking itself or its topic but rather on what may be called the ratio's destinal principle.

With the final epoch of our history we catch a glimpse of the shift from the practical to the poietic character of philosophy.

The ratio established in the Kantian position starts with the destinal principle that is initially the *fact* of freedom, finally its *idea*. The corresponding thinking is initially the respect for its concretion in the categorical imperative and the manifold duties attached to it and finally the enlightenment of the understanding that tends to evade those duties. The *Sache*—in this case the object of acting accordingly—is not, as traditionally understood, felicity but rather the moral dignity that justifies it.

The Fichtean ratio sets out immediately with a transformation of the last Kantian term, namely, with the pre-objectivating, pre-reflective, and thus originary actions of the human mind: positing, contra-positing, co-positing. These are enacted by the pre-empirical ego, which is initially its own concept—absolute, though abstract identity—and finally its idea; this includes not only the position of identity but also the negative action of opposition and thus the formative labor of reflection in positing both sides together. Thus the only truly absolute ego is the destinal principle for the complete enactment of liberty. For the corresponding thinking, it is the self-produced ideal—the destinal principle that attracts the fundamentally practical thought—that makes it strive.

The Hegelian ratio immediately transforms this striving of reflective consciousness into the methodical movement of the pure concept. Its *Sache*, or realization, is the product of thinking, the totality of the conceptual system. Its destinal principle is the transformation of the Kantian idea of freedom into the freedom of the idea that has determined itself—absolutely: the *idea adaequata* of philosophy.

Are these ratios a series of paradigms? Their configuration allows of no ordinary philosophy but is rather the completion of a singular conceptual task. Which? Here we arrive at the point where it becomes clear why and how philosophical thinking makes all the difference. As Kant pointed out, for instance: the critique of theoretical reason is devoted to the task of saving freedom, demonstrating that under the conditions of natural causality, freedom is not impossible. The critique of practical reason does not go on to demonstrate how freedom is possible but to defend man's autonomy—presupposed for all duties—against the sophistry of mundane arguments that corrupt the purity of the self-conscious moral response. Philosophy does not teach what men have to do and to avoid. This is already known to anyone who has a sense, if not the idea, of freedom. The sense of freedom is the dominant issue of the σοφία envisioned by Rousseau's imagination. It is he who speaks of the demand characteristic of any σοφία: man ought to distinguish himself from himself—a formula Kant repeated.

The reference of a φιλοσοφία to a σοφία, which is not of the former's *own* making, is already essential to the beginning of philosophy in the establishment of natural reason. Ἱστορίη παντῶν (the observation of everything) is in itself the outright rejection of a knowledge offered by the Muses. Rejected is not only the Homeric insight that we know nothing but also the Solonian, which warns against δόξα. When, by contrast, Xenophanes sees the results of observation as δόκος, he at the same time asserts that this is the only path on which to proceed. The finitude of human knowledge based on observation is insurmountable.

Equally oppositional to a given σοφία is mundane reason. Yet it not only tries to reject the former but also to replace it as such, recognizing its guiding function for society, whether this be only a circle of friends in an Epicurean garden or the *ecclesia* of the Gnostics.

The thinking of both natural and mundane reason makes all the difference over against the thought of a given wisdom. But the apex of differing is reached when reason differs from itself—both from its natural and its mundanc types. The motive for such an event lies in the accepted task of conceiving the truth of a wisdom within the limits of pure reason, of providing the appropriate logic for conviction.

What if there is no such truth to be conceived? The accomplished conceptions of metaphysics allow for the modern severance of our world from its history—a world which is modernity in a singular manner. In its sphere the types of reason outlined are not just abandoned but transformed: natural reason into technical, mundane reason into temporal, conceptual reason into hermeneutic. As long as we see no means of another transformation from the sphere of our world into the sphere of a speech that constitutes its own totality; as long as we banish such a transformation by eliminating the possibility of rational and architectonic configurations; our thinking makes no difference but is a *différance,* a deferment of thinking. There we are: amidst the postponement which characterizes so-called postmodernity.

AN END WITH DISTINCTION

> But our lot crawls between dry ribs
> To keep our metaphysics warm.
>
> – T. S. Eliot, "Whispers of Immortality"

Metaphysics has come to an end. So they say. Let us assume: so they know. How do they know? And about which metaphysics are they talking? Of what unity are they thinking?

Others have protested: metaphysics is still going on—as it went on and on in the schools. Is it not still being taught? It appears to survive in textbooks. And the historians of philosophy point out: contemporary thought still shows traces of that tradition. Even when unnoticed, it rolls on and on in our habits of thinking.

In that vein we are every now and then offered an introduction to and even into metaphysics. What do we meet there? A contemporary metaphysics? A renewed First Science?

The impetus for such introductions already suggests some "modernizations" of old "problems" traditionally considered to be typical of metaphysics—this all the more so as it itself seems to continue only as a problem. Is it still going strong?

What makes it a problem is the legitimacy of its problems. Especially after some rude remarks from respectable quarters asserting that these problems make no sense. Of course the criterion of sense has duly become a problem itself. To quote "Mr. Eliot's Sunday Morning Service": "the masters of the subtle schools are controversial," even if they are not "polymath"—at any rate, not with regard to the entire field of metaphysics.

Over the last decades the mood has swung around such that the sense of the metaphysical problems is given the benefit of the doubt. Even the project of a "descriptive metaphysics" has turned up—in bold attachment to the old name, yet with the security clause of its difference from "revisionary" metaphysics. To safeguard that difference, even Hume, who was formerly felt to be rather skeptical about metaphysics, is given a position of ambivalence between "revision" and "description." In a fit of caution.

So we may fairly conclude that the prevailing situation for considering the end of metaphysics is rather complex, if not confused. Seriously?

I

But why be so vague as to what we are talking about? There is the undisputed tenet that metaphysics is both ontology and theology. One might want to add henology. It is obvious that "rational theology" is nowadays at best a problematic case. But we are still firmly left with ontology—and, if we are to believe the learned, with henology as well. Both may go on and on since they thrive on an undisputed linguistic basis of investigation—however remote the ontological tradition may be that is thought to derive from Aristotle, however remote the henological tradition may be which the renewed interest in the so-called Neoplatonic strain has unearthed. Even if these traditions have shrunk to rivulets, how could they come to an end? Who would feel its benefit? Who would be relieved? Those who promote the problems in question? And who else takes notice?

The assumption that metaphysics has come to an end appears, however, not to be deterred by the survival of its ontology, let alone by the historial revival of an interest in henology. There is no opposition because it is unlikely that the protest against the assumption refers to the same thing. So what do those making this assumption have in mind?

Which reason asserts: metaphysics has come to an end? Presumably this end is to be understood as an historial phenomenon. Of what sort? If taken in its own right, i.e., as First Science, one would expect it to fall in the history of science. But in the contemporary reflections on such histories it goes without notice. Kuhn and his followers did not attend to the revolutionary structure of metaphysics, though such is prominent in the latter. But apparently it is not to be considered as a science at all, let alone as the primary science. The philosophy of science or of logic may be granted such a status, but not metaphysics.

When it comes to the reflection on the history of the basis of science in life, we find metaphysics also considered—not as science but as worldview. And here we meet Dilthey's assertion that its history has come to an end. Once and for all it is historical consciousness that has put an end to this way of thinking, which is held to be adverse to life itself because it denies the essential relativity of the appropriate understanding, a way of thinking which in every worldview can only grasp and emphasize one aspect of life. It excludes "eternal truths" and rejects the pretense to systematic knowledge. The multi-sidedness of life itself resists all efforts to construct its various and ever varying aspects as a systematic unity.

The history of the worldview and its types will go on and on, but its hybrid, i.e., metaphysics, has collapsed and the error overcome. Already for Dilthey himself, however, there remained a certain uneasiness about the consequences of the relativity indigenous to historical consciousness. This led early in this century to numerous, mostly spurious, essays on the reinstitution, and even to the illusion of a resurrection, of metaphysics. Characteristically the ontological tradition became a promising favorite in different schools. And yet Husserl, whose position really made a difference in the sense-explicative dimension opened by Dilthey, had strong reservations about integrating the tradition. His "radical" approach tended to break with it, notwithstanding its usefulness. That its use amounts to contracting a contagious disease, to which we remain ever prone, was in the end Wittgenstein's effective warning.

II

But the theme of the end of metaphysics was restated by Heidegger in view of a history which is utterly different both from that of science, or technology, and from that of life, or the understanding of it. Drawn to a different history he is the first to ask both seriously and competently: what is metaphysics? No longer taking the answer for granted. The scope of this question appears to be so remote from the traditional academic preoccupations and views, that both the answer and the way it envisions the end of metaphysics have remained at odds with the research into the history of philosophy. Heidegger's question issues from an experience that situates him in the neighborhood of Marx and Nietzsche. They also find themselves confronted with an historical end: the result of class-struggle and the disintegrating belief in the Christian god. Heidegger, however, does not consider the same history, for the reality is not the same. Not the history of the producer society nor of the positing of values but rather that of Da-sein. It is this that history modifies, mediating between its world and its speech.

If Da-sein is historical, then so is the thinking and even the destiny involved in it. It is the latter, the There (*Da*), that evokes thinking in order to be realized in Da-sein. As the clearing, the There inaugurates the correlation of Being and thinking, it appropriates them.

However, the clearing of this appropriation does not imply its clarity; it has remained obscure; thus the appropriation of Being and thinking has amounted to their expropriation. The destiny of Being has turned out to be the singular event of an "epoch" in the literal sense of a retention: it keeps to itself in Being while offering only the beings for the inquiry into their Being.

In this epoch, thinking is, so to speak, deluded. It responds to Being in an oblique way, remaining in the oblivion of the clearing itself and turning to Being only as its own correlate. In the end the inaugurating of the correlation of thinking and Being is usurped by thinking itself. This is the provocation of its voluntary nature, which finally—beyond Nietzsche's will to power—perverts itself as the will to the will alone.

With these—albeit sketchy—terms of destiny and thinking in Heidegger's ratio, we return to its topic: Da-sein.

Its "There" is the whereabouts of man and, with reference to him, first of all the world. How is it affected by the destiny, i.e., by the reticence? It appears in the retiring propinquity of things. Strangely enough, with a resulting lack of distance, or rather: reserve among them. Propinquity demands an opening that allows for an approach from afar. Such an opening is the world with its four quarters: earth and heaven, the divinities and the mortals are far apart, but each of them allows for the approach to the others through the medium of things, which in themselves bring the four into one focus. Their resulting propinquity and the accompanying propinquity of the properly "mundane" things is obviously different from the natural proximity of bodies according to their distance.

Heidegger's world as world is the necessary foil for an insight into the different world, which prevails and "is" and testifies to the thinking realized in it. The dominant experience of phenomena that characterize our world as "technical" would never lead of itself to the question concerning its technicity. Neither its unity nor its singularity would ever be conceded by the multitude of vastly different techniques and their products. It derives its singularity from that of the world as such; only its elucidation permits the assessment of the world, which actually modifies Da-sein, as "technical." This setting refers to the denial of the world as world.

The technicity holding sway in the present world reveals it as that of the *Ge-stell*, i.e., the "sy-stem" par excellence. The radically mundane *systema mundi* totally perverts the "harmony" of a world seen initially by natural reason. The στάσις in the "sy-stem" of technicity is revolting in that it engages everything and everyone with its all-pervasive challenge to become a servile and constituent part of its stocks.

History in the strict Heideggerian sense is properly introduced only as that to which this world of technicity refers. Should we follow this reference if history emerges as just an appendix to the world? The usual reply of historial self-justification, that to understand the present one must look for its past—a vaguely causal and "scientific" proposition—will not do here, where we are bound to understand our world as differing from the world as such.

It is this difference and this alone that destines Heidegger to consider history—that which encompasses every world instituted in an "epoch" or retention of Being. In its totality the world as world is denied. This totality is in turn to be regarded as one epoch only: an accretion of layers covering up the originary ground of decision, where contemplation is offered once and for all the Being of beings, while Being itself is reserved and therefore unwittingly neglected. With each layer or world-stratum, oblivion is intensified until all trace of the originary "mission" is expunged. This is the case when the difference in the Being of beings disappears and thus the "transcendence" of a first reason and first cause collapses. This is the end of metaphysics: a world which is the sy-stem of mere beings. Their indifference gives free reign to the will that is immanent in the technicity of our world.

The end of metaphysics is not an event in the "history of ideas." It makes a difference and in fact all the difference only in Da-sein. Its world is affected neither by the disputes of the schools nor by the rejection of the metaphysical type of "worldview." Metaphysics had been immanent in Da-sein not merely as a set of varying doctrines but rather as the reality of a transcendence constitutive of its world: transcending the *entia* in the quest for their common reason and rationality, and transcending with their first cause to the *entia* as its effects. The *summum ens* had been the *summum bonum* and had evoked a desire in the rational animal, stimulating and directing its will. While the collapse of the transcendence, the devaluation, of the highest values is experienced in Nietzsche's world as a tremor and thus still as indicative of the metaphysical difference, Da-sein has finally settled into a world of complete indifference. Again: this is the end of metaphysics—"not with a bang, but with a whimper," and even this has died away.

Within the scope of the Heideggerian ratio the question as to whether metaphysics has come to an end makes no sense, for it comes into view as such only from out of the world resultant upon its end. All the more—or less—so as history is here not an historial object; this is emphasized by the regress in the characterization of Da-sein with reference to the world, to history, and finally to speech. History appears to be that of speech, even when the latter is distinguished according to the destiny of thinking in Da-sein: the present clearing of the expropriation of Being and thinking is in itself deictic and is that which gives what is to be thought—as it gives what is to be thought in the beginning of metaphysics. The clearing dictated all its "basic words," indicating the various levels in the growth in oblivion.

Speech is by its very nature deictic—both clarifying and obscuring. Therefore, it might—in the form of the occidental languages—be the insuperable barrier to a transformation which allows for the "speech that speaks" and thus the advent of the world as world. That would be the decisive reformation of Da-sein.

It is the expropriation of Being and thinking that entails a mode of thinking that is basically rational—as seen in its principles: that of identity and that of reason. The end of metaphysics is manifest when the primary relation of Being and beings disintegrates, when thinking is left with the computative relations of the mere beings and their network. In the world of technicity, even the former trace of Being as such is expunged. And therefore the end of metaphysics, of this "first" history, becomes Heidegger's concern.

He does not and could not pretend to put an end to it himself. Taken as a body of knowledge, it may be proved to be erroneous, it may be discovered to be an illusion, the result of a delusion in the grammar of our language. But Heidegger is not talking about the same phenomenon as Wittgenstein's "metaphysics."

On Heidegger's view, attempting to put an end to metaphysics would be just as absurd as trying to put an end to the world. His critique must not be confused with the academic humdrum of that name. This makes just as little difference to the world of concern to Heidegger as do the textbooks that keep on trying to give some metaphysical "problems" a renewed relevance. For "us." For whom? Heidegger asked—mindful of man's distinction from himself, of his destiny as the "mortal."

He emphasizes: the distinction of the modes of thinking—that of its "first" and "other" beginning—does not entail the envisioned change of the world as such. Thinking may wait—not *for* but rather—*upon* this change, but cannot possibly cause it; all the less so as the technicity of the present world is also not its effect. And thus the end of metaphysics is not the result of anyone's efforts.

This end is not historially representable but rather present by itself as the history that integrates the world of technicity. In it, the mission of metaphysics has come to an end: even the trace of the oblivion of Being *qua* Being in the Being of beings has been successfully expunged, so that we are left with mere beings. In this very end, metaphysics becomes an obsession for Heidegger insofar as the remnants of relational thinking not only pervade our world but primarily obstruct a language that is free for a mode of speech corresponding to the other beginning of thinking. The origin appears to be obstructed in the languages of our metaphysical heritage. And this is the most redoubtable obstacle of Heidegger's final attempt to leave metaphysics to itself. He suffers from his inability to escape from the language of *Aussagen*, of statements, in a futile attempt at the "poem," the building of speech, which houses the mortals.

III

For Heidegger—in a manner different from Wittgenstein—metaphysics remains an obsession. Leave it alone. Such would be proper advice only if its present depended on our representiation. This is the case for its historians but not for him who is mindful of the present world characterizing Da-sein.

This mind, however, may take another step—resigning itself to the seemingly obsessive metaphysics, instead leaving it to itself by leaving it to its own self, as distinguished from the technicity of the world.

We ask again: what is metaphysics? If we leave the answer to metaphysics, then we seem to hear its own λόγος and that reminds us of its own logic, which is ultimately the Hegelian *Science of Logic*. And this, according to its sequel, the *Encyclopaedia of the Philosophical Sciences*, attracts us to another "end" of metaphysics: the certainty that philosophy has finally become equal to its idea, has fully realized its concept. Has this end been denied by any subsequent metaphysics? Which then? Lotze's? Who comes forward? Or should we acknowledge the academic concoction of textbooks and introductions?

But have we not been too rash in assuming a reply from metaphysics itself? Which is its present? Would Hegel himself not remind us that within the "system," history has its place not as that of philosophy, let alone of metaphysics, but rather as the history of the world and its ἦθος? Hegel's own historial presentation of philosophy is a corollary of the system. And there he does not distinguish metaphysics from a variety of other ways of philosophy. What would justify its restriction to metaphysics? Moreover, how could we hope to keep hold of history by reinstating the logic of the λόγος? Its mere application to a history of metaphysics—would that not amount to a contamination of the development of the pure concept with the ἦθος of objective spirit and even to the historian's history abandoned by Heidegger? All the more, referring to the history, or rather the event of appropriation, that Heidegger alone brought into view? And what else could be achieved in such a muddle but an oblique restitution of Hegelianism—regardless of what Heidegger did?

So we had better not look for a "reply" from metaphysics but instead ask once again: what is it?

Leave metaphysics to its self. This is difficult to try without concealing or rather shunning its own present. It is easier to fall back on an academic representation of this history of metaphysics along the Hegelian lines of a single development of the pure concept. Still, leaving metaphysics to its self is a laborious task and not to be despised. Where would one start if not—with Hegel—in the "Orient"? And if one were to follow Heidegger's suggestion of a Parmenidean beginning, would it not all the same be bound to start with the Hegelian assumption of the utterly determined concept, bent on its development?

Leave metaphysics to its self. Does this advice allow for a transformation of its oppressive present? It does—provided that, without neglecting its presence, it is seen to be secluded from the world of technicity. Then it would be we who are left to ourselves. Then it would be our reason that is left to itself by metaphysics—to use Bacon's expression: *ratio sibi permissa.* Left to its own devices.

Of which ratio are we talking? Not of reason considered as a divine or natural gift of man. But of that reason which is discerned only in light of its fruits or rather seen in its ways. The ratio which is left to itself by metaphysics has completely had its own way (cf., e.g., "Reason in Modern Thought," pp. 133-148 below)—first revising the sense of the life which supports and demands science (Dilthey, Husserl, Wittgenstein); then the sense of that science (Frege, Schlick, Kuhn); finally the destiny of man (Marx, Nietzsche, Heidegger). All of these revisions indicate what appears to be a break with our tradition. However, this appearance distracts us from the event of our reason—which is, due to its scope, "mundane" reason—having been left to itself by metaphysics. By its "departure."

Does that make any sense? Would it make more sense to say: metaphysics is dead? In view of that history which metaphysics is, Heidegger speaks of the "epoch," the unique event of a retention. His oppressive experience in the present of metaphysics is that of a withdrawal: that which lets man come into his own as the mortal has never occurred to him, has been and still is retained like a treasure full of promise. Therefore, the other, non-metaphysical way of thinking has as yet nothing on which to dwell and with which to build; it remains for the time being "utopian."

What sense does it make to speak of the "departure" of metaphysics instead of the withdrawal of Being as such? Resigning oneself to the departure of metaphysics means: attending to what it has achieved: the completion of its tasks with consummate skill. Our *Topology of Metaphysics* has shown what these tasks were and accordingly what metaphysics is. First of all by referring it to what Heidegger alone saw as what is primarily given—so that thought is given to it. But we are reminded: in its peculiar ratios and thus in its ways and above all in the sites of their orientation, metaphysics is referred to a σοφία. Its various forms—the knowledge of the Muses, the Christian doctrine, and finally the civil consciousness—distinguish its epochs.

On the other hand, metaphysics has been defined by separating its ways from the philosophies of natural reason, which is not at all what one might infer from its epithet 'natural': it is not the originary form of reason, does not show the originary ways of thinking, but rather refers to a given wisdom by replacing it with something of its own making, whereas metaphysical reason "conceives" the given wisdom, i.e., offers it the conceptual logic of pure reason. The consummation of its three epochal tasks—there is a coherence in the types of logic required for it—explains the intention of the statement: metaphysics is departed.

The end of metaphysics is determined by the fulfillment of the ends to which its reason—correspondingly purified—has been devoted. Mundane reason has been its critical companion all along, a critical companion even of natural reason—to mention only Epicurus as an example. The end of metaphysics is an end with distinction, both by the nobility of its achievements concerning the wisdom of a given epoch and by its absolution from the end Heidegger attributed to it: perishing into the indifference of calculative thinking.

Metaphysics as shown in its topology—differentiating its sites and its ways, its ratios and their configurations—has for its part achieved what Heidegger expects as a cultivating, building, though not edifying, thinking. It offered a dwelling. But not on our ground, not within the bounds of mundane reason as distinct from natural reason. For such a dwelling, reason's distinction from itself, and not only man's distinction from himself, has been essential. Just like Marx and Nietzsche, Heidegger was concerned with the latter only—a distinction possible within Da-sein: that of the mortal.

In philosophy cheating never pays. And it would be cheating to suppose that we stand in the same historical region as that of metaphysical or natural reason. Such pretensions may serve some self-indulgence but not the task that opens with regard to the achievements of metaphysical reason. They appear to us where we have resigned ourselves to its end with distinction.

Heidegger saw his way among the open fields. Returning to its origin, he noticed: the topics of metaphysics—the immortal soul, the created universe, and the existent highest good—have relinquished their hold on our thought. They have ceded their place to their emerging mundane origin as indicated by the world, the history, and the speech determining Da-sein. There resignation is their last word.

We may gather from this: Heidegger listened to the subjects of natural reason. Amidst the oppressive present of a metaphysics in decay, he entered the stillness of the origin of these subjects, following the hint of their abdication. With this same hint, one may proceed into the present of the other-than-natural metaphysics. It flourished in the present of a tripartite wisdom, which natural reason had not sustained, had not been able to replace by instituting a wisdom of its own. Metaphysics was devoted to a knowledge which in its own rationality appealed to a reason for the attendance of a corroborating logic in him whom it concerned. In every epoch of wisdom, reason has offered that wisdom a corresponding logic—shedding its natural character in distinguishing itself from the ways of natural reason.

Only the departure of metaphysics allows for its replacement by mundane reason as *sibi permissa*, that is, as it is left to itself. And only after it has had all its own ways, is it prepared to recognize the achievements of metaphysics. Why not take heart from the distinguished ways of the departed?

WORLD

REASON IN MODERN THOUGHT

Wernero Marx amico
septuagenario
differentiae mundi memori

There is scarcely any need today to repeat Hegel's warning to philosophy against indulging the desire to be edifying. Such a desire, concerned with the feeling for an "indeterminate divinity," has evidently yielded to another, which is moved by the feeling for an equally indeterminate humanity. Both the one and the other remain indeterminate, not having attained the form of the concept, not even that of reason—'not even', insofar as the realization of reason is prior to philosophy and consequently prior to conceptual thought.

Nowadays it is more appropriate to warn philosophy against indulging the desire to please and to be agreeable. This desire is paramount when reason is determined by the nature of man—as observed in his behavior—and not the nature of man by reason. The latter had been thought to be something proper to man: the use of this property appeared to distinguish him from other animals. And this distinction was understood to determine man in a unique sense: he seemed endowed with reason precisely in order to fulfill his destiny. The reasonableness of such a destiny was the topic of what in Kant's day was called the 'science of pure reason' or 'metaphysics'.

Is there such a science today? No, not even of the type formerly produced by the method of natural reason. Although the injunction "Be reasonable!" and the call for rational discourse are familiar nowadays, such does not imply that those so addressed should consider their destiny as men. What such a call demands requires no science of pure reason but rather factual knowledge about human behavior. When this is distinguished according to its desirability, there is no reference to a destiny of man but only an appeal to a consensus about what is socially desirable.

That such a criterion differs *toto coelo* from the fundamental conviction of a science of pure reason may easily be gathered from the *Critique of Pure Reason*: "Pure reason is in fact occupied with nothing but itself and it can have no other vocation" (A 680). It is not man's servant but rather his legislator, the ground of his autonomy and duties. The respect for the moral law that realizes the idea of freedom is always—Kant reminds us—initially accompanied by the feeling of displeasure and even pain, because desires and opinions are unavoidably affected that tend to disagree with the legislation of pure reason. It demands of man that he "distinguish himself from himself" (*GMS*, 452.7/69). Only thus is the essential purity of reason to be safeguarded against influences that transform this property of man into a commodity which is at the disposal of his nature.

In the contemporary "enlightenment"—if there is such—the call to "be reasonable" amounts to nothing more than saying "Help yourself to reason"—as if this were something naturally available. This may seem to hold all the more so whenever that which is agreeable appears to depend on mutual agreement and thus has a social quality. No wonder some present-day "thinkers" are attracted by the obvious and dominant fact that in order to reach agreement one must first make oneself understood. The significance of the notion of agreement for a consciousness that is no longer that of the pure ego but rather of society was alluded to when at the outset we mentioned the feeling for humanity which has taken the place of the feeling for the divinity.

Stating and explaining this opposition, Feuerbach concludes: "The unity of you and me is God" (*GPZ*, § 60). And what about man's reason in this context? "Thus if the old philosophy said: only that which is rational is true and actual; the new philosophy counters this by saying: only that which is human is true and actual" (§ 50). This is not so much the statement of his knowledge as it is that of the feeling which Feuerbach was convinced would sustain the "philosophy of the future."

This future is the present with which we are here concerned, and from what follows it may be gathered that this present is about to end. In spite of today's cult of pluralism and the pretense of open horizons for infinite progress, I intend to argue that the possibilities of the essentially "anthropological" philosophy which Feuerbach pitted against the "theological" tradition have been exhausted. How so?

I

The name 'philosophy' has always seemed to be there for the taking. Its use is most simply justified by association with what is commonly recognized as philosophy. Where do we see it today? Even if we restrict the use of that name to academic teaching, we are immediately confronted with an immense diversity of opinions and convictions. If out of this *mer des histoires* one prefers to pick up this or that episode, this or that school of thought, such amounts basically to nothing more than a confession of one's own preferences. That these are arbitrary is rendered acceptable only by the existence of a wide consensus as to these or those parts of the doctrine representative of contemporary philosophy.

Trying to speak of philosophy as a whole would be a monstrous undertaking were it not for the system, which only reason itself provides. Which reason? Leibniz reminds us: *simplicissima ratio est relatio*—a thought which found its conceptual transformation and accomplishment in Hegel's logic. Thus we expect the relevant relations to be either those of identity or difference or contradiction. And as far as the proper subjects of reason are concerned, Kant's critique of the transcendental ideas—of the immortality of the soul, the createdness of the universe, and the existence of God—leads us to expect a system of totalities.

If there is a similar system in modern thought, the respective totalities must testify to its all-pervasive anthropological intention; however, this implies the denial of any form that characterized those metaphysical totalities as ideas. And post-metaphysical thought is by its very nature indifferent or even hostile to their former content.

The totalities of concern to modern thought are exclusively determined by human existence. History, world, and speech betray a reason which cannot be solely occupied with itself inasmuch as it is bound to deny these totalities an originary rationality. What is, or what is given, appears to be not only different from thinking as such but also prior to it. The idea, however, was not only the manifestation of what is but also of what is insofar as it is to be, it being what is reasonable.

Why do we speak of a reason that "betrays" itself in those totalities? They do not reveal reason of themselves—as did the "transcendental ideas"—but rather offer it a refuge since it is not what it is to be, namely, occupied with itself. Instead, it remains a tool in the service of man. What do these strange utterances mean? They have already found their explanation in the architectonic of modern thought. So let us consider it.

The denial of ideality to the totalities with which modern thought is concerned must be reflected in the ratios of reason and their sequences. However, the relations of identity, difference, and contradiction can prevail only obliquely in a reason whose actuality is—to borrow an expression from Plato's *Timaeus*—a bastard of reasoning. It is no wonder, therefore, that we find identity not at the core of the envisioned architectonic—as in the "divine" reason of metaphysics—but on its periphery, where reason explains itself in terms of scientific rationality. Epistemology has the immediate appeal of a philosophy that is itself science and the true guardian of rationality. With reference to the totalities already mentioned, we see a progression of three stages: the first is concerned with the speech of science; the second, with its world; and the third, with its history. In each instance the difference from their natural counterparts is brought to bear and this provides us with the first indication of a shift in reason itself, from its natural to its mundane determination.

First then we find the demand to establish a language that conforms to scientific rationality, a language that not merely consists of formalized notions that imitate mathematical signs but a *Concept-Script*, an ideography of signs capable of representing judgments of empirical content and thus of scientific information. Being systematic, it demands the appropriate formalization of logical consequence obtaining between sentences. Only with such a complete sign-system is it possible, as Frege puts it, "to break the domination of the word over the human spirit" (*BS*, xii/7)—the word as it lives in natural, or rather in everyday, language. The embodiment of language in unambiguous written symbols serves to disembody thinking, to make it purely operational in accordance with scientific design. Hence thinking is to proceed in symbols and not merely in conjunction with symbols, the symbols of a language being now thoroughly technical.

The definiteness and clarity which in the first stage pertains to a rational sign-system is, in the second stage of epistemological progress, applied to the knowledge of the world. Schlick, the founder of the Vienna Circle, says in his *General Theory of Knowledge*: "The one essential virtue of a coordination is its definiteness (*Eindeutigkeit*), and since truth is the sole virtue of judgments, truth must consist in the definiteness of the designation for which the judgment is to serve" (*AE*, 81/62). The latter "designate not merely a relation but the obtaining of a relation" (85/65). The relevant way of thinking here amounts to a "correlation of judgment and fact," and the totality of facts is the world.

In everyday life the world is understood as "a multiplicity of infinitely many different qualities" (318/284). But what about the world of science? "Coming to know all qualities, be they objective or subjective, is always the same: the sign-system of natural scientific concepts is introduced instead of them, thus eliminating them from the world-conception of exact science" (322/287 f.)—just as the word or language of everyday life had to be eliminated from a thoroughly rational language. The qualitative reality of "lived experiences" (321/287) has to be abandoned in favor of a reality that is determined purely by means of quantification.

"The quantitative conceptual systems of the natural sciences" (319/284) do not designate Nature but allow the daily experienced world to be recognized as Nature. Reality is then paradoxically called 'physical' only because it is scientifically represented. And insofar as the whole realm of reference is available in terms of the scientific system, everything real, including so-called mental or conscious life, is to be regarded as something natural. Scientific description and interpretation, however, could not for their part be less natural since their elaboration is "only a practical question of expediency" (318/284) and thus manifests their purely technical status. Nature is the world technically conceived.

But what about philosophy? It is "not a system of cognitions but a system of acts; philosophy is that activity through which the sense of statements is determined or revealed. By means of philosophy, statements are explained; by means of science, they are verified. The latter is concerned with the truth of statements; the former, however, with what they actually mean. The content, soul, and spirit of science is lodged naturally in what in the final analysis its statements actually mean; the philosophical activity of sense-bestowal is therefore the Alpha and Omega of all scientific knowledge" (*WP*, 8/56).

With the final stage of the epistemological movement, this activity of bestowing sense itself becomes an object of observation—namely, for a history of science that is not so much concerned with its former theories as it is with the progress of their production. This approach brings into focus the productivity of the paradigms that guide ordinary research. It is on the basis of these that scientific statements make sense. The paradigms determine their meaning in a technical context.

The distinction between philosophy and science, which survived only as a *distinctio rationis*, vanishes here altogether, and we are happily left with what Kuhn calls an "admirable set of tools." After science has ceded its old theoretical status, it is only honest to discard the traditional assumption that science approaches truth—if only by increasing the verisimilitude of its hypotheses.

And a reaction as vehement as, e.g., Lakatos's proves only that Kuhn has betrayed something lying at the core of the epistemological movement. The attempts to salvage the assumption of a theoretical approximation to truth cannot hide the impact of sociological factors on the production of a science divorced from natural reason. A science is to be assessed according to its productivity, not according to the truth of its theories. It is the technicity of science which finally led epistemology to consider its history as determined both by progress and conflict. However, what it expressly denies to history is a goal. After its concern with a seemingly systematic language and its corresponding world, epistemological reason has finally overcome the vision of a totality in view of the endless production of science itself. In the epistemological periphery it is this history that has finally offered mundane reason relief from its proper topic: the fiction of a totality.

II

In determining its own place, philosophical reason formerly established the triad of Being, life, and knowledge. Such reappears in the architectonic of reason that is presently and unavoidably our concern—however, in a reversed or even perverse sequence: with scientific knowledge in the peripheral instead of the core region. Below the epistemological periphery, we enter the region of human life as lived and articulated in pre-scientific δόξα, or opinion. Here reason and rationality find themselves at odds with lived experience. This is expressed in Dilthey's basic conviction that "the context in which thinking is active forms the latter's irremovable precondition. Thinking cannot get behind its own reality" (*GS* VIII, 182). This preconditioning reality is life as it is lived through. And the widest field of understanding this lived experience is history considered as the objectivation of life in its endlessly varying aspects.

The genuine relation to this life is not scientific and technical knowledge but rather an understanding of what one has lived. Such understanding manifests itself in an abstract way with reference to what is said—proceeding from the elementary activity of relational thinking, namely, comparison, separation, and connection. It enriches itself as the understanding of an individual life-context and its particular world. Finally all expressions of human life are gathered for the understanding in the history of humanity. Only there do we find the succession of worldviews which arise from different experiences of the various aspects of life. It is never the case that all aspects are revealed. Nor is there ever a total view as supposed by several worldviews and especially by metaphysical systems. And what is achieved by the appropriate historical consciousness? As with Frege, here we encounter once again the hope for liberation: "The historical consciousness of the finitude of every historical phenomenon, of every human or social condition, of the relativity of every sort of belief, is the last step towards the liberation of man. With this step, man attains his sovereign right to draw from every lived experience its peculiar content, to abandon oneself to it without restraint, as if there were no system of philosophy or faith by which man could be bound" (*GS* VII, 290 f.).

Although Dilthey's thought concentrates on history, it does not exclude the consideration of world and speech in their own right. However, proceeding in this dimension of the experienced life, we find, strangely enough, that the corresponding thinking becomes ever more restrictive, ending with the sole consideration of the functions of speech. Bearing in mind Dilthey's rich experience, this impoverishment becomes obvious through Wittgenstein. The intermediate position is held by Husserl. He remains critical of philosophy—which he holds to be basically a theory of historical understanding—all the more so as, in history, he becomes aware of a growing concealment of man's originary experiences.

His science of the understanding of lived experiences also begins with their linguistic, or rather logical, expression. The corresponding logic holds onto a stream of such experiences as that which is originarily given but interprets it as a stream of consciousness in virtue of the intentional character of such experiences and thus explains their phenomenality as that of ideas. Their intentionality does not lie in their content but rather in their qualities—that is, in the various modes of representiation of one and the same content. In this way the basic relation of thinking is one to Being only. Anticipating the self-presentation of the object, thinking corresponds to simple Being with a simple belief, with what Husserl calls 'proto-doxa', as related to that which is evident insofar as it presents itself.

Logical analysis, however, does not yet yield to reason the proper totality in this second stage of its progress. Though the presence of the relevant world for any representiation is the primary context of belief and its certainty, it remains to be seen which is the originary and which the final evidence at the base of all judgment. It is even more important to be clear on this point since it is concealed by a scientific worldview, that of the modern era which has even penetrated the views of everyday life. This induces Husserl to recur to a pre-predicative evidence.

It is not historical consciousness but only the reflection on an essentially prehistorical experience of the world in which we live that protects the originary dimension of lived experience and the understanding peculiar to it. This reflection justifies simple opinion and its belief, which remains at the root of all methodical knowledge, of every mathematical and physical idealization of reality.

In this dimension—which, in contrast to that of epistemology, we may characterize as the dimension of doxology—reason restricts its field finally to speech. Thus, eliminated is not only the vagueness of a life that is productive of history and its worldviews but also the problems of consciousness and the constitution of its objects.

The complex relation of the understanding and facts is downgraded to the simplicity of a picture referring to what it represents. How is this possible? Wittgenstein shows that reason and thus philosophy is concerned neither with the "That" of the world—for this is only felt and cannot be meaningfully represented in a statement—nor with the "How" of the matters of fact that are the elements of the world: this is a matter for scientific description. Philosophy, which is nothing more than the logical analysis of scientific statements, can be concerned only with the "What" of the world.

The exposition of what a fact, a thought, a meaningful sentence, and a truth function of an elementary proposition are, leads to the general form or the essence of a proposition. Here is the proper field of philosophy. To give an account of that essence is "to indicate the essence of all description and thus the essence of the world" (*TLP*, 5.4711). Consciousness and its ego are here the mere limit of the world as represented in the totality of true propositions. Consciousness is nothing more than an activity that controls the sense of propositions. It develops no doctrine of its own about the world and brands all questions that arise from a confusion of the "That," the "How," and the "What" of the world—in particular, the inquiry into the "sense of the world"—as nonsense.

Metaphysical reasoning appears as the very essence of nonsensical questions, and in the end it is only metaphysics that remains disturbing for the reason prevailing here. Considered not as knowledge but rather as a way of thinking, the remedy for this disease can be found only by exposing the aberrations of everyday language: metaphysics must have arisen from the misunderstanding of its uses. The idleness of language is at the root of this vice. The concern for language is motivated by the rejection of metaphysics and this finally leads to the suppression of the conceptual reason that had produced it. In the end it dawns on modern reason that it is still being seduced by its conceptual counterpart so long as it dwells on a *concept* of language. All generalization must be avoided.

Only the radical rejection of conceptual unity in favor of a family resemblance among linguistic phenomena makes it truly impossible to consider speech as a totality. This is the definitive self-denial of *reason* in this second dimension—prior to the self-denial of *philosophy* on the periphery.

The dominant role of the sciences for the self-presentation of reason is dismissed with the rejection of the logical ideal in the demand for the clarity of speech. There can be no exemplary clarity for all purposes of communication. Technical reason comes into its own when it realizes its practical nature and satisfies the needs of practical clarity and surveillance.

The use of language is practical in the manifold techniques of communication, all of which embody various forms of life. The control of the understanding is most effective when it remains unobtrusively present below the effortless functioning of instrumental language, in the pursuit of social games.

III

Reason as determined by its service to man—to him who in turn primarily belongs to society—is engaged both in technical progress and in fostering communication and agreement. But at its core it knows very well that agreement is to be gained not in the dimensions of scientific knowledge and vital opinions so much as in that of Being—as we may call it according to the traditional sequence. Disagreement reigns basically in the realm of bringing-into-being, or poiesis—prior to praxis and theory. It is human productivity that lies at the core of an entirely human self-determination of man. This core sense-explicative dimension is differentiated with respect to the traditional constituents of divine productivity: power, will, and knowledge—these no longer referring to Nature but rather modified according to the sequence of the characteristically human totalities: history, world, speech. The peculiar rationality that apparently pervades them gives rise in each instance to a thinking that contradicts its reality, that strives to see that reality overcome. Such a thinking no longer claims to be philosophical, and this renunciation is true to the modern determination of reason. It acknowledges its difference from what was formerly natural reason. Instead, it is resolutely and openly mundane. What then are its features? This question demands a systematic survey of the positions of Marx, Nietzsche, and Heidegger. Its bare skeleton may be traced as follows: in Marx the basic distinction from which to proceed is that between Being and consciousness. Not only the latter but even Being itself is relational since it is nothing but the process of human production realizing the relation between Nature and man, his power. Life itself is not—as Dilthey saw it—beyond thought but only beyond academic theorizing about human praxis. This "actual process of life" is man's production of his own life, is therefore open to complete perspicacity—both in the production geared to meet his manifold needs and in the progress of the modes of production.

Which now is the secondary relation of consciousness to the process of production? Its proper place is a society that—as Marx emphasizes—does not consist of individuals but rather is the totality of their relations as determined by the production process. Consciousness is like an attribute inherent in this process as in its substance. And in accordance with its office in productive society, it is the economic consciousness. What is its concern?

In all products it takes account of the labor that they uniformly represent and its intention is to economize both their production and distribution, most of all to increase the productivity of the production process. Therefore, it first of all induces the division of labor. On the corresponding market, speech develops its primary function.

Related to the production process, consciousness is universally economic. In particular, however, it is political. One part of society is set free from production in order to deal with matters of the so-called state. As a consequence, a distinction of classes is established. The originary power-relations, labor- or production-relations, are subjected to those of government. The political consciousness reflects this dual relation, which is first recognized in the world of domination, then in the world of servitude. Only in the latter is the difference of classes reduced to a single opposition reflecting the totality of political power. That reflection is pure where the ownership of the means of production is exclusively that of one class, which is no longer characterized by its former state-function.

The universal economic consciousness is in particular the political consciousness. Its singularity, however, appears only where it is molded by the following contradiction. What the consciousness of the wage-earner knows immediately for certain is that he, in truth, i.e., with respect to production, is a force that is to be realized in labor, and further that he makes a living—quite an apt expression here—only by selling this power, not the products of his work. For the purchaser, however, the same ware does not represent the same amount of value as for the seller because such merchandise is only bought with a view to its being productive in value. In his speculation on surplus value the purchaser cannot have the same certainty of himself as does the seller. The consciousness of the one and that of the other differ in one and the same respect. Both are historically determined, are subject to an historical phenomenon, to "capital" as it dominates production solely in modernity. This unique determination is the topic of Marxian science, and for the economic consciousness it is the First Science of man as determined by his productivity and not by his reason.

This science is thoroughly dogmatic—based on the conviction that Being determines consciousness. What in consciousness appeared to be mutually contradictory sides, prove to be the necessary constituents of Being or the production process of modernity: on the one hand, manpower; on the other, speculation on its surplus value—both sides cooperate in the self-realization of the essentially historical capital.

The development of consciousness is historical. Which is the corresponding development of history itself? According to the modes of the movement of Hegelian logic, we see first a "transition to the other" as manifest in the change of production methods or in technical progress. But where do we see what corresponds to "reflection"? In the revolutionary change of society within itself; thus the relation of the classes itself changes.

Finally history is a development towards a certain goal: on the one hand, the restitution of the power-relation of man to Nature to its pristine state, abolishing the exploitation of the earth; on the other, the transformation of the power of the ruling class into the self-control of productive society as a whole, abolishing the exploitation of the laborer.

To prove the necessity of attaining this goal given the peculiar nature of capital is the main intention of Marxian science. Beyond the end of history, of class struggle, there is only the endless progress of economizing necessary labor and the corresponding expansion of the realm of free activity. While the economic and communist consciousness is preserved in the representation of such progress, its historicity becomes meaningless—just as Marxian science must disappear with the destruction of capitalistic domination. Strangely enough, by its own intention this science is bound to vanish. It is itself thoroughly historical.

The vision of a terminated history is the first achievement of mundane reason—an appearance which does not delude reason itself so much as it deludes productive man, whose instrument it claims to be. Having no ideas, this reason cannot be occupied with itself—as even dialectical reason in Kant's *First Critique* was. It does not follow the train of reasons but rather the attraction of an origin. It is drawn from the power-relations to those of the will as they pertain, prior to the manifest production process, to a concealed life. Understood with Nietzsche, life is "that which must always overcome itself." Dispersed into manifold forms, it organizes itself into structures of domination and is in all its appearances the "will to power."

Thus understood, life is the cause of spirit, which remains in a relation of dependence upon the former. It is "the life that cuts itself into life" with the intention of exalting it. With the spirit, the subjection of something else becomes self-conquest; and estimating, which is proper to all forms of life, becomes a positing of values.

The first determination of spirit corresponds to the last and definitive determination of Marxian consciousness: its historicity—here with respect to the history of the positing of moral values. This too is about to be terminated in a present crisis, in the devaluation of the highest values. Morality deteriorates finally according to its own demand for unconditional veracity. Spirit is immediately determined by the nihilistic result of the history of morality; it distinguishes spirits according to the contradictory possibilities of the will, either to deny itself or to will the negation of all moral values already posited.

The extreme decadence of the will to power coincides with its destructive realization. In it the will elaborates its universal determination. Beyond the destabilized opposition of good and evil—presently it no longer cuts into life—it is the spirit of a creative man who reaches beyond himself and his traditional goals in self-exaltation, establishing a new hierarchy. Beyond this second stage Nietzschean spirit attains its third stage and its accomplishment when it subjects itself explicitly to a destiny derived from life alone. It distinguishes itself from itself so that the creative man is not only the superior man dominating others but is also resolved to produce the overman, who will differ from the last man in no longer being deprived of his own world.

The Marxian sequence of production–consciousness–science has its equal in the Nietzschean sequence of life–spirit–faith. The latter refers to a thought which spirit does not itself produce but rather by which it is overcome: the eternal recurrence of the Same. The corresponding faith rests on the skeptical interpretation of how life and spirit are related—just as Marxian science rested on a dogmatic interpretation of production and consciousness. Nietzsche's skeptical sense is revealed by his judgment that the will to truth is only a peculiar species of the will to delusion and to be estimated according to its particular value. This estimation has the world as its measure. So which world is to become the *differentia specifica* for the man who transcends himself?

At first it is the world that contradicts the remembered world which differed according to the distinction between delusion and truth. Along with this, the after-world of the god who justified traditional moral values vanishes.

Thus the restituted unique world is the modern horizon of a creative activity from a life beyond good and evil—a life that calls for total assent, first of all to the destruction of the values already recognized.

At last it is a world loved as the "ring of eternity"; as such it appears to be perfect, to possess Dionysian beauty. Its vision is beatific because it has overcome the nihilistic feeling that a final reason is lacking. This world is justified in itself as a play and merges into a totality again and again through the center of time, which is what Nietzsche calls "the great midday."

Being as production process; Being as life-struggle: the concern for its origin draws mundane reason finally back to Being *qua* Being—more precisely: it attains the relation no longer appropriate to power and will but rather to knowledge, and that is the relation between Being and the There (*Da*), between Being and the clearing; this is realized in a process of unconcealment, originarily seen in the dawn of φύσις.

This relation also provokes a complementary one, namely, the Da-sein of the productive nature of man as Heidegger sees it. Whereas the Marxian relation of consciousness resembled that of substantiality; and the Nietzschean relation of the spirit, that of causality; the Heideggerian relation is reminiscent of the final relational category, that of reciprocity. In itself, Being refers to "Da-sein" and this in turn refers to the mission of Being.

According to its first determination, Da-sein is what the Nietzschean spirit attained in its final stage: worldliness. Its world is now that of the apprehension of one's authentic possibilities. Da-sein is specified by achieving a resoluteness that causes it to differ from its prior state of irresoluteness. This difference or particularity refers to an appropriated death and the consent to be a mortal.

Da-sein attains its peculiar singularity in its historicity—in a violent unconcealment whose realm is that of errancy. The authorization for authentic action—particularly when it is lacking—appears only in retrospect. As for the knowledge involved in action, its radical finitude appears in the thinking that acts on the world as such—that of the authentic thinkers. The history established thereby is the sphere of oblivion in view of authorizing Being as such. It withdraws itself to the point where oblivion is actively expunged and thinking is left with a world dominated by technicity. However, this in itself provokes a distinction in the historicity of the world: the "other thinking" becomes aware of the other world—no longer present in history but only in speech.

The last and definite, the universal determination of Da-sein appears to be of equal standing with the previously conceived rationality of man. Speech now seems to be his distinctive trait. Yet this implies that speech is no longer understood as an ability and property of man but rather as the proper presence and place of human being, that is, habitation. The productivity of man is finally "poietic." Here the presence and even absence of language is speech.

That which Marx realized as his science and Nietzsche as his faith, is for Heidegger the "*Besinnung*," or recollection. It is of a gnostic character insofar as it is inspired and summoned by a kind of transitive Being or donation—even when it is being denied. Left without authorization, thinking has to ask for a directive and finds it in the counter-sense to the progress of metaphysics. The end of this progression allows only for what Heidegger calls 'the step back'—namely, beyond the first beginning of metaphysics.

How then is speech experienced in such a recollection? Neither as a product of society nor as derived from gestures of power and dominion. Heidegger's manner of speaking already suggests a speech that is no longer consumed by its communicative functions; thus, it is often felt to be strange and even repulsive, if not ridiculous.

Speech is first of all engaged in indicating; its indicating distinguishes the world of the mortals from that of beings or from Nature; the world is as such closed, including its four quarters: earth and heaven, the mortals and the divinities. Secondly speech is an address to thinking that in its "fatality" is singular and unique; with its silence, speech closes the history of the already spoken work of authentic thinking. Finally, however, speech is the annunciation of the "event of appropriation" when Being and thinking appropriate one another.

Speech closes itself in its beginning, as the Nietzschean world in its center and the Marxian history in its end. The totality of speech that appears to be occupied with itself seems to link mundane thinking to the λόγος and even to pure reason, which is indeed occupied solely with itself. But such a link is an illusion above a separating chasm. Mundane reason can never of itself attain the purity by virtue of which it would correspond to its equally pure object alone.

If we look back on the peculiar ratios that this reason has established, it is obvious that they become more and more obscure to an average understanding.

It is all too easy to dismiss these thoughts as fanciful speculation, though one is certain of much company in relying upon the common confusion of what one does not understand with what cannot be understood. In view of Marx, Nietzsche, and Heidegger, one should exercise caution, lest in dismissing their thoughts one dismisses one's own reason. Let us remember that reason is a mere fiction at the point where it cannot realize itself in a basic and objective ratio. What then is the basic content of our own reason if not just the abstract forms of mundane thinking—namely, the economic consciousness, the spirit of nihilistic decadence, and finally a Da-sein of dubious authenticity? To refrain from the corresponding concrete ways of thinking—that of historical consciousness, of mundane spirit, and of a poietic Da-sein—does not exempt one from the sphere of mundane reason. But what is the good of confessing it to be our own? The progress from each of the abstract beginnings shows how philosophy is excluded. "So what?" asks the reason that hides its idleness in the games of modesty, renouncing the view of its mundane totalities, retiring into the careful organization of its thoughtlessness, jealous of its "finitude."

IV

We have traced the hidden ratios of mundane reason at the core of modern thought. They are all the more hidden as this reason has successfully avoided all signs of systematic unity in its positions. So how could we even try to expose it? Only the recognition of what pure reason had achieved in the epochs of metaphysics gave us a clue. And this achievement cannot be altogether foreign to the ratios explicated here. Indeed, they touch the ratios of metaphysical reason in a strange and amazing way. How so?

Marxian science is concentrated on the following ratio, whose abstract terms are the topic, thinking, and the destiny of both. The topic is the ware 'manpower'; thinking, the speculation on its surplus value; both are destined by the liberty of capital to realize itself. Thus, Marxian thought touches the ratio which is at the heart of the Hegelian system; in it the topic is the pure concept; thinking, the method of its development; both are destined by the freedom of the idea to realize itself as physical and spiritual Nature.

Nietzschean faith is critical of the following ratio: thinking as diversion toward a transmundane goal; the topic being the spirit of a man who only apes his like; the destiny, however, which here holds the intermediate position between thinking and the topic is the abject greed and vindictiveness of the demoralized flock. Here we encounter the obstruction of the Augustinian ratio. In it thinking realizes itself as conversion towards the supreme God; the topic is the significant creation, predominantly the human spirit speculating the divine Trinity; the middle term of both thinking and the topic is the destinal principle, which is the enacted love of the Lord.

Heidegger's recollection finds itself faced with the following ratio: the destiny is the technicity of the "sy-stem"; the topic immediately determined by it is the available substance, whereas the corresponding thinking is the taking into account of everything available. This is the Parmenidean ratio in disguise, where the destinal principle is the indication of the allotting divinity; the topic, that which is true because it is destined to be; and finally thinking, the reasoning within the bounds of what has come to be.

In each instance the present destiny appears to be repulsive for man and his productivity: capital, morality, and technicity. And in each instance it refers to an epochal principle of metaphysics. Mundane reason achieves the involution of the latter by a regression, finally transgressing originary metaphysical reason towards what is originarily "given" and to what gives it. In stepping back from truth to the originarily privative ἀλήθεια, thinking becomes aware of the "positive" sense in λήθη (oblivion) itself; it accepts the message of a withdrawal. However, speaking with the proverb, though thinking hears the bells ring, it knows not where they hang. As for where, the places of the aforementioned "touch" give us an indication. They belong to a reason that has become conceptual in that it conceived a given knowledge concerned with the destiny of man. These given expositions of wisdom have been the knowledge of the Muses, the Christian doctrine, and finally the civil consciousness of duty and the certainty of being free which presupposes it (cf. my *Topology of Metaphysics*). Only for the love of the wisdom proposed there and in order to support the conviction that must accompany its truth did the originarily "mundane" reason time and again become philosophical and therefore "natural" and finally metaphysical reason.

Whereas the immediate form of reason is to be seen in the relation between object and understanding, this two-termed ratio becomes three-termed in that it offers itself to the truth of the destiny—thus integrating the destiny into human knowledge, recognizing a ratio where the destiny transforms what was the object into its presentation and the understanding into being mindful of it.

Post-metaphysical, or for that matter post-philosophical, reason asserts: for authentic man, nothing but the ratio of Being and thinking or understanding and object is admissible; and further: there is no destiny other than its present repulsive manifestations; and still further: there is only a destiny which withdraws itself—even beyond the oblivion of metaphysical reason.

However, the apparent withdrawal reflects only an essentially transitive λήθειν (to deny someone a share in a certain knowledge) on the part of mundane reason itself; it admits only of a presence without extension—dividing an oppressive "hitherto" from a future world. Λήθειν is indeed the most "originary" activity of mundane reason: its supreme thoughtfulness in avoiding a given knowledge that has been esteemed as wisdom.

When there is no knowledge of a destiny of man distinguishing what is to be from what is, then there can be no σοφία and hence no philosophy. Metaphysics alone can teach us how in its philosophical pursuits natural reason responded time and again to the demand that it be pure and therefore that it distinguish itself from itself. The completion of the sphere of mundane reason as left to itself, subjects it to an ordeal in which it suffers the transformation of its totalities and accordingly the restitution of its dignity of being occupied solely with its equal.

DILTHEY "AND" HEIDEGGER: ON THE HISTORICITY OF MAN

The "existential-temporal analytic of Da-sein is resolved to foster the spirit of Count Yorck in the service of Dilthey's work" (*SZ*, 404). So read the concluding words of Heidegger's exposition of "Temporality and Historicity"—this in the course of the preparation which *Being and Time* yields for the "question concerning the sense of Being in general" (403).

To serve Dilthey's work, from whose appropriation the Da-sein-analytical "discussion of the problem of history" arose (397). To what does this emphatically expressed intention testify in Heidegger's later work? Nothing.—That's the answer. It thus remains astonishing when already at the outset of that work, the analytic of Da-sein is dissociated specifically from the so-called philosophy of life, in particular from humanistic psychology (46). It could already be expected from this that the said service could not amount to an emulation. Nevertheless, following the words just cited, the disappearance of Dilthey from the horizon of the Heideggerian sense-explication remains odd.

Whoever searches for effects may indeed find a number of things in this sense-explication's later, mature form—down to the consideration of the neighborhood of poets and thinkers. But things of that kind can hardly be read as testimony of the aforementioned resolution: to serve Dilthey's work and, what is more, to cultivate Yorck's pensiveness—the spirit, of course not the letter, of it.

Are both later forgotten? Obviously not if in the essay "The Age of the World Image" a cutting remark is made concerning the anthropological reading of beings within the horizon of lived experience (*ZW*, 86/133); all the less so if in a further remark it is said there: "Through anthropology the transition of metaphysics into the process of the mere ceasing and stopping of all philosophy is introduced. The fact that Dilthey disavowed metaphysics, that basically he no longer even understood its question and stood helpless before metaphysical logic, is the inner consequence of his fundamental anthropological position. His 'philosophy of philosophy' is the elegant form of an anthropological abrogation—not an overcoming—of philosophy" (92/140).

It is not only in view of Dilthey that this judgment is cutting. If it does not meet with approval, it should at least be clear that it seeks none. Its offensiveness, its unpleasantness, does not yet put it in the wrong. At any rate it ought not be passed over when the talk is of Dilthey and Heidegger. It draws our attention to the rift that separated the latter from the former—so decisively that not even the relation of opposition prevails there any longer. The elucidation of this rift shall be attempted in what follows.

I

In *Being and Time* Dilthey's sense-explication is taken up, deepened, and enriched as a bequest—much in the way Husserl, whose position on Dilthey Heidegger specifically cites (*SZ*, 47 note 1), took it up. Neither for the one nor for the other is there any question of dependence and yet both are able to claim to continue a tendency initiated in Dilthey. Thus Heidegger remarks in introducing the problem of historicity: "Basically, the sole concern of the following analysis is to promote, for its part, the appropriation of Dilthey's researches, to prepare the way for an appropriation which still lies in store for today's generation" (377).

Heidegger sees these researches divided into three thematic groups. First we have the theory of the humanities and their dissociation from the natural sciences; then the history of the sciences of man; finally a psychology which is to exhibit "the entire fact of man"; and all of this is aimed at one goal: to open up life in the sense that it is the mode of Being proper to man—this mode being understood as both the subject and root of the humanities. In this characterization, the bequest for Heidegger's own intention, namely, the analytic of Dasein, is obvious. Beyond such an intention, however, it remains indefinite to such an extent that he himself has specifically to fend off the impression of the "wavering and unsure, haphazard way of experimenting" in Dilthey's work and at the same time to reduce it to an "elementary restlessness" (398).

But what is the significance of the fact that neither Dilthey nor Husserl nor even Wittgenstein were able to provide their main works with the reassurance of systematic unity? As is well-known, Heidegger himself remains akin to them in this regard. Now as far as the cited characterization of Dilthey's work is concerned, it no doubt serves the appropriation of the work, though not an elucidation of the later rift. How is this to be grasped precisely with a view to that intent? Within itself.

Where the most extreme simplification of a thought is necessary, a phrase from the later Heidegger offers itself as a guideline. It reads: "The destiny of the topic of thinking." It is precisely in view this that Dilthey and also Heidegger himself shall be considered here in order to discern what separates each from the other. This phrase is actually of help in such elucidation only when its terms in the former as well as in the latter case are each taken on their own and brought to determinacy; only then are their respective proportions disclosed; only then can the transformation of the proportion and finally the distinguishing force of the Heideggerian destiny and the directing intention in Dilthey also be shown.

For systematic reasons, which can be passed over here, we begin with the topic of the Diltheyan sense-explication and in fact according to its determinacy as mediated by thinking and its directing intention. It is the social reality—though not in the way it is simply given to him who lives in it but rather as a kind of material already processed by the relevant sciences (*GS* I, 24/76). Why this? Of concern to Dilthey is a foundational science that is to be of equal rank with the former metaphysics (I, 384/217), in fact as anthropology, and no longer as the science of pure reason. Here the talk of humanity is not in terms of the rational determination of man but rather in terms of the experienced fact, which is the general context of social interactions (*GS* V, 250). This context is also termed the 'spiritual world', since the formation of values and the positing of ends are proper to it (V, 4). Thus the dissociation of the so-called humanities from the natural sciences is simultaneously a restriction of the field of the foundational science called for.

How is the social reality, distinguished into the systems of culture and the associations of family and state, a totality of its own apart from and within Nature? Only insofar as everything given for the humanities is something produced by man and thus is historical (*GS* VII, 148). History is life with regard to the whole of mankind (VII, 256). If the latter lives upon the strata and ruins of its products, its past (I, 25/77), then likewise in and with the latter, since history is not only a past life but at the same time an understood life, which remains understandable in its products (VII, 255). From this the priority of the sciences of the spiritual world over those of Nature becomes clear and thus also the status of the formers' foundation as First Science. Their subject is in fact to be understood in terms of itself. For the researchers of the historical world are of the same nature as those who have made and continue to make it—individuals whose understanding is founded in their own lived experience, who can relive and understand what in their world and in its products was always already lived through in former times, and who precisely on account of this are in an historical manner.

The socio-historical reality is in fact not conceived in terms of itself but rather understood on the basis of itself, which is why the topic is determined with respect to its origin, not in its ground. To which directing intention is it subject? To that of its many constituent parts; these are the various individuals insofar as they are creative. Their will, their struggle, their work, their arousing and satisfaction of desires brings forth the history in which the one life, which in itself remains a mystery, becomes objectivated (V, 131). In the formation of values and the positing of ends, individuals as vital unities bestow sense on the individual appearances of the social reality; and from the latter the totality of its history also derives a sense in each instance (VII, 172)—though no end; for shared ends can only be those of a society within the bounds of its particular world (VII, 185).

But how does the individual come to bestow sense and thereby to be determinative? Within history he appears as an intersection in the network of effective contexts, stands there as a self interacting with his milieu (VII, 161). He is a self, however, only by virtue of his consciousness of the self-ishness of the vital process proper to him, as is explicated in willing, feeling, and representing (I, 50/100). The self-ish vital unity is an end-in-itself and this in the network of that unity's vital estimations and drives (V, 373). Its most vital interests are aimed at the subjection and alteration of what is external, since they are aimed at the procurement of the means for the satisfaction of the vital unity's desires, ultimately at the protection of itself as well as of its property (I, 77/126). But a self is at bottom only there for itself where it knows itself to be independent of the natural order and in fact as it is derived from the experience of devotion and renunciation (I, 385/218). Actually, the self becomes the determinative moment of the historical world only by virtue of the former's awareness of its independence—in such a way that it combines, represents, and advances the world within itself (VII, 255).

This determinative moment is known in its historical effectiveness via the analysis of the course of a life in those structural unities (VII, 237) which reveal the interaction of ego and environment (VII, 21). Those are the lived experiences. They are the primordial cells of the historical world (VII, 161), and the knowledge of the latter has to take these as its point of departure since this knowledge cannot get back behind life as it is exhibited in the determinacy of lived experiences (VII, 237), for already thinking is given only in the context of the psychic structure (V, 5).

Now which thinking corresponds to the said topic and its directing intention? Not scientific knowledge, in the treatment of which the material of history is given, but rather self-reflection. It conjoins historial knowledge of individuals with the researcher's awareness of the value relations his will and his feeling find in life (I, 34/86), brings his knowledge in understanding into interaction with his lived experience, and precisely thereby revives the known history (VII,

119). Accordingly it sets a twofold task of an epistemology and a psychology (I, xvi/48)—ultimately of a method of understanding—for the foundation. These are to assure the structured knowledge of the humanities (I, 119/167) so that they prove their usefulness for vital praxis, out of which they have arisen (I, 21/73). Only insofar as they cognize the desires of practical life do they gain influence upon the latter (I, xvi/48) and, what is more, the power (I, 342) to participate consciously in the formation of society (I, 3/55).

Just as they are organs or instruments, so too is philosophy, in which self-reflection grasps itself. It is a function of society (V, 366), one of the cultural systems of its household. "It is the means of a world-relishing existence and effect that is independent in the force of thought" (*GS* VIII, 176). It is precisely in this connection that the sense of self-reflection for its part comes out: in the autonomy of thinking (ibid.) to establish the values, ends, and rules of social life (V, 371). This requires of philosophy that it become a worldview. In what way? Only as such does it reach down into the eternal interior of religious lived experience (I, 141), over which scientific knowledge cannot prevail (I, 137). Only as a worldview is it able to intervene in the sentiment of the unconditional dependence of the active man (ibid.). Not in order to expunge it but rather to penetrate it, and in fact with the historical consciousness. This yields the "complete acknowledgment of the immanence also of those values and norms that appear as unconditional" (VII, 290) and thus of the finitude of life expressed in them. It is precisely thereby that the historical consciousness becomes the ultimate liberator of the human spirit (V, 9) in the historical process of the freeing of the psychic life from its originary bondage. In this process the task of Diltheyan reason is fulfilled.

The following proportion manifested itself as the fundamental position of this reason: the topic is the self-comprehending, namely, socio-historical reality, as it is given as a whole in historial treatment; its prior directing intention lies in the awareness of the independence of the productive vital unity; the thinking corresponding to this intention is the self-reflection in which the knowledge of the humanities is utilized in the formation of the historical consciousness in order to attain historical significance therein.

II

How does Heidegger meet the Diltheyan ratio? Obviously via the corresponding Husserlian proportion. Instead of with the directing intention, it starts with the topic, which is the phenomena of consciousness, in order to attain first the sense-bestowing determination, namely, the acts of the *cogito*, and then thinking, namely, the reflective scrutiny of the fulfillment or non-fulfillment of sense. It is precisely this that becomes an impetus for Heidegger to find a transformed determination in the question concerning the sense of Being—not of beings—as his point of departure. From the "free-floating sequence of the lived experiences of 'subjects'" (*SZ*, 388) Heidegger looks back to Dilthey's history of objectivated lived experiences in order to open up "history as the enaction of being-in-the-world" and to show with respect to the historicity of Da-sein in what way the sense of Being is temporality.

Whereas Wittgenstein once again attains a sense-bestowing subject, namely, the group which communicates on the basis of acknowledged rules of communication, Heidegger does not return to any subject whatsoever, contrary to the custom of recent philosophy. The question concerning the sense of Being soon proves for him to be a dead end. He realizes: the sense-question itself and the consideration of understanding inherent in it prevents the proper answer—especially in accordance with the There (*Da*) of Da-sein. He breaks out of the entire dimension opened by Dilthey, namely, that of the sense-explication of the vital ground of science, insofar as he turns the question concerning the sense of Being into that concerning the truth of Being. It is further determined to become the question concerning the originary untruth and finally concerning the failing truth of Being. With the latter question Heidegger descends into the dimension of the Marxian and Nietzschean thought of the nature of man.

Yet was this not already thematic in *Being and Time*? Certainly, and in fact in the sense of the phenomenological distinction between fact and essence. It is precisely in view of this that the ground-breaking essay "On the Nature of Truth" introduced '*das Wesen*' with a transformed meaning—this by going beyond the understanding of truth in the philosophical tradition, even beyond ἀλήθεια as discoveredness. Whereto? This becomes clear on the basis of the following outline of the Heideggerian sense-explication. Yet prior to this, an aside.

According to a widely held opinion, soon after *Being and Time* Heidegger distanced himself from philosophy, especially academic philosophy, and as a result became increasingly incomprehensible. It is not our intention to contradict this, even less so if one expects that average comprehensibility whose average can also be established by the rules of communication by which a group of experts abide. The growing incomprehensibility is all the more striking as Wittgenstein, in the dimension Heidegger left behind, becomes ever more comprehensible and even generally so, insofar as he expressly complies with the obvious. That this opposition does not appear by accident becomes evident from the different position of each on speech. Inasmuch as Heidegger leaves its instrumental interpretation behind, its communicative function also fades in importance—this all the more so as what is communicated about the sense of whatever is said shatters time and again in his sense-explication. Why?

This is elucidated in the aforementioned essay, whose movement appears to him in retrospect to be "the saying of a turning within the history of Beyng" (*WW*, 199/140). Of which Being? Not of beings in general, not of the highest being, but rather of that which for him is "the event of appropriation" as such. Not a history that has its continuity in lived experiences, that has its roots in the latter. But neither is it a history as it was regarded as objective spirit. The said Being itself has no history; rather, it is history's sole event of appropriation, and in the manner of sending, that is to say: of a donating that keeps to itself, that in this sense is "epochal." It is precisely here that Heidegger reaches the point where the fundamental proportion of his sense-explication is unfolded.

With the transformation of his question concerning the sense of Being into that concerning the truth of Being and thus concerning the There of Da-sein, the destiny of the topic and thinking appears without mediation and in fact as the clearing, as ἀλήθεια, as the desheltering of a concealment experienced in the relation of Being and man as a withdrawal and withholding of Being itself. What does this odd talk mean? It speaks of a destiny whose fulfillment is out-standing and which concerns the distinction of man in his nature—spoken with Kant: his distinction from himself. Heidegger speaks out of an experience of withdrawal that was familiar to both Marx and Nietzsche—the former in view of the social relations of production, the latter in view of the relation of the creative man to his self. From the topic, which in both of the latter cases is antecedent, the out-standing fulfillment of the destiny there becomes comprehensible. Not so in Heidegger. Whatever he offers by way of its elucidation, the topic already has this destiny as its bequest. It is precisely for this reason that his introductions to it time and again require a leap. The originary character of withdrawal proper to the truth of Being can be explained by nothing else. It is, so to speak, a pure *factum* with no possible recourse to a Who as cause or to a What as substance—actually, it is not even a *factum* but rather an address.

The thinking corresponding to this address or to the desheltering of an originary concealment is commemoration as the remembrance of a growing oblivion. What this commemoration yields is the setting-apart of its other over against the first beginning of thinking, the step back into a more incipient thinking that takes its leave of history insofar as it is metaphysics and in fact as a sequence of concealing strata which finally does not even reveal the trace of the beginning as a decision. Yet commemoration does not proceed disclosively; rather, it lets the desheltering be which is proper to the destiny itself. It develops nothing, inquires into nothing, explores nothing. It knows itself to have been called forth and listens, is pure acknowledgment or thanksgiving—though without thanking for something, since it remains reticent in the face of that which in its donating keeps to itself while retaining itself, in the face of that which is a mission (*Schickung*; *ZS*, 8/8).

Didn't Dilthey already want to sever thinking from that of metaphysics? The part of his *Introduction to the Humanities* which he himself published is chiefly concerned with the dominance and decline of metaphysics, his intention being to show that the time had come for a non-metaphysical foundation of these sciences. Metaphysics appears there as an error whose refutation is long overdue, and yet the work of scientific consciousness was required throughout the entire modern era in order to redress the error, especially the ideal of the logical world-context. The epistemological systems of that epoch amounted "as it were, [to] the euthanasia of metaphysics"—as Dilthey mollifyingly expresses himself (*GS* I, 405/238). A phantasm of knowledge disintegrated there. For lived experience, such knowledge has passed away just as painlessly as irretrievably.

Not so for the Heideggerian sense-explication; not so for the topic of thinking subject to the destiny mentioned above, namely, not for Da-sein. Due to the latter, metaphysics, thus the history denoted by this name, is and remains extremely oppressive and as such testifies to its present. Which? A present that denies the propinquity of world and thing, the There of Da-sein.

For *Being and Time* this did not yet pose a calamity. Like the life lived through, Da-sein seemed always already given and in fact as the mode of Being proper to man. This mode made possible the distinction within Da-sein between inauthenticity and authenticity. Within the horizon of the question concerning the truth of Being, however, it becomes manifest: the existentially interpreted anticipation of death does not yet allow men to be mortals. For Da-sein, or their nature, they lack the world of remoteness and thus of propinquity. Subject to the destiny, which is the clearing of the event of appropriation, of its withholding, released (*gelassen*) thinking prepares for the turning into Da-sein but is unable to bring it about.

Man is not in the, so to speak, authentic world, namely, that of the event of appropriation, and yet is related to it inasmuch as his world is that of the lack of distance among his kind and the things—a world of challenge (*Stellen*) or the sy-stem of mere beings, which in fact are also free of the relation to a first cause and to a first ground, to a supreme being.

It is precisely the man who is mundane in this way who is likewise historical—not because he, in the process of his own lived experience, always already understands the history of the human race, namely, its products, and himself intervenes in this history by producing. Yet neither is he historical just because his thinking is still under the spell of what one might consider to be the effective context of metaphysics. He is historical only insofar as he, by virtue of his world, is exposed to the mission of an originary denial of the truth of Being, of the mission of neglect, and precisely on account of this has a future. And how is such there for him? Only in speech can this future attain determinacy with its difference contrary to all prolongation of what has previously been.

Historical man is likewise linguistically determined. If the history of his world, contrary to all progress, is focused on the decision of its beginning, then only speech goes back to and beyond the latter. In itself, speech makes possible the distinction of the mode of naming from statements, a mode which is proper to the advent, which corresponds to calling, to calling-forth, as it is known with reference to remoteness and propinquity.

In his mundane, historical, and linguistic characters, man is related to the fulfillment of the mode of Being proper to him, namely, dwelling, and prior to that is related to his nature, which is yet withheld, namely, Da-sein. In the fundamental proportion of the Heideggerian sense-explication, the event of the appropriation of Da-sein is the topic; it receives its determinacy in that threefold relation: to world, history, and speech. Thinking, which the destiny lets be, which is the clearing of the said withdrawal, enters into the topic as reticence.

III

Dilthey and Heidegger—their positions with respect to one another are not determined by the acceptance and transformation of the influences and impulses from what preceded them, so much as by the different version and even different dimension which "the destiny of the topic of thinking" finds through their respective positions. They come into contact, strictly speaking, in none of the terms of this proportion but rather in the historicity which in the former as well as in the latter case belongs to the determinacy of the topic: in Dilthey, the historicity of man in the history of his social reality, thus a reality brought about by man himself; in Heidegger, the historicity of the man who becomes cognizant of the said withdrawal and of the history of its beginning.

Unlike life, this history is without process, is given neither in the endless context of mankind's lived experiences nor in the originary succession of individual lived experiences. Rather, it is the momentarily desheltered stratification of the concealment of its decisive beginning.

As far as its sense is concerned, the history which arose from lived experience was that of the self-liberation of man from the originary bonds and estimations of his life. This event attained its utmost power in the historical consciousness. It no longer allows any metaphysics nor any worldview dependent upon it to arise. Everywhere it secures the pluralism of worldviews as it is appropriate for the unquashable multifariousness of life, which in itself is inscrutable. And thus, in the end, the whole of history must also become conscious as a network of histories of which each lives out of its own center, not merely with its own representations and estimations but with a way of representing and estimating that is different in each instance, a way issuing from a "psychic life" that is different in each instance.

And Heidegger's history? Like Marx's and Nietzsche's, it is rigorously singular—all the more so as it springs from the sole mission of the incipient concealment. The strata of metaphysics in accordance with this mission first emerge, however, as the one history where metaphysical thinking descends, has descended, into technical thinking. Yet the latter derives its determinacy only from the world of technicity. It is only the insight into its nature that is the desheltering of concealment as such, thus it is only this that brings to light the history of this world—above all, however, brings to light the decision of its beginning and thus of the possibility of the separation from it, a separation effected in the turn towards a world that arises beyond the beginning of metaphysics out of the originary speech of propinquity or that is failing along with the latter. Here history is completely focused on this undecided future. What is decided here is the entrance of man into his nature, namely, Da-sein. As for Marx and Nietzsche, this entrance would be a distinction of the productive man from himself, that is to say: from the How of his previous producing.

Could Dilthey see in such an anticipation a development or even a deepening of his own conception of the historicity of man. Certainly not. He would have had to interpret that distinction as a relic of metaphysics, as a transformation of its distinction of man as a rational being from himself as a sensuous being. The psychic life of man certainly changes in the course of history; yet such changes remain without the uniqueness of a distinction which would and can set-apart all history insofar as it is determined uniformly in that distinction. If Heidegger saw in Dilthey's philosophy of philosophy a kind of abolition of the latter, then certainly not with the intention of saving it. His intention was aimed at overcoming philosophy. To this end he did not allow himself to be provoked by its anthropological decadence but rather by the strength of metaphysics, through which everything thought historically asserted its present, and in fact in the oppressiveness of technicity. That which was thought requires no animation by one's own lived experience, for such also makes no difference in what was thought. Husserl's topic was able to absorb a history that has its "germ cells" in lived experiences but not the history determined to its end and to which Heidegger returns from out of the historicity of Da-sein.

Due to the aforementioned distinction of man from himself, Heidegger attempted to overcome metaphysics. If he was not even, more precisely: not at all, able to leave it to its self, his intention—and Marx's and Nietzsche's bequests remain included in it—neither was senseless nor remained without significance. For—if the history of metaphysics was ever completely determined within itself, then it becomes clear: natural reason had already considered repeatedly the possibility of man's distinction from himself. Beyond that, the task presented itself to reason in each instance that it distinguish itself from itself. Should the reason of modernity not be obliged to do the same?

Such a distinction fulfills no vital need, such cannot refer to the most vital interests of man. According to its sense, it is not necessary, but neither is it contingent. It is—once again—free.

MORTAL OF WHICH DEATH?

What separates Werner Marx's projection of a new ethics from the mass of similar approaches? Striking is first of all his concern about the actuality of evil; it overtakes the common efforts to communicate that which ought to be regarded as "good" and therefore binding. He then characterizes his ethics as non-metaphysical; taken on its own, such is not a sufficiently distinctive feature, for today all sorts of ethics "without metaphysics" are offered, and after all the ethics of Epicurus and Hume were already non-metaphysical—though integrated into the whole of a philosophy and imbued with a corresponding solidity.

Non-metaphysical—this recalls in Marx's work that metaphysics which not only had a history but which is a history ended on the basis of its beginning. In view of this history, the escape into the ancient antagonism between religion and philosophy is ruled out. With respect to ethics, he sees history as that of man, who leaves his self-conception as *animal rationale* behind in order to become—anticipated by Heidegger—the mortal. Mortal of which death?

The talk of men as mortals has no place in our usual speech. Heidegger takes it from Hölderlin, and already in the latter's thought it retained the strangeness of a translation from the Greek world. All the same, Heideggerian thought has, so to speak, a right to it, though one that cannot be taken from Greek philosophy. This is attested most emphatically by the Parmenidean distinction between the heart of truth and the views of the mortals. Pure insight excludes precisely this human being from the rational nature of man. Heidegger meets the latter so decisively that he brings out the necessity of an other beginning of thinking over against the first and, precisely with respect to the heart of truth, obtains for the mortal an altered status.

It is only late that Heidegger talks of men as mortals, and in fact at the point where it becomes obvious to him on the basis of the nature of truth that and why men are not at all mortals, actually never were, but rather can only now become such. This is attested by our abysmal separation from Greek thinking. There it is the immortals with respect to whom the mortals understand themselves as such, but in Heideggerian thought they are determined to be mortals solely with respect to death. It is precisely this that requires that death especially be distinguished and in fact right in the midst of the life-phenomena of the terminal form of the *animal rationale* for which the will to immortality has passed. Neither Hölderlin nor even the Greeks saw it necessary to think death itself with distinction—unless with the one which the court of the dead makes in passing judgment on a mortal's entire life. Yet as for the dead, it remains extremely odd that they find no place in Heideggerian thought, especially not in his world. Despite all attention to the Greek distinction between being-absent and being-present.

I

In order to be able to locate the place of death itself in Heidegger's thought we first ask: what is this thought? It has to be articulated as a whole in accordance with the phrase 'the destiny of the topic of thinking'. We take a step back from it, let its immediately experienced unity fall into its three terms and their proportion or ratio. To what end? In order not to have to follow the manifold ways of Heideggerian thought or even Heidegger's one path of thinking, a path which would have the continuity of the course of a life. Instead of this, we consider it as a closed and stable whole, though with a distinction of its—spoken with Kant and Heidegger—"reversals" or radical changes. Only in this way does it become clear where Heideggerian thought stops, where it—as *From the Experience of Thinking* says—"has swung into its harmony" (*in sein Gefüge eingeschwungen ist*; *GA* 13, 82).

We simplify this, just as we do every thought that makes a difference as a whole, in terms of its destiny, its topic, and its thinking, attending to their shifting architectonic. This simplification does not claim to possess any didactic value. For the time being, it accommodates the demand for comprehensibility only insofar as it starts out from that average comprehensibility which Husserl's sense-explication bequeaths to Heidegger's. Though it will be seen why the latter loses some of its comprehensibility with each radical change.

The Husserlian sense-explication started with the distinction of thinking, or cognition, more precisely: of its attitude into the natural and the phenomenological, in order to reach with respect to the latter the determinative ground of thinking, namely, the sense-bestowing *cogito*, so that it is finally completed with the analysis of its productions in the field of pure and yet world-oriented consciousness (and of its lived experiences) by precisely this "topic."

a) Heidegger counters all this in that he rejects the preliminary determination of the topic by the *cogito*; thus he takes the region of pure consciousness back to Da-sein, starts with it as the immediately given, distinguishing it as the nature of man from everything that becomes thematic in anthropology and the human sciences.

Then the thinking proper to this nature is no longer characterized by the task of the constitution of the world but rather by the fundamental trait of care. And this in turn has its destiny finally in the sense of Being. The question concerning the latter's disclosedness regulates the analytic of Da-sein, in particular that of its temporality, its finitude, its mortality.

If Heidegger elucidates human being as being-towards-death, then towards which death? *Being and Time* distinguishes it from both the perishing of animals and human demise, in general from factical dying. How else could its necessity be experienced as the "ownmost, non-relational, and unoutstrippable possibility" and even as that with respect to which Da-sein is offered its totality—regardless of whether it represses or accepts it?

Unlike the completion of a What, the totality of Da-sein is that of the How of its existing. This totality reveals itself in Da-sein by means of a twofold "not." The latter is determinative insofar as it nihilates (*nichtet*) and in fact as the impossibility over against all the possibilities that Da-sein itself projects: on the one hand, it nihilates as nothingness and in fact in the anxious sinking of every being; on the other, as the difference of Being over against all beings, as this difference enables the transcending to being-one's-self.

In both cases it becomes obvious that already here, despite their apparently shared question concerning the sense of Being, Heidegger has to eliminate metaphysics as onto-theology. Being-towards-death excludes it insofar as death assumes the rank of precisely that destiny which means for the What of man, for the *animal rationale*: *habet ordinem ad Deum*. Yet this comparison holds only so long as Heidegger remains in Dilthey and Husserl's sense-explicative dimension, so long as he holds onto the "idea of a fundamental ontology" and has not yet descended into the sphere of Nietzsche and Marx.

b) Here in the core region of modernity the first radical change occurs in the proportion of the aforementioned terms and in fact in the sequence: thinking, topic, destiny. This implies first: Da-sein is no longer an immediate datum. It wants to be, so to speak, excogitated and in fact in a thinking or poetizing that is the donation of Da-sein; as such it is historical. Accordingly Dasein now is to be disclosed with respect to the history of thinking as this history is subject to the destiny no longer of the sense of Being but rather of the truth of Being, of a truth of the "simultaneity of desheltering and concealment" and therefore of the errancy that Parmenides sees in the reason of the mortals. It is precisely here that Heideggerian thought collides with the beginning of metaphysics, which had opened the path for the mortals out of errancy and in fact by way of reason's distinction from itself. The history of this realized possibility appears to Heidegger henceforth as the history of the oblivion of the concealing-desheltering twofold nature of truth.

The history of thinking has in turn—like Da-sein—its own totality; it also has, as it were, a being-towards-death and in fact in the exhaustion of the possibilities of the beginning of metaphysics. This exhaustion lets death be experienced in historical, no longer only in mundane, significance. Thought anticipatorily by Nietzsche as the death of God. By Heidegger, as the death of that What which, in its supratemporal perfection, obstructed the truth of Being in favor of that of beings. The death of God affects Da-sein only insofar as death affects the belief in God beforehand and thus thinking. The latter enters its denatured state insofar as it is, in its indifference to the death of God, at the same time indifferent to the history of that oblivion whose theological science represented precisely this God as the supreme topic of thinking.

c) Heidegger transformed the Nietzschean experience of the death of God, of the expired belief in him, into the experience of the death of the historical, the missively misled, way of thinking proper to metaphysics. With respect to this experience, he entered into the strength of his opponent, namely, of metaphysical thinking. Yet the overcoming of metaphysics, which the submoderns take up so gladly because they are relieved, is overtaken by a second radical change in Heideggerian thought. Said in terms of *From the Experience of Thinking*, there thought swings into its harmony, there it reaches the age where it becomes aware of the precedence of the destiny over thinking and its topic. This implies: thinking has disposed of the willfulness of its understanding and the autocracy of its research or inquiry. Thus it has expunged immediate comprehensibility as well, which was still able to assert itself in the guise of the hermeneutic explanation of philosophy.

The destiny of the topic of thinking—how is it articulated in the architectonic of Heidegger's mature thought? The following outline draws attention to the totalities with which the core region of modernity occupies itself—no longer, like natural metaphysics, with the immortal soul, the created or uncreated world, the existent All of the divine reality, but rather with history, world, and speech.

The Heideggerian destiny—such is the clearing of sheltering and desheltering. It is first of a linguistic character—as the stillness that calls and gathers; then of a mundane character—as the nearing of the remoteness; finally of an historical character—as the mission that keeps to itself in donating. In precisely this concretion the destiny proves to be as much expropriating as appropriating (*vereignend*), both in the event of appropriation—first of all: of Being and thinking; supremely: of Being and human being. In each instance, thereby calling forth thinking as much as human being.

Subject to its destiny, thinking is first historical. It is sent—on the one hand, in oblivion; on the other, in the recollection of "what has been," in thinking anticipatorily of the advent of what is withheld in what has been. Thinking then experiences itself as linguistically determined, namely, as a bringing-to-speech of what was previously heard, in short: as a corresponding. Finally, thinking knows itself in mundane significance—thankful to the approach of what is most remote, which sets it on its way. Not as thanking for something but rather with regard to the fact that it is as it is, which is to say: that it may give thanks. As such it is an acting and, more precisely, an accomplishing.

This thinking has abandoned its former rationality. It becomes the middle term for the event of the appropriation of Being and human being. With respect to the latter, truth takes on the meaning of preserving; this on account of the neglect of human being as it brings with it the perishing of metaphysical into technical thinking.

Thinking approaches its topic in accordance with the sheltering-desheltering clearing and therefore as much with the denaturing as with the naturing of man—with both first of all in mundane significance. The extreme of the event of desheltering is realized in that world which reveals the nature of technicity. In a manner formative of the world, this nature reaches beyond thinking, subjects it to itself as calculative in order to exclude it in precisely that determinacy according to which it was itself a way of thinking proper to mundane reason, namely, as thanksgiving. In the world of the nature of technicity, not only thinking but also the nature of man in general is claimed by the extreme movement of desheltering, which not only challenges so-called Nature but first of all precisely that Da-sein which man is in relation to his destiny.

The one-sidedness of the desheltering of beings, including man himself, is converted only by the clearing itself which shelters as much as it deshelters and in fact, in accordance with the world, in such a way that the prevailing lack of distance in the nature of technicity is torn open by the inauguration of the remoteness in which the things let earth and heaven, the divine and the mortal, approach one another. Only in this fourfold does mortality have its own world.

Human being is first that which is distinguished in the sense of its world. It is then that which, out of its previous history, is contradictory and thus is drawn into its ground (*zugrundegehend*) insofar as it carries out the contradiction of a neglecting nature of truth. And finally human being is characterized by the identity of precisely that non-metaphysically stamped originary speech which protects and thus shelters that which is yet unsaid.

II

Human being, as just sketched with regard to the totalities of world, history, and speech, shows the place of mortals in a world that is lacking. There have always been various experiences of mortality—we refer here only to Ariès's superb observations in *The Hour of Our Death*. But it was first and only Heidegger who interpreted mortality in terms of man's distinction from himself. With respect to the distinguished man we now ask: man is the mortal of which death? It is not merely the distinction between kinds of death that is demanded here; rather, the difference that is yielded in human being only by the other death over against the first.

To begin with, mundane death must be distinguished from its natural type. As for the latter, as for the experience of its necessity and the horror of it, Spinoza's reminder still holds here that the intelligent man "thinks about nothing as little as he does about death." The experience that one has to die because one sees that all other men actually die, such is an *experientia vaga* and as such is least of all suitable for the foundation of an ethics—assuming now that such a foundation is proper to cognition and that this ethics ought to possess the binding force of knowledge.

It should be clear already in the first stage of Heideggerian thought that the said difference is not yielded by the consideration of natural death, thus of perishing or demise, but rather only by the distinction of being-towards-death on the basis of an inauthentic and authentic being-in-the-world. Here the denaturing of death is always the one prevailing first of all and for the most part; it prevails where the destiny—thus the sense of Being, temporality, and, more precisely, the finitude of Being itself—is obfuscated.

In the second stage of Heideggerian thought, death is distinguished on the basis of the differentiated being-in-history. A thinking that wishes to establish Da-sein in this history must be open to the destiny which is the truth of Being, thus for its concealing-desheltering nature, in short: for errancy. Each thought determined in this way takes on the mission of the decline in the face of the thought that is unfathomable, historically rising—this in distinction to historically indifferent thoughts. They cannot die but only become obsolete and turn to dust—for the maintenance of those who have to eat dust.

In the third and final stage of Heideggerian thought death is distinguished on the basis of man's differentiated being-in-speech, and here it is truly the other death on the basis of which men can become mortals. Death in the other world over against the first, which is stamped by the nature of technicity. The other world of the aforementioned fourfold, however, is present not in history but only, since it is to come, in speech. In the building speech of thinking, neighboring that of poetizing.

The setting-apart of human being first appeared to be that of its world. In keeping with the latter's first side, death became the topic of calculative thinking; dying itself, a bother which can be dealt with by employing various perfectly intelligible aides. In keeping with its other side, death is the topic of thanking thinking—solely regarding its being entrusted with thanksgiving. That is its capacity.

With respect to death, this thinking becomes that accomplishing in which man attains his nature—to be mortal, and in fact in the sense that he is capable of death as death. This capacity needs death, needs it in the concretion of a habit as only dwelling knows it. In such a habit, human nature lasts, namely, as mortality. But it is led into lasting "so that there may be a good death" (*BWD*, 145/151). An unheard-of phrase in Heidegger's work—this 'being-good' otherwise justly avoided. In its uniqueness it assumes the rank of the past phrase: "God alone is good." It is only as accomplished, however, that death is good. And this is the sole accomplishing which is essential to human production. Only via the latter does man distinguish himself from himself as the "working animal," which is an animal because it has exteriorized its rationality in work.

So that there may be a good death. This is the sole τέλος of dwelling. No *ars moriendi* will gain anything from this thought. And certainly no "ethical science." Yet Heidegger is obliged to attend to the ἦθος itself.

III

And how would a good death be? On the basis of the thinking that lets its world be distinguished, but prior to that on the basis of the destiny that lets death be accomplished. It is just on account of this that we ask once again and now more precisely: which is the other death of the other world? Heidegger answers: "Death is the shrine of nothingness, namely, of that which in every respect is never merely some being but which nevertheless natures (*west*), even as the mystery of Being itself" (*D*, 171/178). Far be it for one to wish to translate this word into the comprehensibility of our everyday language—be it the usual, be it the conventional, be it even only the language of an academic flock and its habits of communication. We respect the inseparability of what has been thought from its word, and we can do this because we do not take this word to be a component part of the continuum of the academic discussion. Such is dependent upon a linguistic instrument of average comprehensibility that does not develop, does not grow and die, but rather is changed according to demand.

Shrine of nothingness—a shrine due to sheltering; and what is sheltered here is the nothingness of all beings and their Being—also of the supreme being. For its manifestation, nothingness is dependent upon precisely that death of which men as mortals are capable. It itself needs the other death over against the one exhibited with respect to that being which man is—with respect to him, for instance, as the separation of the soul from the body, or even merely as demise, as it preoccupies calculative thinking. Put more rigorously: it is not for its manifestation but rather for its naturing that nothingness needs the sheltering of the shrine, which alone is the other, for its part not appearing but inconspicuously naturing, death.

The nothingness of every being and of the Being of beings natures in death only insofar as it is subject via the aforementioned thinking to the destiny, which is explicated in a threefold manner: linguistically, mundanely, historically. In the corresponding elucidation of human being, it is manifest: men are mortals insofar as death:

1) contrary to the lack of distance that holds sway in the technically determined world, tears open precisely that remoteness which makes possible every approach of earth and of heaven, as well as of the divine, in terms of the things;

2) contrary to the endless procession of history understood temporally, brings forth precisely that keeping-to-oneself, that ἐποχή, which sets free the other beginning of human being: of the mortals in the fourfold;

3) contrary to the inevitable utterance of speech understood instrumentally, lets the stillness arise which gathers in calling. Its gathering is the bequest for the building in speech as the dwelling of the mortals requires it.

Remoteness—ἐποχή—stillness: nothing but modes of the nothingness of beings that are sheltered in the other death. By virtue of the latter, the concealing-desheltering clearing is there. Without the distinction of human being on the basis of its destiny, there can be no death in terms of which men can be mortals. Because of this, all attention is still directed to ἀλήθεια, to the clearing, to this, if not mortal, then at least finite, nature of truth.

If Heidegger's thought does not hold up, then by no means due to its unsuitability or lack of success in ethical "problems," but solely due to the shattering of its destiny of the topic of thinking. Here would be, here is, the leap; precisely that which brings us to the point where we can see the sense-explication of modernity and thus of our world as a closed one. Turned towards it. Our world obtains its closedness from that of its history. Only from these two taken together are all the grounds for the donating and denying, for the taking and refusing, of the measures of human dwelling manifest. Nothing more is lacking for a judgment.

ACTION OR/AND DWELLING

Repeatedly Heidegger demanded of his students: read Aristotle for ten years. Ten years—that's a round time, for ten is (as already Pythagoras showed) a round number, namely, the one that indicates something complete. As a first testimony: in its tenth year the Trojan War reached closing crisis. Such a while also needs the thinking that makes all the difference and thus is constitutive of history.

Heidegger's demand sprang from his assessment of First Philosophy as it was first fashioned by Dilthey and Husserl with a view to laying a foundation of the sciences. But Heideggerian thought already parts with the Husserlian insofar as it leads the latter's decision concerning beings and non-beings—which is based on the evidence (*Evidenz*) pertaining to the fulfilled or unfulfilled sense of the contents of representation (noemata)—back to the understanding of the sense of Being, thus from beings to the Being—so it seems—of beings. Because he understands First Philosophy as a theory of the Being of beings, Heidegger believes he finds in the Aristotelian theory of being *qua* being the prerequisite bequest for his question concerning the sense of Being. And the Husserlian demand "To the things themselves" fulfills itself for Heidegger, on the basis of the self-givenness of the phenomena, in the Aristotelian being as it is understood as the true—not as the differentiated true and false of the understanding and thus of judgment but rather as the true of the simple being, to which only ignorance and concealment are opposed.

Conducive to Heideggerian thought is not the Aristotelian theory of being *qua* being, not the theological science, but rather the latter's reinterpretation as and reduction to a theory of the Being of beings, of the sense of Being, which is therefore restricted to the four senses in which beings are understood and thus in the end and eminently to truth in the sense of the unconcealment of the things themselves—prior to any phenomenon of consciousness. Typically enough, the Aristotelian requirement of the simplicity of the being and of its essential relation to reason is of dwindling significance to Heidegger. Such is—as I have shown in *The Rational Architectonic of Modernity* (pp. 322, 329 f., and

332-338) and "Why 'Being of Beings'?" (pp. 19-43 above)—inevitable for a sense-explication within the architectonic of modern thought.

On the other hand, that which in the reinterpreted Aristotle gives Heideggerian thought its impetus—namely, Aristotle's recollection (*Erinnerung*) of a truth as unconcealment which is prior to truth as a property of judgment—brings out that limit in metaphysics which the recollection (*Besinnung*) of the nature of truth transgresses. To be more precise: the return from truth as a property of judgment to the more originary unconcealment was nothing new within the sense-explicative architectonic of modern thought. Rather, new was the attentiveness to the hint that in the philosophical tradition the name ἀλήθεια alone provides. Only this name, through its privative meaning, points the question concerning the more originary experience of truth in the direction of an originary concealment. Aristotle becomes—as no later type of metaphysics is able to—the impetus to take the way back through Greek philosophy in order to find the trace of the experience of concealment in its origin. Heidegger finds this trace solely in the Heraclitean dictum about φύσις, which tends to conceal itself. The concealment to be heard in unconcealment is based on a self-concealing of what Heidegger still calls 'Being'. Thought incipiently, φύσις testifies to this: the sense of Being, which in the whole of the history of metaphysics is *Anwesen*, has opposed to it not merely absence but rather a more originary making-absent, letting-be-forgotten. In this sense prevails a reticence, an ἐποχή, a self-withdrawing on the part of Being itself. Being withholds itself as itself from thinking, withholds from thinking its proper topic, in order to direct thinking to the Being of beings—in the end to the expropriated being under the sway of the nature of technicity. Out of this sway technical thinking emerges as the descendent of metaphysical thinking.

By its own testimony Heideggerian thought unfolds solely in the recollection of the "nature of truth" as it is announced in the name ἀλήθεια. This thought comes into its own precisely at the point where the question concerning the sense of Being turns into the question concerning the truth of Being. With this shift, practical philosophy, insofar as it takes its point of departure from Aristotle, is dismissed, never to be seen again. Let us consider this more closely.

The "Letter on Humanism" mentions the desire for an ethics that confronted *Being and Time* (*BH*, 349/231), one Heidegger expressly rejected as an unreasonable demand. In what he considers as ἦθος, a practical philosophy cannot appear. And yet, is it not the case that while working out *Being and Time* he read the *Nicomachean Ethics* intensely? But what of it? As can be expected from the foregoing, he focused his attention entirely on the elucidation of the modes of ἀληθεύειν, touching only marginally on the proper topic of practical science in an ethics or politics. This topic is, however, the "human good," its architectonic structure and, in accordance with their guiding intentions, the correspondingly differentiated modes of human life—this topic has the scope of εὐδαιμονία (happiness). Who would claim that εὐδαιμονία has any significance for the analytic of Da-sein?

Indeed of significance for such an analytic is that mode of ἀληθεύειν which φρόνησις is—yet only insofar as φρόνησις can be translated as 'care' (*Sorge*). Although *Being and Time* does come into contact with the *Nicomachean Ethics* in this respect, the principal difference must not be overlooked: the disclosedness characteristic of Da-sein knows no τέλος as cause or as principle, let alone the "theoretical life." Along with the architectonic of principles falls that of the "human good" and the modes of life corresponding to it. Instead of a final cause in the sense of the practical best, death is determinative in Da-sein. Thus what remains of the preference of what is better, which is essential to πρᾶξις, i.e., what remains of προαίρεσις, is only a temporally-stamped protention (*Vorhabe*)—pervaded by the anticipation of death as the unoutstrippable possibility, unoutstrippable because death is the denial of a future. When for Da-sein in its Being this Being itself is at stake, then this "for-the-sake-of-which" (*Worum-willen*) is absolutely no longer a good—let alone a highest value.

This Being—never thinkable as a first principle or, more generally, as a ratio—which is understood in Da-sein and which is "sub-rational," is and remains irrevocably finite; this Being is disclosed in attunement as nothingness and in fact in anxiety. This is not a nothingness of beings but rather of the world of being-in-the-world. Thus it is a nothingness of the sole understandable Being as such. If for thinking—to use a phrase from Heidegger taken from Hölderlin—"the trial has passed through the knees," then by way of the non-disposable anxiety that paralyzes, with the sinking of the world, even a non-metaphysically closed action in itself. It is precisely with respect to the disclosedness of death that *Being and Time* no longer knows the distinction between 'good' and 'bad', let alone between 'good' and 'evil', and thus has left behind what Hegel terms the 'judgment of the concept'. By contrast, the lived experience of values nevertheless remains *sub omnibus canonibus* both of rational comprehension and of the understanding characteristic of Da-sein. *Being and Time* certainly asserts a distinction between 'inauthentic' and 'authentic'. Yet such merely heralds the event of appropriation.

The question concerning the sense of Being initially confines itself to the understanding of that Being at issue for Da-sein. But Heidegger's recollection of the nature of truth comes up against an originary untruth that lets Da-sein be experienced as yet out-standing because it is denied by Being itself. This originary untruth is of an historical character and pulls the ground out from under the phenomenological analytic of Da-sein. But when Being becomes no longer ascertainable through the understanding characteristic of Da-sein, the question concerning its sense also loses its footing. It collapses into the question concerning the "truth of Being" as it is to be experienced historically and in fact in the history of withdrawal which metaphysics proves to be. The anxiety of thinking not only detaches itself from the death as-it-is-solely-mine (*jemeinige Tod*) but it also detaches itself—to speak with Nietzsche—from the historically experienced death of God; anxiety is transformed into the experience of an historical calamity, in fact of the calamity of thinking and its topic. How is this experience to be attained by a practical philosophy? Least of all by way of an ethics that serves the desires of the contemporary public domain.

Heidegger foresaw in the "Letter on Humanism" the pressure of the public's desires. Hegel says at one point: philosophy must refrain from the desire to be edifying. There is no need for this today. Nevertheless, the warning is fitting: philosophy must refrain from the desire to be agreeable. Therefore, let us listen to the relevant passage: "The desire for an ethics presses ever more ardently for fulfillment as the obvious no less than the hidden perplexity of man soars to immeasurable heights. The greatest care must be fostered upon the ethical bond at a time when technological man, delivered over to mass society, can be kept reliably on call only by gathering and ordering all his plans and activities in a way that corresponds to technicity" (*BH*, 349/231 f.). Not only has Heidegger no intention of satisfying this desire. He leaves it to technical thinking, from which his own thinking is distinct *toto coelo*—or better, by a whole world.

This distinction draws the following cuts in thinking itself: disputation is cut off insofar as it belongs to the critical business of "minds"—this cheapest way of performing philosophical critique through idiosyncrasy. Then the effect that no longer disputes is cut off—an effect on others, especially on later generations as it is portrayed by hermeneutics as the effective history of thought in the hope of securing duration for itself through the exertion of its influence. But then even action is cut off, namely, the active preference of the better—especially the familiar realization of everyone's own predilections in the field of thinking. What remains is simply this: to be, and in fact to be within itself, as was familiar to that reason involved with itself. With the next cut, however, even this mode of Being is abandoned. Such is necessitated by the experience of the nothingness of all beings and even of the highest, which has been spirit.

Thus only 'naturing' (*wesen*) remains, and no longer 'being' (*sein*). It is precisely this cut that the recollection of the nature of truth makes with its turn into the truth of naturing. Such marks the parting from previous thinking, even from Plotinian metaphysics. And Heidegger makes another cut by taking the verbally understood '*wesen*' (to nature), namely, the present mode of the mission of all history, of the mission of any stamp of Being, back into truth itself as "reserving" (*Wahren*); this is a desheltering that is simultaneously a sheltering. And yet there is one more cut: the reserving is also taken back in favor of appropriation. It is precisely here that this purification of intention, which carries the Heideggerian sense-explication, reaches its extreme and simultaneously attains its proper abode. An ἦθος far removed from any ethics. If there were going to be an "ethics," then of which thinking?

The "Letter on Humanism" begins: "We are still far from pondering the nature of action decisively enough" (*BH*, 311/193)—even after reading the *Nicomachean Ethics*, the *pars secunda* of the *Summa Theologiae*, and the theory of objective spirit in the *Encyclopaedia of the Philosophical Sciences* for ten years. Still far from pondering decisively enough—even after the intense reading of *Being and Time*. The "nature of action is accomplishment" (ibid.). Did Aristotle not already know this? Indeed. But how? In the horizon of science and thus of the knowledge of principles and causes. Precisely within this horizon he distinguishes between science as theoretical, as practical, and as poietical; here he cognizes for πρᾶξις itself the distinctions and the hierarchy of the modes of life, holding the theoretical mode to be the best. And what is the topic of θεωρία? First of all that being which requires no movement because it is with itself as the best and, as the immovable, is the cause of the best movement, namely, that of the heavens.

The nature of action is accomplishment. This is in turn a thinking. Is it θεωρία? In Heidegger's case—and this is in general the case of modernity, namely, the case of Dilthey, Frege, and Marx, then of Husserl, Schlick, and Nietzsche, and, finally, of Wittgenstein and Kuhn—strictly speaking, no. Which thinking is accomplishment and thus the nature of action? Exactly the one purifying itself and therein a thinking released into appropriating. This thinking "accomplishes this relation of Being to the nature of man" (ibid.), thus to Da-sein. Precisely this relation is the event of appropriation. The nature of action is either no action or else the action of that thinking which brings the aforementioned relation to speech. To build speech as the house of Being, to take up residence in its ἦθος, is its sole action. What for? Not for that which one each time intends in acting but rather for that which is human dwelling. No ethical science is formed there but rather a peculiar "ecology."

In order to bring its structure and thus the place of dwelling clearly into view, let us turn once again to the opening words of the "Letter on Humanism." Accomplishing thinking "does not make or cause" the correlation of Being and the nature of man. "Thinking only offers this correlation with Being as something transmitted to it from Being. Such offering consists in the fact that in thinking, Being comes to speech" (ibid.). Here we recall into view Heidegger's mature thought: the question concerning the sense of Being was taken back to the experience of the truth of Being. This experience, however, is finally condensed into the focus on ἀλήθεια as "the clearing, the desheltering of the self-withdrawing authorization" (*GA* 13, 224). The clearing is the appropriation of that giving. With Being, it shares only finitude.

Should we suppress what is thought here due to a lack of immediate comprehensibility? Why should it not for its part lay claim to ten years of learning? And what comes to light therein? Let's wait and see. And if the ἦθος of Heideggerian thought, namely, the said clearing, appears strange, then this is also to be read as a sign and not to be covered up.

In the first place the clearing is of a linguistic character. Its finitude becomes audible as the stillness of speech itself. The failing donation of the summoning names lets one attend, in the midst of the business of information, to the primacy of stillness, which only the corresponding word breaks. Then the clearing is of a mundane character. Here also the withholding of things or their neglect lets one attend to the remoteness out of which alone the things are able to approach. Finally the clearing is of an historical character. Once again, the withdrawal of that which gives and has given what is to be thought, namely, the contemporary lack of mission, makes one think of what is reserved, incipiently sheltered.

Thinking corresponds to this tripartite clearing firstly as historical, that is: as anticipatory commemoration—concentrated on the parting from its first beginning, that of metaphysics, because through the experience of withdrawal it is directed to the other beginning of a more incipient thinking of a future destiny. Then waiting thinking is a listening because it is called to build in the sphere of speech. Finally corresponding thinking is stamped with a mundane character because it is claimed by the remoteness of the failing world of the thing.

Precisely this world is the first topic of thinking and in fact as obstructed by the nature of technicity. It denies with Da-sein the being-in-the-world in which dwelling is founded—not action but rather dwelling as the nature of man. This state of affairs is then historically determined and in fact by the sole history of metaphysics, which closes itself in the world determined by the nature of technicity. Finally it is only the speech in which the other world of the thing, of the fourfold which is gathered by the thing, makes its advent. This is the speech of a thinking that knows itself in the neighborhood of poetizing and hears from it that man dwells poetically. This dwelling is that of the mortals.—Thus far we have given the most concise outline of the Heideggerian ἦθος and in fact in terms of Heidegger's own "destiny of the topic of thinking."

Poetic dwelling of the mortals in a world which is present in speech only. Of which mortals? This is to ask: of which death? Obviously not in the sense of the necessary perishing of all animals. Thought in the sense of Da-sein and its There (*Da*), its openness, its clearing: precisely that possible and accomplished death which attests to the sheltering character of truth thought originarily. And how does its sheltering manifest itself? Let us pause to consider first the world in which alone the mortal is able to achieve his mortality. Obviously not by his own efforts, for the world is not that of spirit, let alone the one constituted by the productions of the Husserlian pure ego, but rather the world which the thing gathers into a fourfold of earth and heaven, divinities and mortals.

Men become mortals only through a distinction of themselves from themselves. A distinction of what kind? Should their definition change? If in accordance with the Aristotelian directive the definition is "the explanation that explains what something was destined to be" (ὁ λόγος ὁ τὸ τί ἦν εἶναι λέγων; *Metaph.* 1016^{a}33), then it must be said: 'the mortal' is no definition of man, if only because no γένος such as "living creature" includes it along with the immortals or with those destined to perish. The mortal of the fourfold stands not only outside of that λόγος which the definition is, but even outside of that λόγος which specifies the defined man. He does not even distinguish himself from ζῷον λόγον ἔχον but only from the *animal rationale mortale* as it has degenerated into the "working animal"—as such it has already forsaken the *genus* 'living animal' and thus its kinship with the immortals; forsaken by the immortals, its *rationalitas* is only that of work. In what respect?

Labor improbus. Work of itself is not to be valued as something good. It is a means and is such still in that sphere of metaphysics in which work is the formation of self-consciousness and the mediated movement of the pure concept to the absolute idea. Through the architectonic of the system, this work (thought teleologically) remained related to that πρᾶξις which Aristotle entrusts to the knowledge of first principles and causes. Wherever a supreme principle and a final Why is lacking, all action as well as all production withers to mere work. What motivates it is ultimately—thought with Heidegger—no longer the will to power but rather the vain nothingness (*nichtiges Nichts*) of the will, of the reason-forsaken will to itself, of the will to the will—testimony of νοησέως νόησις sunk into irrationality. The distinction of the mortals from working animals is thus grounded in a distinction of nothingness itself as it is on the one hand the vain nothingness and on the other the nothingness of the sheltering death. This distinction once again refers to that truth which was Heidegger's sole concern. It is in relation to this that the ἦθος of the mortal is to be understood. Again: it excludes an ethical science. This all the more so as Heidegger felt obliged to part with philosophy in general. Although it may be unpleasant to hear: the "Letter on Humanism" already says this and the later lecture on the task of thinking still says this. What help are evasions via equivocations?

Again: how does the sheltering of death manifest itself, a death on the basis of which men are mortals? Heidegger leaves this in the dark—as well as the dead, who at least formerly were constitutive of the world of dwelling; all the more so as building created the distinguished places of the dead. Is the speechlessness in question due to the fact that "speech"—in Heidegger's experience—"withdraws from man its simple and high manner of speaking" (*BWD*, 142/148)? We recall here the simple and high activity of reason, of which Aristotle speaks with regard to the being that is as simple as it is supreme.

In originary untruth, sheltering remains dark; this is shown by Heidegger's appeal to homestead (*Heimat*) and steadfastness (*Bodenständigkeit*). By contrast, its self-concealing becomes manifest and in fact in the Heideggerian experience of the reversal in Being itself. By withdrawing itself from even beings, the things are left to themselves. In their neglect, it dawns on thinking "that the things have never yet at all been able to appear to thinking as things" (*D*, 163/171) because they are veiled by a Being that conceals itself by desheltering them as beings. But when with the twilight of metaphysics even the Being of beings no longer provokes thinking, then not only does the thing and its world fail to appear but the world of the nature of technicity also deforms the thing into a piece of available stock, which this world is. Here for thinking, sheltering remains only as the other of the setting-upon, challenging desheltering proper to the nature of technicity. Dwelling in the world of the fourfold can be envisioned only in a world-isolated remainder, namely, in the Black Forest farmhouse. Such a vision, however, can provide building with even less guidance since historicity is peripheral to such an edifice.

If we are called upon to learn dwelling, then how? How does it become possible to devote thinking to dwelling and to build on the basis of such a thinking? How is learning to think possible here when "the things have never yet at all been able to appear to thinking as things"—thus not even the world which is gathered in them? Can the hint of the Black Forest farmhouse really give what is to be thought? Is there really a view here that would give what is to be thought, to say nothing of what is to be learned?

Is the jug, whose world Heidegger discloses, present? Certainly not. Since it cannot be encountered as a thing. Why not? Because of the technically determined desheltering. How did Heidegger think of the jug? Attached to a poetically anticipated world: not in our world, not in its history, but rather solely in their speech. Which one? In that which he called the "house of Being." Is it possible, however, to learn thinking as poetizing building? Must it not be learned when dwelling is—to speak with Hölderlin—a poetic dwelling? And what justifies Heidegger in taking up this word thinkingly? Or is one off the track in thus questioning while on a path of thinking?

Learning to think. Once again, are we to read Aristotle for ten years? No. Yet we are to take up that which alone is notable of Heideggerian thought: ἀλήθεια, and with it the question concerning the sheltering in that which conceals itself. In this regard we are once again to consider metaphysical thinking—in Heidegger's thought we are to observe the directive to make a "second voyage" (δεύ–τερος πλοῦς) for ten years through the history of metaphysics as a whole. No longer concentrated on the first beginning—in view of which Heidegger stepped back in the attempt to evoke the other beginning—but rather on the totality of a history, concluding its beginning (*incipit*), middle, and end. More precisely, on the con-clusion of the epochs as indicated by the incipient thought (*isqui primum capit*) of Parmenides, of Augustine, and of Hegel. In what sense 'incipient'? Obviously not in the sense of a temporal succession but rather of the *prin-cipia* in which the conceptions of reason are accomplished. In what sense? Metaphysical reason was literally philo-sophical reason; that is, one that saw and accomplished each time the task of sheltering the truth of a σοφία, one not brought forth by this reason itself, in a logic and thus of conceiving it such that it becomes certain to everyone who accepts reason. The mission of history becomes perspicuous in the reception of a type of σοφία. The ambiguous talk of the end of metaphysics takes on its singular determinacy here precisely due to the fact that its reason has departed in the knowledge: it is accomplished. The sheltering of the truth concerning the vision of man's distinction from himself—as set forth by Homer–Hesiod–Solon, by the Synoptics–Paul–John, and by Rousseau–Schiller–Hölderlin—has been accomplished. If death is the shrine of nothingness, then what does it shelter? That history which metaphysics is, contains the types of that sheltering reason which was in each instance capable of a so-called death upon its having accomplished its task, fulfilled its destiny.

The history of this metaphysical thinking knows no transition to technical thinking and its world. This world has articulated itself completely as the world of modernity through its sense-explications—each time testifying to its having been severed from that history. Our world, however, cannot be uniformly articulated. In the sense-explication within the realm of the doxic presentations of life, within the sciences, within the scope of the productive nature of man, different types of reason assert themselves in the transformations of what was formerly conceptual, natural, and mundane reason; they become hermeneutic, technical, and apocalyptic reason, respectively.

The explicated world of modernity is in the first place as much the technical world as the lifeworld. In this Janus-form, this world lacks a destiny and denies with the predominant lack of distance precisely that remoteness out of which alone—as Heidegger saw—the thing and its world may approach. In the world of modernity the corresponding future is expected only on this side of the specter of philosophy and in fact precisely where the thought of a future, of an apocalyptically determined, distinction of man from himself—an afterglow of σοφία—is reinstated—with the advent of the communist society, the masters of the earth, the mortal. In this way the remoteness of the world itself is preserved in the other region of dwelling. However, if the world of modernity is in its explication every bit as concluded (because it is complete) as is its history, then the expectation of the other future fades. It has faded, as is obvious today in view of the communist society. The modern will-o'-the-wisps of what σοφία has been for the Occident die out.

Having shed their future, the projections of Marx, Nietzsche, and Heidegger urge the corresponding reason towards the discharge of its temporality. Not only "Being and time" but even more "time and Being" is a theme of dwindling significance. However, the thought of poetic dwelling takes on a new face, for speech reveals that stillness which the word had already broken. Which word? The reply "the spoken word of poetry" no longer holds. It already ceased to do so as soon as the selection of the poetized was questioned concerning the basis of its distinction. Its historical place, and even more its mundane place, had to remain without clear determinacy. In particular, the reference to poetizing as τέχνη and the contrasting of the fine arts with technicity in mundane significance indeed remained a welcome but rather misleading association, which then could escape only into a questioning—for want of what might be heard.

The stillness is to be entered with no word of one's own choosing. What was spoken in it is already decided: the words of the configurations of wisdom, to which conceptual reason has corresponded. All the words that aroused the question: who is speaking? "Speech speaks" is no answer to this but only an omen. Legible only in cognizance of the aforementioned history of metaphysics. It cannot be one's concern to bring back the departed types of reason out of this history. Not even an Orpheus would be capable of such. These types remain within themselves, that is: converted into what they accomplished, what they completed. We no longer know a truth that desires to be sheltered in a certainty. The logic characteristic of our world is and remains technical.

Which other truth, one without need of certainty, is to be gathered from the spoken word of the configurations of wisdom? Heidegger's recollection of the nature of truth provided the direction. Back to the difference between sheltering and self-concealing. But this beginning is released only when the will-o'-the-wisp of φύσις κρύπθεσται φιλεῖ is extinguished. As the earliest philosophy knows φύσις, it is a concept strictly related to that appearing with which observation remains concerned. Φύσις is essence—which Aristotle still made clear, for example, in his treatise *On the Heavens*, where he speaks not about the whole of Nature but rather about the nature of the whole.

It is precisely not the self-concealing of φύσις that discloses the originary understanding of the privative sense of ἀλήθεια; rather, such emerges from the transitive sense of λήθειν. Here reason is affected first and foremost. Accordingly what is at stake with the ἀλήθεια of saying, as in the case of communicating knowledge, is the granted or barred participation in knowledge (*con-scientia*) and in fact with respect to the reliance of any knowledge on the attention to (*Anwesen bei*) what is there to be known. An *Anwesen* precisely not in the sense of the appearance or manifestation of something but rather in that of attentiveness and even devotion to it.

The communication of knowledge respects a limit, namely, the difference between what one is and is not entitled to know. It is precisely on account of this that αἰδώς (reverence) is to be understood in the relations of the mortals to their likes, to the immortals, and to the dead. Fundamental to dwelling, it is just this reverence to which technical thinking—that is, the unconcealment characteristic of it—has to be indifferent, for its kind of thinking does not allow of the distinction between what one is and is not entitled to know. Yet it is by no means technical thinking that causes the corresponding publicity of unrestrained publication. The lack of restraint and even of distance experienced by Heidegger, that failing of remoteness in the technical world as well as in the lifeworld, has to come to hold sway because the spoken word of the epochal configurations of wisdom has been swept away into the departedness of their philo-sophical conceptions.

Heidegger reproached even Homer for having spoken in the manner of enunciations (*Aussagen*), for not having attained the naming that calls and upon which the thinking neighboring on poetizing waits. Within the bounds of modernity Heidegger has to remain deaf to the Aristotelian hint that Homer's speaking first and foremost either praises or reviles and thus respects the difference between what is not to be and yet is, and what is to be. It is precisely with regard to this difference that Homer is an expert concerning the ἦθος and its pertinent dwelling; thus he is a σοφός and a teacher. And Aristotle sees also: the Homeric account is a building of a "dramatic" architectonic. Architectonic reason becomes not merely a neighbor but rather a guardian of this architectonic.

Homer teaches dwelling by bringing it into view in an authoritative manner for the first epoch of our history. Such is not possible for Heidegger. Is he able to teach the thinking devoted to dwelling and even the corresponding building? For such he lacks a reason with architectonic significance.

On a Neapolitan building a word belonging to the middle epoch of our history remains silent: *sapientia aedificavit sibi domum.* Wisdom has built a home for itself. Even the house of the world. The edifice of wisdom offered a dwelling. In an accomplishing action, its spoken word brought a dwelling to light which is in itself inconspicuous. From the accomplished action, it was possible to learn dwelling.

Yet not only σοφία but also φιλοσοφία has been a teacher. There is a philosophy—different from the philosophy of appearances—that has taught by taking care of beings and thus of things. Within the bounds of modernity, thus of our world, Heidegger experienced that the annihilation of things "has happened and continues to happen so thoroughly that not only are things no longer admitted as things, but that the things have never yet at all been able to appear to thinking as things" (*D*, 163/171). So it seems so long as the continuum of metaphysical and technical thinking is not torn asunder. It is so torn with the excavation of philo-sophical history as a concluded history. There it becomes clear: the things have appeared to thinking indeed as things, have obviously taken on their historical determinacy from thinking, because they have been thought specifically with reference to a perfection that is proper to each thing. It is on account of this that they were destined to be beautiful. Our history is replete with examples of beauty, i.e., of things that testify to their destiny of perfection.

The "judgment of the concept" has authoritatively molded the formation of the things in our history—embracing even the characteristic things of dwelling: first in favor of the dwelling of the immortals and of the dead: temple and grave; then in favor of the dwelling of the mortals: the edifices of political as well as of familial dwelling; finally in favor of the things of daily use, such as bed and table. The thought to which the things appeared precisely as things has answered to them with their formation according to beauty.

Speech—more precisely: the spoken word of the epochal configurations of wisdom that accomplishes speech—opens up the view to the accomplishments of the dead of our history because it opens up the view to the accomplished conceptions—to the reason which departed with them. Having come into the open of the corresponding recognition, we breathe a sigh of relief—in the wake of the phantasmata of an oppressive memory.

THE LIMIT OF MODERNITY AND HEIDEGGER'S "LEGACY"

As is well-known the talk of 'modern'—having meanwhile also grown old—always had a distinguishing sense; it set a present mentality and its constructs off from a previous and at the same traditional one; for the former as well as the latter fell in the same time. But what if an age is itself distinguished as "the" modernity, while with respect to the latter the repetition of such a distinction is failing? A mere post-modernity testifies only to a succession of times, without letting "the" modernity pass away as a temporary one. Should it thereby fear becoming in turn unmodern? Why is "the" modernity not also subjected to that historical distinguishing proper to it? Might the "stream" of history thereby silt up?

A modernity in singular significance has become apparent. What is singular about it? This is to be gathered only from its delimitation. That drawing up of limits seems, however—at least with regard to its historical beginning—to be arbitrary. For it is not available as an historial fact; rather, such facts are assigned to it and thus allow of description always only secondarily. Sustained by an anticipatory decision. Thus, for instance, by the decision according to which the emancipatory program of the Enlightenment must finally be fulfilled; it is for its sake then that "the" modernity is not yet allowed to—and only for that reason: cannot—be at an end.

Modernity is no datum that could be limited in itself. It derives its limitation only from what it may be for someone, for many. According to which measure? On the basis of the need of many or of most? Or dependent upon the predilections of the socially progressive forces which still require modernity's impulse?

Or should we think: "the" modernity is an *ens rationis*? Perhaps '*ens*' is still saying too much—or too little. At any rate, it should be asked: which ratio? Yours? Mine? A faculty of many men? Of all? Provided that it can no longer be assumed that reason comes to us from the contemplation of the celestial order or as a gift from the creative God or as a predisposition "of Nature in her wise provision for us," provided that our reason does not know itself on the basis of any such cause, it is appropriate to take it back to a ratio, to a proportion constituted of precisely those terms which the Heideggerian phrase 'the destiny of the topic of thinking' provides. In isolation from the phylogenetic explicability of the understanding.

Our *Rational Architectonic of Modernity*, which is built of the differentiated ratios of these terms, testifies in a renewing transformation to the traditional characteristic of reason to think totalities, to be the faculty of conclusion. Modernity, which is explicitly represented as an *ens rationis*, is a closed construct of sense-explications into which our world has been completely articulated. The private view of an ἴδιος κόσμος? All the same, it arose from modernity itself. How?

The view to the rational architectonic of modernity was first opened by our *Topology of Metaphysics* and in fact because the history of that world of the modern sense-explication proved in turn to be a closed construct—a history which was articulated into First Philosophy and its other. It came into view as a result of the transformation of Heidegger's question 'What is metaphysics?'—freeing the latter from the continuum with technical thinking; therefore, no longer determined to leave metaphysics to itself (*ZS*, 25/24) but rather in a position to leave it to its self and thus to let it be. But how does this situation arise if not from some unfounded fancy? How does it border the locality of modernity, in particular the place that the Heideggerian sense-explication created? How does it remain mindful of his "legacy"? Yet does not the word also hold here with which Aristotle begins his *Posterior Analytics*: "Every intellectual teaching and every learning proceeds from a knowledge which was provided in advance" (*APo.* 71^{a}1)?

Heidegger's legacy is contracted into this sole task: "To say ἀλήθεια as: the clearing" (*GA* 13, 224). Not merely ἀλήθεια—it was already brought to speech—not merely the clearing—it has not yet come to speech—but rather the clearing as it can be brought to speech alone with respect to ἀλήθεια. For that, however, the experience of the Greek name first had to be regained. This on the basis of the sole necessity of an experience of the neglecting desheltering under the sway of the nature of technicity.

The way to the truth of this "nature" was opened by Heidegger's recollection (*Besinnung*) of the nature of truth, with its sequence from correctness via unconcealment to originary concealedness. It is only with respect to the concealment prevailing in that concealedness that the sense of the aforementioned bringing-to-speech of the clearing is disclosed: "The desheltering of the self-withdrawing authorization" (ibid.). It is precisely this that first claimed Heideggerian thought by its own testimony—with the dignity of what was a principle for metaphysical reason.

Desheltering—no longer of beings, no longer of the Being of beings, no longer of the "first grounds and causes"; for desheltering is just as little that of thinking as is the preceding self-concealing. It is—in oblique talk, since it steals a glance at the theory of the Being of beings—that of Being itself; put more purely: of the event of the appropriation of Being and thinking. Here desheltering is first of all that of the "mission of Being" (*Seins-Geschick*)—of a mission possessing a fundamental "epochal" trait, that is to say: desheltering of a self-concealing, of a withholding of Being itself from thinking. It is precisely on account of this that thinking is let loose so as to deshelter being, that is to say: as metaphysical thinking, to deshelter only the Being of beings finally as technical thinking: mere beings. It is precisely in this respect that the desheltering of Being itself is the revelation of its character of withdrawal.

What withdraws itself from whom? In the sense of the event of the appropriation of Being and thinking, the "authorization" withdraws itself. At its extreme (ἔσχατον) the withdrawal awakens the recollection which distinguishes itself from technical thinking as the absolutely unauthorized one. The tearing open of the difference is owed to a "turning" in the mission of Being. Technicity deshelters its concealing, its disguising "nature," and with respect to the latter the entire history of withdrawal as the history of metaphysics. So much in memory of Heidegger's legacy—with no attempt at explanation.

Which is authorized thinking? That which was given its topic. Again Heidegger: metaphysical thinking was given the desheltering of the Being of beings; the other thinking over against this one is given the awareness of the self-concealing and the withdrawal in precisely that desheltering, ultimately and simultaneously first in technical desheltering. In the Greek beginning of thinking, it notices a trace of the experience of self-concealing and in fact at the point where ἀλήθεια is thought as φύσις in the sense of emerging. It "tends to conceal itself." Faced with this testimony by Heraclitus, our ways have parted, and in fact with the distinction of λήθειν in ἀλήθεια from the κρύπτεσθαι of φύσις (cf. my "The Early Greek Usage of the Words *Logos* and *Aletheia*"). But it is only the occasion, not the reason, for our departure from Heidegger, for our transgression of the limit of his place. Where does this reason appear?

I

As ἀλήθεια was earlier given voice, it draws attention to the transitive sense of λήθειν, on which ἀλήθεια is based—already different thereby from concealing as κρύπτειν. It calls to mind the possibility of the refusal to let someone know what is already known, eliciting the question concerning the authorization for shared knowledge. But how could metaphysical thinking be affected by that?

To attend to the "first beginning" on which the Heideggerian departure concentrates in the "other beginning": how does it commence then? What is the "mission" in the sense of that ἀλήθεια? A completely open "mystery." The beginning sighted with Heidegger—its trace (preserved in self-concealing) of the originary withholding, or the "epoch," which destines thinking to be metaphysical—is a result. In what way?

The *Topology of Metaphysics* has shown: this is to be understood in the strictest sense as philo-sophy—related to a σοφία whose truth philosophy itself did not produce. Wisdom—such is generally speaking: knowledge of the destiny of man, of a destiny which he fulfills only insofar as he distinguishes himself from himself—as hero, as saint, as citizen. On the other hand, his distinction from other animals is secondary; it falls—spoken with Plato—in the non-delimitability of the "more and less."

However, for the σοφία with respect to which φιλοσοφία commences, the following holds: it knows "how it is" in the open of the difference between "how it is not to be" and "how it is to be." This knowledge is given to the "wise," namely, to Homer, Hesiod, and Solon, and in fact by the Muses as those who know as such because they attend to everything.

On the basis of the knowledge of what one is entitled to know, one is authorized to let the truth be known or not. For the aforementioned σοφοί the knowledge in question is merely given to them, not based on their attention (*Anwesen*) to the topic. Philo-sophy arises precisely when πειθώ (persuasiveness) withdrew itself from the truth of what is known by virtue of the Muses' letting-know. This withdrawal calls that reason forth which, in keeping with the conditions of "mortal" perception, is itself able to attend to everything. On the basis of the knowledge to be cultivated by it, this type of presence takes on the meaning of ἱστορεῖν, of observing. Such views everything in terms of the distinction between "how it appears" and "how it is"; in its gaze it explicitly fixes the φύσις of what appears; with respect to φύσις, the reason in question is "natural." It is such not at all in the sense of the unquestioningly repeated presumption that philosophy initially took an interest in that Nature which is always already there, namely, in the All of what occurs naturally. Early Greek thinking does not know such a Nature, and Aristotle will instead continue to talk of the "Nature of the All" (cf. my "What is *Physis*?").

If that incipiently thought φύσις tends to conceal itself in what appears, its concealment is nevertheless essentially different from precisely that which precedes ἀλήθεια. For natural reason the possibility of a λήθειν is of dwindling significance—as much as is the ἀλήθεια of letting-know. Nor is there any talk of it in pre-Parmenidean philosophy. For everyone can himself attend to what is there to be known here. The All of natural reason is no longer that about which the Muses know; rather, it is determined on the basis of the former's own attention. Thus as observing, it also stamps the manner of exhibition, rejects with the σοφία "metrical" discourse as it corresponds to the knowledge of the "Muses" and becomes "prosaic."

Natural reason is not concerned with ἀλήθεια but rather with the σαφές, with the perspicacity, of the φύσις within what appears. Due to its self-concealing, it will never be reached, and instead of knowledge, opinions of endlessly increasing probability are attained. Here σοφία consists in acknowledging the difference between the knowledge of the gods and the opinions of the mortals to be insurmountable.

The "first beginning" of thinking is not just one; rather, due to the distinction of the reason called forth by the said withdrawal, it is a twofold beginning and thus there has never been only *one* history of philosophy (cf. "The Distinction of Reason," pp. 101-109 above).

Have we lost sight of the limit of modernity? Certainly not—if Heidegger's claim that for metaphysical thinking the sense of Being was regarded as *Anwesen* (being-present) and if today the latecomers abiding by this claim endeavor to expunge the "privilege of presence"—without a clue about the incipient wrong or right of this privilege and about the necessity of thinking *Anwesen* with determinacy and thus with distinction.

In the construction of its ratio, natural reason takes its starting point from its own attention in distinguishing between what appears and its φύσις; the other, namely, "mundane" reason, starts with the presence of its topic. Which is it? Perhaps what appears? This only in its totality. And how is its presence determined for reason? As κόσμος. Present here is: not just what appears but rather its κόσμος, further: the harmony of this κόσμος, finally: the λόγος of this harmony. From this it already follows: being-present and appearing must certainly be distinguished. This all the more so as the κόσμος is a κόσμος only on the basis of the opposition of the φύσεις of what appears or on the basis of a φύσις that acts contrarily. The corresponding thinking understands itself no longer immediately as observing but rather as an entry into the harmony of the principle from which the order of appearances arises.

In this regard the wisdom of mundane reason is on its view the knowledge of the possibility open to everyone: on the one hand, that he himself take on reason, that he establish the pregiven order in his polity; on the other hand, as a mortal who has attained reason, that he gain the life of the immortals.

In natural as well as in mundane reason, an inclination grows for the wisdom that it itself yields. For an accompanying thinking, the latter draws its persuasiveness on the one hand from its own attentiveness to "how it is"—as far as the φύσις of what appears can be disclosed—on the other hand, from the presence of a "how it is to be," which is pregiven in the κόσμος of what appears.

It is only with a third type of reason, "conceptual reason," that ἀλήθεια comes to bear in the beginning of philo-sophy; for here a letting-know is necessary for what is first to be thought—similar to that of the Muses. Of concern here is a directive that gives what is to be thought in such an exceptional manner that it brings thinking first of all onto the sole path of accomplishing, that it becomes the destiny for thinking. Thinking finds itself at a crossroads; its place is the House of the Night, of Death. Here "how it is" is no longer—as φύσις—to be distinguished from "how it appears" but rather solely from "how it is not." Faced with this forking of the paths of "how it is" and "how it is not," the possibility of a λήθειν remains excluded. It is precisely with regard to this that ἀλήθεια assumes a different sense and in fact from the middle form of that verb, which is usually rendered as 'to forget'. The House of Death is then also regarded as the "House of Oblivion."

Yet in what sense does the letting-know on the part of the Parmenidean "goddess"—she calls to mind the first verse of the *Iliad*—bring ἀλήθεια to bear? What is its "heart"? That reason must not deceive itself, as is the case with respect to the views—those that have "necessarily come to be esteemed"—of the mortals. They are incapable of escaping their errancy by their own efforts because their reason is not capable of distinguishing itself by its own efforts, for the force of habit fetters reason to presence—not only its attentiveness to everything, in its quest for "how it is" in the φύσεις of what appears; what is more, it is "violated" by the presence of "how it is to be" in the form of the κόσμος, which arises from the contrary φύσεις of what appears. The views in question cannot dissociate themselves from the eye and ear and tongue.

Even as philosophical, the reason of the mortals leaves itself in the dark about the errancy that must be its place. Λήθεσθαι—instead of this, Plato still usually says: λήθειν ἑαυτόν: to deceive oneself. Only a divine letting-know of ἀλήθεια as the destiny of thinking brings that reason into the open; ἀλήθεια is such in the previously decided separateness of "how it is" and "how it is not" as the "sole paths of inquiry." No story is told here but rather thinking is brought onto the sole path of its own accomplishing and in precisely this sense is removed from λήθεσθαι, from so-called forgetting. The path of "how it is" is as a path the one of that thinking which persuades itself through pure reflection—here βουλή becomes λόγος—through its distinction. From the signs of this path, it becomes aware of "how it is to be": that which is perfect. 'To be' in this sense—it first becomes the topic of thinking for the incipient form of "conceptual" reason, that is, Parmenidean reason—is not only nothing that appears but also no longer anything present, because it is isolated from every relation to what appears, a relation that is essential to presence. Rather, the pure present of the destiny as it was familiar in the knowledge of the Muses is exhibited in that which "is" perfect. Conceptual reason sheltered "that which fulfills itself" in Homer, Hesiod, and Solon in "that which is perfect."

In light of the threefold beginning of philo-sophy, how are matters regarding Heidegger's continuously reconsidered assurance: from the beginning of metaphysical thinking, the sense of Being is *Anwesen*? And how about the prior view: ἀλήθεια is "incipiently conceived as a fundamental character of φύσις" (*GA* 65, 329)—on account of its self-concealing? Corrections make no sense here, but this does: to clear up what has been thought—set on its way by the metaphysics which has been left to its self: listening to it with a releasement that becomes possible only beyond that sense-explication of modernity which is concerned with the separation of the future man from the previous one.

What becomes of the "desheltering of the self-withdrawing authorization" in this connection? It withdrew itself from the "first beginning" of thinking. What does this still mean in light of the distinction of this beginning as presented here? If thinking is to be an authorized one, then it holds for natural reason: thinking authorizes itself and precisely because of this may be unauthorized—for mundane reason: thinking takes its authorization from its topic and in fact via the middle term of its governing principle, thus it has the character of an entry into harmony; nevertheless, more closely considered, it is first and only authorized when it becomes cognizant of its own φύσις—for conceptual reason: without consideration of a pregiven topic, thinking is authorized purely by its destinal principle, by its directive, and reaches its topic—the said "being"—only by virtue of such an authorization.

These differences hold for each epoch of philo-sophy, each determining its task on the basis of the threefold possibility of referring to a σοφία. Accordingly the "self-withdrawing authorization" is of dwindling significance exactly for the comprehension of metaphysics as it is proper to conceptual reason. This does not hold, however, for Heidegger's experience of the said "desheltering" insofar as it is completely intrinsic to the sphere of modernity—our world as different from history, which is closed as that of philosophy and which admits of no continuum extending from metaphysical to technical thinking. For the closedness has its sense with respect to the purely accomplishing conceiving of the truth of an epochal σοφία in the logic which gives it the virtue of persuasiveness. Each epoch of philo-sophy is concluded in the certainty: it is accomplished. It is only with reference to the fulfillment of its tasks that the departure of pure, that is, conceptual, reason can be understood. And it is only with regard to this that that death discloses itself by virtue of which men are capable of becoming mortals. That which Heidegger thought as the "shelter of Being" is to be translated into the truth of the epochal wisdom which took shape in the middle epoch through the authors of the New Testament, in the final epoch through Rousseau, Schiller, and Hölderlin. If the respective conceptions are thought in their departedness, then the stillness, the remoteness, and the mission become perceptible in them which are proper to the Heideggerian "clearing."

II

But how can the talk be of a limit of modernity when to this point only Heideggerian thought has come into view? Only his answer to the question 'What is metaphysics?' gave rise to a new approach to metaphysics and further to philosophy. And only the distinction of reason which has grown out of it allowed for the distinction of the sense-explicative dimensions of modernity. Finally, only the corresponding architectonic reveals the closedness on the basis of which the limit of modernity becomes apparent, and with good reason.

But what does the tearing of the Heideggerian continuum from metaphysical to technical thinking mean now? Does the latter and thus its present come, so to speak, to lack a mission? What does the distinction of reason and thus of the modern sense-explicative dimensions say to this?

Concerning the first dimension: in the sense-explication of the interpreted life—of its history (Dilthey), its world (Husserl), its speech (Wittgenstein)—the figure of hermeneutic reason takes shape. It occupies the place of what was formerly "conceptual" reason. The latter's conceptuality was completely developed in the said history. However, the pure concept has lost its principal significance entirely for sense-understanding reason: since the latter is primarily related to the doxic construct of lived experience, which is not already rational in itself. This thinking which simulates First Philosophy draws its authorization from a sense which in each instance has already been lived.

Concerning the other dimension: in the sense-explication of the sciences—of their speech (Frege), their world (Schlick), their history (Kuhn)—technical reason develops the figure of ratios peculiar to it. Certainly to be distinguished from the traditional understanding of techniques, it occupies the place of what was formerly "natural" reason; its natural character was completely exhausted in the said history. For technical reason, a φύσις that conceals itself no longer has any sense whatsoever, since "Nature" for the sciences in question is the real, which is determined by its network of denotations. Their puzzles have their place in the particular problems of research and not in a Nature which exists somehow in itself. Thus this reason takes its authorization from its own fundamental technical trait.

Concerning the final dimension: in the sense-explication of the nature of man—of its history (Marx), its world (Nietzsche), its speech (Heidegger)—the figure of temporal reason comes to light. It occupies the place of what was formerly mundane reason. Its world appears, namely, in the present that is still determined historically, or by what has been, to be an absolutely a-cosmical world. That which corresponds to presence in the κόσμος is present as the "future" of the transformed nature of man. That which holds this future together in the same present with what is offensive in what previously was, is only time. Therefore, time and Being, not: reason and Being. Thinking draws its authorization from that division of time which is focused on a distinction of man from himself, from the expropriations of his nature. Unlike the said history, the present in the sense of modernity no longer knows the intuition of the man who is already distinguished. The communist society, the overman, the mortal remain outside of experience—heralded without a clear shape.

Bringing man's distinction from himself into view is a fulfilled task of each of the epochal configurations of wisdom. Philosophical reason distinguished itself according to its possible positions with respect to σοφία. But what do the sense-explications constituting the sphere of modernity know as φιλοσοφία?

First of all the sense-explication of the interpreted life; it has us understand:

1) After the collapse of metaphysics, it has to observe once again its foundational function and this firstly with the study of the historical objectivations of life and its socially effective contexts, since it is itself a "function of society."
2) It is to be restored as the philosophical activity in all sciences and especially in First Science—on the basis of the method which is "pure phenomenology." In shedding light on the "subjective" constitution of the world, philosophy once again fulfills a "humanitarian" function.
3) Its final function, however, is a therapeutic one and in fact in view of the pathological problems that busy "philosophical" man—generated by his misunderstandings of an idle use of language.

What does the sense-explication of the sciences say to philosophy?

1) Philosophy is extraneous to First Science, namely, to logicized arithmetic, though if it wants to be science, it should reap the benefits of the purely technical language of logicized arithmetic.

2) It is intrinsic to the natural sciences; it itself is not a science but rather the clarification of the sense of scientific statements, separated from their verification in research.
3) Since it itself is not a science, it can be neglected in the history of the social production of knowledge on the part of scientific research; it can even be neglected in the investigation of the crises of its puzzle-solving.

And the sense-explication of the expropriated nature of man? It breaks with philosophy:

1) as a form of "ideology," of a reflection of civil society which overshadows the truth about the capitalistic relations of production, about the expropriation of the power of productive man;
2) as a form of decadence and negation of life which deceives the acting man about the expropriation of his will by the moral values given to him. The "love of truth" is to be overcome out of a "love of life" and its folly;
3) as the decisive testimony to the forsakenness by Being of a thinking that has forgotten the withholding of what itself is still worthy of thought in what is questionable in the historical present.

The philosophy business has, to be sure, been unable to take these refusals seriously; instead, it has subsumed them under its usual "critical" practice.

III

As a rational architectonic of its sense-explications, modernity is a closed sphere. Where does a transgressable limit become visible in terms of modernity itself?

The sense-explication of the interpreted life reveals no such limit. First the stream of sense-indicating life and its objectivations continues without end. With the sole exception of metaphysics, the types of worldview are preserved and, with their particular content of lived experience, confront the hermeneutic disciplines with ever new tasks. With the stream of lived experiences itself, endless is then the business of phenomenological analysis; endless is finally the therapeutic task regarding the consequences of the violations of rules in the language games of everyday comportment, games which are continually constructed and deteriorate. Metaphysics has likely disintegrated as a worldview, to be rejected as unscientific work preliminary to "scientifically rigorous doctrines"; it arises, however, time and again in the form of "metaphysical propositions." Its first diagnosis sets an historical limit; therapy remains, by contrast, an endless task.

Nor does a limit of modernity come into view for the sense-explication of the sciences. Even and just in consideration of its revolutions, the history in question remains an endless progress. Technical thinking expands without restraint—this all the more resolutely as it alone is able to remedy even those defects which remain a reminder in each instance of the need for the social control of environmental conditions affected by technologies.

Neither the one nor the other sense-explication allows even the thought of a transgressable limit of modernity to appear. They reveal only the transgressed limit: the new beginning of philosophy. By contrast, for the core sense-explication the limit that it itself has transgressed is of subordinate significance over against that which has yet to be transgressed. "How it is" as well as its provenance are seen in an exclusive relationship to the future—the necessary, the possible, the not impossible future. It is that of man as distinguished from his previous nature. Whether and how such is achieved does not fall within the autocracy of thinking but rather is due to—similar to the presence of the κόσμος for mundane reason—a "Being": of the state of the social process of production, of the rising and falling tendency of life, of the "mission of Being." It is precisely thereby, however, that the future becomes a barrier for thinking itself. In this exceptional sense it claims its finitude.

In so-called postmodernity the prevailing mood replies to this, saying: no future. It indicates the paling of the Heideggerian, the Nietzschean, and even the Marxian experience of expropriation (not: alienation). Along with it, "temporal" reason itself disappears, as does the division carried out by it of the present into that of what is prior and of what is to come. In this way the sole modern trace of the former configurations of wisdom, their demand that man distinguish himself from himself, vanished; the consequence of this is the weariness of his will to his distinction from other animals. The decaying future stimulates, first, the imagining of social utopias. However, they only bring out all the more emphatically the sole right and task of the intellect to concern itself with the—ultimately also "ethical"—requirements of the everyday and its shifting "today." Always already endless, the business of "philosophical" discussion—immortal like the clouds—is embedded in this concern.

What remains here of the said "Being"? What, above all, gives what is to be thought here? Violence—in view of its legitimacy, an indistinguishable sub-economic, sub-conscious, sub-linguistic violence. Thinking feels challenged by it and in fact to a critique in the sense of counter-violence, of resistance and emancipation. It is precisely this sense that is predominant in the contemporary understanding of modernity.

With its most conspicuous appearance—the violence of men against men—the discussion of the said violence goads on the vanity of a need-oriented "ethics" to conduct itself—in advance of sociology, psychology, and linguistics—like First Philosophy (Levinas) and therefore to pit itself once again against the alleged dominance of "ontology" in all previous philosophy. The beneficiaries of the Heideggerian "recuperation" (*Verwindung*) from metaphysical thinking—already concerning the simple knowledge of this, they feed on it—reinterpret it, in keeping with their own critical practice, as a critique of metaphysics. Athens or Jerusalem: however the clichés of submodern thought may read, they have not made any advance on Heidegger's judgment about the beginning of metaphysical thinking—decisive for the determination of the other beginning over against the first. If there is no thought whatsoever of the difference between "what is" and "what is present" here, to say nothing of the difference of presence itself, one talks without second thought of the "privilege of presence" in the occidental tradition of thought.

While Heidegger's "temporal" reason was focused on the missive division of the present and therein especially on the advent of the world of the thing, the contemporary critique of metaphysics in the horizon of Husserlian lived experience—though pared back to its determination by the transcendental *cogito*—is confronted with a future that arises from a "postponement"—of what?—and in fact one on the part of a man of passing determinacy. Moreover, this reinterpretation of the future obstructs the access to the core sense-explication of modernity, to say nothing of the access to the departed conceptual reason of our history.

Nevertheless: the submodern critique of metaphysics, its aversion to the old "faculty of principles," to the object of reason as a totality—maligned by the association of it with the "totalitarian"—its passion for pluralism, also its penchant for the plurality of histories, worlds, and languages, indicates a certain accommodation of the investigation of reason itself as a philo-sophical and thus different reason.

IV

The sense-explicative architectonic of modernity has been left behind. But in what sense? Is submodern thought, in the wake of the fulfilled tasks of the rational architectonic of modernity, perhaps merely left to itself? What is indicated here—is that already a type of reason whose transgression of the limit of modernity is motivated by modernity itself? That such is not the case shows the blindness to modernity as a closed construct. Thus, as is fitting, the latter does not open a way out by its own efforts. Yet in what was presented here at the outset, a way into the open has become apparent and in fact in the renewal of Heidegger's question 'What is metaphysics?' But to what extent can the aforementioned legacy speak for the whole of modernity?

In each of its sense-explications, the traditional sense of truth has become questionable and has everywhere provoked the rejection of its conventional interpretation as *adaequatio rei et intellectus*—a relation between the topic and thinking that disregards the destinal term.

Thus in the sense-explication of the sciences. What becomes of "truth" there? Frege shows it in the significance of absolute objectivity—rigorously separated from all representation and lived experience; the objective concept is immediately subject to the directing intention, mediately: relational thinking is subject to the latter. For Schlick it loses not only the rank of the directing intention determining thinking and the topic but also allows the positive sciences only an approximation of truth. Whatever they know of the real can lay claim to only greater or lesser probability. Further, Kuhn expunges the idea of such an approximation due to the indeterminability of its end.

In the peripheral sense-explication of the interpreted life, of concern is a more originary truth, namely, the one of the fulfillment of sense or of the lack and failing thereof. Dilthey shows how the one or the other is lived through primarily self-ishly—not yet egoically. Prior to all statement. Husserl thinks truth in terms of the self-givenness of the phenomena; the fulfillment or non-fulfillment of what is intended in what is represented are to be shown with reference to these phenomena. Having begun from that which is lived through pre-predicatively, Wittgenstein eliminates the conventional privilege of "apophantic" saying, which is referred to its truth-value: truth cannot even be shown in the same way for all assertions; such a demand has sense only in certain cases. Above all, however: the "unwavering foundation" of the rules of communication in language games is in turn not true. The guiding question here is no longer "How is it going?" but rather "How does it work?"—seen in terms of the functioning of everyday speech.

In the former dimension that truth withdrew itself which was incipiently understood in terms of attending to the "true," namely, the φύσις of what appears. In the latter dimension the truth that incipiently attained insight on the path of self-persuasion by way of pure reflection and in fact in the determinacy of "being." And in the core dimension of modernity? The "truth" that was incipiently that of the topic itself, namely, of its presence in the form of a κόσμος whose determinative ground gave what was to be thought.

Here in the sense-explication of the nature of man the predominant experience is that of untruth. First with Marx in the relations of production as they are reified by the fetishism of wares and money—with the consequence of a merely hypocritical humanity. Then with Nietzsche in the value-positings of Christian and socialist morality, in which the decadent life does not tolerate the truth about the truth, nor on account of this the art of the beautiful illusion—with the consequence of the "longest lie" and the approach of the "last men." Finally with Heidegger in metaphysical thinking's forsakenness by Being, in which "the self-withdrawing authorization" remains concealed—this with the consequence of the solely technical, namely, "positing" and challenging, desheltering.

Starting from "agreement," Heidegger's recollection of the "nature of truth" can speak for the whole of modernity. He alone deals with the renunciation of the "common concept of truth" in a way that reaches "de-structively" back to the beginning of philosophy. With respect to the true in the sense of the φύσις of what appears, there he takes up the sole hint in the fundamental trait of self-concealing. The turn into the beginning of thinking, however, first yields the attention to the sheltering sense of self-concealing, to granting, even in the desheltering determined by the nature of technicity, more precisely: in the desheltering of the withdrawal characteristic of desheltering. But here Heidegger's thought, spellbound by the "temporality" of its reason, runs up against the aforementioned barrier of the future. "Temporal" reason remains dependent upon an advent that is absolutely unavailable to it—much like the former "mundane" reason's dependence upon a presence unavailable to it, namely, that of the κόσμος of the contrary φύσεις of what appears.

That this thought runs up against the said barrier is expressed exoterically in Heidegger's assurance: "Only a god can save us." As if he had not already saved us! More precisely: those departed within the realm of modernity, or rather those whom the "savior Zeus" or Christ as the redeemer of the world or the necessarily self-endangering humanity of man could have saved. An indeterminate—that is, nameless—and thus non-summonable god will not save anyone.

But it would be and is just as facile as it is vain merely to go beyond the limit of modernity into the way of thinking proper to so-called postmodernity. Though the latter's will-o'-the-wisp is to be read as a sign. Of what?

For the thinking of technical reason, the relation to a self-concealing nature, moreover, to the *arcana naturae*, had already become meaningless. The unmasking-strategies of submodernity are directed no longer to such relations but rather to self-concealing, what is more: to deceiving, as it alone is proper to man—more precisely: directed to the veiling and concealment of the socially prestamped sub-structures of violence. It is precisely on account of this that Foucault recognized the special status of structural anthropology and psychoanalysis among the human sciences: they penetrate the no-man's-land of man, blur the boundaries with respect to which he conceived himself. Man's reverence even for himself—it is precisely in this connection that the "positive" sense of deceiving and further of the reticence in letting-know is expressed which was the originary place of ἀλήθεια—has, as it were, become false where the distinction borne by all of the configurations of wisdom between "how it is" and "how it is to be" has foundered. For the, as it were, true reverence had its first and decisive exposition in the relation of the "mortals" to their "immortals" and to their "dead." It is precisely this triad that was constitutive of the speech-world of the knowledge of the Muses; it arises from the simple distinction between attending (*Anwesen*) and not attending (*Abwesen*) to everything (cf. my *Ground and Present as the Aim of Early Greek Philosophical Inquiry*, pp. 225 ff.).

We recall: λήθειν prevents a possible share in knowledge, what is more, the testimony of presence. In submodern thought the striking "irreverence"—not only: lack of distance; such prevents a coming-near out of an pre-established remoteness—in human relations expunges a reverence (Αἰδώς) which has become groundless. Hesiod already foresaw that in the "Iron Age" she as the last of the gods will leave man's earth. Translated into the decline of civil society: the self-conscious acknowledgment, the respect for the self of the ego, for its "humanity," was constitutive of this society; and the human dignity of the modern era, the dignity of the free citizen, of a man who distinguished himself from himself in the self-determination and formation of his personality was based on such humanity. If such a distinction remains without a present, if there is no σοφία here that brings this distinction into view (Aristotle, *Poetics,* ch. 2), then it falls into oblivion, more precisely, because it is thought in terms of violence: it is repressed. How is the Heideggerian "preserving" in the "nature" of truth still to be thought here?

As far as its sheltering is concerned, it has its exceptional place in death as the "shelter of Being" (*D*, 171/177). Which death is that? Obviously not the demise of a man. With respect to which death could men—those who are "capable" of it—become mortals in the world called forth by the thing? With respect to its fundamental sheltering trait, Heidegger speaks of the "shrine of nothingness" and explains: "of that which in every respect is never something that merely exists but which nevertheless natures, even as the mystery of Being itself" (ibid.). But the latter is still thought in reliance upon the self-concealing of φύσις. It is on account of this that that talk requires no explanation but instead a translation, for the illusion of obscurity rests here in the futurity of the world and its mortals.

The requisite translation is possible only for the reason which frees itself from the said temporality—much like the conceptual reason of each epoch of philosophy distinguished itself from its natural and mundane types. The translation in question attains a present which is no longer divided into that of what is prior and that of what is to come, thus it is no longer "temporal."

The limit of modernity is transgressed only insofar as modernity's characteristic rejection of the former or prior is conceived as a fulfilled task. That is to say, it completely articulated our world and separated it from its history. If this is finally thought as detemporalized, then it takes on the determinacy of the under-world of our world. It is with regard to this that the present sense of the said death now becomes apparent: from the departedness of that reason which alone was "capable" of death and in fact with the knowledge: "it is accomplished"; the epochal tasks are accomplished which called forth this reason as a "philo-sophical" reason in a distinguished sense.

It is no longer necessary to "recuperate" from metaphysics—for who presently thinks metaphysically if not in the sense of a concoction of metaphysics?—but only from the departedness of conceptual reason. What it has accomplished demands a new "reverence"; but prior to that the respect for that which endowed the accomplishing with what was to be thought. As is well-known, submodern representation and exhibition help themselves as they like to what the sense-explication of modernity rejected. In all its "de-constructing," however, it is unable to grasp that which was given there, since the submoderns leave themselves in the dark about the "construction," about the epochal architectonic, of philosophy and, most of all, of σοφία.

Once again: the limit of modernity is not at all to be transgressed into a postmodernity but rather into the present of "detemporalized" reason, which reflected in the world upon its under-world, encountered acknowledgingly what was accomplished by conceptual reason in order to preserve the configurations of wisdom which called the former forth. Heidegger's "legacy" is taken on and transformed in this way.

TWILIGHT OF MODERNITY

Whoever would provide only that understanding which insists unreservedly on its right to a "plain and familiar language" (Locke) will find Heidegger's *Contributions to Philosophy (Of Appropriation)* insufferable; it has to remain—judged with the pertinent language—"mere verbiage" for him. Whoever insists unreservedly on comprehensibility for everyone, or at least on that which is usual among experts, may grow morose when he reads: "Making oneself comprehensible is suicide for philosophy" (*GA* 65, 435).

But how should the reviewer meet the assurance: "No one understands what I am *thinking* here . . ."; and once again: "No one grasps this . . ." (8)? Should he give way to the "once" of a future still counted on, one in which "this attempt finds its interpreter" (83)—from the "once" of "centuries" in which Heidegger's question "wishes to determine the will and style of thinking" (19)? The reviewer makes his escape in confessing to be "no one" in order to meet as such what has hitherto gone unheard: "to let Da-sein emerge . . . from the truth of Beyng in order to ground therein beings in the whole and as such, in the midst of these, however, man" (8). Thus first the truth of Beyng as the origin of Da-sein; it is precisely this relation that is in its reciprocity "the event of appropriation." Then within this event the grounding of beings in the whole and as such, after the theory of first grounds and causes, thus metaphysics, veiled the failing grounding. Finally the grounding of man within the said beings so that he—not reason—ultimately "attends to himself" (50); this in a transformation (84) of the *animal rationale*, of the "former rational animal" (62), and today of the "technicized" one (98). All of this is thought here.

As far as its incomprehensibility is concerned, it won't do to translate what is said into the generally comprehensible language of the everyday on the one hand, of philosophical "science" on the other. Since the author, as is well-known, was as capable of the one as of the other, he could have done that himself—wherever possible.

Even if "Of Appropriation" is the "essential heading" of this book, the legitimacy of the "public title" first has to become clear. Contributions to which philosophy? Certainly not to the contemporary types in their "increasing desertification" (354), in their cultivation of "aporetics" (94). No contributions to a systematic and historial "philosophical scholarship" (461) but rather to the philosophy of those who are "affected by Beyng," thus of the thinkers of the "first beginning" up to Nietzsche. In the "other beginning," however, "the essential version of the concept of philosophy in the present and the future . . . is an historical one" (421)—not: historial—that is, it has to carry out "the decision for history or the loss of history" (98).

The structure of the *Contributions* cannot—the author repeats Dilthey's well-known word (5)—be a system. It is a "fugue" of resonance (*Anklang*), serve (*Zuspiel*), leap (*Sprung*), grounding (*Gründung*), those to come, and the last god; a preview and a retrospect of this whole; continuously a "persisting with the Same" (82).

I

Where does the event of the appropriation of the truth of Beyng and Dasein resound? In the midst of the "confusion of un-beings" (7), which are seen as such only with regard to the Being of metaphysics, and in the renewal of the question of Being, not in the "analyses of the 'spiritual' and 'political' situation of the times" (309), which are everywhere offered at bargain prices. With the exhaustion of the metaphysical question of Being, "the age of complete questionlessness" has dawned. Once there is no longer any need regarding what was formerly questionable, however, "the need of needlessness" (107) remains: the experience of the "forsakenness by Being." This is permeated by "calculation," the "fundamental law of comportment," by the acceleration of the ephemeral, by the "uprising of everything *en masse*" (120). All of this driven by "machination" (*Machenschaft*), the "denaturing (*Unwesen*) which itself is still essential to naturing (*Wesen*)." Here the preponderance of the "makeable and the self-making prevails" (126). This throws light on the "first beginning": φύσις as that which "makes-itself-by-itself" is disempowered and in fact in a history of the "machinative exegesis of beings"; its doctrine of causality also extended to God, determined him to be the *causa sui* (127).—Augustine's and Thomas's objections to this should be heard here.

Machination—even if this name is not to be understood morally, it nevertheless retains such an offensive tone that already an appreciation of the economic understanding has to be failing on account of a superficial notion of "business" (392)—to say nothing of an appreciation of technical reason. Yet here 'machination' names an enaction of truth: "The more decisively it unfolds, it conceals itself as such all the more obstinately." In its "growing self-concealing" appears the "predominance of lived experience" (127). Here the concealment proper to the nature of technicity veils itself beyond recognition. "'Machination and lived experience' is formulistically the more originary version of the formula for the guiding question of occidental thought: beingness (Being) and thinking (as re-presenting con-ceiving)" (128). Both are first to be seen in the predominant worldviews (140), then as their academic functionaries (134, 142), finally in the university business which moves into its technical determination (147, 155)—as is attested by the history of the understanding of "experience" (164). "The concealed end towards which every this and that hurries without having or being able to have the slightest clue about it, is the state of complete boredom in the horizon of one's ownmost achievements . . ." (157): the resonance of the forsakenness by Being, which could give one at least a scare.

II

From the contemporary sciences the awakened recollection (*Besinnung*) turns to the former First Science. It alone serves to thinking the provenance of the resonance—the history of its world. What guided metaphysics? The opinion that "Being can be found in beings and this such that thinking goes beyond beings" in order to come back to them again immediately (170). So it seems when one's sight has not gotten clear about the Husserlian provenance of both fundamental ontology and the question concerning sense. In order to do so, the translation of what is given in the phenomenological attitude into Aristotelian being is insufficient—nor is the self-critique of "ontological difference."

The guiding question of metaphysics testifies by way of its exhaustion to its inability to "inquire into Beyng sought in its fundament" (173). The "fundamental question" corresponding to this serves to the former guiding question its possibility. Contrary to the traditional way of representing Being as the most general in the sense of beingness, *Being and Time* already brings about the turn to Being in the horizon of time and no longer of thinking (183). It prevents the relapse into a first being (185), overcomes the rule of the correctness of representational thinking, its demonstration through intuition, and the corresponding decisiveness of presence, finally of φύσις (195).

According to the truth of Beyng—not: of Being as it was thought with respect to beings—metaphysics is a history of decline. The first and decisive interpretive thrust in the sense of "beingness" is made by Plato. The consequences are seen principally in Aristotle, Descartes, Kant, Hegel, and Nietzsche; among them, the one most nearly equal to the Greeks: Kant (426). In the Middle Ages a semblance of "philosophy" (350) under the dominance of Christian dogmatism which befalls even "the idealistic representation of the absolute." The labels 'realism' and 'nominalism', otherwise despised by Heidegger, are supposed to say something here; even more, principal differences are concealed by the term 'German Idealism'. Beyond all demands for correctness, it remains difficult to say of the judgments in question that they give what is to be thought. An example: "Machination as the fundamental character of beingness now takes the form of the subject-object dialectic, which as the absolute dialectic plays out and classifies all possibilities of all known regions of being . . ." (203). It is difficult to restrain oneself and to turn such a distortion into the question: why must Heidegger obfuscate the rational intention of each type of metaphysics despite his painstaking reading?

The presumption of an "essential dominance of Platonism" in the "history of the treatment of the guiding question" (216) generally suppresses, with the denial of every "essential change" (232), the epochal differences in the tasks and intentions of metaphysical reason. As far as the non-metaphysical types of philosophy are concerned, however, the asserted guiding question does not at all let them come into view. But are, for instance, Hobbes and Hume to be neglected if of concern is occidental thought, which has become historical? They came into the world no less than did Cartesian thought. The serve to which Heidegger's projection of a history of metaphysics responds betrays everywhere Nietzsche's pre- and counter-word (219), even if he is in turn pushed back into Platonism in order once again to take up its "overcoming" as an "historical decision of the greatest proportions" (221).

III

The "serve" was supposed to have introduced thinking to the possibility and necessity of the "leap"—not over a chasm and to another ground but rather into this chasm as it opened with the collapse of the truth of metaphysical reasoning. It becomes necessary here "to sacrifice every being"—even an understanding that is no longer subjected to any reason—"to Beyng" (230). The results of *Being and Time* should be taken up once again: the exegesis of the temporality of the There, of the "originary unity of self-lighting-concealing displacement (*Entrückung*)" (234). The latter can succeed, however, only when Da-sein is thought in terms of the being-away (*Weg-sein*) which precedes it—from history to the world of un-beings.

The "leap" has the character of projection, though it is at the same time an adjected (*zugeworfen*) possibility (239); it is exactly this that is the "Beyng" which is impossible to think in terms of beings. In the jump (*Absprung*) from the being-away of previous thinking, Da-sein opens as the "temporal play-space" (*Zeit-Spiel-Raum*) in which man obtains his self—in opposition to the gods for whom the There becomes the place of conflict in which they decide about their advent or flight (244). With that the warning: "'man' and 'god' are ahistorical, empty clichés unless the truth of Being brings itself to speech in them" (476). The aforementioned decision of the gods, however, remains related to a change in the nature of man—to the decision about whether the "fall of the *animal rationale*" into its *animalitas*, into its life as it is interpreted by science and worldviews (479), persists or not. Not beings, not the gods, but only Da-sein is proper to Beyng—this due to its "being-towards-death"; for "the presentiment of Beyng comes from nothingness," the "excess of pure denial" (245). Man is "used" for the experience of this denial. Beyng needs him as historical and as such he belongs to it; this reciprocity "constitutes Beyng as the event of appropriation" (251). It can be nothing "arbitrarily representable for everyone at any one time." Hence the "incomprehensibility" of what is thought here. Only he who is informed, in the sense of Da-sein, understands. Whoever is away does not know Beyng as that which conceals itself. As such it comes to bear only where truth "natures in sheltering as art, thinking, poetizing, deed" (256); this is the span between earth and world (259)—the former as it is related to history, the latter as it is formative of history, "thus nearest to the event of appropriation" (275). An earth that is more originary than Nature. "What was this once? The place of the moment, of the advent, and of the abode of the gods, as it, still being φύσις, rested in the naturing of Beyng itself," in order to fall directly into the violence of machination. "Must Nature be abandoned and left to itself?" Still in his later work, Heidegger cannot bring himself to affirm this, to take this liberating step, at last disregarding Hölderlin.

Metaphysics thought Being principally in terms of modalities. *Being and Time* already breaks with the precedence of actuality (281): in "being-towards-death," possibility and necessity collide—prior to all "ontology," with its "pale and empty mixture of modalities" (283). Should this characterization apply, for instance, to its exposition in Kant, Fichte, and Hegel? Or to an historically inconsequential school-discussion? How should "the fidelity to the history of the first beginning" (468) be able to hold up if it ignores the fundamental difference between actuality and reality?

The leap, thus being-towards-death, as "it is a duty only for the thinkers of the other beginning" (285), means for them: resolute singularization. The "thinking of Da-sein," which has turned away from the universal of beingness and therefore is "non-conceptual,"[1] no longer knows any community founded by the species 'man' but rather is immersed in the said duty.

IV

The leap into (*Einsprung*) Da-sein is concentrated on "grounding." How? The Being of the There is care—explicated by *Being and Time* only in mundane but here in historical significance with respect to the "crisis between the first and the other beginning" (295); being-away was "insufficiently indicated in inauthenticity." Historical care aims at the "transition into another history of man" (309), attains—bearing in mind the event of the denial—the "deepest question concerning man" (314). Thus it seems that there are "two fundamentally different depths of occidental history" (431)—an inevitable phantasm already given Marx's and Nietzsche's experiences of expropriation.

The previous nature of man, his rationality, obstructed the nature of truth, that is, the self-concealing proper to it. Yet the rule of reason "one day has to shatter, and the current centuries effect this shattering, but [such is] necessarily accompanied by the continual intensification of 'rationality' as a principle of machination" (336). Where truth "is shrouded in the form of 'reason' and of the 'rational', its denaturing is at work, that destructive power of what is valid-for-everyone, whereby everyone is arbitrarily authorized and that pleasure taken in the fact that absolutely no one has anything essential in advance of the other, arises" (343). Yet how could the former "faculty of principles" and its architectonic character be the predecessor of this straw man?

The grounding in Da-sein excludes the ground in the sense of the ratio; nevertheless, for the "grasping of time-space" a recollection of its "provenance from the history of the first beginning is indispensable" (373). Despite his painstaking study of Aristotle's *Physics*, however, the author passes over its reference to the first, that is, Zeno's, exposition of space and time. This is all the more instructive as in it a thinking comes to bear to which—prior to the presence of "ideas"—"correctness" alone is essential, a thinking that excogitates a time-space which no phenomenal analysis attains in its "originary unity" (379).

The temporal play-space of Da-sein is the "abyss" as the "originary chasm" in the hesitating "self-denial" of Beyng (381). This self-concealing is obstructed by the "un-ground" as it prevails in the un-being (380). The abyss appeals in the manner of displacing, that is, temporalizing, but at the same time in the manner of implacing, that is, of spacing (384)—both "on the basis of the unity of the hesitating denial." The harmony of the self-denial that displaces and the hesitation that implaces emerges from the "hint," the "self-inauguration of that which conceals itself as such" (385).

V

The leap into Da-sein and the grounding are alone the task of those "to come." In fright, freed from the spell of today (396), they become those who "expect in retrospect"; they "slip-under" (*unter-laufen*) what is coming (397) and therefore do not fear their decline—open for "the decision about the advent and the failing of the gods." In this being-towards-death, they are surely the singularized; yet the grounding of man in beings, which are in turn grounded, requires the prospect of a people—not a people understood biologically (99) but rather one projected in a manner characteristic of Da-sein (319). This people moves into its history, where it adopts its god (398), "traveling beyond itself" (399). As the prophets, the "seekers" transmit the god's hint to the people "belonging" to him—in the historical crisis, the hint of the "last god," whose "passing by" once again calls to mind the Old Testament. A regression from the New Testament?

VI

The concluding "fugue" announces the last god emphatically as "the wholly other over against those who have been, especially over against the Christian god" (403). The rejection of him runs through the entire work—especially as far as his consequences and the belief which is contaminated with metaphysics are concerned (24, 228, 350, 483). In the other beginning of thinking, "no redemption, i.e., basically the subjection of man, occurs but rather the institution of the originary nature (grounding of Da-sein) in Beyng itself: the acknowledgment of the belongingness of man in Beyng through the god, the confession of the god, which neither diminishes him nor his greatness, that he needs Beyng" (413). All of this has to appear to be so within the bounds of modernity.

Is "the wholly other" once again a Dionysus? Such would make sense of: "The most terrible jubilation has to be the dying of a god" (230). For the man who has moved into his being-towards-death. He has subjected himself to the divine law of the "great singularization in Da-sein, of the solitude of the victim, of the singularity of the shortest and steepest course" (408) and thus corresponds to the momentariness of the passing-by (*Vorbeigang*). His god is nearest "when the event of appropriation enters into the denial" (412). "To create silence" for the passing-by—that silence of which Heidegger, "on the way to speech," will say that it is proper to the speech that itself speaks; here it is initially only the "speech of our history" (501).

In the moment of the passing-by, "Beyng, as the innermost Between, is equal to nothingness, the god overwhelms man and man outstrips the god, immediately, so to speak, and yet both in the event of appropriation" (415). Such is not met by any waiting for Godot; rather, the illusion that "man would have to wait for God is perhaps the most insidious form of the deepest godlessness" (417). On the other hand, no beatific vision but rather belongingness to the "fissuring of Beyng" and its "wretchedness" (416).

Looking back on the whole once again: the continuum of history projected from out of the resonance; all differences in this history "cannot veil the simple uniformity of the entire history of this questioning" (426), which from Anaximander to Nietzsche is directed towards "beingness," "the fundamental occidental determination, then, from which all alterations of the exegesis of beings arise" (450). Here it still seems: the philosophers have merely interpreted differently.—This semblance is dissolved through the expunction of the "Same," as supposed by Heidegger, through the tearing of the continuum between metaphysical and "technical" thinking. This regarding the epochally distinguished tasks which philosophical reason has fulfilled.

Even without seeing this, one has to wonder at the "guiding question": where is the oft-cited ontology attested, then, except in the business of the schools of the modern era? Or perhaps in Duns Scotus? Where does Aristotle bring a "Being," inquired into with respect to "beings," to speech? Is it to be gathered from the "Being of beings"? When Thomas Aquinas speaks of "Being"—distinguishing between God and creatures—can that be retrojected into the Greeks? Isn't the question instead called for: why "Being of beings"? (cf. pp. 19-43 above). This question has to run up against the epochal difference in the Plotinian principle. And where do Kant and Hegel follow what is asserted to be the guiding question? Perhaps in the exegesis of beingness as objectivity? Would the *Critique of Pure Reason* then have to—could especially its "doctrine of method"—express still more clearly the sole rational intention of distinguishing the object and in fact in order to "save freedom"? Among the numerous remarks in the *Contributions* on Kant, no trace is found of an appreciation of this destinal principle; thus what 'subject' principally means here and how the "ego" is to be thought with distinction (426) also remain obfuscated. Mundane being and rational being, thing and object—Kant distinguishes between these; it is all the more urgent to attend to this if "the attempt at the originary question of Being at the same time has to be an essential event of the appropriation of the history of metaphysics" (468).

The "guiding question" is a will-o'-the-wisp over the cenotaph of metaphysics. It still affects contemporary thinking like one of Circe's spells. For the

Heideggerian "crisis" of history can be easily reminted into a critique of metaphysics. What could urge one to an appreciation of the latter, when beingness has been "only the thinnest thinning of beings and, even more, itself such a being" (466)? The attempt is still being made "to break" "the privilege of presence" as the sense of Being (460). Following the Greeks, one might have at least distinguished between appearing and being-present (*Anwesen*)—and further distinguishing the latter within itself; then the question would be whether and how in the case of "being" as it is discussed for the first time, namely, of the Parmenidean being, the talk can be of "being-present." Once the said "privilege" has been presumed—was it not broken long ago? By Plotinus in view of the originary "donating," by Kant in view of the "positing" of the moral law.

In metaphysics, thinking is first in relation to Being. Thus Calypso, who forces her way into memory, is more dangerous than Circe's transforming spell. "Thinking in the sense of the statement becomes the guiding thread for the thinking of occidental thinkers" (457)—hermeneutists of Being and, prior to this, of thinking. This presumed, it is demanded: "Renunciation of every logical exegesis of thinking"—of one of the "greatest prejudices of occidental philosophy" (460). Which clarification accompanies this violent blow to metaphysics? Where does Heidegger produce the "transfiguration of its essential, fundamental positions" (411)? Closer to the said thinking: where does he produce an appreciation of the "statement" and its decidability? This precious—so it may be said—invention of our history. And which logic was here a mere exercise of "acumen," a "doctrine of correct thinking" (177), and finally a "remnant" of the impotence of thinking (170)? Even the speech of technical thinking and logic in mundane significance deserves appreciation.

Yet how does logic appear in metaphysics? It "is, with reference to the essential grounding of the truth of Beyng, an illusion but the most necessary illusion that the history of Beyng has as yet known" (461). Is Kant's "logic of illusion" outdone here? Who has been successful in grasping it on the basis of the other beginning of the thinking of Being? Its origin remains unthought in Parmenidean thought. Corresponding to Θέμις and her directive, thinking takes the sole "path of inquiry" that leads to the end—the path of "persuasion" accompanying truth. It is precisely the former that thinking has to produce for itself, not the latter. In pure reflection, it attains the topic in which what has already been decided becomes insight—what "is completed." By contrast, Zeno's logic: there is a persuasion on the basis of pure reflection which thinks through un-truth and even constructs it. A logic of another kind. But concerning the intention, asserted and repeated time and again, that the philosophy of the modern era understood truth as certainty, it fails to see that Descartes and still Hegel insist on the difference between the two; it expressly governs the twofold movement of the *Phenomenology of Spirit*.

In accordance with this difference, Kant emphatically recalled the "logical" task of philo-sophy: it is not philosophy's place to teach man what duties are but rather to shelter these, against the contestations of sophistic reasoning, in the logic of "science." Accordingly in the history of metaphysics, even logical formalism had an epochally diverse character. The reason called forth by such a task of sheltering was always an architectonic, a "building," reason. What it accomplished for the "dwelling" of occidental man is obscured by Heidegger with the, to be sure, necessary illusion that "the history of Being and the history of man begin only now" (454)—after the "the loss of his nature, a loss long in coming"; thus man's becoming man is to be expected—after Marx and Nietzsche, still a, when not thought-taking, then breath-taking self-assertion of modernity.

It always warns: "do not resort to reason" (453 f.). Certainly not to the one which was to have been the "perception of the Being of beings" (440). The destiny subject to which its thinking had to be the first in relation to its topic for Parmenides, for Plotinus, for Kant, remains completely dark. Or would "mission" (*Geschick*) be an answer here? If the "guiding question" is a projection that fulfilled itself in the obfuscation of the rational intention of all metaphysics, what then becomes of the "fundamental question"? Is its "ground" to be taken back to the ratio, which, to be sure, cannot be a natural gift of man but rather the mediate "proportion" of the terms in Heidegger's phrase 'the destiny of the topic of thinking'?

"Being" is no subject of research for the Heideggerian recollection, even less a concept, but rather a "title" that demands to be understood completely in keeping with its intention (433)—along with the latter it is totally transformable; even when "Being" is to be crossed out, that which is "most worthy of thought" in it is not expunged. Is "time" also such a title? It became the "first indication of the nature of truth" (ibid.), and thus thinking—in accordance with Heidegger's "legacy"—will find its directive only in the latter. This directive opens the view to the "sheltering" within the history of metaphysics itself and lets its end be grasped on the basis of the fulfilledness of the conceptual tasks; their reason can utter the word of passing away with good reason, of the solely conceivable "dying": it is accomplished. Heidegger never found nor could find any reason to think of the "dead" involved in the "being-towards-death." Even for the other world over against the one of machination and lived experience, no underworld could open up.

The departedness of metaphysics lets the core sense-explication of modernity gaze steadfastly at an event of expropriation that seems to have arisen from history—of the capital of the modern era, of Christian morality, of machinative θεωρία. Spellbound in the corresponding experience, reason is one-eyed—without an eye having been snatched from it; it is, so to speak, "cycloptic" and possesses a violent gaze. The Cyclops is the brother of precisely those Titans whose character Heidegger projects into metaphysics and its history (462)—penetrating a veil—thereby also testifying to the projective character of his view.

Heidegger took up the event of the appropriation of Being and human being at first in mundane significance, then unfolded it—above all in the work discussed here—in historical significance. The concluding references to speech also remain determined by the latter (497); for, as the "donating naming of the truth of Beyng" (177), it is also ultimately the "historical, history-grounding word" (510). Only where Heidegger's thought is especially "on the way to speech" does it also bring into view, and even as a matter of priority, its appropriative character.

"Of Appropriation"—although this work belongs to the middle phase of the Heideggerian recollection, it testifies not only to the limit of modernity but is moreover a *monumentum* to its limit, if one hears therein that *monere* is the *causativum* of *meminisci.* A parting belongs to the transgression of the limit, a parting that is foreshadowed in this work. Not least of all, however, is the "logic of its other thinking," namely, "sigetics" (78), a bequest that once again lets one listen in *silentium magistri.*

NOTE

1. The published version of Heidegger's text reads "inbegrifflich" but clearly ought to read "unbegrifflich"; see *GA* 65, p. 286 (top) [Editor].

SPEECH

ON REASON'S INTEREST IN LANGUAGE

It has not been so long since language seemed to be, if not the common interest, then at least the common subject, of the most diverse philosophical trends of our day. In the meantime the span between Heidegger and Wittgenstein has come to lack all appeal. This becomes most conspicuous in the fact that the misgivings of both concerning the feasibility and possibility of an ethics have been set aside. The "brave new world" of modernity seems to be giving way to a moralizing one.

However that may be—it remains necessary to shed light on what destined the sense-explication of modernity to thematize language and, in contrast to this, what destined philosophy in general to consider it.

Averse to such a distinction, those under the spell of the historial habit of thinking in terms of continua would like to reply: have there not been since time immemorial philosophical considerations of language out of which a special discipline finally arose? But how did it arise? Through the systematic construction of a totality of philosophy—as in the case of the ancient disciplines of logic, ethics, and physics? Or through the conceptual division of a totality—as in the case of general and specific ontologies? Or bound to a context of specialized philosophies which has become opaque to itself, philosophies that, indifferent to their degree of generality, do not stand in any order of generic unity?

Did the philosophy of language borrow its topic from one of the "positive" sciences? Does it thereby continue those dilettantish reflections which, prior to the appearance of linguistics and in fact at the turn from the eighteenth to the nineteenth century, entertained cultivated society? Or does it lay claim to a "regional" ontology? Or does it esteem itself as linguistic theory, being dilettantish in this as well? Now—it should not be surprising if today philosophies of language were quite diverse.

When one looks back on the systematic works of First Science in the history of our world, one should be surprised that neither Aristotle nor Thomas nor Hegel have a special philosophy of language—despite a complete division of the realm of philosophy. As far as Hegel is concerned, this is all the more striking as he was familiar with the attempts of his contemporary Schlegel, but also with the older attempts, at a philosophy of language.

The *Encyclopaedia of the Philosophical Sciences* knows no science whose subject would be language, although language is mentioned repeatedly. Where? Unlike the history of the world, in which the formation of objective spirit is brought to completion, it is mentioned in systematic places of subordinate significance: above all, within the development of subjective spirit, more precisely: of the one which is not yet the free, not even the practical, but only the theoretical spirit. In this connection, language does not, strictly speaking, attain the dignity of something conceived. It is merely taken into account and in fact where imagination and memory are conceived: for its appearance belongs to a phase of development that precedes the proper activity of the intellect, namely, thinking. Thus it is considered only in the form of names, as something external to representation.—This externality allows language to appear in another systematic context: with regard to its "elementary material" as a physiologico-psychological phenomenon, but with regard to "formulas," namely, in view of its grammar, as a product of the understanding (*GW* 20, § 459 note/214 ff.).

Here it becomes apparent: what in fact destined metaphysics not to thematize language, though it does consider it, was the delimitation of thought, what is more: of the concept. It required the latter's separation from names.

I

This preliminary account of Hegel's calls to mind another distinction in the inauguration of modernity, more precisely: its sense-explication of the sciences: Frege's rigorous scission between scientific, that is, mathematical, concepts and all representation and its states of consciousness. But just how decisively the Fregean concept is of another nature than the Hegelian concept, is manifest already in the different character of consciousness from which the concept is removed in the one as well as in the other case. Whereas Hegel sees in consciousness a form of knowledge that is as capable of methodical formation as of systematic completeness, Frege refers to a consciousness that belongs to the element of lived experience and that, unlike the "natural consciousness" of the *Phenomenology of Spirit*, cannot descend into its ground (*zugrunde gehen*) but rather asserts itself irreconcilably as the first over against the scientific concept.

It is precisely this state of affairs that requires reason not only to consider language but also to clarify the linguistic character essential to scientific cognition, what is more: to inference. The complete detachment of inference from the "language of life" can have recourse only to mathematical formalism and must develop it into an artificial language. However, its desire for security presses for its withdrawal especially from every phonetic language and for its elaboration as a "concept-*script*." Only in this reification does it attain the purity of the technical instrument that is appropriate to a cognition which is in turn determined technically.

It is not language in general that becomes thematic here but rather the linguistic character of scientific cognition—this, however, in contrast to that of representation and further of lived experience. Hence, talk of the philosophy of language in this connection would be ill-advised, especially as Frege himself abstained entirely from characterizing his investigations as "philosophy." That they would not be particularly honored by this name becomes clear in view of the peripheral dimension of the sense-explication of modernity.

There of concern is first the historical (Dilthey), then the mundane (Husserl), finally the linguistic (Wittgenstein) characters of the "basis of life"—also of the sciences, and in this respect, of concern is a "foundation" that aspires to the rank of the former First Philosophy, of metaphysics. Now in Dilthey and Husserl matters of language do in fact become thematic—thus, for instance, with regard to the origin of the categories or in the context of a "genealogy of logic"—without, however, leading to the development of a philosophy of language. Consequently, such is all the more obvious—it seems—in Wittgenstein.

Unlike Schlick, Wittgenstein does not take his point of departure from the directing intention, which is the unity of all scientific knowledge, but rather from his topic, namely, the world—this, however, being understood on the basis of the said foundational intention first as the totality of the facts "in logical space" and thus as the world corresponding to the Fregean concept. Not the Husserlian world, which was to be elucidated in terms of its constitution by the productions of consciousness, in particular, of the *cogito*.

However, Wittgenstein's topic first appears immediately at the point where language detaches itself from the language of inferential and depictive knowledge in order to appear for the first time as having been left to itself: rescued from the predominance of the name, now in the entire manifold of linguistic action, namely, as a network of "language games" among which the logicized languages of the sciences can no longer lay claim to any exemplariness. They have in turn become languages of life; every technique of communication is and remains intrinsic to everyday life. Such is the homogeneous field of communication.

Did Wittgenstein do philosophy of language? Are his descriptions of the workings of language or of linguistic life, which the sciences and their logic also have as their basis, to be understood as a special discipline in the academic philosophy business? How could this square with his earth-shattering insight that the unity of the concept is to be kept apart from language? It is just this insight that Wittgenstein unfolds into a critique of the "philosophical" concept in general and thus of the language of traditional philosophy in order to demonstrate the denaturing of its topic. Yet the concept proper to it proves to be a "super-expression" (*Über-Ausdruck*), a disease of language, caused by its idle use. It is on account of this that a topic of philosophy assumes the form of a problem. What is needed here is, as it were, a homeopathic and thus "philosophical" therapy—not with a "concept-script" but rather with a pragmatic "grammar." Such is the fundamental technique for the dissolution of the illusion of "philosophical" problems; and even Dilthey's and Husserl's foundational intentions were still moved by such a problem, by the will-o'-the-wisp of the metaphysical concept in the idea of a First Science.

Like Fregean reason, Wittgensteinian reason is also not destined merely to consider language. The linguistic character of everyday life and its praxis here becomes the proper topic of this sense-explication. This, however, in starting from the limit marked by that "about which one cannot speak" and about which metaphysics had nevertheless spoken—nonsensically—i.e., about the non-everyday.

Now did the offense taken by Wittgenstein draw attention to the language of metaphysics and especially to the concept proper to it? By no means. Immersed in a "plain and familiar language," which as a result of Moore's efforts had become even plainer and more familiar than Locke's language, one busied oneself on the one hand—in the manner of the analytic philosophy of language—with arbitrarily invented "metaphysical propositions," while on the other, one sought out what is immediately comprehensible in the mass of the tradition and took pleasure especially in the technique of interrogation proper to a Plato who allegedly thinks "dialogically."

Meanwhile the everyday of vital praxis has been made even more everyday. World and history have also been included in the deconceptualization of language—as a network of worlds and histories.

II

What then was the non-everyday about which metaphysics had spoken? One points all too easily to its fundamental theological trait. To recall Marx here: even the everyday has its gods, its religions, and even its theologies.

By contrast, non-everyday has always been a σοφία which urged men to distinguish themselves from themselves and in fact to take on reason—obviously not that ratio which one, even lacking a ratio, i.e., ground, still ascribes to all men as an innate (since it is essential to them) faculty. In the epochal configurations of wisdom of our history, a ratio is articulated which takes a simple relation between topic and thinking back into a third term, namely, the destiny. Corresponding to the σοφία of an epoch of this history, each work of φιλοσοφία exhibits the proportion and the content of precisely these three terms. Such a ratio, as it is realized in the work, is the only one we can experience and from which we can learn pure reason.

Here it is manifest: the ratios combine into different figures. There is not just "one" reason, for reason is determinate only insofar as it distinguishes itself. Its figures concentrate on the elucidation of either the topic—and such is initially the rationally disclosed world—or cognition—and such is in the first place the agreement with the rational constitution of this world. The former we call 'mundane reason'; the latter, 'natural reason'. It is from these that conceptual reason distinguishes itself; it is a reason which conceives precisely that destiny which is given in one of the configurations of wisdom of our history—be it the wisdom of the Muses, of the Christian doctrine, or of the civil consciousness. Here, to man's distinction from himself corresponds reason's distinction from itself. The latter and only the latter furnishes the logic appropriate to the destiny. It is precisely in this that that which is traditionally called 'metaphysics' consists. It is devoted to reason's chief interest in each epoch, and we therefore direct, as far as our history is concerned, our question concerning reason's interest in language to metaphysics—more precisely, only to those metaphysical positions that are decisive for the architectonic of an epoch.

As for the first epoch, such a position is to be seen in the work of Parmenides. It conceives the destiny to which the knowledge of the Muses—above all in Homer but also in Hesiod and Solon—had given the appropriate expression: the μοῖρα. It is the share allotted to each: firstly of existence; then of esteem within the community; finally of goods. This destiny is realized in the enaction of right as it is brought to completion in a given instance by the insight of the father of the gods and men.

Parmenides translates this entire state of affairs as follows: the sole share that draws its limit beyond the totality of appearances, namely, in the House of the Night, is truth itself, which is accompanied by the power of persuasion. This destinal principle reveals itself in "being," more precisely: in its How: it must *be* completely and unshakably. For the λόγος, for pure reflection, this topic becomes the path on which it learns "how it is"; it is completed in insight, which itself *is* because it is complete and firmly grounded. The whole consisting of the destinal principle, its realization, and the cognition of the latter comes into view as what is perfect, namely, as that which has always already fulfilled its destiny.

Where does the consideration of language occur in this proportion? Insight expressly has to eliminate the modification of 'to be' (*sein*) by the modes of transition which "the mortals have made up, convinced that they are true"—firstly generation and also corruption; then within this span and related to a determinate There (*Da*): to be and also not to be there; further in the distinction of the There: now to be here, then there, thus occupying another place; finally the transition within the movable itself: changing the shining color. That which the mortals have made up here are names, although they name neither someone nor something. Only so long as these verbs are not known to be names can they lay claim to the persuasiveness of the true itself, namely, of "how it is." To discover their nominal character means: to separate them as something extrinsic to being, or the true, from the insight that is in being itself. In order to safeguard it from untruth, reason here takes an interest in language, and in fact in such a way that it completes the sense of the name with the complement of the predicates of transition.

The field of views which was excluded from truth now proves to be the proper place of names. Unlike insight, these views remain without a destinal principle and subject to change. Their field is wholly occupied by names—here in the proper sense of the naming of a What. Its thetic character and its instrumental function have been familiar from time immemorial. In the horizon of θεωρία decisive for Parmenides, they serve to distinguish the sensible. The simplest difference, however, is the opposition as it is disclosed when the first side is given by mere relating—this starting from the relation of a What to itself: "completely the same with itself but not the same with the different." This is philosophy's first formula of identity and belongs, it should be noted, to the views of the mortals, not to truth; it belongs to a distinguishing by means of posited and made up names that are assembled into a κόσμος ἐπέων, an order of words. The first elements here are what are originarily opposed, namely, light and night; due to the said identity, they take on the determinacy of elements and it is precisely on account of this that the manifold—including the gods understood genealogically—emerges by virtue of mixture. Within this world the mortals are themselves to be understood as mixed beings and their views as products of the changing mixture of their bodies, to which the tongue also belongs.

That which is thought by Parmenides as truth is ἀλήθεια, which prior to all philosophy was understood with reference to a possible λήθειν, deceiving, as it can affect always only a knower. And who could ever have understood precisely this deceptive power of the name better than Odysseus, since he gave himself the name 'no one'. In Parmenides it is manifest: deceptive are not the names the mortals have posited as signs of their views for the manifold What of the things of their world so much as those signs which are not recognized as names and which seemingly show "how it is." The difference of the name from the named has been known for ages, not, however, the segregation of being—that is, of truth—from the modifications of Being by transition. The corresponding insight was absolutely unattainable within the network of human views. Parmenides attained it in the entirely non-everyday experience of a mission which—only comparable with death—removed him from the totality of appearances and the corresponding world of words.

His insight became the bequest for both logic and rhetoric—and they are the sole disciplines in which the philosophy of the first epoch attended to, where not language, then nevertheless linguistic phenomena.

The history of our world would not have known a middle epoch without a conception equal to Parmenides'. It is Augustine's, related to the knowledge of the New Testament, to the destiny appearing there, which is not merely God but rather his glory. Its decisive version is Paul's, achieved with the distinction furnished only by the incarnate God. In his doing of truth the concealed glory of his provenance and the obvious but paradoxical glory of his humiliation (not only to become man but also to become the Crucified), a glory recognizable only through faith, are distinguished. Thus only faith catches sight of the glorification of the deceased in the resurrection and thus the justice of this God.

What becomes of this in the Augustinian ratio? It also starts with faith, unfolds it, in keeping with tradition, into thinking and assent, and recalls in thinking the ground of assent. The latter is given the meaning of love, which refers to the ground as wisdom: thus the *cultus* of precisely that God is *amor sapientiae.* The *fides* must at the same time be knowledge and this is related to the destinal principle (which is in turn differentiated) and in fact to the verb—it should be noted: not to the noun; it is, namely, the word of a promise and in fact a promise of presence (*Gegenwart*), that is, attendance (*Beistand*). In the fulfillment of the promise, the word is as much substance as subject, the latter in the literal sense of being the subjected; the Word subjects itself to itself in that it becomes not only soul but also flesh, thus becoming capable of both human action and suffering maltreatment. Finally the topic in which this destinal principle is to be realized is also a differentiated one: first in the seeing of truth on the basis of the depictive relation to the creative word, then in the doing of truth, which is related to the Word's *humiliatio*, to its self-humiliation.

Unlike the Parmenidean ratio, this Augustinian ratio, which consists of *intellectus fidei*, *verbum subiectum*, and *mens speculativa*, annexes itself to a preceding metaphysical ratio: the Plotinian. The latter marked the most thorough negation of Christian knowledge because it already excluded the possibility of the incarnation of the "Lord"—Plotinus also refers to the first Nature by this name. This "ineffable" One cannot go out of itself, to say nothing of being the word which acts as its own subject. Only its beauty lowers itself to those subordinate to it—namely, the hypostases: spirit and soul—in order to reveal itself to them as κόσμος. It is precisely the latter that gives occasion to reason in the human soul for *conversio*, for the turning back and the return into the first, which is no longer only the origin of spirit but also the ground of its κόσμος, and in fact due to the first's goodness.

Augustine's cognition converts not on the basis of an illumination but rather of a call to "read" and in fact to read a passage from Paul on man's distinction from himself. This *legere* is the bequest for reason's distinction from itself, in particular from its post-Plotinian, namely, mundane (in Iamblichus) and natural (in Porphyry), characters. It separates itself from the autocracy of self-deification as well as of the "running up into one's own true self," separates itself from the self of spirit. Only the said *legere* sets the *intus legere* of the inner word free, sets the *intellectus fidei* free which inaugurated the ratio just sketched.[1]

Now how does language come into view within this ratio? As the language of the doing of untruth, related, as in Parmenides, to the final term of the ratio, which is here no longer cognition but rather the topic, in short: the image of God. Of central significance here is a word that Augustine, following Paul, takes from the Old Testament: *omnis homo mendax*: every man is a liar. This state of affairs goes back to the practical language of the promise of the equality of a created spirit with God, thus in the denial of the absolute difference. The promise is ambiguous, is fulfilled not in the sense of the glory of God but rather in the sense of distinguishing between good and evil. Such distinguishing penetrates the language of man in that he goes beyond the incipient naming of animals as his companions to the practical language of self-apology and thus from the name to the statement in the sense that the latter is made specifically before him who judges and in fact before the divine judge.

The untruth that destines the Augustinian conception to consider language is the self-justification which is easily concealed in statements. In such justification lies self-glorification by virtue of one's own justice and thus the denial of the dependency of the image. It is precisely on account of this that the fabricated statement in the mere statement, the former belonging to the doing of the speaker, has to be distinguished from the mere statement. Only in the former does the sense of the statement, or the "inner word," speak.

How does the metaphysics of the final epoch answer our guiding question? The decisive position here is the concluding one, namely, the Hegelian position, in particular the *Science of Logic*. For its "labor of the concept" reveals the fundamental poietic, productive trait of the thinking of this epoch: truth as worked-out, after being for the middle epoch essentially the truth that is done, and for the first epoch, that of which there is insight.

The Hegelian ratio is opened by the topic, which only absolute labor in itself permits and accomplishes: the pure concept as the cause of itself, namely, of all its determinacy. It determines itself in that it distinguishes itself within itself—starting from the two moments of pure immediacy and also indeterminacy, namely, Being and nothingness, the unity of which is the first concept, namely, that of becoming. The term following this topic is cognition and in fact that of the contradiction inherent in the topic, a contradiction which sublates it into a determinacy that is in each instance new. For the topic, cognition is, more precisely, the element of the method of its progressive determination which moves the concept, being of contradictory determinacy and thus impossible truth, towards precisely that truth which is its destinal principle: the idea which as absolute does not leave any determinacy, not even the negative determinacy, outside of itself. It is reason's completely realized self-determination and is in this sense freedom.

But what Hegel said of spirit also holds of freedom: a force "is only as great as its exteriorization." In the absolute idea, however, it is not the moment of its mediation—for it is already accomplished—but only the moment of immediacy which is capable of exteriorization—and in fact as the exterior which Nature is—which first as spiritual Nature goes into itself up to the forms of absolute spirit: art, religion, and philosophy—as the absolutely free form of spirit; for in it spirit remains completely with itself and enjoys itself.

This conclusion of Hegelian thought refers to the decisive event in the knowledge of this epoch: the setting-apart of the destinal principle itself, a principle, namely, that appears immediately as Nature—precisely that concerning which Kant assures that its "ultimate intention . . . had indeed, in the constitution of our reason, been directed to moral interests alone" (*CPR*, B 829). This Nature clearly is to be distinguished from that which seems to the natural scientific understanding to exclude a causality arising from freedom.

The Hegelian ratio conceives a wisdom which has as its content the moral convictions of the "common reason of man"—conceives it in the scientific form that Kant had given it and in fact in defense of its essential purity. Therein lay the necessity that reason distinguish itself from itself—and in fact as a practical, legislative reason from its theoretical utility for the understanding in its cognitive operations. In the rational form of that wisdom, the destiny, namely, the idea of freedom, appears not only without any mediation but also as being incapable of mediation. It is realized in the moral law, more precisely: in the categorical imperative, and the rational feeling of respect corresponds to this topic.

This "sole feeling effected by reason" recalls that the wisdom of moral human reason had already been articulated by Rousseau. It demands not the distinction of reason so much as that of man from himself—in the release from all bondage into which he had steered himself: ultimately, political bondage. The self-infliction of this condition is what here inaugurates the historical span of the prevailing counter-Nature first with reference to the Nature of the origin, then with reference to the civil freedom of the other future, which is attainable only through the sublation of the existent condition.

The history of the formation of man by his own efforts awakens a new interest in the language that distinguishes him—as it is realized first by Herder, then by Humboldt, in the context of an anthropology. By contrast, Condillac's efforts remain bound up with the previous interest as it is alive on the one hand in Leibniz's "characteristics"—concerning language's utility to cognition—on the other—with regard to its utility to society—in Hobbes and also Locke.

We shall pass over all these positions, regardless of whether they have in view man's distinction from himself or only—as in anthropology—from other animals, and turn once again to Hegel—with the question: what destines his reason to consider language? Is an impulse provided by untruth also visible here? If in Parmenides untruth affected cognition; in Augustine, the topic; then it may be expected here: the destinal principle itself, namely, freedom.

It was interpreted by Kant as an idea, as a pure concept of reason, and therefore the destinal principle remained, according to its form, related, if not to cognition, then at least to the representing proper to the moral consciousness. Then Fichte offered freedom, according to its form, if not to the realized topic, then at least to that which is to be realized to infinity, namely, the ideal. Only Hegel succeeds in positing freedom, also according to its form, in the accomplished destinal principle itself.

And where does the untruth appear here that urges the consideration of language? Not in the *Science of Logic* but rather at the point where the latter's possibility, that is, the possibility of absolute knowledge, is denied—not in the concept but rather in natural consciousness, which is obsessed with its own finitude. Insofar as it cannot renounce itself, its own concept compels it to skeptical experience and directs it to its ground (*zugrunde richten*). The history of the formation of this consciousness is the *Phenomenology of Spirit*.

Accordingly untruth appears there in absolute significance and in fact in the moral self (*GW* 9, 354/399), for the latter opposes in the particularity of its conscience the universality of morality in that it knows itself to be "above the specific law and every content of duty" (*GW* 9, 352/397). Conscience can assert itself in this opposition, however, only so long as it does not express itself in specific actions. Such freedom of conscience, which keeps itself pure of the deed, would be morally meaningless were not this self-consciousness nevertheless to express itself and in fact in language. It expresses its conscientiousness before those of its kind—in the congregation of beautiful souls, which produce and socialize themselves in mutual praise. Freed from the universality that knows itself to be subjected to duty, they open in their communication of praiseworthy intentions the particular congregation of speaking. From this it follows: their language is the "hypocrisy" (*GW* 9, 356/401) of morality as it accompanies the good, more precisely: innocent, conscience.

The untruth of such expression is absolute insofar as it sets the destinal principle itself, namely, freedom, in contradiction with itself. Since freedom is nothing without its realization. The conscience that in its particularity sets itself against the universality of duty and nevertheless knows itself to be blameless since it does not expose itself through specific actions to the judgment by all the others, gives in its speaking the appearance of realized freedom. This is finitized through the opposition of the particular to the universal and thus negated as a destiny of absolute significance. Only the language of the pure ego, of the pure self-consciousness and conscience—which expresses itself in the reciprocal acknowledgment of the expressions of those of its own kind—offers itself as the element of this absolute untruth. Such is no longer the language of the statement but rather of self-expression in the strict sense, namely, of the self.

III

What sense would it make to search the history of philosophy for opinions about language? If the epochal conceptions of our history were sketched in the foregoing, then first in recollection of the non-everyday ground of their non-everyday speech, then in the elucidation of the occasion for and limits of its consideration of language. If this occasion lay each time in the threat to knowledge by untruth, more precisely: by the illusion of truth, then therein lies a hint of those sense-explications of modernity that in each instance take their point of departure from an immediate experience of untruth; thus they do not exclude it from their final term as do the metaphysical ratios but rather bring it to distinction in their first term. Strangely enough, these positions of the core region of our world come into contact with the epochal positions of our history just sketched, though in reverse order. Here too language comes into view in conjunction with untruth.

Here it is first the language of the topic, with which the Marxian ratio begins, namely, the relations of production. In them, hypocrisy appears not as that of the pure ego and its goodness so much as that of things which speak of their value as wares in such a way that they veil the social work in them through the comparative values of material properties.

Then language is that of cognition, with which the Nietzschean ratio begins, namely, faith. In it, the lie appears not to be that of the soul so much as that of the body and its life, which, out of its will to power, perverts the highest value, that is, it perverts the art of the beautiful illusion into the knowledge of truth. With this exchange, the will to power is deceptive about itself.

Finally language is deepened into that of the destiny itself, with which the Heideggerian ratio begins; such is the clearing of errancy. This appears, however, no longer as in Parmenides as that of human reason but, oddly enough, as that of the latter's mission, thus of that which gives what is to be thought. It disconcerts in that it disguises itself, in fact gives itself and yet withholds its proper gift. This distinction within itself has cleared (*gelichtet*). And it is just this that makes all the difference in the relation of this mission to human being. Since it becomes obvious that and how the latter is admitted into the fundamental challenging trait of the nature of technicity, but precisely on account of this, that and how it is capable of distinction in unison with this nature.

The difference in the untruth of the destiny itself was solely that the originary untruth, or errancy, has cleared. This clearing occurred not in the world, not in history, but only in speech, and in fact as the address of that which is withheld from human being and yet preserved: the world of the safeguarded thing, which has been rescued from its neglect. Man belongs in this world not as he who produces in society, not as he who creates himself in isolation, but rather as the mortal. This with respect to a death whose fundamental trait is sheltering, thus related to truth as unconcealment. Therefore, no death by demise or even perishing but a death that, strangely enough, is prior to Da-sein—prior as the concealed is prior to what is desheltered.

The world of the mortal in this sense is given only in language. But this gift allows the prevailing language of the technical world and, prior to that, the language of the history of metaphysics to become oppressive to Heidegger's thinking. In the separation from the one as well as from the other, the language of his own thinking became virtually absurd and seemed ever more repulsive. Contrary to the Wittgensteinian development, which presses into everyday language and settles into it as the primarily senseful language. By contrast, Heidegger's language is the absolutely non-everyday testimony to a listening that precedes speaking, a listening to the non-sounding language of a "destiny of the topic of thinking."

Keeping to language: it is striking in the core region of modernity that in the sequence from Marx via Nietzsche to Heidegger the immediate comprehensibility of what is said fades. This fading itself is to be read and respected as a sign. It gives reason's interest in language a turn without leaving untruth out of view. Which turn?

So-called postmodernity does not know what our world had in the sense-explications of modernity: its complete articulation.

Such is first legible for that reason which has learned its distinction and thus also its present task from the epochal conceptions of our history.

NOTE

1. Cf. my "The Philo-Sophical Conceptions of the Middle Epoch," where the sequence of terms has been reversed: namely, topic (the relation of *Deus et anima*), destinal principle (the subjected word), and cognition (*fides quaerens intellectum*).

THE DIMENSION OF SUBMODERNITY

The following reflections are dedicated to a friend, a neighbor. In which neighborhood? That of present thought. How are the boundaries of its present determined? The sense-explication of modernity had installed in our world as an explicated one the departure from its history. Not only is this departure noted with mere indifference in so-called postmodernity. What is more: a separate sphere of thinking has been formed which in a word and on the basis of a preliminary distinction can be indicated in contrast to the spheres of history and world as "speech," a sphere which is to be thought neither—in view of the history of philosophy—intrahistorically nor—in view of the world of the sense-explication—intramundanely; like the two spheres that have already been determined, it is to be thought as a totality that is closed and articulated "rationally" within itself. Accordingly the sphere of speech should also allow itself to be distinguished into three dimensions—if it distinguishes itself as much within as from itself. We shall have to leave this qualification for the time being as a hint—as an initially dark one.

In order to delimit our neighborhood through its locality: in which dimension do we meet? Not in school-filiations and effective histories of "philosophizing" but rather in a present that we anticipatorily characterize here as "submodernity." First disclosed in Merleau-Ponty's thought—already taken up by Masullo in his work *Structure, Subject, Predicate*, but also in a treatise concerned expressly with speech, "The Play of Significance and the Solitude of Sense." In these the themes of intersubjectivity, fundaments, and the pathic come to bear.

Which common locality of thinking was opened by Merleau-Ponty? According to its position, it recalls that dimension which formed the hermeneutic reason of modernity—bound up with the names Dilthey, Husserl, and Wittgenstein. It had set itself the task of a First Philosophy. But it failed to fulfill it each time—not least because the metaphysical conception of a bequest of "truth" was simulated; however, the bequest was no longer to be taken up in the form of a pregiven knowledge, more precisely: of a σοφία, but rather as pregiven "Being," or "life" as it is prior to all thinking. No philo-sophy was possible here, namely, the sheltering of a truth about the destiny of man in the bastion of a logic. The bequest of life and its doxic constructs permitted only the former conception's simulation, which, to be sure, is certainly to be distinguished from the imitation of an exemplar.

Just as the sense-explication of modernity formed its peripheral dimension via the hermeneutic simulation of philosophical conception, so too present thought forms its periphery via the simulation of the core of modernity, that is to say: of the Marxian, Nietzschean, and Heideggerian sense-explications. Now what reveals the respective positions of Merleau-Ponty, Foucault, and Derrida as—as it is called—"postmodern" is their abandonment of, as it were, "apocalyptic" reason and its projections of the other world of the other man of a necessary, possible, and not impossible future. "Anarchic" reason, as it were, expunges this last trace of the thought of man's distinction from himself. It was this thought that stamped the configurations of σοφία of our history and time and again provoked a philo-sophy, whether to the rejection or to the autocratic replacement or to the conception of the σοφία's truth.

Whereas the core sense-explication of modernity found its place outside of philo-sophy, the simulation of the former retreats into the surrounding haze of the latter, thereby entering into the "bad and confusing danger," which is how Heidegger had viewed "philosophizing" (*GA* 13, 80). An assessment that Wittgenstein shared for other reasons. Submodern thought no longer insists, as did the core sense-explication of modernity, in an experience of expropriation with regard to the *operationes* proper to man as well as formerly to God: power, will, knowledge. Not moved by an other future, it drags Marxian, Nietzschean, and Heideggerian thought into a philosophy which is continued without crisis beyond all "discussion." The opportunity for such continuation is offered it especially by Husserl, particularly by his alleged "idealism." Even where the difference between 'transcendental' and 'empirical' is of dwindling significance, thinking abandons itself to the inquiry into "possibility" in the sense of what is made possible by the empirical findings that it adopts from the human sciences. Yet it no longer makes any sense here to reproach the reason in question for impurity. It has no grounds for purifying itself, for distinguishing itself within and even from itself.

How is the locality of submodernity structured for the view that knows its limits and, moreover, their transgressability? We shall unfold this locality according to its simplest proportions, or ratios, which are built out of the terms 'destiny' (translated in submodernity as the 'reigning impulse'), 'topic', and 'thinking'.

I

The first of these comes to bear in Merleau-Ponty's work.

B) Like the Husserlian proportion it begins immediately with the term of the topic. But since the "lifeworld" is released from the dimension of transcendental subjectivity, here it holds prior to the Husserlian: like the Marxian proportion. In it the topic—namely, value—is developed as follows: it appears first in mundane determinacy—as a thing in its use—then takes on the speech of the wares, in order finally to become historical in the form of the eminent, that is, productive ware 'manpower'. With the latter the topic is unveiled in its totality: the relations of production or the historically resultant society. On Merleau-Ponty's view, however, the productivity proper to that society is reduced to a particular productivity (*PhP*, 199/171 (note))—over against that universal, likewise "material," productivity, which means: "to make sense and to communicate it" (*PM*, 197/141). If this is in fact "what is most proper to me," then it is, all the same, integrated in a society which is formed not only by intersubjectivity but prior to this by "intercorporeality."

1) First for the bodies in question is their linguistic character. If the latter can no longer be that of a soul which voices its thoughts, then especially the body itself has to undergo an exegesis that radically separates it from its objectivistic representation on a physical basis—with reference to the philosophical tradition: from the *res extensa* and its further categorial determination.

Percipere is the actuality of the ego, which the body is—this viewed not as it occupies a position in space but rather as it inhabits it; perceiving and moving, it discloses its specific situation—out of "latent intentionality." The body-ego is included in the "spatializing-temporalizing vortex, which flesh is" (*VI*, 297 f./244), because it is "of interiorly worked-over mass" (193/147).

The "incarnate" existence is stamped in its comportment and its corresponding habits not only by so-called material needs but, prior to these, by the fact that it is a "sexualized body," no longer merely reproductive in the sense of the "proletarian" (cf. *proles*) body—prior to this: it is sexualized with regard to speech and in fact due to the structure of expressive relations which are precisely peculiar to sexuality, relations in which a body-ego is there for its kind and in which others encounter it (*PhP*, 184/157). Here an entire body speaks to an entire body—not speech as it is understood as a sign-system of and for the ideas of the "intellectual soul."

But how is that speech understood which has to distinguish the body-ego in order to replace the former *differentia specifica* of man, namely, his ratio? It asserts its equal rank with reason at the point where it as speaking speech is distinguished from spoken speech (*PM*, 123/87). For speaking speech is "always occupied with itself alone," that is to say: with the differences between expressions, between gestures, and between verbal chains (161/115). It is not as if it, like pure reason, essentially attended to itself, not as if it were occupied with pure rational concepts (Kant, *CPR*, B 708). The words "leave in our mind no empty corner for pure thoughts" (*PM*, 161 f./115). For speech in itself "never says anything; it invents a series of gestures which between them exhibit differences sufficiently clear for the conduct of speech, to the extent that it repeats itself, trims itself again, and confirms itself, and irrevocably purveys to us the course and contours of a universe of sense" (46 f./32). This in endless work; for "the expression is never absolutely expression, what is expressed is never completely expressed; it is essential to speech that the logic of its constructions never yields such constructions that can be conceptualized" (52/37). Its logic is decisively not that of the rationality which determined the *animal rationale*. Thus the man in possession of the said speech is radically other. How is that?

2) "Speaking" speech understands itself only in its differentiation from signs, which are not yet representatives of certain significations (35/24). It has to come into the world of human communication. Such discloses itself to the foregoing perception (174/124) as the "carnal relation" of the body to the world (193/139), in whose flesh the body is a "cavity" or "fold," which is once again smoothed over upon death (*VI*, 308/254).

Everything that is lived through is perceived in the expression towards which it presses (*PM*, 106/75). Man perceives his kind in gestures he knows to be shared modes of comportment (60/42). The communication of perceiving bodies first becomes egoic where the gesture is transcended towards the word—as naming, as signifying, sense-imparting word (196/141). It is only here that an other is present as the other—representiated in turn as one who representiates and in fact in a shared present.

The egos communicating in this way bear—unlike the former self-consciousness—"the germ of depersonalization" within themselves (29/19); as in this connection it holds in a new sense: *esse est percipi*—to recall Beckett's *Film*. For the speech spoken in the world of corporeal perception is in each instance one shared in its totality (59/42)—not at all according to the former community of reason and its concepts (56/40): "Discourse speaks itself within me. [. . .] I put myself into the other, I introduce him into myself" (28/19). Exposed to one another, mutually accommodating one another (27/18), "the limits between mine and not-mine" disappear (202/145). What is more: insofar as he communicates, everybody is capable "of letting himself be destructured (*défaire*) and restructured (*refaire*) by the others" (30/20)—no longer in the image of the Lord but rather in that of the *socius* in a submodern *societas*, which is "communistic" no longer in economic but rather in originary significance, that is, it issues from the linguistic being. The "social totality" is so penetrant here that Merleau-Ponty can say: "If I wanted to render precisely the perceptual experience, I would have to say that the They perceives in me and not that I perceive" (*PhP*, 249/215). With this They, an existence becomes apparent that is no longer receptive to the Heideggerian distinction between inauthenticity and authenticity. The demand essential to all wisdom, that man distinguish himself from himself, has become inaudible here. Instead it holds: change the style of your world-comportment (*PM*, 198/142), let yourself be restructured by the others (20/13). The communicative experience says: "There is an ego which is other, which has its seat elsewhere and deprives me of my central position" (187/135). The perceiving body, which reaches beyond me, has always already prepared such a decentralization of the individual, of several, and even of all, individuals.

3) The world of verbal communication is firstly a cultural one (112/78); in it the standard of adequation, the viewpoint of similarity, no longer holds sway as in the natural world but rather the viewpoint of transformation; on account of this the cultural world grows layer by layer. It is a sedimented world (195/141) and it is precisely in this sense that the relations of communication are of historical concretion.

The sedimentation of signifying acts (114/81 (note)) and thus of the genesis of sense (116/82) "accumulates not only creation upon creation but it integrates" (142/100) them at the same time—even other cultures into the same history, since into the same present (122/86) of a shared future and a tradition that causes the origins to be forgotten (96/68).

A) Viewed with respect to the historically concretized relations of communication (no longer: of production), the reigning impulse becomes apparent to which the topic of Merleau-Ponty's ratio is subject.

1) As historical, however, that impulse consists of the demand for social progress through the transformation of the relations of communication themselves.

2) But what keeps this progress going is the reigning impulse in linguistic significance: the demand for a creativity that breaks open the sediments of sign-systems already instituted, and enters into the "initial situation of a non-signifying world," as it "is always that of the creator" (82/58).

3) The reigning impulse attains mundane concretion where it sets its goal for progress in the relations of communication: "the social" (*S*, 155/123) as it is to be persistently perceived by the body-egos.

C) What is thinking?—philosophy asks this time and again (20/14). It now asks: what is the thinking that is subject to the cited reigning impulse, conditioned by the relations of the aforementioned communication—once again: no longer of production?

1) Thinking "seeks contact" with "raw being," as it is imparted to thinking by the body's perceiving and imagining (*VI*, 49/29). Its highest calling is to "enlighten" the belief intrinsic to perception (139/103). In that it commits itself each time in a certain situation (126/92)—primarily one of "exploitation and oppression" (*S*, 399/320)—in that it gets involved, regarding "the social," with the perception in the "flesh of the present" (*VI*, 10/xxxv), enlightening thinking has to be immediately politicized.

2) Light is shed on it here, however, always by a perceiving and imagining within an historical horizon (*PM*, 159/112). In a situation which sees modernity reach its limit this means: the Marxist notion of the structure and aim of a history of class struggles (*S*, 298/235) is to be dismissed; it has been worn out "as a matrix of intellectual and historical experiences" (15/10)—and with it the fixation on "revolutionary praxis" (13/8). With regard to history, philosophy becomes "action at a distance" (20/13), namely, critical theory. Marxian thought does not disappear here, however; it will henceforth summon up the "echoes" of a "classic" (16/11).

3) The thinking-term attains its concretion in linguistic significance. For it, of concern is ultimately the transformation of the "fetishes" of traditional representation into "art" (*PM*, 111/79)—into precisely that which is possible only by virtue of the veiling of the speech in speech, namely, of what is spoken in the speaking speech (35/24). It is only on account of this that critical thinking can come to transform not merely ideas but rather their matrices (126/90), to impose a "coherent deformation" on the visible (128/91). The literary work is able to "distend, to incite our *imago* of the world"—it is already the transformation of a perceived world into a spoken world (173/124)—"towards a new sense" (128/91). It is only the thinking which translated the "I think" into the "I speak" that reaches the creative dimension of speaking speech; here "it continues beyond, it conserves destructively, it interprets deformingly" (95/68). A critical thinking that not only employs speech but rather, focused on "the secret of its inventions of style," speaks of the word itself (143/101). Here critique becomes creativity in the field of that world of perception which is "the system 'ego–other'" (27/18). Of concern here is no longer the truth of an "adequation with things" (93/66) but rather the truth of anticipation (181/129)—to be sure, not: projection. It is only in this way that creative thinking actualizes itself as emancipatory.

And which other reason (34/23) comes to bear in this connection? It has its rationality—in accordance with the relations of communication—in association with the "*accord des esprits*," with the agreement of "emancipatory" thinkers. Such no longer requires "that we all reach the same idea on the same path or that the significations be enclosed in a definition; [rationality] requires only that every experience carry with it points of stimulation for all ideas and that the 'ideas' have a configuration" (198/143). Here the pluralism of the idea in submodern society finds itself safeguarded—in the midst of stimulating experiences which are common to those who are persistently others, as they are perceived.

II

The second ratio in the figure of anarchic reason is unfolded by Foucault—no longer simulating the Marxian but instead the Nietzschean sense-explication.

C) It begins immediately with the term of thinking—without the support of a previously elucidated topic or reigning impulse. But how is such a thinking structured within itself?

1) With respect to a speech that speaks no longer on the inside of an ego but rather on the outside of an id—without ever falling silent. An incessant murmur. Speech's speaker does not have the identity of the ego as a *res cogitans*, is not the author of what is spoken, for that which he articulates or to which he gives voice is the originarily perceived murmuring of the id, particularly that of its unconscious desires.

2) This "thought from the outside" comes into the world insofar as it runs up against what has already been spoken by the others, their articulated desires. As for how such articulation meets this thought, it is already regulated, usually having already fallen under the spell of the "orders of discourse"; it subjects the interlocutor in many different ways and even forces him to acknowledge the specialized languages from whose game he is excluded. Confronted with such barriers, which are in turn always social, thinking learns to help itself to the freedom of "transgression." It wants to be deregulated—especially in the voicing of individual desires. This implies that thinking thinks subversively against the prevailing orders. Yet for thinking, the peculiar means of such subversion of all artificial barriers is primarily the exposure of the genealogy of order.

3) It is precisely in this respect that thinking realizes itself as historical. Its theme is the subjection of the individual to the will to truth, to the forms of social violence, finally to an originarily Christian ethics. Especially the scrutiny and guidance of one's conscience subjects the latter to the commandments, to a universal and its alleged necessity.

B) The topic of this thinking which understands itself historically is the individual man:

1) as he is primarily an historical subject of that knowledge of himself which the modern human sciences produced regarding his life, his work, and his talking. They created the representation of man to which the individual subjects himself as his universal. Finally, for him the will to the knowledge of himself represented his sexuality. Its history points, however, beyond the epoch of representation back to the Greek and Roman world, where self-knowledge was part of the technology of living, the "care of the self"—care in the sense of the economy of desires and pleasures, of one's management of one's own well-being. As the annihilator of ancient technologies of living, namely, as excessive subjecting regulation, as the advocate of a universal "thou shalt" contrary to one's own will, Christianity intervenes in this historical distinction (cf. "Technologies of the Self").

2) However, the topic, which is thereby disclosed historically, takes on a linguistic significance in the present and in fact in the self-dissolution of humanism, ultimately of the representation of man by the human sciences; for their subject gets lost in the "no-man's-land" disclosed by structural anthropology and psychoanalysis. The id mentioned at the outset appears here as a linguistic structure (cf. *The Order of Things*).

3) The ground on which the mundane realization of scientific humanism stands becomes all the more shaky and brittle. Namely, this humanism's authoritative knowledge created authoritarian institutions that exercised exclusive violence within society: the asylum, the clinic, and in general the manifold facilities for the correction, supervision, and discipline of individuals, finally the steadily deepening network of a public administration that intervenes in the self-regulation of the individual, in his selection of the means for achieving well-being, even demanding of him the notion of a stable identity as a person—interfering not only with his being other than the others but also with this: himself becoming an other over and over again. It is precisely at this possibility, however, that the reigning impulse in the Foucaultian ratio aims.

A) In a world permeated by the violence of disciplinary structures, that impulse takes on:

1) firstly the significance of a counter-violence; it is concentrated in the resistance not of a class, not even of a political party, but rather in protests by masses of individuals, each of whom insists upon the de-limitation of the realization of his private distinction between pleasure and displeasure. The positive side of such emancipation is the demand made upon society that it foster the self-actualization of each and every individual. The self of such actualization, however, is not that of any identity somehow preestablished, it is no ideal, but rather the particular projection of an alterity which is related to the others, which attains determinacy only on the basis of this relation.

2) The demand *en masse* for individual self actualization necessarily stands in a negative relation to a history of *mancipatio*, as Christianity decisively required it and in fact as the task of placing one's own will in God's hands, a task that was renewed by the demand inherent in the modern era that man subject himself as citizen to the universal rational will as it takes shape in the social contract.

3) Contrary to the universality essential to the concept, self-actualization assumes finally a linguistic form, and in fact in the voicing no longer of noetic but rather of aesthetic values, which allow one's existence to be made into a work of art, though a work that neither knows nor wants any completion; it is precisely on account of this that it asserts a creativity for which the self, as one that is to be actualized as always an other, remains open. In a game whose outcome is always unpredictable. Self-actualization—such means the unrestrained self-management of one's own desires and pleasures. Without letting oneself be subjected by a morality of universal obligation.

Now has the They, which became apparent in Merleau-Ponty, disappeared or been at all expunged in Foucault? The "individualism" for which he is usually reproached has its individuality precisely in the They, for the self of self-determination is—whether a majority or minority—one procured *en masse*, one which cannot at all urge the ego to its distinction from itself.

III

The third ratio—Derrida has presented it—concludes the figure of anarchic, or better: polyarchic, reason. With the latter this submodern way of thinking simulates the Heideggerian sense-explication. Derrida's ratio begins with the term of the reigning impulse and in fact in such a way that it understands the universal law as the justice of God, who is the epitome of alterity, namely, the Wholly Other. Not only is he de-logized in his alterity; he cannot be thought as ground because he is contradictory within himself and in fact to the point of indeterminacy. Everybody can be this god, for the Derridian motto reads: *tout autre est tout autre*, which in fact means that every other is wholly other. Here the primacy of alterity without identity is expressed—the last step after making a start with the others, who are constitutive of the ego, and the progress towards precisely this individual's alterity. In the solidarity of each other with the others, with respect to whom it is other, the submodern god appears as the other who is wholly other. He rejected the "privilege of presence" marking the entire occidental tradition—according to the noetic attention to himself, he even dismissed from himself the aisthetic attention to the others. But the presence was privileged because it is essential to the master and his mastery.

A) It is precisely on account of this that we can say: the reigning impulse immediately appearing here is emptiness. In it the way of thinking proper to submodernity in general is exhausted.

1) Let us first take it up in linguistic significance: of the reigning impulse as de-presenced, nothing remains "save the name" (cf. *Sauf le nom*)—though not an unequivocal one. Rather a name such as 'god' insofar as it suggests names of many kinds. Radically pluralistic as Foucaultian society already was. In his inconceivability this god is similar to the epitome of the ἄλογον, namely, of the χώρα, in Plato (cf. *Khôra*). He is the impossible, who cannot be excluded on account of his self-contradictoriness. As the Wholly Other he is the mystery, though an empty one.

2) How does this linguistic being, who does not even murmur, come into the world? As the "*différance*"—a distinguishing that presupposes nothing identical. Of this it is said: "It governs nothing, reigns over nothing, and nowhere exercises any authority. [. . .] Not only is there no kingdom of *différance*, but *différance* instigates the subversion of every kingdom" (*Dif*, 22/22). It appropriates the emptiness of space and time and in fact as "elsewhere" and "some other time," no longer in reliance on the present of here and now, as was proper to reason's attention to itself, proper to its omnipresence. The originary disclosive force of desire places itself beyond the exclusion of the contradiction of "being for oneself an other."

3) In the groundless play of its world, divine desire, which leaves and covers over its trails, is directed as much towards wasting itself, towards self-consumption, as towards the postponement of its satisfaction. Its self-consumption is its complete burning within itself: is the Holocaust. By contrast, the side of the postponement is its history in which the originary mystery is repressed. Its extreme is the other Holocaust, which does violence to precisely that people who alone knew: "Justice is an experience of the impossible" (*FL*, 946/947). Here there is no room for the question: how was the Holocaust possible? It indicates the end of the occidental history of reason and its culture of right.

C) The reigning impulse is in itself empty and cannot as such call forth any reason; as the Wholly Other it remains the "inconceivable unknown."

1) It is only in its historical concretion as the monstrosity of the Holocaust that it stimulates a thinking (cf. *Cinders*) of primarily historical determinacy. It turns against its philosophical tradition as whose result it imagines the technology of "giving death" *en masse* to be (cf. *The Gift of Death*). In view of this gift, of the perversion of the originary "it gives" (*es gibt*) in Heideggerian thought, it empties itself of all content of the tradition's so-called logocentrism. It "deconstructs" the tradition's constructs, scans it for cracks that allow its cohesion to

be decomposed. It regards it as being oriented towards an outside, to which these constructs have closed themselves. This thinking causes the systems to slide in pieces towards the outside and thus to collapse; it sounds the "death bell" especially for the Hegelian system, which is the most mature system (cf. *Glas*).

2) Its linguistic determinacy is gained by the thinking released from the dominance of the λόγος in that it expunges the present constitutive of the λόγος: the representiation of what has previously been thought or known. The priority of the utterance corresponding to the latter over its written form is in turn inverted in favor of a writing which, no longer as a phonetic writing, is bound to thought on the inside of the speaker (cf. *Of Grammatology*). If what was formerly said is reduced to what has been spoken and this in turn to what has been written, which is now only a fragmented "trace" or "tombstone" of that which has been thought, then the thinking that moves about within the intercorporeality of such signs has a free hand to bring their "polysemy" into play; it itself thus becomes radically pluralistic.

3) What does this mean for the mundane character in which thinking becomes concrete? It enters into the world of the others, each of whom has the right to think differently. However completely differently one may think—he thinks like the They thinks, for in the public of his everyday life it is decided what is and is not relevant in what is thought. Here it is always already understood that the ontological difference thematized by philosophy is not of primary relevance but rather sexual difference is (cf. *Of Spirit: Heidegger and the Question*). This is confirmed by peering through the cracks of metaphysical systems; here in logocentrism the phallocentrism of the occidental tradition becomes visible.

B) Emptied of the tradition, this thinking meets its topic in what is forethought by the They insofar as it claims relevance (*FL*, 972/973).

1) The topic shows itself to be primarily of mundane determinacy with the claim that it concerns every other. Here are the problems whose "elsewhere" and "some other time" no longer permit any indifference—through the traditional fixation on the here and now. The entire world claims the attention of the pluralistic society. Where every other stands in comparison with every other—simultaneously as individual and *en masse*—the unequal share of the possibilities of life has to be the most pressing problem here and in fact under the title of "injustice"—not related to a concept of justice but rather to many different views on equality.

2) The prevailing injustice, however, is to be understood as an historical result. For here, there is the history of the dominance of men who have asserted their specialness as "adult white male Europeans, carnivorous and prone to

sacrifice" (*FL*, 950/951). Thus history is that of Eurocentrism, of the oppression of youths, women, and non-whites, that of the animal-butchers and, not least, of those who were able to set the Holocaust into motion. Contrary to such flagrant injustice the rights of those beings who are always other are to be demanded.

3) The topic of thinking finally has to attain linguistic determinacy. Starting from a "sensitization" of society in the sense of a responsiveness of the particular others to the others. With respect to this responsiveness the "unlimited responsibility" of everybody for everybody is likewise to be understood. The impossibility obvious therein of a demand made from all sides is not admitted as an objection that could abolish such responsibility but rather only as a recollection of the said experience of the impossible or of the god of submodernity.

The responsiveness of the They has to be immanently of global significance. It is articulated *en masse* in the body language of demonstrations; their signs are intended to be slogans, effective in the world of intercorporeality. Lacking a concept, as must be so in the case of justice, more of it is demanded to infinity. Translated into social power-relations this means: more democracy.

Of concern here is not a well-defined form of constitution. Its concept is surpassed as merely formal in an endless process of the "democratization" of all social relations. This concrete topic of thinking has its relation to the empty mystery of the reigning impulse only in literature: "No democracy without literature, no literature without democracy"; for it alone realizes the right to say absolutely everything (*P*, 65/28); such is possible by virtue of the separation of speech in what has been written from the author as a legal subject. This unique right to place even the prevailing right into question, to assert justice contrary to it, refers to the mystery of democracy, which alone is safeguarded by literature—with precisely that emptiness of determinacy which allows the demand for "more democracy" to be made to infinity. Those who demand this constitute the They, who is everybody who is an other over against others and precisely this: who is Wholly Other, who demands that this fact be safeguarded by the others.

IV

Is the dimension of submodernity unfolded here everything in the totality of speech and so in the horizon of our shared present? No: it knows a second dimension. Which?

We recall: the hermeneutic reason of modernity had dealt with "sense" in the doxic data of life and lived experience in contrast to the techno-scientific cognition of the world. Once the simulation effective there of the former metaphysics had been exhausted, in postmodernity linguistics assumes the rank of the former First Science (Jakobson). It is firstly "pure linguistics"—no longer pure of all empirical data but rather of the ego of the speaker and the peculiarities of its "tongues." It is then expanded into semiology (Barthes), finally concretized into the treatment of precisely those linguistic structures to which structural anthropology (Lévi-Strauss) and psychoanalysis (Lacan) attend.

This structuralist dimension also harbors the possibility of disclosing the speech in question "logo-tectonically"—not by chance in reliance on the system of the Kantian categories of relation. Accordingly the, as it were, substantial mode of speech understood instrumentally is to be seen in its expressive function; then the, as it were, causal mode, in its informative function; finally the relation of reciprocity, in its communicative function. Here it becomes clear: the functions completed in this way have in the latter their first and definitive function. This all the more resolutely as verbal language has been integrated into the expanse of body language—in Merleau-Ponty's terms: into "intercorporeality." The traditional standard of the λόγος or of "enunciations"—of saying-something-about-something—for the comprehension of what speech is, is thereby radically expunged. Along with it, the reliance on the utterance of that which is comprehended "in the soul." What would this "soul" be in sub- and postmodernity? It has fallen silent. The sense of the sign as such—as Derrida makes clear—has been transformed. This already becomes visible in its de-limitation, which results in an infinite plurality of interpretations.

Whereas this dimension of the explicative totality of speech is only the *complementum* of the first dimension, the They enters into an exclusive relation to the configurations of wisdom, thus of knowledge, which were conceived in the history of philosophy: the knowledge of the Muses concerning justice, the knowledge of Christian revelation concerning goodness, the poietic knowledge derived from the humanity of man concerning holiness. The They in no way spoke there. It is not as if the They would not take note of all this, but not as what has been said, not as the admission of man into his distinction from himself, but rather merely as what was spoken, as "texts" woven into the previous social relations.

In this dimension all our neighborhoods come to an end. Yet the prospect of that which is alien in contrast to the neighboring regions, namely, the prospect of the pre-philosophical configurations of wisdom—mediated by the seemingly "implausible" "*grands récits*" (Heidegger's, Nietzsche's, and Marx's projections of the singularly other man)—decides the question of friendships in thinking. How does Cicero say it in reliance on Aristotle? *Idem velle et idem nolle vera amicitia est* (To will the same and to reject the same is true friendship).

IS TOTALIZING THINKING TOTALITARIAN?

Let us begin—as is fitting—with what is familiar. Now, familiar is by no means what "totalizing thinking" is, but rather what 'totalitarian' means. Today this word rings in everybody's ears, is common in public life—not so much as a descriptive as more a defamatory epithet. It brands political systems of our time that not only had terrifying consequences but, what is more, spread terror through their form of domination. Now, rule by means of terror is in fact no recent invention; new here is rather the technique of the complete penetration of every expression of social life. Were the latter perhaps susceptible in a special way to such penetration?

Totalitarian—even if this word looks like a technical term, in its use it is nevertheless saturated with every bit as much aversion as was the word 'evil' formerly. The earlier impression of evil has been preserved for contemporary society in nothing so plainly as in the experience of the technology of domination employed by totalitarian systems. The sight of evil has always been exciting. This is even corroborated by the attempt to expose its banality, to deny it the spirituality of the diabolical. Thus the research into totalitarianism cannot and does not wish to conceal its genesis from excitement, especially about the National Socialist system. The, so to speak, ultimate and at the same time most extreme evil has become the motor of a branch of research. But was not political science already introduced as a substitute for theology in the canon of university disciplines? (Cf. Jefferson's founding of the University of Virginia.)

In the inquiry into the nature and especially the origin of totalitarian domination, its moral assessment—in the wake of Heidegger's translation of Nietzsche's conviction that the decisive philosophical tradition is the ideology of Christian-socialist morality—had to run up against the history of the former First Philosophy, named metaphysics. This all the more so as the structure of the sense-explications, into which modernity has been articulated (cf. my *Rational Architectonic of Modernity*), had already regarded metaphysical thinking as futile, disconcerting, and even disastrous. Already here a socially animated critique in philosophical guise was encouraged. In the Platonic beginning and in the Hegelian end of metaphysics, the first enemies of the open society were unmasked. The others were found in modernity itself. Oddly enough, within our world precisely the fiercest opponents of the metaphysical tradition appeared to be the heirs of the totalitarian thinking endemic in philosophy—namely, Marx, Nietzsche, and Heidegger.

Modernity knew a submodernity in all quarters and in fact with regard to the bequests of the former's sense-explications, to which submodernity adheres and on which it still—left to itself—dwells. In the latter it clearly emerges what the talk of the "open society" amounts to: the horizon of judgment is in the first place not that of political-scientific research but rather a political, and what is more: social, conviction; it is grounded in a mentality known and valued as pluralistic. So a society is not open just because it happens to be democratically constituted—in the sense of the classical doctrine of right concerning republican forms of government—rather, only when its democracy is determined from the standpoint of the pluralistic mentality. The region peculiar to this mentality is, namely, not the state, let alone the family, but rather social everyday life. It is here in this region that what totalizing thinking is and how it becomes totalitarian, opposing pluralism, is disclosed to contemporary man. Which plurality is claimed here?

In everyday life an experience holds sway to which Sterne referred at the outset of his *Tristram Shandy*: ταράσσει τοῦς ἀνθρώπους οὐ τὰ πράγματα, ἀλλὰ τὰ περὶ τῶν πραγμάτων δόγματα (what excites people are not the facts but rather the views concerning the facts). A plurality of views as they are ever mine—hence: plurality of opinions (*Meinungen*). Opinions about what? About anything that an open society can leave open; about anything that calls for one to take a stand, so that one not so much expresses one's opinion but rather reveals one's attitude. Thus: a plurality of attitudes—to provide it with the unlimited accessibility of a public, however, is in turn a matter of attitude, precisely of the pluralistic mentality.

Whose? Not that of an ego as it asserts its opinion; rather, that of a society which has in this mentality its so-called "basic consensus." In it is based the peculiar force of this mentality, which is buttressed by what is taken for granted: the agreement to differ openly not only in opinions but already in attitudes—which themselves are ever changing. To be excluded here are only those who break with the consensus concerning such openness. Just as little as a crime can count as an alternative to legitimate action, so too the totalitarian mentality cannot count as a mere *oppositum* to the pluralistic one. The former is rather the privation of the latter. It is just such a distortion that especially Heidegger had already ascribed to metaphysical, and in the end to technical, thinking. The pluralistic mentality's account of itself—most tangible in Lyotard's *The Postmodern Condition*—takes its point of departure from this and assures: totalizing thinking is totalitarian. And from the former's collaborators we hear: "The flip side of totality is constraint and terror" (Welsch, 39). Now does this characterization of the thought of totality also hold for metaphysics?

As for the claimed totalizing, we first let Kant speak: pure reason is preoccupied with nothing but itself. It becomes its own object in its ideas. These concepts of pure reason are all totalities according to form and content; according to the metaphysical tradition, they are not indefinitely many but exactly three: the soul as immortal, the world as either eternal or created, and God or the most perfect being as the *omnitudo realitatis*. Reason thinks of each of these predicates as founded and does so in each instance in a syllogism—it is after all the "faculty of conclusion." The conclusively determined totalities in turn form a system and in fact one corresponding to the distinct forms of the rational syllogism: the categorical, the hypothetical, and the disjunctive. The system is thus a totality of totalities, brought to completion in Hegel's *Science of Logic*. This work knows only one idea, the pure concept, which determines itself by way of its methodical distinction within itself. It is precisely this self-determination, and in fact to be that totality which Hegel calls 'the pure personality', that gives rise to the concept of freedom, which Kant was only able to presuppose as idea and which Fichte could only anticipate as ideal.

What is thought in this way has to give the impression within the horizon of the pluralistic mentality of being mere quibbling. Its interest would much rather be engaged by the Kabala. Even the scholarly preoccupation with Kant and so-called German Idealism does not change the fact that today the signs of a kind of reason are nowhere to be seen which as pure reason would be occupied always and only with itself. Without it, however, the said totalities are lifeless imitations, and thus scholarship manages no more than to bring reason up for discussion as a matter of opinion.

Yet the talk of totalizing thinking does not have such rational totalities (whether substance or subject) in view so much as it does the concept of the understanding insofar as it subsumes a multitude of individuals under a universal and thereby has always already disregarded the individual in its individuality in favor of the universal, be it species or genus. Now anyone with some acquaintance with history could easily see just how resolutely the natural theology of the late Middle Ages and also the philosophy of consciousness of the early modern era—for instance, from the former, Cusanus; from the latter, Leibniz—had respected individuality. What irritates the contemporary critique with regard to subsumption, then, is rather the projection of the critique's aversion to the relation between function and argument, as Frege established it for our world with logicized arithmetic in the language of the sciences and as it, in the guise of economic calculation, penetrates the so-called relations of production. To blame Aristotle for the subsumptive force of the universal shows only that even Heidegger's adversaries live off his knowledge and his judgment without penetrating the intention either of the one or of the other. Aristotle's definition of the definition could teach otherwise, for it reads: ὁ λόγος ὁ τὸ τί ἦν εἶναι λέγων (the explanation that explains what something was destined to be; *Metaph.* 1016^{a}33). Yet how could this be thinkable for the submoderns: to fulfill a destiny?

Subsumption is subjection—so the pluralistic mentality judges. Here its concern only seems to lie with the individuality of things; in truth, of concern is the diversity of attitudes and in fact in the claim to so-called self-determination. It is for the sake of the latter that one gladly refers to the tradition of the Enlightenment and professes that its program remains to be fulfilled. But since it is obvious that Kant understood something about the Enlightenment and about the freedom called for by Rousseau, it is easy to see that the emancipatory intention of the pluralistic mentality has its origins elsewhere. We need only recall Kant's talk of 'heteronomy': every human being experiences it first and foremost in himself and in fact in being determined by his own desires. It is precisely on account of this that the liberating work on himself, namely, formation, is demanded of him as a rational being; it is in fact the work of the moral, and thus the legal, or more precisely: the civil, self-consciousness. Already the modern consciousness of lived experience, which was decisively articulated by Husserl, can have nothing more in common with such a formation. Nor do the contemporary endeavors to gain emancipation aim at the heteronomy inherent in everybody, not even—or only secondarily—at that arising from the so-called other, but first of all at the subsumptive social orders, especially at the unconsciously effective orders of the force of speech, such as, e.g., Barthes tried to demonstrate with respect to the exclusive, anti-democratic effect of the group-specific orders of discourse.

This directs our attention once again to what in metaphysics was the concept and its definition. The explanation of what something was destined to be, not only guaranteed its knowability but also the concentration on the possibility of fulfilling its destiny. To represent it perfectly means in Greek metaphysics: to be good; what is more: to be beautiful; and most of all: to be accomplished. It thematized the so-called beings first of all in the determinacy of what is accomplished, and thus brought to bear the difference between "how it is to be" and "how it is," between truth and correctness. The talk of "ontology," which first occurs in the modern era, drops this distinction.

If the universality of the concept is thought as an abstraction possessing subsumptive force, then the aversion has to be directed against everything that was once regarded as an exemplar, namely, an essence in which the fulfilledness of its destiny is to be discerned. In the Wittgensteinian sense-explication—Lyotard is explicitly led by it—the expunction of exemplariness affects even logic as it was regarded as the exemplar of scientific clarity; it can no longer be considered to be an exemplar of linguistic clarity, for there are always only many languages, each of which has its own standards of clarity.

Here a shift is indicated from the former determination of man to his so-called self-conception, from the *specificum* of the λόγος or ratio to the specificity of possessing language; in the latter the logical is merely a special case. Even theology has conformed to this trend insofar as it interprets its name as a "talk of God" that follows special rules of discourse.

Far more forcefully than in terms of the concept of man, the expunction of the exemplar is manifest in connection with man's visualizations or projections as they were fashioned—speaking with Lyotard—in the "*grands récits*"; not only in the ancient stories about man's destiny but even in the projections advanced in modernity. Admittedly Marx's communistic society, Nietzsche's masters of the earth, and Heidegger's mortal in the world of the fourfold have meanwhile come to be regarded as will-o'-the-wisps of totalizing and even totalitarian thinking that have finally died out.

Metaphysics is held to have been ontology on the one hand, but theology on the other. As for this other side, it first opens the view in the line of attack characteristic of thinking in the pluralistic mentality. Against principles, more precisely: against that which unifies in a totality, against what is in itself unconditioned and completely uniform. Even against the non-divine unity of the world as it was thought in modernity. First of all by Husserl in the sense-explication of the interpreted life: with respect to the stream of lived experiences the pure ego guarantees with its identity the unity of the world, which is constituted through the ego's sense-bestowing productions. Then by Schlick in the sense-explication of science: the world which is diversely lived through is unified through the scientific description of the real. Finally by Nietzsche in the sense-explication of the productive being of man: the perspectivally stamped worlds of the positing of values remain a part of the world of the eternal creation and destruction of power-constructs. The decomposition of even these projections of unity along with the principles of metaphysics is the decisive event in contemporary thinking. Its motto reads: originariness of difference.

Unconcerned with the social needs for consensus that keep the ethics business going, Lyotard draws attention in his *The Differend* to an originary dimension of dispute. It is no dispute that can be justly mediated in society according to familiar rules, in particular through the dispensation of justice. Impervious to such a verdict, this dispute springs from the diverse kinds of discourse—request, command, praise, assertion, etc.—as well as from the diverse orders according to which sentences can be combined. Once the statement has lost its traditional precedence among the kinds of discourse, the non-uniformity of speech not only asserts itself in utterance, thus in so-called tongues, but, what is more, in the rules for the formation of communicative expression.

The semblance of unity fades away for the pluralistic mentality, however, not only with respect to what is spoken but likewise with respect to the speaker. This trend becomes particularly clear with respect to the submodern attack on modernity's last bastion of identity, namely, on the pre-mundane or transcendental ego in Husserlian thought. Sartre already allows for only an intramundane ego—it provides its mere existence with the unity of an essence in free engagement.

Merleau-Ponty reduced such a unity to the consciousness of one's own body as the precondition of every interaction. The decisive blow to the unity of the pure ego, however, was brought by Lévi-Strauss from the standpoint of structural anthropology and by Lacan from that of psychoanalysis. As Foucault recognized, here the sciences, which realized the modern interest of man in himself, in his life, speech, and work, transgress their limits and in fact enter into the "no-man's-land" of man.

In Wittgenstein's *Tractatus logico-philosophicus* the ego-subject is still regarded as the limit of the world. The dissolution of this limit into the group-subjects of language games and their sets of rules, the consequent blurring of the limit of the human, is unsettling for many but is welcomed by the pluralistic mentality as a relief, as the progress of emancipation, as the final release from the dominance of the sense-bestowal of the transcendental ego. For the plurality proper to lived experiences needs no unity arising from hermeneutic reason but only a regulation by technical reason. Foucault's proclamation of the death of man is a matter of even greater indifference to the pluralistic society than the death of God as experienced by Nietzsche.

One must not think that in the said expunction of the principal unity the prevailing concern lies with facts. At issue here is not even the forming of an opinion that could be contested by another. Rather, of concern is the articulation of a mentality and its characteristic intention. It is on account of this that debates with these endeavors, viewed as if they were philosophy, plunge into emptiness. They themselves demonstrate their honesty in confessing to be non-philosophy and can thus least of all be refuted by recourse to a former philosophy.

Even if the submoderns dwell upon Wittgenstein's dissolution of the unity of language, due to that of the unity of the concept, their concern is in fact no longer the—still hermeneutic—scission between sense and nonsense in what is spoken but rather the social emancipation from the largely unconscious force in the orders of discourse. Thus the contemporary critique of metaphysics also aims at unmasking not the nonsense in metaphysical propositions so much as the totalitarian character of its totalizing thinking. Rather than contradict this critique, we now finally raise a question: what prompted philosophy to think totalities? Was this thinking a totalizing?

Among scholars no less than among dilettantes the conviction still holds sway: philosophy sprang from an interest in Nature that arose somehow and at some time. And which Nature would that be? Aristotle still makes it clear: exactly not what becomes self-evident for posterity, namely, the whole of Nature. Nature is thought by the Greeks as a Nature of something determinate, even if it be the Nature of the All. The question concerning the Nature of something is secondary to a concentration on everything—more precisely: on the totality of what appears and its unity. So it is with the earliest philosophy—but why?

The pre-philosophical Greeks are not familiar with any unity of the world, not even by name. When Homer speaks of a comparable All, a whole is viewed to which shared dominance is essential. Zeus, Poseidon, and Hades each has at his disposal a limited share of the realm. Conflict over the shares to which one is entitled is in general the theme of the Homeric songs. Admittedly it is a conflict that can always be mediated by an arbitral decision, finally by the decision of the father of the gods and men. Nor does Hesiod speak of a world but rather of the unity of precisely that dominance which the father of right had won; by contrast, the origin of everything is one that is radically distinct within itself: Chaos and Earth—not even the progeny of both can be united. Finally conflict over the shares of land pervades in turn the Solonian πόλις—a conflict that has to be arbitrated in accordance with supreme right, which is accompanied by the greatest force.

Once again: what destines philosophy to think totalities? Nothing but the σοφία just addressed, namely, a knowledge that understood itself to be a gift of the Muses. There are only three possible positions of thinking concerning this knowledge: on the one hand, that—which is doubled in itself—of the rejection of what has been given; on the other, that of its conception. What does this mean?

First of concern is the self-assertion of thinking against a knowledge that is granted to man and not produced by him. It asserts itself, however, in the observation not of what is made on the basis of one's own knowledge but rather of what appears of its own accord. In the latter, one must distinguish its essence, which is in each instance concealed and thus yet to be discovered, from that which is conspicuous. It is precisely this essence that early philosophy called φύσις. Distinguishing in this way, observation itself thus determines its topic; it reduces the manifold of appearances to a simple contrariety of Natures, such as moist and dry, and distinguishes with respect to the contraries the determinative first over against its other. It is precisely in this way that thinking becomes the knowledge of a totality. With such knowledge, what we call 'natural reason' comes to the fore for the first time.

The other rejection of the previously given knowledge takes its point of departure not from thinking but rather from its topic, namely, from the totality of what appears, a totality which already proves to have reason in itself, and in fact as κόσμος, that is to say, as the order of right. Once again, this order is grounded in the first side of an opposition. Thinking has to correspond to it so as to be ordered itself and to be able to have an ordering effect. Hence it is the thinking characteristic of mundane reason.

The distinction of this reason from the natural type approaches the contemporary presumption of a plurality of reason. Such does not admit of philosophy. Rather, the said difference is essential to philosophy, given its constitutive relation to σοφία, and this difference is accomplished where a third reason is called forth, one that is related to wisdom conceptually. How so? By way of the distinction of reason as much from its natural as from its mundane types, and such distinction was the event of purification in every beginning of metaphysics, whether in Parmenides, in Plotinus, or in Kant. Only pure reason is capable of conception.

Let us stay with the Greek beginning and view the Parmenidean purification. Here reason parts, on the one hand, with the observation of everything that appears in the space of the opposition of its Natures; on the other, with the κόσμος of the totality of what appears. According to both sides, it holds: reason severs itself from a knowledge grounded on correctness. In the end, such knowledge is always of concern just when what matters is finding the means and ways for satisfying needs, for escaping difficulties; but most urgent is time and again the restoration in the polity of the disturbed order of right. As Parmenides learns, ἀμηχανία (helplessness) regulates the bustling reason of the mortal, compels it to cultivate every τέχνη and μηχανή, namely, all useful knowledge.

But what justification would the liberation of reason from such servitude have? Can it ever be superior to the demands of human helplessness? Does the idleness of metaphysical thinking not announce itself in its purity—precisely that nonsense which Wittgenstein believed he exposed? It seems all the more so as its purity is precisely the birthplace of that logic which severed the concept from the name and acknowledged the former's exemplary clarity. The logic of conceptual, of pure, reason prompts natural as well as mundane reason, respectively, to cultivate their own logics, which correspond to their own tasks. Yet it is first with respect to the conceptual logic, finally in its Hegelian form, that the violence of totalizing thinking imposes itself upon submodern thought—as harbingers of totalitarian constraint.

Let us once again consider the Parmenidean purity of reason. It purifies itself insofar as it, proceeding logically, takes a path whose signs let one think "how it is" only within the bounds of "how it is to be." The movement is accomplished in the insight into what is accomplished, as mentioned earlier. But what first sets this thinking on its way is that truth in which the critical nature of right has its present—a truth to which all correctness is subject. The name of this truth reads ἀλήθεια. What does it mean? It is all the more urgent to raise this question insofar as the Heideggerian sense-explication received its directive from precisely that name, a directive that led to the limit of our modernity. Beyond it, the path leads either into the open or to a dead end.

When Heidegger rejects truth as correctness and with it the usual nominal definition 'the agreement between knowledge and object', he stands in harmony just as much with Dilthey and Husserl as with Frege and Schlick. He stands alone, however, in his attempt to take his directive from that Greek name, a directive leading from unconcealment to an originary concealment in order to distinguish the latter in turn—as, on the one hand, a self-concealing and, on the other, a sheltering. The precedence of that which conceals itself over all that has been desheltered is common to all the submodern tactics of unmasking—particularly as far as the aforementioned unconscious orders of constraint are concerned. Thus what was thought metaphysically is also searched today—especially by Derrida—for so-called cracks through which that which conceals itself shines forth in what is said, and it is in fact precisely this self-concealing that allows Derrida to talk not only of the logocentrism but even of the phallocentrism of totalizing thinking. We mention here only his attempt to understand Heidegger's "ontological difference" more originarily as sexual difference (cf. "*Geschlecht*"). The social epiphenomena of such originariness need not be extrapolated here.

Now back to the said truth. The fact that it is considered for the first time in philosophy in the Parmenidean beginning of metaphysics already gives pause, for this means: truth is thematized only in unison with the distinction of reason from its natural as well as its mundane types—thus in departing from the totalities which were on the one hand the totality of what appears determined by observation; on the other, the pregiven order of right entailed by this totality. What is correctly known in such a totality is always only something probable (διάκοσμος ἐοικώς) since it is a matter of views; in light of this it becomes understandable as to why the views in question must time and again gain prestige.

Now contrary to all views, what is the knowledge of pure reason? What is its truth? What does ἀλήθεια mean here? By no means 'unconcealment' if one here thinks back with Heidegger to a self-concealing φύσις. With the passing of the aforementioned totalities, the difference between what shows itself and what conceals itself no longer has any significance either. But not even the revealedness of Parmenidean knowledge is addressed by ἀλήθεια. What else? The talk of its "heart" calls to mind the only instance in early Greek in which ἀλήθεια is the mark of a mentality and not, as is usually the case, of a discourse. Hesiod ascribes ἀληθές to Nereus, the old man of the sea (*Theogony* 235), and explains: οὐδὲ θεμίστων λήθεται: he never loses sight of decrees, that is to say: of what is always already decided. And even this is further explained: δίκαια οἶδεν: he knows what is right. Parmenidean truth, unlike that proper to discourse, can be understood not on the basis of the transitive λήθειν (to deceive someone) but only on the basis of the middle λήθεσθαι (to deceive oneself about something), which is misleadingly translated as 'to forget'.

The truth first thematized in the beginning of metaphysics is the present proper to Δίκη, to right, and it is of a critical nature precisely on account of this. However, Δίκη was prior to all philosophy, namely, it was in turn the present of the destiny in the Homeric σοφία and in fact as the directive which is issued from the μοῖραι, the shares, which decree and delimit that to which one is entitled. It is just this destiny that is conceived by Parmenides; he in turn ascribes to such a directive precisely that present which ἀλήθεια is, that is to say: the directive of what is always already decided must constantly be kept in view as that of right—disregarding the plurality of whatever in continual change attracts the attention of the eye and ear. To never lose sight of the critical nature of right—this task is fulfilled only by the departed reason, which was removed from manifold servitude. What the mortals think, does not hold for it: better to be the slave of a man of no estate than the master of the underworld (cf. *Odyssey* XI 488 ff.).

The departed reason takes the path of its convincing-itself, of the consideration that is occupied with its move, that is, the path leading to the insight into what is accomplished. This indeed is also a totality but not a whole composed of different parts, and by no means the result of totalizing but rather an identity of "how it is" within the limits of the identity of "how it is to be."

Modernity, to say nothing of submodernity, no longer has any idea about this identity of truth. In its discussion of identity and difference, submodernity still holds onto that identity which an individual being has for itself and contrary to others—which was first grasped in Parmenides' account of "views." Derrida brought the dissolution of the opposition of both relations no farther than to difference in the horizon of time, namely, as "postponement" and in fact just as it is always already familiar in connection with the satisfaction of human drives.

To understand Being in the horizon of time—such was, in following Husserl's bequest, Heidegger's intention. His submodern following requires us to seek out so-called totalizing thinking in the first beginning of occidental philosophy, for it is precisely contrary to it that the other beginning is to make all the difference. Derrida's "deconstruction" of the history of the first beginning depends on Heidegger's assurance, which has been unquestioningly accepted by the former and has also remained otherwise unexamined: in the entire occidental tradition, Being is understood as *Anwesen* (being-present), this sense of Being is privileged (cf. "Privilege of Presence?", pp. 81-90 above).

By contrast: in the middle epoch of metaphysics, Being is understood as self-giving or as having-been-given; in the final epoch, however, as self-positing or having-been-posited. The ground of this state of affairs becomes visible in Plotinus, given the fact that the One, which is absolutely transcendent, is neither something nor ever occurs but has its present in the beauty of the descent of its power; in Kant, given the fact that the idea of freedom cannot be known in itself but has its present solely in the moral law. And in the first epoch? The difference between being-present (*Anwesen*) and being-absent (*Abwesen*) is not preserved for conceptual reason. Such has significance—as it is understood in terms of appearing—only for natural and mundane reason.

As far as the submodern critique of metaphysics is concerned, one's patience may easily wear thin due its lack of knowledge regarding what it is talking about. But this occurs only when one expects something correct from it and thus fails to appreciate the signs given by the pluralistic mentality, signs which are very much worthy of interpretation. One may be outraged that Derrida thinks he uncovers sexual potency fantasies in Hegel's work and thus reads the whole in conjunction with Genet's effusions. And yet this ought rather to give occasion to ask: which reason of which task do we ourselves possess? For without a task to determine reason, the assurance that one has reason is no longer even a pious belief.

In the subtitle of the text in question, Derrida raises the question 'What remains of absolute knowledge?' and thereby names that which is even more provocative for the pluralistic mentality than totalizing thinking. The question itself makes no sense, for it is easy to see that of such knowledge only the nothingness of its everything can remain and by no means something, namely, this or that remainder. Such is beneath the dignity of that reason which was the "faculty of principles." The title of the said work is more becoming to this reason: *Glas*—the toll of death. However, this calls to mind a saying cited by Hegel: they heard the bells toll but knew not where they hung.

The sense-explications of modernity sounded the death of metaphysics long ago. The submoderns auscultate a corpse in their critique of metaphysical thinking. But the latter's reason leaves no corpse behind and so they then auscultate a home-made straw man of metaphysics, and thus must hear themselves and therein the conflict of manifest and unconsciously virulent force, of violent right and of the belief in a justice demanded in protests.

What else is there to listen to? Perhaps to that silence which Heidegger noticed in the speech of the poem? Yet the oft-cited neighborhood of poetizing and thinking is a milieu that veils the relation appealed to here between σοφία and φιλοσοφία. It makes the silence of the configurations of wisdom audible and in fact precisely the silence of those that called forth that reason which distinguishes itself. This was possible only insofar as they were in themselves rational. The speech of just this rationality, which allowed the latter to be understood as a "doctrine," has been silenced. Deaf to this ἐποχή, to this reticence, one assures: their speech has, as that of a former world—for instance, of the New Testament—become incomprehensible. Hence the demand to translate them into our world, but that means: into that of everyday life, which is to say: into the communication operative today. It operates, however, only in preserving the irrepressible plurality of diverse sets of rules—whether now for linguistic action itself or for the relevant kinds of texts. But what if the configurations of wisdom spoke of the distinction of man not from other animals but from himself—of a distinction that makes, contrary to the mentality of everyday life, all the difference? Because this distinction was one thoroughly contemplated, it required no peculiar speech; rather, it allowed its speech to become, in the strict sense, an inhabited one. In an everyday life that excludes such a distinction, it runs in idle. Here the honest word is not that of wisdom but rather the word of pure folly, which the non-distinction of man brings to speech in exclusive everyday life. In no way do we have the submoderns to thank for this word but rather the poet Beckett. It possesses a purity contrary to the "efforts" that do not even amount to foolish attempts to distance oneself from the network of the languages of everyday life.

Their technique is the so-called "alienation" (*Verfremdung*) of the most everyday. The cutting force of modernity which severed our world from its history is only simulated here. Everyday life then becomes the master of all alienating gestures; they remain protests which show society the scope of the pluralistic mentality—as the self-affection of everyday lived experience and the exhibition of an individuality which itself is a feature of the masses.

Along with its privation the pluralistic mentality belongs to exclusive everyday life. Its days never become all the days but derive their content from endless changes. Totalitarian here is the notion that everything has to change—an everything, however, that in the social sphere can mean only: most things. Thus totalitarian thinking also remains caught up in everyday life: the pluralistic mentality in fact sees in it the evil of its own privation but is not able to understand itself as the mother of this invention.

Metaphysics said: everything is already different and in fact insofar as it has been conceived or as the Being that has been thought has made all the difference in contrast to the Being of everyday life that is prior to reflection. The reason of metaphysical thinking, however, grows only as old as is required for the accomplishment of the epochal tasks of sheltering the truth of a given wisdom in a logic. Modernity condemned such thinking due to a necessary blindness to the sense of this corresponding expiration of reason. Its last word about metaphysics was this: it is the history of the withdrawal of that which grants thinking its proper topic—ending in a technical thinking possessing an openly totalitarian and, prior to that, totalizing character whose determination Heidegger termed the '*Ge-stell*' (sy-stem). Only with the tearing of the continuum of this history does it become possible to leave metaphysical reason in peace and in fact in the peace of the conceptions this reason accomplished of the sight of truth in the knowledge of the Muses, of the doing of truth in Christian knowledge, of the production of truth in civil knowledge.

But what if in the de-limitation of everyday life even the retort of modernity against such knowledge dies away? Must not the view then arise that the totalizing thinking of metaphysics not only has a totalitarian thinking as its consequence but that totalizing thinking even springs from the latter?

Unum est necessarium—the pluralistic mentality has forced the provocation of this word of distinction into the no-man's-land of man and precisely in this way absorbed it in everyday life. Since to its speech belongs the latter's underground—precisely that which the analysis of so-called wild thinking and that of the unconscious opened up here with the pressing question 'Who is speaking?' The answer preceding the question reveals the baselessness of the decision to ask after a Who. It must read: what is speaking?

Can the Who of the speakers of the aforementioned configurations of wisdom still be saved? What was spoken by them called forth each time a distinction. For already there, who is speaking became questionable in each instance. Let us recall the well-known answers: prior to the bard Homer, the Muse speaks, that is to say, she who knows from the oldest memory. Prior to the Evangelist Luke, the Holy Spirit speaks, that is to say, the love of the self-revealing God. Prior to the poet Rousseau, the genius of the humanity of man speaks, that is to say, the productive imagination of his natural freedom.

These answers have become so incomprehensible that they can no longer be repeated in their simplicity. Here too the protests against the hermeneutics of modernity are of no help. Yet a discretion is possible in view of the given answers. Such becomes necessary when we follow the hints of that conceptual reason which is at last left in peace, back to the conceived configurations of wisdom—not in order to repeat what has already been accomplished, thus to restore the metaphysical logic, but rather in order to lay bare the architectonic of those configurations, namely, the closed figures consisting of the proportions or ratios of the terms 'destiny', 'topic', 'thinking'. Only that which is in itself rational was able to call forth a philosophical reason. The Who of the said speakers first gains its proper ground in the architectonic, in a structure built out of ratios. In view of this structure, the question that has occupied us here vanishes.

JUDGE CONTEMPORARY ART?

In which respect does philosophy meet art? On the one hand, in that of thinking, more precisely: in the judgment of its works; on the other, in that of the topic, more precisely: in the kinds of its works. However, for as long as there has been philosophy, the destiny to which the relation between thinking and the topic is subject has been one shared with art. How is that possible? Insofar as art is a type of knowledge.

Focusing on the former respect here: what can philosophy contribute to the judgment of works of art? How are matters especially with its present contribution to the judgment of contemporary, more precisely: postmodern, works of art? As far as they are concerned, one encounters them today frequently with a certain embarrassment and even with doubt as to whether what is offered as art is at all such. Moreover: the embarrassment can be found in exactly those who have no doubt about this matter and who act as experts in contrast to the many laymen. Ultimately, however, even the judgments based on such expert opinion—for instance, in talks given at exhibition openings—can cause the listener a certain embarrassment because they typically remain strange with respect to their criteria of judgment—it is especially at such openings that, despite the obvious fact that in modern and especially postmodern art the criteria operative in history have been expressly abandoned, the urge to cling to a continuum in art history arises everywhere. In this way a contemporary judgment concerning contemporary artistic productions becomes completely confused.

What is one to do in such confusion, which not only costs the private buyer dearly but, what is more, the public purse? One cultivates the faculty of judgment. This begins by becoming attentive to the seduction of the same name 'art' for fundamentally different things; by expunging the deeply entrenched superstitious belief in an endless progress, in a history of art which continues much like the generations of life. What has happened since the middle of the last century in religion should already make one hesitate to make such a presumption; most of all, modernity's obvious break with what has been philosophy. Its mission is reflected in works of art—though only for him who has attained the faculty of distinction from that history which philosophy has been.

Balzac wrote a novella entitled *Le Chef d'oeuvre inconnu*—the unknown, more precisely: misjudged, masterpiece. It tells of a master painter from the heyday of Dutch painting who ultimately spends ten years painting a picture of a woman which is to testify to the height of his art. Yet the woman depicted fades more and more into a "chaos of colors, tones, indeterminate nuances" and in the end is only recognizable by the tips of her toes.

It is no accident that Picasso (in 1931) illustrated this story. He shows the painter with his model, who has meanwhile grown old, whereas his canvas is covered only with curves and straight lines that no longer reveal any figure. The disappearance of the image as an image of something visible is far too obvious in modernity—down to Ad Reinhardt's monochrome panels—for one to be justified in doubting whether there has been a break with our history's image-tradition. Even if one wishes to claim that in this history the pictorial character of a work in the visual arts is already of dwindling significance, one has to admit that the judging of works of art has at least been transformed in an earth-shattering way.

Which judgment? Not that concerning how correctly the painting renders what is at hand but rather that concerning beauty. Regarding everything that is, such a judgment presupposes the consideration of what has to be. And, in each instance, what has to be is the thing in its completeness. The so-called aesthetic judgment had its basis in the teleological judgment. But because teleology asserted the conceivability of the world according to ends, art and especially the visual arts were concerned with the man of this world and its things. What one today only understands as "objectivity" was no extrinsic accessory to art. The common distinction between 'objective' and 'non-objective' in the visual arts is null and void; it conceals what is proper to an art which sprung from the judgment in the horizon of a rational idea of beauty. It asserted itself not only in the painting but likewise in the cultivation of the observer. Here we have to distinguish an art which is de-structive of just this judgment and in the end supersedes it. This occurrence is legible precisely in the unfolding of contemporary thinking. Such an unfolding also reveals that and how, despite all exhibition and reproduction, the accessibility of what art has been in the epochs of philosophy is becoming increasingly closed to us.

There is no continuum reaching from the Greeks down to our day in the judgment of works of art. For, prior to that, there is no continuum of artistic formation itself as presumed by art history according to its hermeneutic conventions. For our history distinguishes itself—insofar as it has been one of the "spirit"—in terms of the crises in the principles of knowledge.

We recall the following in brief: firstly in early Greek culture: the determination of all artistic formations according to the insight into "what is complete," more precisely: according to the knowledge of the κόσμος of all appearances, of the ἁρμονίη of their Natures, of the one λόγος, namely, of the proportion in this harmony.

Secondly in the core of the middle epoch and thus in the Augustinian age: the determination of artistic formations according to the knowledge of the *ordo* of all created things and their disturbance by man's fall from his creator as well as from the awakening and return from fallenness to the "divine" beauty of divine power.

Thirdly beginning with the Florentine Renaissance: the determination of artistic formations according to the certainty that the visual arts themselves have assumed the rank of free science; this with Alberti's outline of the *costruzzione legittima*, then with Leonardo's artistic intention of a *rappresentazione evidente*, most of all, however, with Michelangelo's assumption of the latent presence of a *vera idea* in the material of production. This implies: art lays claim not only to the understanding but also to reason as it is the faculty of conclusion from principles.

The most intimate neighborhood of art and philosophy is reached, however, where works of the imagination—and in fact of the imagination on the basis of human freedom in absolute significance—give what is to be thought to Kantian, Fichtean, and Hegelian reason. Yet the supreme destiny, namely, freedom as it is understood by them, could be exhibited there only in literary works. It is precisely on account of this that Hegel's much-chided judgment is right: "For us art is and remains, in keeping with its supreme destiny, a thing of the past" (*Werke* 13, 25/13). The task of exhibiting the said freedom in absolute significance was fulfilled in the letters making up Rousseau's *Nouvelle Héloïse*, in Schiller's dramas, and in Hölderlin's hymns. Thus it is precisely in this neighborhood that the conceiving penetration of the judgment of taste and its cultivation moves, a neighborhood in which the beautiful and, most of all, the sublime are distinguished from what is pleasant in art.

Closer to our question: which distinctions are instrumental for the judgment of works of art in modernity—that is to say: in a world which, on this side of philosophy and its closed history, is explicated in the sense-explication of future human being (Marx, Nietzsche, Heidegger), of the technicity of the sciences (Frege, Schlick, Kuhn) and the data of an unanticipated life, finally of the lived experience and understanding of sense (Dilthey, Husserl, Wittgenstein)? Each of these levels of interpretation offer modern artistic products their own horizon.

As far as the first of these horizons is concerned, it is, to be sure, questionable as to whether it can grant art, and especially the visual arts, an abode.

How could, for instance, the experience of the expropriation of man—of his power, his will, his thinking—prevailing there set an artistic task?

As far as the last of these sense-explications are concerned, however, it is obvious that the visual arts of modernity were able to gain a foothold on the ground of an originary lived experience of social man and his environment—including the natural one. Here the artistic tasks of the art of our history can be, where not merely imitated—as, e.g., in Tissot—then at least simulated—as, e.g., in Renoir or in Rodin. Yet it is not only the objectivations of life that preoccupy formation based on lived experience but also the somnaical worlds of the ego and the id as they are constituted in dreams, such as in Ernst or Dalí; ultimately, however, the sign-worlds of sense and nonsense in language games—as in Klee and Miró.

But that which incisively asserts the modernism of modernity in artistic significance lies on the level of the consideration constitutive of technical reason—which is to be distinguished from the understanding of techniques. It is precisely within this horizon that an art is established which step-by-step executes its severance from the epochs of our history, from art as a type of knowledge and thus of truth; this art returns to its "technical" origin. It abandons:

1) The *aequalitas* of the representative work along with the Nature of the object as something represented; artistic language—e.g., Manet's—asserts its independence from that of "life," of the lived experience and representation of it; such leaves this art cold. Here the "statement" adopts a method of composition which recalls Frege's dismissal of the relation between subject and predicate in favor of that between function and argument, whereby the sequence in both relations is reversed. Unlike the former subject, a function can have an arbitrary range and also remain "unsaturated." In the functional context of a painting, empty spaces are possible; such can be arbitrarily shortened and expanded or transposed. There is no longer any "Nature" of the objects here which would be a "system"—a closed idea which distinguishes and thus determines itself within itself.

2) The *similitudo* as it was constitutive of the relation of the *imago* to its *exemplar*. Modernity's artistic break is manifest most clearly right at the point where it seems to have been most accommodating: Braque and Picasso's cubist revolution collides most of all with Cézannes's bequest. The *imago* is now explicitly negated in the painting—with the entire manifold of color-"arguments" which Cézannes's painting brought to fruition.

3) The *rationalitas* and thus the proportion in the construction of the painting according to "measures." In the end the artistic reduction of art breaks with that which distinguished it as "beautiful" from other *artes*; we can

also say: breaks with its reason, with the thought of architectonic necessity. We recall here the late panels by Jackson Pollock. Even the artistic de-struction of what have been the fine arts in our history attains its proper end.

It already becomes apparent in this context which difficulties the judgment of artistic productions on this side of modernity has to address. In force here is obviously the motto: "anything"—by no means "everything"—"goes." Rightly so, for the old question concerning truth: "How is it?"—to say nothing of the consideration of "how it is to be"—is superseded by Wittgenstein's concentration on "how it is going" or how it functions.

Where would the judgment of contemporary works of art have its footing? In the midst of a way of thinking that testifies to a radical pluralism—even if the many opinions are homogeneous *en masse*—this seems out of the question. And thus a judgment made on the basis of common knowledge or common taste as they were once formative of style is also entirely out of the question. The artist who is convinced that he can give, if not a beautiful, then at least a generally legible, sign which surpasses his accidental individuality, today finds himself sooner in a rather desperate situation. How is he, without the acknowledgment that accrues by way of knowledge, to accrue demonstrative force in his speech? How will he achieve something said and not only utter something spoken, which pays off more or less as do non-artistic products?

What is to be done in the midst of the obvious confusion concerning the judgment of contemporary works of art? Learn to distinguish. But how? By learning to distinguish what is already distinct—contrary to the confusion entailed in the notion of the endless procession, if not progress, of art.

One can best learn to discern what is already distinct, however, in the history of philosophy—in its principal, since they are epochal, crises in the judgment of what is beautiful, good, true.

Secondly one can learn to discern what is distinct in the world of modernity as separated from its history, a world which was completely explicated by its sense-explications. It is precisely the knowledge gained in this way that for the first time gives rise to the idea that and how a sphere has already articulated itself on this side of modernity. Which differences can be read in thinking on this side of modernity, where its projections of a future, generally the *grands récits*—as Lyotard calls them, a phrase that endows the slogan "no future" with its full sense—have been abandoned? On the basis of which distinction of thinking does contemporary art in its various facets become a mirror and in fact of the man who no longer summons up the willingness to distinguish himself from himself?

Here we summarize succinctly his self-understanding, thereby attending especially to his linguistic character: the first position of thinking in this dimension was formed by Merleau-Ponty and in fact in a simulation of Marxian thought—though translated into a decisively anti-totalitarian type.

Rejecting the prevailing position of consciousness and its world-constituting ego, the topic of this thinking is the perceiving body as it finds itself as likewise perceived in a natural and social environment, discloses in it a space of its motility, is primarily a sexualized body and as such encounters the other body and forms a language which is initially that of gestures: body language. The "incarnate" existence creates sense and communicates it to those of its kind.

Determined in this way, man is always already subject to the reigning impulse of the social—yet this not only means in a social world but also in the horizon of an intersubjectivity that lays claim to him, one which remains originarily intercorporeal. This world is culturally determined only insofar as speech proves itself time and again in the creativity involved in distinguishing between signs which in turn results in new products of sense.

Conscious of himself as the producer of all products of sense, man liquefies the objectified sedimentations of former sense-bestowals, sublates what has already been spoken in "innovative" modes of expression. Realized in this way, the linguistic character of submodern man offers his art the first scene. In particular, the submodern artist sublates the fetishes of the everyday—such as comic strips (Lichtenstein) or a Campbell's soup can (Warhol)—into art; he "alienates" (*verfremdet*) everyday things through a deformation that yields a new, or even no, sense; he excites by way of a disfigurement of the familiar (Oldenburg).

The other submodern scene, likewise testified to by "Documenta," is laid out on Foucault's view as follows:

The starting point is no longer the body language perceived by the They as the former's subject but rather a speech of the body as it speaks as the speech of the id (*Es*) and its desires. In this way it permeates thinking immediately.

This id proves to be a linguistic structure which can be disclosed by structural anthropology and psychoanalysis. In view of this structure, however, the form of man fades away as it was produced by his representation in the modern human sciences. It becomes blurred, as becomes manifest, e.g., in Francis Bacon's and Dubuffet's canvasses.

But how is the linguistic character of man more precisely articulated? The possibility of just that subject disappearing which was bound to the "I think" becomes apparent with the originariness of the "it speaks" (*Es spricht*): the endless murmur of desires. Its articulation is undertaken especially by contemporary literature. In view of the historical continuum of art, it holds: "From this moment a work whose only meaning resides in its being a self-enclosed expression of its glory is no longer possible" (Foucault, *LI*, 48/60). Thus no longer a transfiguring speaking, no—thought with Nietzsche—creating beyond oneself; an incapacity which becomes virtually aggressive in Segal's mannequins: the likeness of those who have already been assimilated—and this, of all things, according to the standard of "self-actualization"; in the mirror of artistic products that are a denial of the orders of discourse, of the orders of social discussion, that are the enaction of an accidental individuality—as, e.g., in Beuys.

Finally a third scene: that of so-called installations. Here the conventional media of artistic depiction are completely dissolved into an endless plurality—unlike when, e.g., Picasso experimented with tin and ceramic. "Nothing save the name" remains of the former "divine" art. Art has—now thought with Derrida—achieved the state of total "alterity"—after the claim of "being other than the others" (Foucault) and, prior to that, of "being determined by the others" (Merleau-Ponty).

The art of installations is also an empty mystery to which each observer may give a content. Even if the artist has designated a content, such does not oblige anybody to anything. Every artifact of this kind remains "polysemic," like the signs of an undeciphered script. What is excited here? A "responsiveness" among mere others whose every "*tout autre*" is wholly other. Everybody is claimed and—having been sensitized—urged to some kind of response. The presence of the observer is what is expressly brought forth in the corresponding fictions of art; its presence is itself a linguistic mirror of the interpretations of a work which itself makes no pretense of making any sense.

The "deconstruction" of what art has been, even of what has been the artistic negation of the fine arts, ends in installations in museum rooms or out in the open, where a work of art might have had its place—e.g., in a park. It then continues to be only the room which urges one to allow something as banal as a double row of bricks to become a stimulus for interpretation.

The regression from the history of art into the continuum of its pre-history—in keeping with this continuum, it is simultaneously the endlessly progressing post-history—allows for the erection of totems everywhere with which no taboo is connected and which therefore remain without any significance for the establishment of a community. And why should it have any? Taken in the sense already indicated, the others are always already socialized.

The thrust of deconstruction targets those forms of dominance of a totalizing, since it is logizing, thinking which oppresses the pluralism of individuals, forms of dominance which are sedimented in society, in its unconscious. And so the topic is ultimately the adversary—as the object (*Gegenstand*) was once thought as resistance (*Widerstand*). The name of this adversary is: the logocentrism of the occidental tradition and thus Eurocentrism. Yet in that tradition's beginning the λόγος was, we recall, the ratio, the proportion, in which the harmony of the κόσμος of all appearances was disclosed. The contemporary art scene of the counter-word to the λόγος, to the concept, to the thought of what is perfect as guaranteed by the concept, truly has no lack of witnesses to this mentality. Its works also are to be judged in accordance with the criteria of so-called deconstruction. In this connection it should become clear that the art of submodernity—that the art in its flourishing subculture—only continues to share the name with what has been art in our history. And it would be just as foolish as unjust to locate it in the continuum of art, as is everywhere attempted through unfounded association.

But does our age not know another type of art? Indeed, and in fact the one which is explicated in the sciences of linguistic communication. Here there are works of art which are to be read as signs, which in fact speak but say nothing. We mention here first just that break—e.g., in Klee—with the hermeneutic way of thinking proper to modernity which is executed consciously in monochrome panels. This is to be seen in Yves Klein, for example. His neighbor Ad Reinhardt paints, as he says, "the sign that refuses to signify" (in Bois, 11). With the consequence, which he himself saw, that there is nothing more to be understood in this painting. Such denial is a sign that the distinction of speech is the proper artistic task of the present. That which is to be understood would always be a given sense. But here no sense is given and no gained sense understood. This too is precisely the situation which Beckett formed poetically. In both cases, we note that the purity of art, a concentration on the fundamental "poetic" trait of speech (Jakobson), is possible as such on the conditions set by postmodernity. Purity which excludes from itself every misuse of a work for the supposed establishment of sense, for the actual borrowing of sense from social clichés. An eminently indexical act of renunciation.

Only from such acts do we learn what in our present is a possible artistic speech. Only the purity of formation grants judgment an abode. Yet such is first and only grasped when thinking has learned what has been purely said, what has been purely thought, which has given what is to be thought, which has set reason itself on its way to the purity of formation. In keeping with the sense of the name 'philosophy', such were eminently the occidental configurations of wisdom—in this connection we cite only Homer, Paul, and Hölderlin. Precisely they—this is obvious in our history—have delivered the relational ground common to both philosophy and art. This ground is concealed, however, where what is said is no longer distinguished from what is spoken, because, prior to that, actuality is no longer distinguished from reality (cf. the Kantian "categories").

Inundated with what is spoken, which says nothing, shows nothing, indicates nothing, philosophy no less than art suffers from the same lack of a master. Postmodern cheerfulness lacks the maturity, the pain, of which Nietzsche said in view of philosophy and art that it is proper to the spirit of a life that cuts into life. Only such cuts set us free.

EUROPE AND THE THINGS OF DWELLING

To begin with, a confession: a dilettante is talking here—that is to say, one who on the one hand has no idea about the circumstances surrounding the planning of a television program but on the other at least has the penchant to watch something every now and again; one who therefore reads daily what ARTE[1] has scheduled; sometimes he also takes pleasure in a find such as, e.g., the recent program on Ionesco.

Though occasionally a certain dissatisfaction with the offerings makes him ask: why, out of the truly rich multiplicity of what today is regarded as a manifestation of culture, why, more precisely, out of the astonishing manifold of what people have even expressly arranged and produced for viewing, is just this and again this chosen? Why 'and again', where surely for almost every evening a new focus is set? Do the station's selections reveal a one-sidedness, even if a broad one? The motive for such a question is dark since it is not at all conspicuous—perhaps it cannot be so due to habit—that on television, alongside various documentaries about Nature and art, it is predominantly the world of actions that comes into view—whether initiated artistically or recorded directly. One may certainly suppose that man regards himself as the most interesting object. But is he then able to view himself only as an agent? Has he not always already seen himself in the things of his dwelling, this expressly attested in various ways by their remarkable formation?

One might think that these questions are trivial. Let us listen more closely. Do they in any way express an interest held by present society? And how would such be discerned? Now—it has already been discerned, since the fundamental pluralistic trait of contemporary society has already found its articulation. There in force is the chief interest in the violence of men against others and against themselves, of men against so-called Nature and especially against the natural environment. The reflection on this violence determines it first to be economic; then sub-economic, that is to say: to be the violence of the orders of discourse which tend to be exclusive; finally to be the violence of the so-called master thinkers of our tradition—with the unifying, universalizing, systematizing violence of what they represent as the first ground or origin. Representative of this interpretation are the names Merleau-Ponty, Foucault, and Derrida. Their respective thoughts are constitutive of what can be regarded as the philosophy of so-called postmodernity. Whether this name pleases our contemporaries or not, in philosophy it rightly testifies to a separation from the sense-explications of modernity.

Yet pluralism, with its necessary thematization of both non-violence and violence, is not the only fundamental trait of present society. The other is communication as it has been disclosed by the scientific disciplines of pure linguistics, semiology, and structural anthropology. Here, Jakobson, Barthes, and Lévi-Strauss are to be mentioned, the latter having just recently been paid tribute by ARTE.

In this other dimension, of concern is not the overcoming of humanism and its egocentricity, not the dissolution of the face man assumed for himself in the modern human sciences, not the expunction of his self-conception based on the λόγος or ratio, but rather the establishment and unfolding of his linguistic character as it is alone human. Starting with the speech of "wild thinking," which is also effective in civilized thinking. The first thought and thus the first word is a negation, a prohibition, a taboo. The first gesture of speech is a negative one to such an extent that its own instrumentality is already borne by it—negating the independent significance of individual sounds. Accordingly the humaneness of the use of instruments begins first of all with the manufacture of secondary ones, that is to say: for the manufacture of usable instruments with instruments. Here an interest in things becomes apparent which, in their instrumentality, respond to properly human speech. Especially insofar as they can become the subjects of semiology.

If the things of dwelling join the instruments of production and action, it certainly has to remain open here as to whether they were to be sufficiently grasped for their part as instruments. Should we define them? Even disregarding Wittgenstein's objection to such a procedure, such would be imprudent for historical reasons, which we shall have to pass over here. At any rate, the following exposition can rely on the illusion of immediate familiarity, an illusion that dwelling along with its things has for everyone. Does just this general familiarity not speak against its presentation on television? What interest could table and bed have claimed for themselves—without thus being the so-called props of a plot? Prior to this, one would have to ask: can dwelling be at all shown? For such to be possible, must not an action, such as, e.g., familial discord, first be introduced into it? Could dwelling be accessible perhaps only by way of its things—by way of house and garden and their arrangement?

Dwelling is well-known but difficult to grasp. Can it for its part be dissolved into something manifold, much as an action into individual actions? Can it be completed like actions? Does it display an architectonic of grounds and causes within itself? Presumably not, for otherwise philosophy would have attended to it, were dwelling not to have become thematic only in the separation of the sense-explication from philosophy at the limit of modernity and in fact for Heidegger. We leave it in all semblance of familiarity and turn to its things.

Now such things are already presented on television and in fact in advertising spots—as on every market, so too on this one, as wares. The merits in use as well as in their design are thereby extolled. Yet the market has to be left to its own global habits of advertising. Advertisement has to take care of itself and is no business of public television, most certainly not of ARTE. Anyway, the contemporary market also reveals: as in other things, here too it is not only their market value that can be discerned but also the determination of each thing's use in dwelling; beyond that, however, a manner of design which suggests a judgment of the attractiveness of the thing—as it were, an answer which may depart from the judgment of its utility. Such distinction is older than Europe. We mention here only a Hittite ewer from the early second millennium B.C. and a Northern Chinese vase from the same period, each of which possesses, for a contemporary eye at any rate, an exquisite form—this ever among a mass of average products. In their attractiveness, such things are not merely things of use but rather are to be read as signs—as signs of the most modest interest of man in himself and in fact in his faculty of judgment. It is precisely on account of this that we shall now talk of Europe and the things of dwelling.

Of which Europe? We should first look—as is fitting—to our contemporaries for an answer to this. In the dimension of the reflection upon the fundamental pluralistic trait of its society, there is much talk of Euro-centrism. Such is, as is well-known, a reproach and testifies to a Europe that is at odds with itself—as it were, stricken with a bad conscience. Why? It was only recently that the widespread aspersions cast on the distant Columbus make the contemporary basis of judgment perspicuous: social violence or non-violence. And how could it be otherwise in light of what we said at the outset? The Europe of violence against the rest of the world—once again, first with a view to the world market with its political substructure; then with a view to the predominance of its orders of discourse down to their legal manifestations; finally with a view to the claim of the superiority of its culture and in fact of its logocentric culture.

The "postmoderns" are at odds with their Europe of colonial modernity, especially with that of the violently imposed European world market. This is manifest in another way with respect to the aforementioned sciences of communication—concretized in structural anthropology. The disclosure of wild thinking, the rescue of its remnants, which have not yet been transformed by civilization, requires—as Lévi-Strauss calls it—a "dis-placement" (*dépaysement*) of the researcher, the departure from the established customs of his country and the ways of thinking of his people, the expunction of all feelings of superiority.

Regarding overt or covert violence, no one speaks of a Sino-centrism, although China has always been far more intensely centered on itself, also in its self-esteem, than Europe has been. Even Leibniz's offer to the Imperial Court to exchange European mathematics for China's technical know-how came to nothing. At any rate, a Europe other than that of the capitalistic world market, a Europe that understands itself geographically and geopolitically, surfaces here—a Europe not of our world but one belonging to a closed history, closed by the concluding of the reason proper to it. It has to remain concealed so long as its history is instead projected as a continuum extending back from Europe's seemingly revolting present.

The other, and in truth first, Europe is not old according to its self-conception, not much older than the world powers characterized as European and the postmodern rejection of this Europe. Only Napoleon has completed its political formation. Which Europe is that? In his *Reflections on the Government of Poland and its Projected Reformation*, Rousseau writes: "Today there are no more Frenchmen, Germans, Spaniards, even Englishmen, whatever one may say of this fact; there are only Europeans" (*CGP*, 960)—they being understood, however, in a negative sense in the wake of the dissolution of national institutions. At any rate, a Europe is known here, though chiefly in the resistance to its cosmopolitan dissolution (cf. the commentary ad. loc.).

Neither the Greeks nor the Romans nor their Carolingian or Salian descendants understood themselves to be Europeans. The Greek and the Roman worlds, however, come to fruition in a European self-conception and in fact due to a political constitution that seems to accommodate Rousseau's principle of freedom—this also becomes obvious in the text cited above. According to the development and standard of this principle, Europe here posits its historical beginning. In accordance with the latter the principle is also completed as an historical construct—despite all contemporary continuation in a hollow repetition of concepts such as 'human dignity' and 'human rights', which in the world of modernity and most of all in the speech of submodernity have been deprived of their rational ground. It is precisely on account of this that it may be a task for television—contrary to the common inclination to "establish proximity"—to leave the history of this Europe, despite the reigning lack of distance, in its remoteness—and this most appropriately with regard to the things of dwelling of concern here.

The myth of Europa already calls to mind the fact that European dwelling is stamped by the legal relations that shelter it. Europe is a young culture and thus the myth professes a pre-European provenance, namely, *ex oriente*. Europa is carried from Phoenicia to Crete and becomes the wife of Zeus, who for the first time linked violence with right. By contrast, the linking of violence with right is a state of affairs that excites the submoderns, a fact recently confirmed by Derrida's text "Force of Law." Europa's three sons become kings who administer justice—ultimately in the underworld.

Still linked with the kingdom of the old Orient in this myth, Europe comes into its own with legal relations that are literally political, namely, where word and deed are to be answered for, what is more: to be justified, in public discussion. This Europe of our history becomes visible for the first time in the works of Homer and Hesiod, finally of Solon, who is the first to constitute a πόλις, to devise—in Greek terms—a κόσμος for it. This κόσμος is a posit, is as such sublatable, and is preserved not by the legitimation of royal judges but rather in the giving and taking of reasons as to why it is better to proceed one way rather than another. Here matures with early philosophy what Hegel called the 'judgment of the concept', that is to say: that is good, that is beautiful according to the knowledge of what an action, what a thing, was destined to be. Here the rational intention to appreciate something in view of its perfection is realized. Such was the proper motive of European formation. With respect to this motive, Europe proved the suitability of its name: the "wide-eyed"—like an archaic κόρη.

It is precisely the culture of such judgment that has widely extended its gaze time and again beyond the bounds of the habitual for what is exceptional in other cultures. This is attested just as much by a sixth century B.C. Corinthian jug decorated with an animal-frieze as by a Sicilian ivory box from the Hohenstaufen period or by a blue and white delft bowl from the seventeenth century. All of them appropriations and translations that remain unrivaled in the open-minded appreciation of foreign achievements, an appreciation of more than the usual influences—for instance, of Chinese ceramics on fifteenth century Persian ceramics. In what sense unrivaled? European technologies found their ground in European science. This, in turn, in the science of reason.

It establishes itself along with earlier philosophy in the attempt to ground the political κόσμος on the pregiven κόσμος of the so-called Natures. There is something similar in China; and this as well: thinking the κόσμος in terms of a harmony. But not this: in terms of an invisible and yet mathematically representable harmony; and this is once again to be taken back to a λόγος, a ratio, and in fact as the proportion of all proportions—most richly embodied in the buildings which for the Greeks alone bear the name 'dwelling': ναός, that is, temple. In them the architectonic of public buildings is learned. The family house remains structurally of little significance. As for the domestic things, however, we know them in their attractive formation mainly from burial objects: vase painting.

This first Europe is open-minded not only in taking but just as much in giving. Uninhibited by ethnic divisions, the Hellenic πόλεις offered that which alone was binding for their entire οἰκούμενη, their world of the housed, namely, the ἑλληνίζειν: a way of life of free sociability based on a common language and education. This was understood in this way not only in the Hellenistic empires but also by the decisive heirs of their culture, namely, the Romans.

With the *res privata*'s achievement of independence from the *res publica*—according to the concept, since Epicurus—a new fertility of the interest in the things of dwelling appears, one which can still be seen today in the remains of Pompeii or of Roman villas. The *ordo* which here became effective says something other than κόσμος, namely, it emphasizes the central intention of a way of life as it is a differentiated one in the second Europe—again with the distinction of reason itself: directed on the one hand to one's obligations to the community which is structured according to the natural whole, on the other to the relief of the body in the company of like-minded individuals from its burdens and of the soul from disturbances, finally to the perfect life in the sense of the *religiosi*, above all in the monastic community.

This second Europe also has confirmed itself according to the diverse intentions of life in the acknowledgment of foreign excellence in the usefulness and formation of the things of dwelling—be it in the appropriation and development of Syrian glass art into objects that are still exemplary or of Sassanidian silverware and also of Byzantinian fabrics or Arabic metalwork.

Whereas in the medieval phase of this second Europe the strength of the assimilation of superior foreign crafts is rather limited, a corresponding talent asserts itself almost eruptively in the fifteenth century, thus at the outbreak of the final—and in truth first—Europe of the said history. Here we mention only the example of majolica. The dominant status of the Arabic tradition is obvious in the Hispano-Moresque ware of Valencia in view of both technique and decoration. Their tin-glaze is imported into Italy and forms the technical basis of a manner of decoration which has no equal in the Islamic world. The conventional figurative elements are dispelled from the picture as it is taken over both thematically and structurally from indigenous painting. Here things of domestic use appear as showpieces as seldom before. In this period the visual arts claim for the first time to be science and not merely craft; they posit their right in accordance with the generality of such knowledge to integrate all crafts productive of the things of dwelling expressly into a uniform formative project—to produce the fittings for a building as well, in particular the furnishings. Michelangelo's Laurentiana provides a first-rate example of this.

In the seventeenth century, however, the way of thinking proper to this epoch begins to get clear about its principle, namely, freedom as self-determination within the horizon of consciousness, thus of the relation between the ego and the object external to it. The contemporary maligning of it under the catchword 'egocentrism' does not know what it is talking about. It is precisely the objectified ego that in its departedness—also from its human manifestation—sets an imagination free which, as far as the things of dwelling are concerned, possessed an unheard of wealth of inventiveness.

Determinative here is not the κόσμος, not the *ordo*, but what Hegel in looking back at the civil society conceived as the "system of needs." In order to bring their diversification into view also in the things of dwelling, one need only visit an English country house, such as Holkham Hall. Here European dwelling in its *commoda vitae* (Bacon) most clearly parts with the dwelling proper to other cultures. By way of comparison, we mention only the Imperial Palace Katsura in Kyoto—nearly empty rooms of the most refined simplicity.

Here in the third epoch of its history of reason, we find, so to speak, the European Europe—prior to all national power constructs, a civility that was cultivated with the said freedom first and most intensely in the Netherlands and England—this based on self-respect and the acknowledgment by one's peers. Just how the entire society is permeated by it is manifest in the fact that the mentality of civil dwelling is able to pare down the representational form of furniture, e.g., such that the eye is especially directed to the natural qualities of the wood, its color and grain. To the semblance of Nature as it is also proper to an English park.

For this Europe the things of dwelling explicitly become objects of a judgment that requires the cultivation of taste. Such is European, it does not think of rescuing provincial idioms. Dutch glassblowers happen upon the Façon de Venise. A Moustier tureen gets its decoration from the commedia dell'arte. Wallpaper from Lyon finds its way to England. The porcellaine de Saxe, namely, Meissen ware, to France. Cultivated taste does not ask: is that German, is that French? It knows no pained endeavor to understand the products of one's neighbors, no "tolerance" for the foreign. With open-mindedness it says, e.g., with the opening words of Sterne's *Sentimental Journey*: "They order this matter better in France." It asks: what is better? And searches for a standard for answering this question, not least because the judgment about the beauty of a thing has its place in civil sociability. Even the demand for the "purity" of taste was able to gain acceptance in the eighteenth century and found such purity in what is "classical"; it thus inaugurated a relationship to the first and to the second Europes, a relationship which was most definitely "inhabited" and not merely reflected upon. We mention here only the architect Robert Adam, who, after years spent studying with Piranesi and exploring Diocletian's palace in Spalato, evolved its architectural and decorative doctrine, transformed it freely, purified it, and concerned himself with the dwelling in his buildings via the decoration of the rooms and furniture down to the last doorknob.

And once again the open-mindedness of this Europe for the superiority of other cultures: for China's horticulture and porcelain, for India's, Persia's, and Turkey's carpet-craft—and also in this case their assimilation by Cuenza, their complete redesign in the manufacture of the carpets of Savonnerie and Aubusson. But enough of this final Europe, which Leibniz saw invested with the mission: *embellir la face de la terre*. This earth on which we dwell has increasingly shown another face, one from which the landscape architect Humphry Repton already expressly sought to screen the views from a house in his design of the perimeter of the grounds: the industrial landscape and its miserable housing complexes.

This foreshadows the earth-shattering event in the formation of the things of dwelling and in fact according to their ware-character, more precisely: to the freedom of self-realizing capital. Moved by the Marxian analysis, William Morris founded "the arts and crafts movement"—typically enough, no longer focused on the whole of the residential building but instead dealing with the things of a household down to the printing and binding of its books.

Yet despite all admiration for the workmanship of medieval crafts, the things of dwelling move into the modernity of a Europe for which nothing is foreign any longer the world over. First of all so-called art nouveau permeates architecture, as it were, reactively. Its forming, not on the basis of the taste of the faculty of judgment and the reason grounding it but rather on the basis of the lived experience of an unreflected life, shows at once a one-sidedness. The other and superior side over against this one is the constructional engineering proper to technical thinking. Wittgenstein held to his rejection of all decoration down to the last detail in his design of the Stonborough House in Vienna. He articulated the resistance to dwelling in a residential building and thereby gave a sign—even harsher than a Mackintosh chair, on which one can hardly bear to sit.

Certainly—Bauhaus and Le Corbusier found the language mediating the "functions" of dwelling. It also expresses perfectly clearly, however, the departure of the "system of needs" and along with it civil society—as well as the sociability proper to it. This holds not only of the so-called residential machines of Marseilles but also for the generously laid out Villa Savoye in Poissy. Even in the paintings, the furnishings themselves testify to the predominance of industrial design. Such completely satisfies the intention of men who are aware of themselves as the "arguments" of "functions" (cf. Frege).

It is no accident that so-called postmodernity, as far as its name is concerned, also comes into view and to fruition from out of architecture. Based on the pluralistic mentality the syntax of signs no longer requires any justification. Thus the glass façade of a New York high-rise can be trimmed with a quotation of the portal of an Egyptian temple. With the fundamentally equal value of all signifying things—so to speak, in their reduction to phonemes that have no significance in themselves—the Europe marked by rational judgment is now only a phantasm for its adversary: precisely the unjustly "Eurocentric" Europe.

In Egypt old Solon heard from a priest: "You Greeks are always children; there is no such thing as a grizzled Greek" (*Timaeus* 22A 4). Never again will the Europeans become children. Have they grown senile? Would they not rather be those of the dead Europe, determined on the basis of its closed history? Yet—as Hegel says—"to hold fast to what is dead, that is what requires the greatest strength" (*GW* 9, 27.26/19). There what is dead, however, is not what has perished but rather what has departed. In order to grasp the departed as such, the faculty of distinction is needed which already knows that Europe's reason has come forth eminently with its distinction of itself—never unanimously, which is also why its philosophy was always in conflict. Such conflict is also to be provoked in so-called postmodernity—regardless of the quarreling of the philosophy business and its endless continuation of problems. Such conflict is to be renewed in view of the difference, mentioned at the outset, between the reflection on the speech of violence and the sciences of the speech of communication. Incomprehensible to both sides, a third dimension of speech becomes apparent here: that of the word of the configurations of wisdom which came to fruition in Europe's philosophy—configurations epochally distinguished as the knowledge of the Muses, of the Christian doctrine, and of that which makes a man a citizen: his Nature, present as freedom, or his humanity. In each epoch the σοφίαι have awakened a corresponding "philosophical" reason, have given dwelling in Europe, despite its nations, its characteristic stamp: a culture that bears a tension within itself, one which is to be animated time and again in crises. Thus let us encourage the crisis which always meant for its protagonists: to get clear about oneself and the world.

Once again to the things of dwelling: as was said, there is much that opposes one's descent into that history in which a wealth of things brings the characteristically European dwelling to speech with distinction. In the idle talk of those who are merely ephemeral, these things cannot be voiced. Would this not also be the appropriate place for a *dépaysement* first of all for television so that we might learn to see what is our own in light of what is foreign? Such becomes an exercise in seeing, however, only when not just the obsolete things of only prehistoric or ethnological interest are sought out there, the things that are to speak while lacking a script, not just fossils of human dwelling, but rather things whose selection is itself alive in the judgment of foreign culture, thus in a learning that allows itself to be led to what is worth seeing by the appreciation that the foreigners themselves have for such things.

In this sense, appreciated is already, e.g., a famille rose bottle, which the Emperor Chien-Lung himself inscribed with a poem; prior to that, however, a vase made of Ting-porcelain from the Sung Dynasty, a celadon ewer inlaid with black and white flowers from Korea's Koryo period, or a red Raku tea cup by the Japanese potter Koetsu from around 1600 A.D. which even bears a name: Woman-Face-Moon. All such things provide a lesson in seeing but also in being quiet before the silence of a dwelling that took shape there.

In the first of the "Four Quartets" one of the moderns, namely, Eliot, takes the movement of word and music back into a stillness which he indicates not by accident by way of the comparison:

> as a Chinese jar still
> Moves perpetually in its stillness.

Is anything to be added to this? No. Enough.

NOTE

1. ARTE (Association Relative à la Télévision Européenne) is a German-French cultural station based in Strasbourg and is oriented towards the European market. It shows films, reports, and documentaries focusing on animals and nature, countries and people, and art and society; three times per week (Sunday, Tuesday, and Thursday) the evening is devoted to a specific theme; music is the subject of other programs; and plays, performances, and short-films are shown [Editor].

THE PRESENT OF CHRISTIAN *SAPIENTIA* IN THE SPHERE OF SPEECH

As far as the configurations of wisdom of our tradition are concerned, the middle configuration plays a special role. Whereas the first configuration—grounded in the knowledge of the Muses—and the final one—grounded in the humanity of man, in its imagination—have been silenced or have become silent, it still seems to hold for the middle one, grounded in the revelation of the Holy Spirit: it speaks; and in fact by way of the "preaching" essential to it. Yet in which determinacy? Does the reading and interpretation of New Testament texts guarantee the present of the "Gospel"?

In which joy would this message be present? In that deriving from the redemption from sin and death? From the expectation of eternal beatitude—of the beatific vision of God "face to face"? Instead of raising further, immediately obtrusive questions, we ask only this: who knows?—once more: knows—and this in the preaching of what has been the *Sacra doctrina*. In view of this, is not even doubt testimony of benevolence?

Let us leave all questions to the side that are provoked by phenomena of contemporary unbelief or even belief. They remain diffuse with respect to a present of answers that have already anticipated such questions. Answers by which our world has been articulated—this insofar as it, as modernity in singular significance, had to take its leave of its history. Christianity also falls in this history, and it seems to have carried its "Gospel" away with it. Thus it is held to be a thing of the past.

Yet in its Nietzschean position, the said modernity knows a Christianity with an oppressive present. This not just as a type of morality but rather morality in its socialistic transformation. And it seems that the Christian churches are bent on confirming Nietzsche's presage. By confusing the Pauline "wisdom of God" not even with the "wisdom of this world" but rather with its prudence or only with the "sensibility" ascribed to our contemporaries.

Considered more closely, however, our present is no longer that of the said modernity nor of the "Antichrist" (Nietzsche) constitutive of it. With the prospect of the distinction of man from himself, with that of his other, future world, the Antichrist's thought remained akin to the wisdom, and thus the message, of the New Testament. Foucault's translation of Nietzsche for our contemporaries has expunged the "Antichrist's" recollection of a Christ, however distorted. In fact, the overcoming of the "thou shalt" by the "it is my will" and further of the latter by the "it plays" (*KGW* VI.1, I) is quite familiar to submodernity, though not the integration of this sequence in a "revaluation of all values" for the sake of the creation of the "overman," since here there is no thinking permeated by the will to power which precedes such creation, nor does the self-overcoming in keeping with a world of the eternal return of the Same follow it. This thought can no longer be asserted as a counter-word to the word of the return of the Son of God as judge, of this former thought which possesses the "greatest weight" (*KGW* V.2, § 341). The word concerning his return has come to lack resistance (*Widerstand*) and thus its object (*Gegenstand*). The question as to whether the message of the New Testament has its own present or is dependent upon the one whose fundamental linguistic trait Foucault most clearly articulated in association with submodern thought, becomes all the more pressing here.

His objections to Christianity—again understood as a type of morality—are of less importance for our question; at any rate, corrections are of no use in this area. What matters is this: of which determinacy is the man to whom as submodern the Gospel is preached? What could he possibly find good and joyous in it? He—who?

To say it straight away: his self-conception, as articulated by Foucault, excludes an ear for the said message. How does one help oneself in such a situation? Best of all with equivocations on 'love' and 'peace' and 'justice'. Thus the failure to hear the message comes to be taken for granted. And how would the simulation of hearing be expunged? By the distinction of speech—no longer on the basis of a "faith" which has itself become equivocal but rather on the basis of an attempt to abide by what has been thought in a configuration of wisdom, a thought inherent in what has been said: *cogitata co-agitare*, and in fact to disclose it in its architectonic. In view of the latter, it also holds for the message of the New Testament: speech has to take care of itself.

It is not necessary here to sketch once again the Foucaultian position in its entirety (see esp. pp. 233-235 above). We emphasize only its rejection of the message of the New Testament: 1) with regard to thinking as it understands itself in historical concretion as "emancipative"—this in view of the genealogy of the subjecting orders of discourse in the Occident; 2) with regard to the topic as it in mundane concretion, namely, in the sense of the individual who has hitherto been subjected, even calls for alterity contrary to traditional standards of identity and thus for the totally emancipated self-regulation or self-management of one's own life; 3) with regard to the reigning impulse as it testifies in linguistic concretion to an individual's self-actualization with a creativity by virtue of which the self to be actualized is time and again a newly projected or pre-spoken self.

Here man's distinction from himself—in the sense articulated in the New Testament of one's subjection to the will of that God who in turn subjected himself—is completely eliminated. Eliminated here is precisely that which through a *mancipatio* (giving oneself into someone's hands) makes all the difference for someone. Instead, on the agenda is: to become "new" again and again through mere "alteration"; without still preserving an identity, to live one's life as, so to speak, a series of novelties. How could it be audible here: "put on the New Man who has been created on God's principles, in the justice and holiness of the truth" (Eph. 4:24)—yielded by him who brings the message of peace (2:17)?

Letting this be heard does not first depend on the circumstances and states or on the world of the listener, but, prior to that, on submodern thought's position on speech: the traditional "orders of discourse" are attacked and expunged as structures of dominance, as instruments of power for social segregations which exclude this or that group from participation in discourse and thus from co-determination. Commandment and prohibition are forms of discourse that are deprived of social respect. In short: the speech of the "Lord" is regarded as impertinent.

The ear for the message of the New Testament, however, is closed not only in the contemporary social actuality of speech—the Word as that of the "Lord" cannot bring joy—but, what is more, with the disclosure of the message as such as it is articulated by linguistics. This in the horizon of semiology, which assigns the message as "text" to certain genres and subjects it to a structural analysis.

However, such objectivating leveling—for instance, to a linguistic account (*récit*)—is still not the decisive event, because, at least to begin with, it remains a matter of scholarship. More important than the formal decoding of New Testament "texts" and the attendant formation of hypotheses is the postmodern speech in the preaching of the message. It is oriented towards what Barthes analyzed as the contemporary "*message publicitaire*," namely, the speech of advertising. Does not the "Gospel" also belong to this genre—namely, advertisement?

Does not the connotative aspect also prevail in it and with it the stimulus to the wishful dream and its poesy, the denotative aspect of certain states of affairs? Does it also hold here: "insofar as one sticks to the linguistic level of the message, that the 'good' ad, the 'good' message is the one that condenses the richest rhetoric within itself"—e.g., concerning 'love' and 'peace' and 'justice'—

"and with precision (often of a single word) attains the great dream-subjects of humanity and thereby causes that great liberation of images (or by images) which defines the distinctive feature of poetry" (*MP*, 246 f./177)? Does contemporary preaching not have to "transmit" the Gospel precisely in the mode of the ad in order to arouse the response 'Yes, that's it'?

No subjection to the truth, to a type of knowledge and its doctrine. Instead, an openness to a "linguistic representiation of the world" and in fact that of praxis. Here what is said connotatively is to be distinguished from what is told denotatively (247 f./178). Yet what is said, namely, the directive given, is in the case of the ad the product.

And what is said, what is the directive given by the Gospel of the New Testament? It is high time to think speech itself here with distinction and in fact in view of the submodern or postmodern understanding of it indicated above. One comes upon such a thought, however, only by way of the insight into the difference of the modern sense-explications that was already yielded and, prior to that, into the difference of reason itself, which distinguished itself according to its position with respect to the epochal configurations of wisdom into "natural," "mundane," and "conceptual" reason (cf. "The Distinction of Reason," pp. 101-109 above).

In each epoch, wisdom guided precisely that speech which urged man to his distinction from himself so that he be the "humane" man and not merely the one determined by a type of speech which distinguishes him from other animals. He is not already "humane" with the speech that has its beginning in the assertion of social prohibitions (cf. Lévi-Strauss, *The Savage Mind*). He becomes "humane" on the basis of the freedom of renunciation, and he learns such from a kind of indication that brings the span between "how it is to be" and "how it is" into view. Only this awakens thinking from its instrumental employment to the attention to the "humaneness" of man.

It is not the speech of prohibitions and commandments that gives what is to be thought but only the span that has been brought into view, namely, the span between "how it is not to be" and "how it is," between "how it is not" and "how it is to be," in this regard the "truth" of an event that completes itself, that claims thinking as such. Only the configurations of wisdom of our tradition give what is to be thought in such a way that the man of concern in each was able to understand himself as a "thinking being"—not only as determined by speech, as is asserted by the pre-historical orientation of "postmodernity." It is precisely for this reason that we take up the present task of recalling that distinction of speech from itself, a distinction which has its actuality in the said configurations of wisdom—distinguishing what is said, which gives what is to be thought in the sense mentioned, from what is spoken. For the philosophy of our history, that which gives what is to be thought there is in each instance a wisdom whose truth expressly wants to be sheltered in a certainty. Now as far as the conception of the message of the New Testament is concerned, we refer here first to its philosophical horizon, as it is outlined in our "The Philo-Sophical Conceptions of the Middle Epoch"; prior to that, however, to the clarification of the historical place in which the message is preached as it is presented in our "Introduction to the Rationality of the New Testament."

Yet both clarifications remain inadequate insofar as our present is severed by the deed of the said modernity from that history and its middle epoch, in particular from its inaugural phase. This deed had to be done because our present knows no configuration of wisdom which would have once again set the task of the aforementioned conceiving. And as for the former configurations of wisdom, their epochal tasks were fulfilled by metaphysics. Furthermore, what is due to be dealt with in view of the linguistic character of man as articulated in submodernity and postmodernity is rather this: to learn to attend to the distinction of speech from itself also in the message of the New Testament, to attend to what has been thought in its saying and, more precisely: to the figures of its ratios or proportions consisting of the terms 'destiny', 'topic', and 'thinking'. A building thinking is necessary here, not a conceiving thinking but rather a, so to speak, logo-tectonic thinking. On this side of contemporary theories of action such a thinking has human dwelling in view (see "Action or/and Dwelling," pp. 169-181 above).

How does logo-tectonic thinking attain—it stays strictly in a present of thinking which is just as much severed from the philosophy of our history as from the sense-explication of the modern world—how does this thinking attain what is said and thus what is thought in the New Testament? How is it exhibited for this thinking in the determinacy of being wisdom?

The message talks first of all—so it seems—of God. Yet what does that mean here? A power which is divine insofar as nothing is impossible for its word (Luke 1:37). He who is powerful in this way dwells in his glory. Wherever this glory descends to men, they dwell in peace and act righteously.

The message of the New Testament appears, however, only in the following determinacy:

I) The Synoptic ratio starts with the destinal term: the shared and simultaneously distinguished glory of God—distinguished to the point of visibility in the "Son" of the "Father": visible in him firstly as the resurrected Lord. Looking back from his resurrection, such is the glory of the Temporarily Transfigured. Thus, transfigured because God expressly acknowledged him earlier in baptism as his Son. Jesus can be acknowledged as the Son of God only because he equals the Father in his love. And this equality is in turn not thinkable except by virtue of the fact that this man is generated by the Holy Spirit. Thus already with his birth, in its proclamation to the shepherds, the glory of God comes to word and this in relation to the peace that the Son and only he as the Son of God imparts to his followers.

After this graduated attribution of glory to the Son by his followers and the Father, after this linguistic mode of the destiny, it is to be thought as an historical destiny. Here the difference between those—Father, Son, his followers—who are united in love is no longer to be emphasized but rather the power of the authorized Son and in fact the return of the Transfigured as judge (Matt. 24:30). The end of the world with the Last Judgment, in the distinction between those called to beatitude and the damned, is the rational vision of history as one that completes itself.

In the end, however, the destiny is of mundane concretion and in fact in view of the present in which Jesus, the Lord, is "the sign that is contradicted," one posited "to fall and rise" (Luke 2:34) for those meeting him. The spirits are distinguished with respect to this sign.

With the turn to Jesus' working of many signs, and in fact in saving or healing, the topic of the Synoptic ratio comes into view. What Aristotle says of tragedy also holds here: actions, not agents, are what are of concern, for only they are subject to the judgment to which everyone is entitled—but not the judgment of a person. At any rate, such holds for the topic in mundane significance. It is precisely with the fulfillment of the Law that Jesus' actions are brought into opposition with the actions of the pious and the teachers of the Law, that his actions incur their hatred, which leads to his suffering and death. But if Jesus does not abolish the Law, how can his fulfillment of it bring about the opposition? Precisely because this fulfillment understands the Law in the purity and simplicity according to which the Law is the will not only of God but of his Father. This will alone is the true Law.

The opposition of the topic taken in mundane significance is deepened with its linguistic character. Action according to the will of the Father is, namely, the heralding of just this will. What he wills, however, is the advent of the kingdom in which the Son is Lord. That he is to be present in the herald himself, opens up the contrast to traditional apocalyptic teachings, to their future without a present. Jesus heralds the present advent of the kingdom of God and thus the advent of the Last Judgment or of salvation.

The linguistic, the heralded, present of the kingdom of God becomes the historically determined topic insofar as Jesus initiates the conflict with the prince of this world. The end of the latter's reign becomes apparent. He has his power in the death understood as demise. The historicity of the topic, namely, of the acting and heralding of Jesus, is contracted into his suffering and death, which he accepts freely. Insofar as obedience reaches its extreme in his understanding of both suffering and death as the will of his Father, both are to be thought with distinction. As distinguished, they are opposed to the natural will to pleasure and self-preservation. Only in this opposition do both give what is to be thought. Ultimately the resurrection of the Crucified as the beloved Son of the Father.

Now as far as thinking itself is concerned, it enters into contradiction with itself in view of the resurrection, a contradiction that expunges its natural and mundane characters. The distinction from itself carried out therein is first expressed with the call of the Baptist as μετανοία, as a change of heart with respect to God, but it shows its historical significance only in the assent to him who has risen from the dead. Such is not subject to the conventional judgment proper to the understanding. Such assent demands an incipience of vision familiar to reason alone. As in the Emmaus-story, one's eyes have to be opened to that. But only he who has been awakened can himself open them, since his presence stands in contradiction, not only in opposition, to his death. To stand in precisely this present means to have faith. Faith thus cannot appear without the separation of thinking from φαντασία as the representiation of something, as the dogmatism of natural and mundane reason represents it.

Thinking is historically determined in that it believes in the resurrection of the Son from the dead and thus in the love of his Father. This belief comes to the world in the mentality expressed in the Beatitudes. They describe the conditions of the fulfilled Law and in fact with the contradiction into which the conventional "thou shalt" dissolves. According to its mundane determinacy, thinking wants to fulfill the will of the Father and experiences precisely the heralded kingdom of Heaven in doing so.

From the beatific experience of his present, in the mentality unfolded in the foregoing, thinking gains the linguistic character proper to it. As εὐλογία, as *benedictio*, it testifies to the overcoming of the slanderer and his reign in one's own thinking. It is a ὁμολογία (agreement) with the love of the Son for his Father; it is expressed as the confession of faith in the presence of men, and this finds its counterpart in the Son's confessing for the confessors in the presence of his Father (Matt. 10:32). The thinking-term of the Synoptic ratio is condensed into precisely this mutual confession. In this thinking, it becomes clear as to what, after power and will, the knowledge proper to God means: it is explicated as the condemning "I know you not" and the saving acknowledgment of a name in Heaven (7:23).

II) Pauline preaching sees itself in a completely different situation than the one proper to the Synoptics, for the former's ratio starts with thinking itself and thus without a previously determined topic. However, thinking cannot attain the distinction necessary for it on its own. As distinguished, thinking has to be given. But how? The skeptical answer of natural reason would read: by τύχη, that is to say: unexplainably, it just happens that way. The Pauline answer, however, reads: by χάρις, grace.

The givenness of this distinguished thinking is grace. Its giving is an immediate call, and thus Pauline thinking is first of all of linguistic determinacy. The present of the caller is not that in the flesh, not even that of the transfigured body, but only that of the voice which calls to the converted thinking.

Distinguished thinking comes as an exhortation. The saying involved in it is a bene-diction, is εὐλογία, and in fact in Christ. With him its ground becomes audible, namely, as he who gives grace. With respect to him the thinking given is first of all a thanking for itself, and this thanks is in turn expressed as εὐλογία, as the "praise of the glory of his grace" (Eph. 1:6).

Since the thinking given is thankfully related to the giver, while the latter is the beloved of his Father, thinking enters into the relation of divine love. It is only in this relation that thinking becomes open to its historicity and in fact on the basis of the belief that God—in a new creation—has "reconciled" us to himself through Christ (2 Cor. 5:18). It is only on account of this that he who thinks may know himself to be for his part "known" and thus loved. In the ground which Christ is for him, he who is blessed knows himself as one "de-limited" by the Father beforehand. With a limit that makes all the difference for his salvation. In such a belief and share in knowledge, thinking finds its beatitude. It knows its reason to be reborn into the originariness of reason's destiny—not into the paradisiacal image of the creator, which man was prior to having eaten from the tree of knowledge, but rather into the image of the perfect cognition of Christ, who comprehends the Law in terms of the will of his Father.

How does this image as such come into the world? It learns in itself to think of its nature, namely, being mindful; it learns from this nature to make a "rational sacrifice" of the body—for the pure ascertainment of what the will of God is. Moreover: to do this will and thus to be holy and irreproachable. But if knowing oneself to be known means: knowing oneself to be loved; then this thinking is actualized only in works of love (Gal. 5:6). Such is the concretion of Pauline faith.

As such, converted thinking sees itself referred to its destiny as it lies in the power of God. Why? It is just with respect to every activity of the servants of God that this power was exhibited in the Law which had to be fulfilled. With respect to the relation 'God–Law–servant' an opposition opens up in the Pauline destiny. The middle term of the Law is obstructed by the Christ who himself is the mediation between his Father on the one hand and his followers on the other as those freed by him, freed for sonship. It is precisely due to this that it holds for the faith which is actualized through love: in the corresponding works, Christ is himself the primary agent (2:19). Only in this way is he acknowledged by thinking as its destiny.

But how does the power of God reveal his glory here? Contrarily, and this first according to its mundane determinacy. Having fallen prey to Nature and the world, the mentality of men was unable to renew itself on its own as the efficacy of a divine love. The gift of the said thinking is conditioned by the self-giving of God—on the one hand, such that the Father sends the Son; on the other, such that the latter "empties" himself of his glory, as God's equal makes himself similar to men and in fact in such a way that he becomes the servant of the Law that makes them subservient. He overcomes this servitude insofar as he surpasses the fulfillment of the Law in the obedience that extends as far as the freedom for death on the cross—that is to say: of the Cursed. The glory of God enters into the opposition to the divinely accepted shame insofar as the Father awakens the Son to his glory.

It is precisely from this opposition that the linguistic version of the destiny arises, namely, the εὐαγγέλιον of the glory of the Christ—the illumination about the proper image of God as it is gathered in the name of the Lord who links the name Jesus with the name Χριστός and thus is "the name above every name." But since this name translates the name of the Anointed One awaited by the Jews, it becomes the challenge of historical determinacy. In what way?

The God of the Hebrews did indeed want to assert his power over all other powers and thus the superiority of his Law. But the sign of salvation, which is circumcision, obviously refers to the principle of lineage and thus is linked to ethnicity. The sign of the cross is now set over against this; it is no longer compatible with such a linkage and, with its directive, asserts strict generality, sets Christ's gift of spirit over against every carnal tradition. His self-communicating holiness does not know the conventional differences between men, does not love these differences, and thus separates the present of God's glory from the temple in Jerusalem. His glory becomes world-historical, for the spirit of God's power, which appeared in Christ, dwells in each of his followers regardless of his provenance.

Now the topic in which the Pauline destiny is exhibited is, in the sense of the said generality of the spirit, the singular congregation of those called, that is, of those who have their ground in Christ. For the call issues from him. The calling to be a member of an ever historical congregation sets itself in contradiction to the wisdom of this world. For the calling presupposes a preliminary decision of God which is inconceivable to the understanding—namely, the precognition and the pre-delimitation of individuals. The justice of God is all the more inconceivable here in that from the calling follows: to make someone just and in the end to glorify him (Rom. 8:30).

That the wisdom of God knows a justice distinct from that of the wisdom of this world is already manifest in the fact that it gives no justification for the exclusion of anyone, in fact so radically that there is no talk whatsoever of exclusion. The acknowledgment of divine wisdom requires only the insight that no one can make himself just—for instance, insofar as he acts in accordance with the Law. Such an individual excludes himself from the calling. The presumption of an anticipatory rejection of someone belongs to the understanding proper to the wisdom of the world.

The congregation of those called reaches the world in the works of the love that springs from the spirit of Christ—thus in the works of those "justified" by him, more precisely: those made just. Here they are the works, on the one hand, of sanctification which, as such, are of sacramental significance—here we mention baptism and the Lord's Supper—on the other hand, however, of irreproachability as it shows a similarity to the traditional virtues, though virtues which are subjected to the so-called theological virtues, namely, faith, hope, and especially love.

The mundane character of the topic in the Pauline ratio, however, only intensifies the contradiction on the part of the congregation of those called—Paul also calls them the saints in the sense of their integration in the body of Christ, which the church is—to the world which possesses its own wisdom.

This contradiction comes to bear as such in the linguistic determinacy of the topic. It is, namely, the κήρυγμα, that is to say: the preaching of the Gospel throughout the world and in fact that of the destiny itself. This preaching is the λόγος τοῦ σταυροῦ—the word of the cross. For the preaching, however, authorization is required, namely, to be the ἀπόστολος, the missionary (10:15). Such an individual becomes the medium, the mediator of the call of the calling from the Gospel of the Lord himself (2 Cor. 5:20). Such a mediator has to have learned to think in the sense of the ratio unfolded here; that means, however, to listen to what is said. The preaching lets it be spoken. Only with the kind of speech that presents the Gospel is obedience awakened in the listener—that means: to abide by what is spoken, which is inherent in what has been said (2:9). Such is a preaching which is not only a representiation of the determinative message but provides a present for it. But that means: the preacher has to withdraw himself, that is, his own present: "It is not ourselves that we are proclaiming but Christ Jesus as the Lord, and ourselves as your servants for Jesus' sake" (4:5). Servants of men—not the liberating εὐαγγέλιον of the destiny. To proclaim oneself—that is the passion of the natural man, of his narcissism. The preacher as διάκονος καινῆς διθηκῆς, as *minister novi testamenti*, is required to completely distinguish himself from himself. But the distinction does not lie within his power, for his ability is insufficient to think up on his own what is to be said. He who has not been freed, will—according to the habit of reading the Law—stick to the letter of it all the more so. But "the written letter kills, the spirit gives life" (3:5). Only he to whom spirit is given, having begun from the said gift of converted thinking, finds his way into the spirit of the Gospel.

The Pauline ratio is completed, typically enough, with its linguistically determined topic as it elucidates κήρυγμα and thus the characteristically Pauline efficacy: to preach the Gospel to all without distinction and thus without the distinction between Jews and Gentiles. It is this that matters on the basis of this ratio. Thus it is foolish to pick out Paul as the missionary among the Gentiles. For he asserts the strict generality prescribed for him by the destiny just elaborated.

III) Preaching is the ultimate and highest task of those called to membership in the church of Christ. Pauline preaching, however, is contracted into the λόγος τοῦ σταυροῦ, of the cross as the sign of salvation. Matters are different with John's task; it is concentrated on the λόγος of the λόγος itself, which is with God but which also became flesh. With the talk of the λόγος, the Gospel according to John seems to accommodate philosophy. And this was already noted by the early Church Fathers. Such induces us here only to make the observation that John's ratio was the easiest to conceive and also prompted the first conception of the message of the New Testament; the Synoptic ratio was the most difficult to conceive since precisely there the *sensus historicus* was to be emphasized whose subject most fervently resists thinking.

John's ratio is opened by the topic. As in both of the ratios just taken up, this topic has to reveal the will of God. Since the topic appears here immediately, it poses the difficulty of not being predelineated by the destiny as it is ever the power of the glory of God. Thus the strange prologue, which anticipates the revelation of the glory in the incarnate λόγος.

What is the will of God? "For God loved the world so much that he gave his only begotten Son so that whoever believes in him may not perish but have eternal life. For God sent his Son into the world not to judge the world but so that through him the world might be saved" (John 3:16). Thus in its general significance the topic is the salvation of the world as it has to be distinguished from the Last Judgment as thought in the Synoptics.

Now as far as the first, that is, the linguistic, mode of this topic is concerned, it is encountered, following the prologue, first of all in the Baptist's testimony: "And I saw the πνεῦμα come down on him like a dove from heaven and rest on him" (1:32). And he continues: "This is the Son of God" (1:35). Now in which determinacy? As "the lamb of God which takes away the sins of the world" (1:29). This testimony is true, but he who is destined to be sacrificed does not accept this testimony from any man: "But my testimony is greater than John's: the deeds my Father has given me to perform, these same deeds of mine testify that the Father has sent me" (5:36). This is not spoken against the Baptist but rather as the testimony of Christ, who proves his authorization to save his followers (1:34). The performance of the works with which he was entrusted speaks for him as Savior. This testimony stands for the fulfilled will of the Father. The works of light.

This attestation concerns as yet only the sonship of Jesus. His first disciples recognize, however: "We have found the Messiah, which is translated by Χριστός" (1:41). Yet the Anointed One proves not to be the awaited King of Israel (1:49) but rather the savior of the world. To be such is the will of the Father in the mission of the Son. With the delimitation of the world to be saved, a world no longer of individuals, the topic takes on historical determinacy.

How is the difference in the whole understood which is ever characteristic of the topic? Not as the execution of the contrast between hitherto and future in the Last Judgment but rather as the distinction of the Last Judgment from salvation itself. He who has come as Christ is the Savior as such. He is Who He is (8:24). And he is such in virtue of the scission between light and darkness. It is here that the topic takes on its mundane determinacy.

This scission is, as it were, the establishment of a new world. The old world did in fact arise through the light; yet as the world of men, it no longer testifies to this provenance. In the λόγος through which everything came into being "was life, life that was the light of men" (1:4). This already implies: the scission between light and darkness no longer concerns the world of the originary human creature but rather the present age of the world. Precisely the world into which the light still had to come since it is the world of human desires. Regarding this, it is said: "the light has come into the world" (3:19); and what did it disclose? "People have preferred darkness to the light" (ibid.). Why? "Whoever does wrong hates the light" (3:20). Darkness thus does not belong to the work of the creative λόγος but rather in the human will, which manifests itself in bad works. Here it becomes clear: there is nothing to be saved here, nor anything to be judged, since such a will judges itself and in fact sentences itself to the realm of lies—contrary to the truth of the light—and to the realm of death—contrary to the life of the λόγος; the slanderer of its work is not only a liar; the διάβολος is also a "murderer from the start" (8:44).

In the topic of John's ratio, the task of saving the world, and in fact on the basis of the divine love of it, is unfolded—the world which is one of darkness due to the love of men. Thus love is distinguished here in the whole; that is, it is distinguished first not by its object, but rather this object is distinguished by the manner of loving. For the light itself loves differently than does the darkness. To be sure, the world is not bad or evil, but rather a kind of love of it is, which is an unmediated love since the middle term, which is the λόγος—"light from light"—is obstructed by the prince of this world, who himself does not appear.

As in the configurations of wisdom of the first epoch it also holds here: the world is only secondarily the one consisting of heaven and earth; primarily it is the world of speech—in the first epoch, thought on the basis of the distinction between the attention and lack thereof to everything (*Anwesen und Abwesen bei Allem*); in the middle epoch, thought on the basis of the difference between the giving and the acceptance or rejection of the light.

But how is the salvation of the world effected? Only in the realization of the intention: "the world should recognize that I love the Father" (14:31). It is precisely this recognition that is unfolded in the thinking-term of John's ratio.

First in mundane determinacy and thus regarding the light and darkness of the world. Only where this difference is recognized does it have to be regarded as an exclusive relation and thus as an opposition. It sets men apart according to their provenance: "born from the will of the flesh" or "from God." Only such a birth discloses the light, namely, "the glory that he has from the Father as the only begotten Son of the Father, full of grace and truth" (1:14). According to what has been said thus far, however, the pertinent vision has to be of practical significance, namely, one has "to do the truth" (3:21). It is only in this way that one is grounded in the truth (8:44).

But how does that birth occur? Only by virtue of the Word which the Savior speaks. Due to this, thinking attains linguistic determinacy. The Word is to be heard and it is to be believed. More precisely: it is believed in hearing. Here the opposite of this is not unbelief but rather not hearing, deafness as it springs from the said love of darkness. And such is also the love of one's own words. When Jesus speaks the Word, it is not his, just as the works are not his, for both testify to but one thing: his love of the Father, and that means here:

his being-within (*In-sein*) the Father. It is precisely on account of this that it holds: "Whoever has seen me has seen the Father" (14:8).

In truth, however, the Word is heard only by him who remains in the Son: "If you make my Word your home, you will indeed be my disciples; you will come to know the truth, and the truth will set you free" (8:31). Which truth sets one free? The truth about the distinction of love. Thus the Word to be heard is contracted into a sole, but also new, commandment: "Love one another as I have loved you" (13:34). Here the old qualification of "as yourself"—of a love that excludes the said being-within (*In-sein*)—is superseded.

The historical opposition ultimately comes after this opposition in thinking, an opposition which allows the grace of thinking to become clear: "It is for distinction that I have come into this world, so that those without sight may see and those with sight may become blind" (9:39). As the gift of sight along with the understanding proper to it is a natural gift, it is reduced to unsuitableness. Only sight deriving from grace is suitable. And in fact that of the present light as it has attained historical determinacy: "The light will be with you only a little longer now. Go on your way while you have the light, or darkness will overtake you, and no one who walks in the dark knows where he is going. While you still have the light, believe in the light so that you may become children of the light" (12:35)—once again, with respect to the self-chosen oppositional provenance. That is to say: being either from this world (8: 23; 15:19; 17:14), from the earth (3:31), from below (8:23), finally from the devil (8:44), or from God, from the Truth. Such provenance is a given one only insofar as it is accepted by those concerned. This acceptance becomes the assent in view of the difference between truth and lie; and this assent is provoked by the present of the divine λόγος: "When you were blind, you may have had no sin, but since you say, 'We can see', your sin remains" (9:41). The response to the Word brings to light the mentality of the provenance determined alternately.

This finally refers to the destiny as it immediately appears in its historical mode: the λόγος of God became flesh and, as such, is the unavoidable occasion for those who are in the flesh of the world and think based on it to judge themselves. The Word speaks in vain not even to the deaf, since their deafness is willed. They can evade hearing but not the decision. That is the power of the divine Word insofar as it became flesh and thus provokes the seeing in the flesh to its distinction from itself. Do those born "from the will of the flesh" remain in the presence of the incarnate Word in this origin? Do they reinforce their deafness by hearing the lie and are they able to evade the present power of the divine Word just in this way? That is the unavoidable decision which the Word as incarnate brings with it. "Light shines in darkness, and darkness has not conceived it" (1:5). It is on account of this that it, in excluding sight, not only remains what it is but solidifies into this remaining.

In historical significance the glory of God shows its astonishingness in the fact that it opens by its incarnate Word for the men who are of this world the possibility of staying in this world and yet no longer seeing the origin in it (17:14), but rather of seeing their own origin in the λόγος that created them and thus in God. But this cannot mean: to be related to the creator without mediation; this all the less so as the determinative ground precisely does not permit of such a relation to a first cause but only a being-within. The insistency of the truth of God, however, is possible only as insistency in the mediator who is the saving λόγος only by virtue of his incarnation. The destiny, which is not merely God but rather his glory, becomes determinative only through the reciprocity of the being-within of Father and Son (14:19), of the Son and his followers. As such it emerges not in the Old but only in the New Testament and in fact first of all with the destiny's historicity. It is historical in turn not as the Word of God in general but only as the Word distinguished from him since it was sent into the world and therefore became flesh.

Having become historical, the Word enacts the contradiction of being a Word in the flesh. In the flesh—for Epicurus this already means: in a body whose principal states are pleasure and pain; it is firstly the diversely encumbered body and precisely on account of this is destined to become unencumbered; it is then the body whose soul is first of all disturbed and precisely on account of this is destined to become undisturbed. Strangely and also typically enough, in John there is no talk of Jesus' πάσχειν (suffering), nor of pain, but rather of the ταραχή, of the disturbance of his soul, and in fact at the beginning of the farewell discourses (12:27), but then even more intensely since the talk is of a disturbance in the spirit, i.e., in the announcement of Judas's betrayal—in view of Jesus' imminent death. For the thinking proper to natural and mundane reason, such a disturbance of the λόγος itself is unthinkable and its unity with the flesh—thus the destiny as historical—is a contradiction. But it has to be such to begin with. "I have my origin in God and have come from him; I did not come of my own accord but he sent me" (8:42). He also leaves again. And nevertheless his temporary existence is a radical transformation of the present of the God of the Old Testament, for his glory appeared only in "passing by." It was impossible for him to achieve historical determinacy.

Then the destiny appears in its mundane version. Here the λόγος says of itself: "I am the Way; I am Truth and Life" (14:6). What is that—the Way? For his followers, not that of coming but rather of going somewhere, of following: "where I am going, there you may also go"—this immediately precedes the answer just cited to Thomas's question concerning the Way. He is the Way into the other origin, namely, into the truth of God. What is truth? Jesus left this question raised by Pontius Pilate unanswered because the answer would have been incomprehensible to the inquisitor. Nevertheless, it aids in the distinction. It is easy to remark: the question is raised by a skeptical thinking, and that means: by the expunction of precisely that "truth" which dogmatic philosophy understood as that which occurs, that with respect to which it is decided whether the understanding should agree with a φαντασία of the soul. Yet there can no longer be any talk of such an occurrence—to say nothing of the ἀλήθεια of the first epoch—in John's Jesus. It does not fall back behind skepticism. If in this connection one speaks of it, e.g., as Bultmann does, as "reality," the matter only becomes blurred. Here ἀλήθεια is solely a datum as it is intra-divine and in fact it is the glory itself in the determinacy according to which it is exteriorized. It is due to this that Jesus requests of his Father for his followers: "Consecrate them in the Truth; the λόγος, your Word, is the Truth" (17:17). As the Wherein (*Worinnen*) and thus the ground of holiness.

And finally Life. It comes last on the Way of Truth because it marks the destination of those consecrated. For the Word—of which it is said in the prologue that in it is Life—says in the world of death or of corpses, namely, of despirited agents: "I am the Resurrection and the Life. Whoever believes in me, even though that person dies, will live" (11:26). Strangely enough, the core sense-explication of modernity was not able to recognize the obvious here: namely, the distinction of dying and thus of death. It is not as if such would be a death in the flesh, but instead one distinguished according to the origin in favor of which the mortal had decided—as the case may be, in his distinction from himself. And it is obviously the glory of God, this manifestation of his power, which makes all the difference here.

It is precisely in this respect that the concluding, namely, linguistic, version of the destiny is understood, that is, a term which asserts with the λόγος the distinction of speech from itself, from its historical and mundane manifestations in history and the world themselves: "I came into the world so that I could bear witness to the Truth. Whoever is of the Truth hears my voice" (18:37). Certainly a voice in the world but not a voice of this world. With this voice—and just this speaks for the force of distinction proper to what is said in it and not merely spoken—with this voice, whose λόγος is as sheltered as it is obvious in the flesh, the following is manifest: the glory of God is to be seen in this world in no other way than in a learned seeing, in a seeing that has achieved a readiness, in a thinking that meets what has been thought and gives thanks to it.

Unlike in the speech of communication and advertising, unlike in the speech of social needs and desires, the releasement of a λόγος is manifest here which, prior to all philo-sophy, speaks without pressure and least of all with compulsion. There is no non-violent discourse because in the presence of the power effective in the glory here under consideration, neither violence nor non-violence makes any sense. There is no discourse of any kind since here a λόγος speaks of itself, a λόγος which only alone, since it is μονογενής, can have a say. A say that has edified itself. It recalls the whole of the message of the New Testament as a message of dwelling—not of a future dwelling but rather of one that has been and therefore is visible in all necessary determinacy.

ACCESS TO THE WISDOM OF THE FIRST EPOCH

What is our intention? To regain an ear for the configurations of wisdom of our tradition—for what they give to be thought. But has this ear ever been lost? Are the texts in question not still read today? And is the assistance of hermeneutic scholarship not offered more abundantly than ever before?

Which ear would need to be produced then? Precisely the one that distinguishes what is said from what is spoken, that understands what is said in the sense of a "teaching." A teaching is meant to be abided by—whether one accepts it or not. But what do Homer or Paul or Hölderlin teach? That to be man is a destiny for men which they fulfill only in their distinction from themselves and not just in their distinction from other animals—even less so as the latter distinction remains groundless so long as it is not grounded in man's distinction from himself. Yet this asserts a permanence that comes to bear only within human dwelling and, only on the basis of it, in ever individual words and deeds.

But how could the ear for the configurations of wisdom understood in this way have ever been lost? First of all they are different such that each has an exclusive relation to its historical antecedent. What one configuration gives to be known seems to be incompatible with what the others give to be known. And each has given not only what is to be known but, beyond that, what is to be thought. Each teaching has aroused misgivings, in particular its contradiction by the thinking that learned to understand itself as "philosophy." On the one hand, the ground of each teaching's way of thinking was pulled out from under it (by natural reason); on the other, the ground of its topic (by mundane reason), resulting in the replacement of this teaching by a philosophical wisdom. By way of such contradiction, however, a type of philosophical reason has in each instance achieved its distinction from itself and has conceived what arose in each epoch as the destiny of the topic of thinking, that is to say: sheltered it in the form of the concept and its logic.

Each of the configurations of wisdom has found the response of a so-called metaphysics, and it is just these responses that also reveal precisely which teaching as wisdom gave what was to be thought and thus called forth a philo-sophy.

Here the knowledge comes into view which first referred to the word of the Muses, then to the word of the Holy Spirit, and finally to the word of the humanity of man. Each time, the speakers of a particular wisdom take up a given word—in distinction to what they themselves might have thought up.

It is precisely in view of the said philo-sophical conceptions, however, that the audibility of those configurations of wisdom taken together has disappeared along with modernity, since they too were dragged down in the oft-cited but little understood "extinction" of metaphysics. Modernity also knows a sense-explication which for its part once again leaves its own trails to man's "necessary" distinction from himself and in fact in the future of the communist society (Marx), of the masters of the earth (Nietzsche), finally of man as the mortal (Heidegger), in a world yet denied.

And the inaudibility of what is said in a particular wisdom intensifies once even those trails have been lost in our present. There is no longer any such future. Instead of on it, the argumentative eagerness typical today is focused on what is supposed to hold in discursive and active communication. In such eagerness, so to speak, a favorable prejudice is expressed which supports a recollection of that dwelling which the configurations of wisdom of our tradition do not, to be sure, discuss but rather bring into view—addressing those men who dwell more or less wrongly and rightly. Now it seems that our contemporaries, like the moderns, cannot see themselves in such a vision. It seems all the more urgent to rationally regulate their relations via an ethics or on the basis of a theory of action. Yet such are only the superficies of a sphere of thought's differentiated positions on speech. Not least because the rationality claimed today is likewise in need of clarification. That it is not enough to appeal to "the principle of non-contradiction" should be obvious—even if, in addition, the necessity of social consensus is called for which in turn has an enlightenment about the "true" interests of the individual as its consequence.

Now is it our intention to propose an alternative ethical project here—with a simple appeal to what the wisdom of our tradition has said? Such cannot be the case already because wisdom is not audible in what it has said—in what it made known as a teaching and in what it gave to be thought—without a distinction of speech. We are, as far as dwelling is concerned, at home in speech and not in our world along with its history. Hence the reliance on historial scholarship is also unnecessary; for regarding wisdom, of concern cannot be the representiation of what was formerly spoken but rather only the present of its claim. Precisely this present is—as everyone will easily convince himself—at least "problematic."

Here we take up the said distinction of speech in view of the wisdom of the first epoch. That Homer was the eminent teacher of the Greeks was even acknowledged by his adversaries. But wherever the Muses are at best an historial reminiscence, the talk of what only they make known remains empty. To be retained here is only the question as to what Homer's work gives to be thought. Yet this question inevitably hits upon what has already been thought—whether in rejecting or in accepting it—in the beginning of Greek philosophy. This draws our attention to a preliminary question: which present does this philosophy have then—and in fact on this side of the arbitrariness of historial representiation?

Even the distinction of the sphere of speech requires—just as in the sphere constitutive of the world of modernity—a simulating first dimension. If in that world hermeneutic reason simulated the task of what had formerly been conceptual reason, here in the sphere of speech anarchic reason—as we shall term it here—simulates apocalyptic reason as it was proper to the core sense-explication of modernity (cf. "The Dimension of Submodernity," pp. 227-239 above). For submodern society Merleau-Ponty translates Marxian thought; Foucault, Nietzschean thought; and Derrida, Heideggerian thought. In each instance here, the apocalypse of the future of the other man is expunged. Only Heidegger articulated this future in terms of the history, no longer of the relations of production, no longer of moral estimations, but rather of philosophy. Every representiation of this history was effected by Heidegger expressly in the element of the present of technical thinking understood as the descendent of metaphysical thinking. Furthermore: the future of the other man cast its present shadow as a distinction of the other beginning of thinking from the first one. It is precisely on account of this that early Greek thinking gained a present heretofore unknown.

If each of the configurations of wisdom of our tradition is able to verify its own present, then not in that history which attained determinacy as the history of philosophy, nor in that world which was completely articulated by the sense-explications constitutive of modernity, but solely as it achieves distinction in the thinking of our present. *Hic Rhodus, hic saltus.* Consequently the present of the wisdom which was the first teaching for the Greeks has to be approached first by way of the Derridian simulation of Heideggerian thought, more precisely: of the latter's distinction between the aforementioned first and other beginning. The simulation does not so much hold to the turning for which the name ἀλήθεια became a directive but instead to the name λόγος, which is after all pertinent in this context. Unlike ἀλήθεια, however, it stands not for a turn within the Same but for a turn within the Other—in keeping with a sense of alterity as only submodern thought has unfolded it: with respect to its linguistic character, the ego as constituted by the others (Merleau-Ponty); then the ego as it actualizes its particular projection of its self in being other than the others, even if in an individuation *en masse* (Foucault); finally according to the hyperbolic assurance: *tout autre est tout autre.* With it we would again find ourselves with Derrida and first of all with his rejection of the "logo-centrism" of the occidental tradition. In keeping with Heidegger's pre-judice that metaphysics is onto-theo-logy, the rejection aims on the one hand at the subsumptive universality of the concept, on the other at the attention-to-itself of the highest, that is to say: of reason.

The desire of Derridian thought remains fixated on overcoming the occidental tradition of thought, which extends as far as Heidegger himself, even if this overcoming—unlike, for instance, that undertaken by so-called logical positivism—is in a certain way concerned with the preservation of what it consumes. Derrida talks a great deal and of all sorts of things and thereby shows, even in the dissemination essential to his thinking—he overcomes the Heideggerian way of thinking already in this way—his reverence for the "pluralistic" ground swell. But even if his thought expressly refuses every commitment, violence may and can be done to it—to be sure, a kind of violence other than that which he, by his own admission, inflicts upon the thinkers of our tradition. Contrary to the violence of the deconstruction of the traditional "sediments" of thinking, we posit the acknowledgment of accomplished building and do not exempt from this the fictions of submodernity.

What preoccupies us here is not the construction of Derridian thought—which can be nothing but: construction after the manner of a burrower—since an architectonic is ruled out by the very desire of the thinking proper to this thought. Of concern to us here is rather this: how does the "deconstruction" of the logo-centric beginning of philosophy obstruct access to the present of wisdom as it is to be disclosed in the difference of its speech?

Derrida does not want his deconstruction to be understood as a form of (moral) nihilism but more as an anarchically oriented endeavor and this in a sense contrary to the fundamental "archic" trait of metaphysics. But how could this affect the aforementioned present of wisdom? Only insofar as the conceptual reason of the first epoch of philosophy safeguards the needed trace of the truth it conceived. It shows not what is to be sought so much as where. As such, however, it is eminently the philosophy of Parmenides.

Following Heidegger, Derrida's attention in the region of early Greek thinking is directed less to Parmenides than to Heraclitus. The affinities with the notion of *différance* crucial to Derrida—it is more a network of representations—remain, to be sure, extrinsic to Heraclitian thought. Deconstructive thinking nowhere takes the opportunity to comprehend its victims in the architectonic of their thought but instead grasps them in that "element" in which it thinks it sees its likeness: a thought determined by a desire which Derrida wishes to understand as "phallic"—this in keeping with the view that sexual difference is more originary than what Heidegger had attributed to metaphysics as the "ontological" difference, namely, that between Being and beings. Derrida has neither scrutinized the legitimacy of this assertion, one he in fact exceeds in order to reach the aforementioned origin but also one by which he abides, nor has he thought with distinction Heidegger's assurance of the privilege of presence in metaphysical thinking, although such presence has become the connecting thread for Derrida in his attack on logo-centrism. It is not as if we would want to turn these omissions into a reproach—Derrida knows what he is talking about always only approximately when of concern is the totality of metaphysics—rather, they are to be understood in light of the necessity of a simulation of Heideggerian thought. Along with all its consequences, this simulation is indispensable for the constitution of the first dimension of thought within what we distinguish as the sphere of speech in contrast to the world of modernity and its history.

Derrida's critique of logo-centrism obscures just what destines Parmenidean reason to engage in conception. It obscures the distinction of the sense of Being, if we may still talk this way in light of our rejection of the oft-cited "privilege of presence" (cf. "Privilege of Presence?", pp. 81-90 above); it especially obscures, however, the ἀρχή and in fact at the point where it takes on the meaning of 'ground' as it is known by so-called metaphysics; but along with this ἀρχή, it also obscures the distinction of identity. Now it would be completely otiose to engage in historial corrections of Derridian views on the logo-centrism of the occidental tradition and its "archic" thinking since a socially supported desire prevails in them.

The necessary distinctions concerning the "origin" of metaphysical thinking come to light when, but then only when, the beginning of Greek philosophy is grasped as a closed construct. On account of this, we shall now sketch its architectonic with the necessary brevity.

To begin with, the rejection of the knowledge of the Muses is to be attended to—this with regard to its reliability. Here it holds, as it did already for Homer: the reliability of a type of knowledge and thus of letting-know requires a presence with what is there to be known. Philosophy begins with the exclusion of such letting-know since it harbors the possibility of a ψεῦδος—not only on the part of the bard but, prior to that, of the Muses. Regarding the reliability of what is known, the appropriate thinking is determined to be θεωρίη and ἱστορίη, that is to say: in the whole as in the parts, determined to be a seeing which is open to anyone due to his own presence with the thing in question. The thing therefore has to be determined to be something that appears (τὰ φανερά). Since such appears in dispersion, the presence with everything is possible only in the distinction of a φύσις, which first must always be discovered, from what appears. Only in terms of it does θεωρίη attain a totality. It sees not only that and that and that, but "how it is"—first of all regarding everything that enlivens the earth: it is moist.

This first φύσις is a unified ground which in turn makes its pure appearance as water. Its primary position is not guaranteed genealogically—the corresponding knowledge would abandon the said ground of the presence with the first—but rather by the fact, illustrated by way of comparison, that water not only (according to the traditional notion) surrounds the earth but likewise supports it.

This bequest of Thalesian thought is taken up by Anaximenes and transformed: the first is air, for it surrounds and supports not only the earth but also the heavenly bodies; as wind it even moves them. In itself it is invisible like the cohering "soul" of everything, but by way of an oppositional action, becoming rarefied and compressed, it becomes visible in simple appearances.

It is precisely on account of this that thinking is required to be a discernment of different φύσεις and their combined actions, then a continuous explanation of the conditions of what appears diversely.

However, the topic of this thinking is, more precisely, a clarification of the actions of those φύσεις which, on the basis of the oppositional behavior of the first, are determined to be the transitions between 'is warm' and 'is cold'. The context of the entire order of what appears is understood in terms of these.

Xenophanes sees such a topic immediately. If within the totality of what appears he represents earth as the first, then not in the sense of a primary φύσις prevailing in all appearances but rather in order to allow land and sea to emerge with respect to this φύσις and then to allow the sun to act on both. Here too the transitional φύσεις are in play: the 'is moist–is dry' and the 'is warm–is cold'; yet they are not determinable for their part with regard to the oppositional behavior of a first, such as air.

Even if the latter remains invisible as the soul that holds everything together, it nevertheless appeared oppositionally. Unlike the psychic ground, Xenophanes' divine first cannot appear and therefore remains incomparable with the form and thought in terms of which men know themselves. If this first is perceived, then only in the commotion of appearances on the basis of his sheer power of thinking, thus without him stirring. This god is entirely engrossed in being present with everything. Thus his knowledge is ever complete.

It is precisely in contrast to him that the thinking proper to physiology, which is resolutely oriented towards man's presence with a thing, is brought to complete determinacy: the observing and explaining of it goes on without end, it remains a quest. Though it improves its notions, it does so without ever attaining σαφές, precisely that perspicacity which would grant its reliability. It remains δόκος (received opinion) and thereby commits itself to precisely that modification of truth which the Muses knew as ψεῦδος (Hesiod, *Theogony* 27). Yet here of concern is not the deceptive likeness but rather a likeness guaranteed by observation and explanation.

In this way the first figure of philosophical reason, namely, physiology, was concluded. It brought "natural" reason, with which it came onto the scene in opposition to the given knowledge of the Muses, to clarity about itself.

This figure of the beginning of philosophy went unnoticed in Heidegger and consequently in Derrida. Though the figure now to be sketched was noticed—to be sure, not as a rational figure but only in the elucidation of the respective thoughts of Anaximander and Heraclitus, without ever taking Pythagoras into account. What is brought to complete determinacy here, however, is not thinking so much as the topic of cosmology—a work of "mundane" reason.

Anaximandrian thought is unfolded starting with the topic, which is immediately taken up in a way that recalls the Hesiodic beginning with Χάος and Γαῖα: immediately distinguished as the earth and the ἄπειρος φύσις that surrounds it. This limitless φύσις distinguishes itself in turn as the oppositional φύσεις of moist–cold and hot–dry; both are excessive in their appearance—similar to the Hesiodic 'Ουρανός and Κρόνος—first in the inundation of the earth, then in the consumption of moistness. Only the phase of the balance of both sides allows for the manifold κόσμος of what appears on the earth and in what surrounds it.

Here we hit upon the governing principle which determines the topic as it is unknown to physiology: the realm of justice—on the one hand, "granting one another what is right" in the manner of balance; on the other, the settlement of wrong as such, of the incipient measurelessness by a measurelessness that destroys both sides. This occurs in the temporal succession, the self-completing cycle of the years—by necessity. Its consequence is the endlessly repeated generation of oppositional effects out of which a κόσμος temporarily appears. It develops until man emerges as a living being. Here the κόσμος loses the artificiality ascribed to it in Hesiod's *Theogony*.

Which way of thinking corresponds to this generation and corruption of the κόσμος of everything once it becomes comprehensible only as an enaction of right? As such the course of this enaction not only has a beginning, a first, but also the "ground." No observation reaches it, but only ξυνιέναι does, that is, the combining of the totality of what appears with φύσις, namely, the transitoriness of what appears itself. Φύσις becomes comprehensible only on the basis of the steadfast validity of right in the temporary presence of all that appears as κόσμος; it calls for a reflection.

At this point Pythagoras enters into this reflection without mediation and elucidates thinking first of all according to the pre-understanding he gained from the Muses, thus with respect to Μνημοσύνη. This thinking reflects on what is known prior to all observation; it constructs symmetries out of the relations of whole numbers and is as such a συμβάλλεσθαι. In this activity, thinking always envisions: the μιμήματα (representations) of the recollected "harmonies." Only on the basis of their bequest does thinking become aware of its topic: the body as such and then those "bodies" making up the totality of what appears: unities consisting of the limitless and the limit. Here σῶμα no longer means 'corpse', though it assumes the relation to a soul as such guarantees the coherence of a living body—either consisting of pure fire or pure earth or, in that which animates the earth, consisting of their mixture. They are ultimately experienced as that mixture of the human body.

And where is the governing principle in the sense of the enaction of right to be found? The totality of what appears no longer knows any wrong, which is also why its κόσμος of their lasting ἁρμονίη is preserved eternally. In the cycle of the return stands only the life and in fact the soul of the mixed being. Here too there is no wrong. The locus of wrong is alone the living being, man. After a violation of life, he—who due to his ability of ξυνιέναι, must have initially been, in Homer's terms, ἰσόθεος (equal to a god)—finds himself transposed into the state of "according someone his right," finds himself with a mortal body whose mixture binds him to the said cycle of all that lives in the air, in the water, and on the earth. The wrong can be settled only by purification and in fact in learning justice from harmonic theory. It is completed in the arrangement of the political κόσμος.

Justice is firstly meant to be recollected justice and is illustrated as a harmonious proportion—as the δύναμις which is the τετρακτύς of the purifying μάθησις (learning); then it is the appearing harmony of the κόσμος; finally, however, the harmony yet to be accomplished and already accomplished in the polity.

Now Heraclitian thought starts immediately with a transformation of the Pythagorean governing principle: not the justice from which peace follows but rather a right that has to accompany contest. Such is decisive and in fact as a φύσις which does not merely have the continuity of the "ever flowing" but rather: "in bringing itself apart, it brings itself together with itself" (B 51). As such it does not have the limitlessness which is the first over against the limit but rather the infinite proportion: related to itself, it changes into its contrary and is thus no longer the harmony manifest in the κόσμος of what appears. It has its unity in the split which allows the split sides as such to clash. Precisely on account of this, its name is τὸ ξύνον (what is shared).

With respect to it, the thinking proper to cosmology becomes aware of its governing principle, which determines it to set itself apart: to separate reason from the understanding proper to observing and thus to furnish a presence with everything which at the same time understands its segregation from everything. It is precisely on account of this that this thinking dismisses the way of thinking proper to those men who are absent with (*abwesend bei*) everything and who distinguish themselves from the dead only insofar as they, instead of being with what is shared, apparently act on their own self-forgetting power of thinking.

Only for distinguished thinking does its topic become the λόγος which it perceives in light of the harmony of the κόσμος of all that appears. Insofar as it gives signs from which it may be gathered how things are, it specifies which φύσις it is that brings the individual appearance into the unity of that which runs counter to it. With respect to the λόγος of the One, which is simultaneously everything, thinking attains the concretion of ὁμολόγειν (saying the Same); it says the Same as that which for this thinking are the signs in the totality of what appears and of the regulating σοφόν, which is segregated from this totality.

What is to be said of the topic? It is firstly the proportion, which stays ever the same, of fire and its continual "turnings" into sea and land. It is then the totality of living beings as they expressly want to be protected in their limits by dominance. It is finally men as they, in keeping with the divine νόμος, are urged to protect themselves and, with the self-chosen ἦθος, to be their own δαίμων. They either do right by the λόγος of their soul or they do not. As such they judge themselves: maintaining themselves in the proportion 'God–man–ape' or, as mortals, attaining the contrary relation to the immortals—their belonging together with those who distinguish themselves from themselves via a death that is understood in terms of ξύνον and no longer as demise.

Just as physiology brought its thinking to complete, since it is concluding, determinacy, so too cosmology its topic. Here of concern is the peculiar presence of the totality of what itself appears—first as κόσμος, then as its ἁρμονίη, finally as the latter's λόγος. Presence modified in this way attains a decisive significance for the man who himself is part of the totality of what appears—first of all as a living being in general, then with the distinction of being reasonable (in particular for the purifying teaching of the harmony in everything), finally with the possibility of saying the Same as the λόγος of everything.

Once again: how is the incipient λόγος of the so-called logocentric tradition determined? It emerges from the modes of the presence of the totality of what appears, first as κόσμος, then as its ἁρμονίη; its ground in turn—and it is the last one of the said presence—cannot appear, cannot even be exhibited, because it is the intrinsically self-oppositional relation 'in bringing itself apart, it brings itself together with itself', in short: the contest. Its sides can certainly be envisioned, but not the fact that it is moved. Only the λόγος remains for it as the element of its manifestation.

What does this mean? Here we run up against the so-called privilege of presence. As that of the totality of what appears, a totality disclosed in terms of its φύσεις, it is essentially a presence for observation and remains dependent upon the latter. With the return of the said presence into that of the λόγος and its signs, the attention to the λόγος is first thematized and in fact in the way in which presence makes all the difference not for the λόγος but for men in their understanding: either they remain attached to the contrary of fire in the appearing κόσμος, namely, bound to the moist origin of their soul, or they perceive the λόγος of the soul as an opportunity to distinguish themselves from themselves and, as mortals in relation to the immortals, to be present with the λόγος of the ξύνον, of the shared contest. That is the prerequisite of the ὁμολόγειν, of the indication of what is equal to what the λόγος makes manifest. The immortals already say this, and so there can be no talk—with a side glance at Heidegger's *Ereignis* (event of appropriation)—of a λόγος whose showing is dependent upon the saying proper to the mortals, unless the relation that binds the immortals to the mortals is taken into account. So much for the incipient λόγος and its essential supplementation of the presence-for (*Anwesen-für*) with the attention-to (*Anwesen-bei*)—a difference which not even Heidegger was able to bring out, to say nothing of the difference between appearing and being-present. In passing, we recall here only: in σοφία the attention-to was decisive for the understanding of *Anwesen*.

It is exactly the importance of the Heraclitian λόγος for an answer, more precisely: for an echo on the part of the mortals that reveals: cosmology—unlike physiology—does not stop with its severe rejection of the σοφία of the Muses, more precisely: of its Homeric version (thus explicitly by Xenophanes and Heraclitus); rather, it attains its own σοφία, if not of human dwelling, then of human comportment.

Considered as a whole the Greek beginning shows: philosophy immediately forms a knowledge—and this also means in Greek: an intention—specific to different types of reason. In this connection it is astonishing to see: the representatives of each type of reason do not think as a herd but rather each forms a position of thought on his own. And yet together they accomplish the common task of a closed rational figure. Now as far as the concludedness of the one beginning of philosophy is concerned, it is first achieved in Parmenides' rejection of the physiological and cosmological figures just sketched.

His position is already radically different insofar as it accommodates Homer's σοφία by acknowledging a knowledge as having been given, disclosed by a goddess who calls to mind the Muse of the *Iliad.* Here arises not only the possibility but also the necessity of abandoning the presence with everything in the manner of observation, the presence of everything as a κόσμος in the mode of the λόγος. A state of affairs that could not be appreciated by Heidegger and even less by Derrida—and in fact due to the former's pre-judice that metaphysics is a theory of the Being of beings.

For the intended opening of the access to the configurations of wisdom of our tradition, it is, as far as the knowledge of the Muses is concerned, highly illuminating that Parmenides himself experiences at the outset the favor of those who rank as the destiny in that wisdom: Θέμις and Δίκη: on the one hand, what is to be done and what not, have been established; on the other, the corresponding directive.

Now within that which is there to be known, the manifold of what has been established is translated into the one truth, that is to say: ἀλήθεια as what is to be kept in view: "how it is"; the directive is translated, however, into that which by itself wins one over: "how it is not, it cannot be." That is the first path for a thinking that has the determinacy of inquiry or seeking.

The other path in the sense of the cohesion of the differentiated sides is already indicated by "how it is not." What has to deprive it of all attractiveness is the contradiction of "how it is necessary" by: "it cannot be so." For thinking, however, this other path certainly can be and has been followed. What speaks against this is just what Xenophanes had conceded as necessary: it does not come to an end, just as the Heraclitian soul comes to no end in making its way.

The goddess prevents not only this path of the former philosophy from being followed, but the third path as well, which, unlike the two sole paths of independent inquiry, knows no θεωρία, for on it, reason is entangled in a search that serves in coping with human dilemmas; they lay claim to a thinking in the sense of reflecting to-and-fro on possibilities. Here too the decidedness of "how it is not" is forgotten.

With these three paths, thinking is itself differentiated and thus determined. What is called thinking is understood solely on the path a given thinking takes—said with Aristotle: on its μέθοδος. In this way the thinking that pursues its own destiny also experiences its distinctive character first in following the path of "how it is." It does not engage in any observation here but rather follows the signs the whole lot of which lay claim to thinking in its purity. What they give to be thought is this: the topic of physiology and eminently of cosmology is itself already to be contested and this in view of its mere possibility, which has its place only in pure thinking. It is manifest: this topic assumed its proper form on the path of "how it is not." Untrue is the multiplicity, untrue is the being-in-motion which was presumed along with the totality of what appears.

"Principles of thinking"—in the course of the conflict of the other beginning of thinking with the first one, the Heideggerian recollection was attracted to them, and Derrida has followed suit in his critique of occidental "logo-centrism." In the same context, both Heraclitus and Parmenides come into view. We needn't bother with how their respective thoughts are distorted here in the service of a "more originary" thinking, since the urge for an originariness pursued by thinking with its leap into the a-byss, into the ground-less suspension, left us long ago. It is not as if we would want to hold onto the principles of metaphysics; rather, we have found our way into a reticence in the face of their strength.

Let us learn how these principles become apparent in Parmenidean thought—before they could and had to assume the form of principles. First of all concerning the later principle of non-contradiction, thought in Aristotelian terms: the state of affairs as state of affairs. Prior to this, Parmenides: Δίκη, that which directs, firmly keeps the topic of thinking within its limits on the path of "how it is." There it says: the contesting of every loosening of the bonds of being has as the ground of its decision: "is or is not." On this ground it has been decided what thinking learned at the outset: to leave the path of "how it is not." Is or is not—this is to be decided; such has been established, is Θέμις.

In the present context we shall have to pass over the so-called principle of excluded middle. It comes to bear historically in the middle epoch and there ultimately with the thought of the Last Judgment.

As Heidegger notes regarding the principle of reason, it first emerges as such early in the modern era. We shall also have to leave it aside for now. Yet the *principium rationis* has its predecessor in the principle of identity. Or does this only seem to be the case? Aristotle knows no such principle, but he does know that actuality which is the sameness in pure reason of him who has insight and that of which he has insight, a reason which, being related to everything, is simultaneously the first ground. The elucidation of this state of affairs rules out Heidegger's notion of a two-thousand-year period of incubation of the *principium rationis*; rather, it refers to an epochal beginning of philosophy, due to which the one Aristotelian axiom has to be reinterpreted as a principle of thinking—with the consequence that identity and reason (*Grund*) have to be represented in the form of principles. For the submoderns such historical niceties are, to be sure, not worth the trouble, for at most such interfere with their desires in dealing with metaphysics. Certainly—Heidegger cites a version of identity characteristic for Plato and thereby presumes to have hit upon the decisive version for the whole of history. But he expressly rejoins it with a Parmenidean word, one said to assert the identity of thinking and Being, in order then to grasp this more originarily.

We listen once again to Parmenides himself: the topic of thinking is obliged to be intact and motionless. It is intact according to the said decision which, based on the 'is or is not', admits of neither a generation nor a corruption nor a void. It is radicalized in the decision also to exclude a change from 'is' to 'is' in the sense of a change of place or an alteration of the thing. Remain the Same in the Same according to the Same—this is the complete version of identity on the path of "how it is." This is followed by the Aristotelian version of the state of affairs as such: something is attributed to this and this in such and such a regard.

In the said identity, thinking, as it had to be an inquiry into reliable truth, comes to rest. It has gained insight. It is precisely on account of this that the identity of thinking and Being as interpreted by Plotinus is now to be dissolved: the aforementioned Same is to be intuited and is also that on account of which intuition "is," that is to say: is true. In that which has the said identity, intuition manifests itself and is communicated in its manifestation. In that which is of the said identity, namely, in "being" and only in it is intuition fully determined—said in the sense of a binding promise: it is so.

What remains here of the asserted dependence of being on the nature of man, that is to say: on his thinking? What remains of this state of affairs, which is fundamental to the event of appropriation as thought by Heidegger? This state of affairs surely continues to subsist, but only for thinking within the bounds of modernity. Only this thinking is subject to the standard of the reciprocal appropriation of Being and human being. Not even in the recourse from Parmenides to Heraclitus is such justified. It has its justification solely in the horizon of the experience of expropriation as it moved the core sense-explication of modernity. Only in the withholding of itself does a dependence of so-called Being on the nature of man become thinkable.

In submodern thought, however, it has already been squandered. It knows only the dependence of my self, as I am among others, on the others, on an other who is other than I, ultimately on the Wholly Other. It is precisely this dependence that first completely closes the originary dependence of human being, namely, of thinking, on that knowledge which is given as wisdom. Could it perhaps be for its part dependent on human being? Should we here, with Nietzsche's Zarathustra, call to the sun: "You big star! How could you possibly be happy if you did not have those whom you light!" (*KGW* V.1, 5.8/121)? That is not the sun of the first epoch. For its σοφία, it holds: Θέμις and Δίκη are always already among their own kind. They fulfill their actuality already among the divine; they are not dependent on men for such fulfillment. They granted Parmenides the favor of his departure from the business of men. Here the differences of thinking, of its paths, were revealed to him.

In their segregation from all appearances, these differences became obvious to Parmenides, as the differences of the topic of thinking did in light of them. Appropriation of Being and thinking—what was previously thought, since previously experienced, therein was: the expropriation of thinking. Such cannot be experienced, however, by submodern thought. Thus the said appropriation is no longer a pathmarker of thinking. Derrida makes his way without such a sign. His thinking itself gives signs and in fact in accordance with *différance*. Thus what Heidegger distinguished as the first from the other beginning becomes in turn an other beginning over against that other beginning executed by deconstruction. It endlessly requires Heidegger's other beginning, which it has made its own.

In order to clarify this, let us listen once again to Parmenides: the mortals also know a πειθώ, and in fact their own, with which they persuade themselves insofar as they, beyond the insight 'it is', that is to say, 'is true', posit names, in fact names that dominate all understanding of 'is' in physiology and cosmology. The starting point is generation and corruption; within them the tenses of 'to be' and 'not to be' are to be distinguished; within these the being-here or being-there of the same with regard to the change of place; in that which has come to occupy its place, its appearing one way or another in the change of color. It is precisely in this way that that which comes to be is constituted—as the *Theogony* already knew—as that which appears. Due to the way in which it appears there, namely, in transition, the distinction of its φύσις from its particular determinacy is essential to it. The said predicates represent the outline of each φύσις as it is clearly to be distinguished from the individual appearance. For the relation to its other is ever essential to it. By contrast, such is by no means essential to a birch. On the other hand, the φύσις remains ever that of appearances, of the many and moved appearances.

But if thinking, having come to rest in the insight 'that "is",' is even segregated from every φύσις, how can a Being thought in terms of beings still be presumed in keeping with Heidegger? Which content remains that of the Parmenidean insight alone? Perhaps being? Which? Precisely the one that arises in the so-called predicate 'is perfect'—this with the sole recollection of everything that the Horae bring, namely, themselves first as Εὐνομία (Well-orderedness), then as Δίκη (Directive indicating how it is to be), finally as Εἰρήνη (Peace).

Is perfect—in originary purity this is what Hegel calls the 'judgment of the concept'. The weary respond: nothing is perfect. But that is not the response of modernity. It says: everything, as it is, is imperfect. Nor is this the response of submodernity. It says: already the desire for perfection does not understand itself. What is more: it is tyrannical; it is elitist; it is anti-social, that is to say: it is evil.

And further: 'is perfect'—all requirements are lacking for this judgment. For what could be judged about in this way? It is a judgment about nothing. Indeed. Yet only when thinking does not remain with its topic but hankers after some thing or other. Though here the talk is solely of that which was known to be justice. Nor is this an appearance—but for all that, is it nevertheless not something present, such as the κόσμος of all appearances? Nor is it the topic of the Parmenidean insight. Insight is not even present with such. It is "in" the aforementioned "Same." Only in this way "is" it itself and in fact as the given assent (πεφατίσμενον) to "how it is," namely: it is so—the Same remaining in the Same, it lies there in accordance with itself. But why, for after all it is not without Why? Answer: it is perfect. Is what? Can we finally grasp it? No What. Is it not at least reason? No. Nor is it any presence with anything which one tends to represent as being. The talk is of an insight which itself "is." We repeat its content: 'is perfect'. What place might *Anwesen* still have here—particularly after we have thought it with distinction?

Let us recall Heidegger's oft-repeated and uncontested assertion: in the entire history of metaphysical thinking, the sense of 'Being' is: *Anwesen*. It has to seem this way, since of 'is perfect', in light of which both Plato and Aristotle think, only the 'is'—naked and bare and as such abandoned by every σοφία; the 'is perfect' is never to be seen again—remained for the sense-explication of modernity. And this mere Being, as it is that of beings, is now supposed to stand for the topic of metaphysical thinking in general. Cold and dead it lies there, an oppressive cenotaph upon our entire history. Indicated by the curse: nothing accomplished.

And this curse echoes in submodernity without causing any pain. In Derrida it echoes as the thrill of self-pleasure in deconstruction. At long last Athens is razed. Yet unexpectedly Elea rises out of its ruins. The word of Parmenides becomes audible: it is perfect. With it the resonance: it is accomplished; finally the echo: it is completed. An entire history awakens out of Parmenides' word, out of the insight 'is perfect'.

Do we notice what is going on here? In anticipation we said repeatedly above: the speech of wisdom has to take care of itself if it is ever to be heard. Furthermore, we note here: the Parmenidean beginning of philosophy also takes care of itself in the purity of its thought. If this purity is ever to be appreciated—and the distinction of the reason of the beginning is integral to such appreciation—then Parmenides also takes care of himself, blows the entire submodern cloud to the side, a cloud which has come to enshroud the history of philosophy under the title 'privilege of presence'. This requires no rectification, for it has become senseless—not as Heidegger grasped it from his experience of withdrawal, but rather as Derrida simulates what is thought in this experience. Privilege of presence—with this title, submodern thought is only annoyed by its inability even to be the other thinking of Heidegger's other beginning, and this even in the very attempt to think more originarily than and thereby to outdo Heideggerian thought as well. (Thus the consorts sit at the table of the twelve and let themselves be roasted by their master (cf. Derrida, "Passions")).

Who thinks originarily? Perhaps Thales? There is no talk of this. Perhaps Anaximander? That remains dark since it cannot be decided. Already Heidegger's intention focuses on the comparative and has decided: Heraclitus thinks *more* originarily than Parmenides. So it seemed so long as the sole measure of originariness was failing. But that measure is in fact the Homeric σοφία. Parmenides thinks in terms of it, though not originarily so much as incipiently. Only with him is the beginning of philosophy reached if in this connection the determinate and thus distinguished reason is to be thought of. Parmenides is the first to understand that it is with Homer that one is to begin. No one understood this before him. But only the reason which is distinguished from itself.

In terms of it we now see for the first time the beginning of philosophy as a closed one. Closed by virtue of natural, mundane, and conceptual reason. As such it is the beginning of all philosophy, of the totality of its history, and not just of an epoch. Here the beginning confronts us in its unique role of being the only one to endure Heidegger's other beginning, of being the only one to make the deconstruction of metaphysical thinking reveal its emptiness.

But is it still able to do this if we, after our expunction of the privilege of presence, enter into the Derridian play on the '*présent*', provided this not only means 'presence' but also 'present' or 'gift'? But which *présent* is meant here? Put briefly: that of the other in all modes of his alterity, begun with the alterity of the body-ego as concentrated in an encountered face. All the morality of one's unreserved devotion to the others remains that of the body-ego and, as such, involved in the limitless dispersion of one's spending oneself on indefinitely many. We are and remain here in the element of social communication and thus of the obfuscation of what has been—for instance, the freedom of the personality in civil society.

Yet the Parmenidean beginning teaches: it is exactly with the insight 'is perfect' that the greatest force of distinction is attained. To it nothing is alien. Nor are the views of the mortals, to which it itself in turn remains absolutely alien. They too are understood in terms of the said insight, and in fact better than they understand themselves. Why? Due to the distinction of the identity of the views from that in which the insight dwells. It is no accident that no one—if I may confess to be no one—has dealt with this distinction, but rather that all have subscribed to that identity which is indeed the identity of a What or of what is mere being, ultimately of what appears as such as it is represented in view of the difference between light and night—the *complementum* to the predicative side of the change in color. In the night all cows are black.

It is exactly in this dimension of what appears that that is also encountered which, together with its φύσεις, Anaximander is first to have termed ἀρχή, that is, a first in the cycle of the presence of a κόσμος. Precisely this is, if one will, the originary philosophical sense of ἀρχή. But this is no longer the sense that Parmenides discerns in the views of the mortals, that is to say: of those destined to demise. Mind you, these views are neither those of pre-Parmenidean philosophy nor of a philosophy apart; they are just the mortal's simulation of philosophy. Their κόσμος is one of names whose element is the positing of differences. Mind you, a speech-world—not only of predicates of appearance but also the denotations of a What as it possesses at once the same identity of that which is to be addressed on its own—completely severed from the Same of insight—that identity which Heidegger, in reliance on Plato's being, will dissolve into the identity of Being, and this with a final assertion of the originary difference in the "reciprocity" of Being and thinking. Precisely not a Same as insight harbors it within itself. Following the trait of the origin that has become groundless, in the Derridian origin such reciprocity ultimately undergoes a slide into sexual difference.

The first names of that which is in each instance identical with itself and which precisely on account of this is in each instance different from the other of concern here, are (in the sense of appearance) 'light' and 'night'. Though they do not remain at all separate from one another inasmuch as together they denote a totality that consists of them in equal proportions. And in this totality they are imparted to everyone. The identity of these sides asserts itself in every named thing as more of one side and thus less of the other. Absolutely nothing in this world of names is thought purely. If the sun is pure, then only due to its shining. If there is pure fire, then only related to pure night. The pluralization of what is firstly posited with distinction occurs, however, through mixture. Such was known neither by physiology nor by cosmology, especially as this mixture is understood in the views of mortals as a sexual one. In this world there is no right (*Recht*); but only violence, and exactly violence, is welcome (*kommt recht*); for in this context equal shares would mean: being a hermaphrodite instead of predominantly female or male. In this realm it is not the limit-determinative Μοῖρα that prevails but rather the Δαίμων who steers everything in that she stimulates births which are followed by death in the sense of demise. It is precisely on account of this that she excogitates the first of the gods as Ἔρως, that is to say: the desire for him who is ever the other, followed by discord. The heavens of this world are, as it were, tenebrous. For its gods remain subject to the law of the simultaneously more or less of a particular opposite.

In this world the mortal—again he who suffers his demise—expresses himself, that is, the mixture of his thinking in the shifting predominance of light and night as they dominate his perception: in attentiveness and forgetting, in waking and sleeping, in being-alive and being-dead. This in a body that is always already distinguished according to its gender. Because the mortals exist in this manner, those views have to gain a good reputation which agree with the sexually-determined body. What do we hear there? No philosophy and yet something that in its all-pervasive completeness resembles philosophy.

In its resemblance to the truth, every deception has its force. It is not overcome where the deception is refuted in this or that particular. Parmenides shows: it is to be presented as a singular construct of names, this in reliance on the immediately many and scattered as well as distracting views. Only this sets a limit to the dominance of the deception. For of their own accord the views are directed solely to differing—not only here and there but prior to that from time to time. This provides them with the mobility and changeability of a Proteus such as Derrida. The power to hold him fast lies in the distinction of identity. Only the judgment of reason becomes a provocation for the resistance of the endless plurality of views. It is only because these views, beneath all insistence on their individuality, are of a fundamental affinity that they emerge *en masse*, that they allow of being disclosed as a totality in proportions built of the terms 'destiny' (translated in submodernity as 'reigning impulse'), 'topic', and 'thinking'.

Is perfect—that is the provocative topic of conceptual and therefore pure reason. The reason of the mortals certainly hears it, but it has to mishear it and can do so precisely because it hears identity differently, that is, not in terms of thinking and its destinal principle but rather in terms of precisely that topic which reason has posited as a differentiated topic with its particular identities. Such difference reaches the extreme of its closure, however, only where that which is always different is understood as the other of the other and as far as thinking is concerned: the other as he is that of the others. He who thinks in this way also expunges that identity which was that of the *res cogitans* instead of that of what appears. It is only in this way that the trace of conception as such is fully expunged. With it, however, the access to the σοφία of the first epoch is completely barred. In this connection the preoccupation of the historians of philosophy with the identity mentioned by Plato, which was already found to be barren by Heidegger, does not help in the slightest. If only because the view in question lacks nothing and formulates this identity in an axiom that gives nothing to be thought, that is not even intended to do so.

Derrida's deconstruction of occidental logocentrism is, to be sure, the significant foam on the surface of the fermentation into which Heideggerian thought is transformed once its experience of withdrawal or of the mission of history has faded. Yet the practice of deconstruction has only sealed the inaudibility of the word of conceptual reason in its first beginning, only mediately the wisdom of the first epoch itself, especially in its Homeric form. It is only structuralist reason—the postmodern transformation of hermeneutic reason—that meets it and in fact as a literary work.

In order to understand the access in question, to begin with we recall that Jakobson is able to assert the central position of linguistics—that is to say: of the structural analysis of verbal language—among all other sciences, once philosophy had become, already within modernity, of dwindling significance (cf. "Linguistics in Relation to the Other Sciences"). And it is within linguistics that poetics is granted a key role. This has to be of especial importance for an understanding of Homer when one encounters him as a poet—all the more so as this has come to be taken for granted. Who would still want—like the early Greeks—to hear first and foremost the teacher in him?

Whence the special rank of poetics within linguistics? Jakobson takes up this issue in his now-famous treatise "Linguistics and Poetics," taking his point of departure from a survey of the totality of verbal functions. To begin with, emphasis is laid on the horizon of verbal communication, at whose center the message lies. Addressers and addressees make up the first relation accounted for. Then for the understanding of the message, the knowledge of the context first of all has to be assumed, on the other hand the contact which both the addresser and the addressee have to have made so that the message, so to speak, "comes across." A final factor is the code of the message which must be familiar to both; in accordance with it the message is encoded and decoded.

Now is Homer to be understood as the addresser of a message or as its addressee? Or is he essentially both? In which context is it given and perceived? At the banquet in the court of the Phaeacian king or of another lord? Or as in Hesiod's case in the lonely foothills of Helicon? Or does the message itself present a context? Which contact do the bard and his listeners establish with one another? What do both parties expect? And what would be the common code in which the addresser encodes the message and in which the addressee decodes it? Is a tripartite relation thinkable in this connection, namely, one that would also include the Muse in the common code? Does it matter that she alone appears as the knower? And does her letting-know in any way have an eminent significance for the message? Is it of importance for the message as such that she makes something known to someone? Above all, however: does it matter to her when she gives what is to be thought?

Each of the aforementioned factors indicates a different function of verbal language—even if they combine in the functioning of a message. Decisive here is the predominant function. For the most part, it is the referential, "denotative," "cognitive" function.

It is no accident that Jakobson first turns to the expression of the speaker's attitude in order to emphasize its "emotive" function. The speaker expresses his having been moved by what he wants to get across to the other. An emotion that finds its pure expression in the interjection. We know something of this kind from the *dramatis personae* of the ἔπος, but hear nothing of it from Homer himself. Whether and how he has been moved, we know not.

Nor in Homer himself does that verbal function become clear which is in turn aimed at moving the addressee of the message—the conative function as it is expressed in the vocative and imperative moods. Homer never says: "thou shalt."

Yet perhaps he makes use of the third verbal, that is, the referential, function, which is focused on neither the first- nor the second- but rather on the third-person. One would like to say: Homer is completely objective since he talks neither of himself nor of the addressee of the message, unless in the break of the immediacy with which he brings the bard and his audience into view. To put our question more precisely in Jakobson's terms: does Homer offer declarative sentences in a certain context, or does he at least raise the questions into which they are convertible? Here we grow hesitant since the truth test is to be applied. One readily draws upon a distinction on which Frege insisted—namely, between poetry and truth. But do we perhaps want to contest the view that the Homeric work represents an instance of poetry? And what could that possibly be in our case?

The bard first of all belongs to the δημιουργοί—that is to say: he produces a work for the people. In this respect he is much like the carpenter, the physician, the seer. And he is related to the latter in a special way. He does not merely construct a canto (*Odyssey* I 328) but is divinely guided in doing so and thus has a knowledge which requires no verification but which proves itself true; this, however, insofar as it relies on a synopsis of how it is, how it will be, and how it has previously been. Not only does the bard know a certain context but also a process to which it is essential that it be completed. Precisely this is its message: it completes itself.

Yet let us first consider the verbal functions which become apparent from the three additional factors of the linguistic structure which have yet to be considered. First of all, the contact in question which—for instance, by clearing one's throat—has to be expressly established and prolonged. Do you still hear me? Are you even listening? The "phatic" function, the only one to which even, e.g., birds are privy and thus which extends beyond verbal language, only draws attention to itself. In advance of all information. The presence with something is touched upon here which Aristotle also terms φάσις.

The common code requisite for the understanding of an utterance becomes thematic as a metalingual function: to assure oneself of one's understanding and being understood, which are always only assumed in object language. The question 'What do you mean?' has its place here, as it is raised *ad nauseam* in the business of the analytic philosophy of language—with the tacit assumption: you are talking incomprehensible rubbish to someone who has understanding.

Finally the "poetic" function of speech—related to the attitude which is no longer focused on the factual context but rather on the message for its own sake. Here of concern is not a true or false statement taken from a certain context. Does that which is proper to Homeric speech find its place here?

To begin with: the poetic function is neither confined to poetry nor is poetry in turn to be reduced to this function. It certainly plays a dominant role in verbal art, but it is of subordinate significance in other linguistic activities. What does it bring about then? "This function, by promoting the palpability of signs, deepens the fundamental dichotomy of signs and objects" (Jakobson, *LP*, 69 f.). For others the latter are sooner regarded as palpable, that is, comprehensible, even as that which is properly to be comprehended; by contrast, the signs are regarded as the means of comprehension.

The poetic function thus emphasizes the independence of creating signs, also those other than verbal signs, in contrast to the utility of signs for the imparting of a certain context. Such points to the fundamental poetic trait of speech in general as a continual process of distinguishing between new signs and the perishing of old ones. This process brings to light what the poetic as such is here. Does Homer elucidate it? Or does he rather make one hesitate in wanting to call him a poet?

In the sense of the poetic function, someone such as Joyce is the true poet—especially in *Finnegans Wake*. Jakobson experienced such poetizing most intensely in the products of his futurist friends. There the poetic function appears as one of language in, so to speak, the cultivation of pure cultures. As much as this function might look like the innocent sign of distinguishing productivity, considered more closely it asserts that for the poetic dimension of speech, completeness and thus beauty can no longer be a criterion in poetry. The poetic function of speech comes to bear after the judgment of the concept has faded.

Yet to what extent can Jakobson's thought here be claimed for postmodernity. Not only can no position of philosophy be seen in his thought, but not even the hermeneutic simulation of conceptual reason, and nevertheless it is not a science restricted to a particular object. Rather, at issue is speech as it forms, after history and world, its own totality. To this belongs the break with hermeneutics and its dependence on the element of the individual's lived experience, just as it was also to be taken into account regarding the language games of groups and their rules of communication. For the analysis of verbal structures, this element is no longer of any importance, not even in connection with the aforementioned emotive factor.

What in Joyce, for instance, strikes one as associative talk, is in truth a displacement of word choice from its selective to its combinatorial axis; it is precisely in this regard that the poetic function of speech as such manifests itself. Typically enough, Heidegger also shifted the originary sense of λόγος from the choice and its distinguishing towards a collection (*Sammlung*). Thus away from judgment. Here it is manifest: his blow to the location of truth in judgment follows a thrust that accompanies the abandonment of metaphysical thinking, especially of the predicate 'is perfect'.

What does the discovery of the poetic function of speech, of its productivity via the combination of signs, amount to then for the audibility of the Homeric ἔπος? The said function extinguishes the poetic trait which, by its link to the 'is perfect', safeguarded a sign of what is thought in the Homeric work, what is more: a sign of σοφία. The impotence of hermeneutics regarding the latter, that is to say: the illusion of its understanding on the basis of one's own lived experience, the deception of reprcsentiation which had imposed itself on the present of the knowledge of the Muses, has been overcome here. And this overcoming by structuralist reason must not be disparaged. Also in this case Hegel's remark about consciousness holds: better a torn stocking than a repaired one. This all the more as here it emerges: to appreciate the Homeric work as poetry and thus in its beauty is already to downgrade his σοφία by subsuming it under an abstract-universal in light of which it is no longer evident what separates the knowledge of the Muses from, say, Horace or Goethe.

Homer's σοφία cannot be retained as knowledge, as the teaching which it has been for the Greeks, for the first epoch of our history. We do not allow ourselves to step back into it after the fashion of hermeneutics. Armed with the illusion of the possibility of representiation. We remain strictly in our present, thus we effect an ἐποχή with respect to all the configurations of wisdom. Not, however, in the manner of a neutralization. The present of each is appreciated not in the acceptance and transformation of knowledge as it occurred in the conceptions of our history; rather, each reveals to us its present with what is thought in it. In order to bring out what is thought as that of reason, the thinking proper to logotectonic reason is needed. It is logotectonic, however, in the entire sphere of speech, just as, prior to that, it was such in the sense-explication of our world and in the philosophy of our history. The sign which precisely Parmenidean thought gave says, however: only with its completion does the traversal of these spheres provide the necessary testimony of its reason. But logotectonic reason cannot repeat the Parmenidean predicate 'is perfect'. For, indigenous to the sphere of speech, it attends not to what has moved θεωρία, πρᾶξις, and ποίησις thinkingly but rather to dwelling. The space of the latter, namely, the space of dwelling, is that speech which alone has distinguished itself from itself. Such is no longer simply the speech of wisdom but rather the speech of that which gives what is to be thought. Just this speech requires for its distinction from itself a preceding distinction within itself, one yielded only by the distinction between anarchic and structuralist reason. It is precisely on account of this that the distinction of speech from itself, namely, from its speaking to its saying, to its indicating, has to become clear.

Hence, let us take a glance at what is to be taken as what is thought in Homer. We hear the reliable clue for that in Parmenides' account of the underworld. Regarding the destiny, there is no need of a translation back into its original language, for he himself mentions whence ἀλήθεια and πειθώ became apparent to him: from Θέμις and Δίκη. That is the destiny in Homeric thought.

What is Θέμις? We can pass over the nominal definition here, nor do we need to provide an abstract-universal notion, a so-called concept of it. What is Θέμις? Something like a custom suggests itself; yet this would emphasize only what is generally posited; here to be thought of, however, is likewise the side of positing as it is carried out from case to case. In each case, however, at issue is what is to be heeded as a rule or standard in social life. This in the entire span which discloses the humanity of comportment—starting with the relationship to those whom we meet as foreigners, unprotected by a specific polity, via the cult of the gods down to the kind of relations among men and women. In each of these cases, the duties are quite well-known—even without any legal regulation. Just as it is θέμις that Telemachus embraces his father upon his return home or that Penelope bursts into tears when someone recalls her absent husband. Such is not properly understood when reduced to an expression of emotion but only as an impulse to which one is bound in familial relations.

What Θέμις is, has to have been learned and thus has to be known, to be kept expressly in view, not forgotten; for otherwise one would end up forgetting himself, he would sink to a barbaric state of cohabitation as the *Odyssey* sees it among the Cyclopes. They are familiar with neither Θέμις nor Δίκη (IX 215). This familiarity, this knowledge confirms our interpretation of Parmenides, for Θέμις is continually linked to 'is' in speech. Therefore it is also inappropriate to speak of a predicative sense of being, since such hankers after a subject with the determinacy of a What. In particular, the reliance on the participial form of being only intensifies the confusion. For at issue is continually "how it is to be," which in Greek can be indicated by a mere ἔστι with a subsequent infinitive. Eminently with the Parmenidean ἔστι γὰρ εἶναι (B 6). Heidegger says of this word: in it "is concealed the incipient mystery for all thinking" (*BH*, 331/214). It concealed itself from him so abysmally that he had to translate it in the sense of his own inquiry: "It is, namely, Being"—just as is the groundless custom of the philologists. Said, however, is: "it is, namely, to be." What? "That which gives what is to be said and to be thought." And what is that? The way in which it is Θέμις. Subject to ἀλήθεια: being.

Everyone already knows what Θέμις is, provided he does not repress his knowledge. Now this indeed occurs and has its consequences. It is precisely on account of this that the judge has to enter with his knowledge and bring right to bear. In a new decision he confirms what has already been decided. The destiny in the sense of Θέμις is—this should be noted—always already of a linguistic character and therefore has its proper place in the ἀγορά, thus where one speaks with a view to a decision. However, in the judgment there is not yet any guarantee that justice has been allotted. Namely, it can be either "straight" or "crooked." Thus it can lack the force of instruction. It is precisely on account of this that Θέμις has to be wedded to Zeus, with his insight and power.

Out of this wedlock arises Δίκη. Heiress of the maternal character. Effective above all where a directive becomes necessary, especially in the conflict of claims to certain shares of goods. Where a balance is called for. She is the standard which forces every arrogation ultimately back into the transgressed limits. Precisely her bequest calls to mind the fact that Δίκη is the sister of Μοῖρα—with the established share of life, reputation, and property.

It is precisely on account of this that the topic is determined in the knowledge of the Muses, namely, what is contested. Life is contested in absolute significance and just because of this the knowledge of the Muses brings its destiny into view first and foremost in a contest in which it is a matter of life and death. It is first of all a conflict with others, then it is—especially in the *Odyssey*—a conflict with oneself, with one's own lack of moderation to which all of Odysseus's companions fall victim. The conflict with others is sparked off on the one hand by the disregard of their legitimate claim to acknowledgment, on the other by one's own greed.

Whether one likes it or not: conflict is first of all the element in which the Greeks move. Not even Achilles liked this. In a central passage of the *Iliad* Homer has him say—and Heraclitus takes offense at this: "Let conflict and rancor disappear from the lives of gods and men!" (XVIII 107). It cannot disappear, however, wherever one thinks, wherever one judges, wherever one distinguishes, down to the absolute difference which life and death can make wherever both are free.

Precisely this leads to the concluding term of the Homeric ratio: thinking in the determinacy of βουλή. Of a thinking that is forced to make decisions. That which is controversial forces one to make them. Mind you, thinking does not precede its topic here; the latter does not determine itself but rather knows in what way it is immediately subject to its destiny, namely, Θέμις and Δίκη. Nor can the topic in question be an appearance as it would have to be conceived with regard to its φύσις. That which gives what is to be thought is justice alone—but only in such a way as it is challenged by conflict.

In which determinacy does thinking correspond to this conflict? As βουλή. What does this mean? A proposal is made and in fact with a view to an imminent decision. The decision is made, however, not according to law or right but rather to reason and right. Reason makes a proposal as to how something should be decided, namely, within the limits of what has already been decided. Thus Homer's reference to that which has already been unalterably decided and which in fact not even a Zeus can overturn; these are the decisions made in the sense of Μοῖρα, the alloter, a daughter of Θέμις. This implies what we already heard from Parmenides: thinking has to be one within limits. Thinking has to be able to move within them according to the Parmenidean, not the Homeric, ratio—only in accordance with the latter, since there, as is never the case in philosophy, thinking follows upon the topic. Yet this is subject to controversy. And that means: one claim is pitted against the other. Each wants to be weighed against the other insofar as something has to speak for each if they are to lay claim to a justifying ground. Even in the case of manslaughter, right can be opposed to right. Precisely this is the context of a thinking that sees itself faced with conflicting claims. It makes a proposal aimed at the settlement of the conflict—a proposal that can in turn be scrutinized in light of other proposals and thereby turn into consultation. As already in the proposal the aim of the consultation is the ascertainment of what is better and that means at the same time that which wins one over, which best promotes a just peace.

A proposal presupposes experience in the controversial matter, above all a knowledge that, as Homer puts it, rests on a simultaneous seeing forwards and backwards. Thus a seeing as it is proper to a seer. He sees, namely, "how it is" in each instance in the framework of a totality. In particular, he sees that the way in which the conflict is solved attests each time: the conflict is resolved in accordance with the decision which the father of the gods and men made in light of the best knowledge of what is best. Thus he makes no proposal to anyone but rather consults himself and decides alone. That is to say: through him, every resolution of conflict is harbored in the best end, in a decision that does not allow it to be continued, but rather establishes peace regarding the matter of contest. It is just this that is the name not merely of the end but rather of completion.

Now this brief consideration of the structure of the Homeric ratio does not amount to a representiation of the wisdom in question. This wisdom has its present only in the speech proper to it, in that which, as in every wisdom, yields a vision. Only this is the teaching. The logotectonic gives only the signs as to where one is to search; in a certain way, it also gives the signs for what conceptual reason translated, since it derives from the relevant conceptions.

Once again: the speech of wisdom has to take care of itself. That which gives what is to be thought and is not to be taken on as a science (ἐπιστήμη) cannot be helped by arguments. Such would be an arrogation in the face of wisdom. Here the present task of thinking can only be this: to awaken an ear for what is said via the distinction of speech in the midst of what is spoken, since thinking, having lain already for too long not in a dogmatic slumber but rather in a critical din, no longer understands its own word. Its own word is, namely, precisely that which through its own rationality awakens reason.

GLOSSARIES

The following glossaries consist of a selection of the key German terms and their English translations; they by no means include every translation. An effort has been made to translate the terms consistently throughout the present volume, and the most frequent translations may be found below; wherever more than one option has been listed for one German term, the first has been used most often, the second less often, and so on. The German-English glossary has been coordinated with its inverse in order to aid the reader. All qualifications and explanations of the sense and scope of terms are located only in the German-English. It should be borne in mind that while the translations offered below (especially those obviously adopted from translations of Hegel and Heidegger) may be used in other contexts, the scope of the application of most of the terms is specifically bound to Boeder's way of thinking.

GERMAN-ENGLISH

abarbeiten: to de-struct (cf. *Destruktion*)
Abgeschiedenheit: departedness
abgrenzen: to delimit
abgründig: abysmal
abschaffen: to abrogate
Abschied: departure
Absonderung: segregation
Absprung: jump
Abstandlosigkeit: lack of distance
an sich: in itself (cf. *in sich*)
Andenken: commemoration
Andersheit: alterity
Anders-sein: being-other, alterity
Aneignung: appropriation
Anfang: beginning, principle
anfänglich: incipient
Anklang: resonance
ankommen: to make one's advent
Ankunft: advent
anwegen: to set on its way
Anwesen bei: attention to, presence, being-present
Anwesen für: presence for
Anwesenheit: presence
Arbeitskraft: manpower
Aufbruch: uprising
ausbleiben: to be failing
auseinanderlegen: to explicate, analyze
auseinandersetzen: to set-apart, confront
Aussage: enunciation, saying; declarative sentence; proposition, statement
das Äußerste: extreme (ἔσχατον)
ausstehend: out-standing
Austrag: originary differing (cf. διαφορά)
Bedeutung: significance, meaning
Befugnis: authorization
Begleichung: settlement (arbitrated)
Begrifflosigkeit: deconceptualization
beirren: to lead astray, mislead
berücken: to implace
Besinnung: sense-explication, recollection, reflection
Bestand: stock(s)
Bestimmung: destiny, determination; (termi-

nologically:) governing principle (for natural and mundane reason), destinal principle (for conceptual reason), destiny (for the configurations of wisdom and apocalyptic reason), directing intention (for technical and hermeneutic reason), reigning impulse (for anarchic and structuralist reason).
Bestimmungsgrund: ground of distinction, determinative ground
Bewandtnis: role, function
Beziehungsgrund: ground of relation, relative ground
Bodenständigkeit: steadfastness
das Da: the There
darstellen: to exhibit, depict, represent
Denken: thinking, thought
denkendes Ding: *res cogitans* (thinking thing)
Dunstkreis: surrounding haze
Eigenmächtigkeit: autocracy, autocratic character
Eigenwilligkeit: willfulness
Einkehr: entrance, turn in to
einräumen: to space
Einsprung: leap into
entbergen: to deshelter
Entbergung: desheltering
Entborgenheit: deshelteredness
enteignen: to expropriate
Enteignis: expropriation
entrücken: to displace
Entrückung: displacement
Entschränkung: de-limitation
Entwurf: projection
ereignen: to appropriate
Ereignis: event of appropriation, appropriation
Erfahrung: experience
erkennen: to cognize, know, recognize
Erkenntnis: cognition, knowledge
erleben, Erleben: to live through, experience
Erlebnis, Erleben: lived experience
Erörterung: exposition, topology
Erschlossenheit: disclosedness
Ferne: remoteness
Figur: figure
Fortbestimmung: progressive determination
Gebirg: shelter
das Gedachte: what is/has been thought
Gediegenheit: solidity, concretion
Gefüge: architectonic
Gegenwart: present
Gegenwendigkeit: reciprocity
Gegenwendung: counter-turn
gelassen: released
Gelassenheit: releasement
Gemeinwesen: polity, community, commonwealth
Gestaltung: formation
das Gewesene: what has been
Gewißheit: certainty
das Gesagte: what is said
Geschehen: enaction, event
Geschichte: history
geschichtlich: historical (cf. *historisch*)
Geschichtlichkeit: historicity
geschichtslos: uneventful
Geschick: mission
geschickhaft: missive [adj: sent or dispatched; intended for sending]
Geschicklosigkeit: lack of destiny
Gesinnung: mentality
das Gesprochene: what is spoken
Gestalt: form, type, configuration
Gestell: sy-stem (cf. *System*)
Grund: ground, fundamental, fundament
Gründung: grounding
Heimat: homestead, homeland
herausfordern: to challenge
Herkunft: provenance
Herrlichkeit: glory
herrschaftlich: dominant
Historie: historial scholarship
historisch: historial (cf. *geschichtlich*)
in sich: within itself (cf. *an sich*)
In-sein: being-within
innerlich: intrinsic
Irre: errancy
Kehre: turning
Kenntnis: know-how, knowledge
Kommunikations-Verhältnisse: relations of communication
Lichtung: clearing

Machenschaft: machination
das Man: the They
Mannigfaltigkeit: manifold, multiplicity, plurality
Menschenwesen: human being
Nähe: propinquity
Natur: Nature
Natürlichkeit: natural character
nichten: to nihilate
das Nichts: nothingness
Nichts an Bestimmtheit: expunction of all determinacy
nötig: needed
notwendig: necessary
Ortschaft: locality
Produktions-Verhältnisse: relations of production
real: real (cf. *wirklich*)
Realität: reality (cf. *Wirklichkeit*)
Rechts-geschehen: enaction of right
Rechtsverhältnisse: realm of justice (first epoch), legal relations (middle and final epochs)
Rettung: salvation
Sache: topic, subject, thing
sammeln: to collect (λέγειν)
Sammlung auf: concentration, focus on
Sammlung: collection
Schein: semblance, illusion
Scheu: reverence (αἰδώς)
das Seiende: beings, being
Seiendheit: beingness
Sein: Being
Sein des Seienden: Being of beings
Selbst-Verwirklichung: self-actualization
Selbstsein: being-one's-self
Selbstzweck: end-in-itself
Seligkeit: beatitude
setzen: to posit, place, set
Setzung: positing
Setzungscharakter: thetic character
Sicherheit: security
Sinn: sense
Sorge: care
Sprache: speech, language
Sprachlichkeit: linguistic character
Sprung: leap
stellen: to posit, challenge
Stellen: challenge, challenging, positing
stiften: to institute, install
Stiftung: institution
System: system (cf. *Gestell*)
Technik: technicity, technique, technology
Technologie: technology
tilgen: to expunge
Trieb: drive
Überkommnis: over-coming
Überzeugungskraft: persuasiveness, power of persuasion
Umbruch: radical change
Umkehr: reversion
umkehren: to revert
Umkippung: inversion, reversal
Umwälzung: radical change
Un-Grund: un-ground
Unentborgenheit: non-desheltereedness
das Unseiende: un-being
Unter-Schied: dif-ference
Unterschied: difference, differentiation
Unterscheidungsgrund: determinative ground, ground of the distinction
Unterscheidungskraft: faculty of distinction
Unverborgenheit: unconcealedness
Unwesen: denaturing
Ursprung: origin
ursprünglich: originary
urteilen, sich in etwas (acc.): to divide oneself primally into sth. (Hegel)
verbergen: to conceal
Verbergung: concealment
vereignen: to appropriate
Verfallenheit an: having fallen prey to
Vergegenwärtigung: representiation
Verhalten: comportment, behavior
Verhaltenheit: reticence, restraint (cf. ἐποχή)
Verhältnis: proportion, (cor)relation(ship)
Verödung: desertification
Versagung: denial, privation
Versammlung: assembling
verschieden (ptp. of *verscheiden*): passed away
verschließen: to occlude, obstruct, close
Verschlossenheit: occlusion, closedness
Verwahrlosung: neglect
verweigern: to deny, refuse

Verweigerung: denial, refusal
Verwindung: recuperation
verzichten auf: to refrain, renounce, abstain (from)
Vielheit: multiplicity, plurality
vollbringen: to accomplish
vollenden: to complete
vollkommen: perfect
Vorbild: exemplar, model
Vorbildlichkeit: exemplariness
Vordenken: presage (projection); forethought
Vorenthalt: withholding
Vorgabe: bequest, precondition
Vorgang: process
Vorherrschaft: predominance
vorstellen: to represent
Vorliebe: penchant, predilection, preference
das Vorstellen: representative thinking
Vorstellung: respresentation
wahren: to reserve
Wahrnis: preserving
Wechsel: shift, change
Weg-sein: being-away; to be away
Weisheits-Gestalt: configuration of wisdom (σοφία)
weiterwälzen: to continue
weltlich: mundane
Weltlichkeit: mundane character, worldliness
Wesen: nature, naturing, essence, being
wesen: to nature
Wesensraum: naturing space
wirklich: actual
Wirklichkeit: actuality
Wissen: knowledge
Worinnen: Wherein
zurücktreten: to step back
Zusammengehörigkeit: cohesion, belonging together
Zuspiel: serve (cf. serving in tennis)
Zuspruch: address
zuwerfen: to adject
Zwiefalt: bifurcation

ENGLISH-GERMAN

abrogate (v.): *abschaffen*
abstain (from) (v.): *verzichten auf*
abysmal: *abgründig*
accomplish (v.): *vollbringen*
actual: *wirklich*
actuality: *Wirklichkeit*
address: *Zuspruch*
adject (v.): *zuwerfen*
advent, make one's (v.): *ankommen*
advent: *Ankunft*
alterity: *Andersheit, Anders-sein*
analyze (v.): *auseinanderlegen*
appropriate (v.): *ereignen, vereignen*
appropriation: *Ereignis, Aneignung*
architectonic: *Architektonik, Gefüge*
assembling: *Versammlung*
attention to: *Anwesen bei*
authorization: *Befugnis*
autocracy: *Eigenmächtigkeit*
autocratic character: *Eigenmächtigkeit*
be away (v.): *weg-sein*
be failing (v.): *ausbleiben*
beatitude: *Seligkeit*
beginning: *Anfang*
behavior: *Verhalten*
being(s): *das Seiende*
Being: *Sein*
being: *Wesen*
Being of beings: *Sein des Seienden*
being-away: *Weg-sein*
being-one's-self: *Selbstsein*
being-other: *Anders-sein*
being-present: *Anwesen bei*
being-within: *In-sein*
beingness: *Seiendheit*
belonging together: *Zusammengehörigkeit*
bequest: *Vorgabe*
bifurcation: *Zwiefalt*
care: *Sorge*
causation: *Ur-Sache*
certainty: *Gewißheit*
challenge (v.): *herausfordern, stellen*

challenge: *Stellen, Herausforderung*
change: *Wechsel*
clearing: *Lichtung*
close (v.): *verschließen*
closedness: *Verschlossenheit*
cognition: *Erkenntnis*
cognize (v.): *erkennen*
cohesion: *Zusammengehörigkeit*
collect (v.): *sammeln*
collection: *Sammlung*
commemoration: *Andenken*
commence (v.): *anfangen*
commonwealth: *Gemeinwesen*
community: *Gemeinwesen*
complete (v.): *vollenden*
comportment: *Verhalten*
conceal (v.): *verbergen*
concealment: *Verbergung*
concentration on: *Sammlung auf*
concretion: *Gediegenheit*
configuration: *Gestalt*
configuration of wisdom: *Weisheits-Gestalt*
confront (v.): *auseinandersetzen*
continue (v.): *weiterwälzen*
counter-turn: *Gegenwendung*
de-limitation: *Entschränkung*
de-struct (v.): *abarbeiten*
deconceptualization: *Begrifflosigkeit*
delimit (v.): *abgrenzen*
denaturing: *Unwesen*
denial: *Verweigerung, Versagung*
deny (v.): *verweigern*
departedness: *Abgeschiedenheit*
departure: *Abschied*
depict (v.): *darstellen*
desertification: *Verödung*
deshelter (v.): *entbergen*
deshelteredness: *Entborgenheit*
desheltering: *Entbergung*
destinal principle: *Bestimmung*
destiny, lack of: *Geschicklosigkeit*
destiny: *Bestimmung*
determination: *Bestimmung*
determinative ground: *Unterscheidungsgrund, Bestimmungsgrund*
dif-ference: *Unter-Schied*
difference: *Unterschied*
directing intention: *Bestimmung*
disclosedness: *Erschlossenheit*
displace (v.): *entrücken*
displacement: *Entrückung*
distance, lack of: *Abstandlosigkeit*
distinction: *Unterscheidung*
divide oneself primally into sth. (v.): *sich in etwas* (acc.) *urteilen* (Hegel)
dominant: *herrschaftlich*
drive: *Trieb*
enaction: *Geschehen*
enaction of right: *Rechts-geschehen*
end-in-itself: *Selbstzweck*
entrance: *Einkehr*
enunciation: *Aussage*
errancy: *Irre*
essence: *Wesen*
event of appropriation: *Ereignis*
event: *Geschehen*
exemplar: *Vorbild*
exemplariness: *Vorbildlichkeit*
exhibit (v.): *darstellen*
experience (v.): *erleben, Erleben, erfahren*
experience: *Erfahrung*
explicate (v.): *auseinanderlegen*
exposition: *Erörterung*
expropriate (v.): *enteignen*
expropriation: *Enteignis*
expunction of all determinacy: *Nichts an Bestimmtheit*
expunge (v.): *tilgen*
extreme: *das Äußerste* (ἔσχατον)
faculty of distinction: *Unterscheidungskraft*
figure: *Figur*
form: *Gestalt*
formation: *Gestaltung*
function: *Bewandtnis*
fundament: *Grund*
glory: *Herrlichkeit*
governing principle: *Bestimmung*
ground of relation: *Beziehungsgrund*
ground of distinction: *Unterscheidungsgrund, Bestimmungsgrund*
ground: *Grund*
grounding: *Gründung*
having fallen prey to: *Verfallenheit an*
historial scholarship: *Historie*

historial: *historisch*
historical: *geschichtlich*
historicity: *Geschichtlichkeit*
history: *Geschichte*
homeland: *Heimat*
homestead: *Heimat*
human being: *Menschenwesen*
illusion: *Schein*
implace (v.): *berücken*
in itself: *an sich*
incipient: *anfänglich*
install (v.): *stiften*
institute (v.): *stiften*
institution: *Stiftung*
intrinsic: *innerlich*
inversion: *Umkippung*
jump: *Absprung*
know (v.): *erkennen*
know-how: *Kenntnis*
knowledge: *Wissen, Erkenntnis, Kenntnis*
language: *Sprache*
lead astray (v.): *beirren*
leap into: *Einsprung*
leap: *Sprung*
legal relations: *Rechtsverhältnisse*
linguistic character: *Sprachlichkeit*
live through (v.): *erleben, Erleben*
lived experience: *Erlebnis, Erleben*
locality: *Ortschaft*
machination: *Machenschaft*
manifold: *Mannigfaltigkeit*
manpower: *Arbeitskraft*
mentality: *Gesinnung*
mislead (v.): *beirren*
mission: *Geschick*
missive: *geschickhaft*
model: *Vorbild*
multiplicity: *Mannigfaltigkeit, Vielheit*
mundane character: *Weltlichkeit*
mundane: *weltlich*
natural character: *Natürlichkeit*
Nature: *Natur*
nature (v.): *wesen*
nature: *Wesen*
naturing: *Wesen*
naturing space: *Wesensraum*
necessary: *notwendig*
needed: *nötig*
neglect: *Verwahrlosung*
nihilate (v.): *nichten*
non-deshelteredness: *Unentborgenheit*
nothingness: *das Nichts*
obstruct (v.): *verschließen, verstellen*
occlude (v.): *verschließen*
occlusion: *Verschlossenheit*
origin: *Ursprung*
originary differing: *Austrag* (cf. διαφορά)
originary: *ursprünglich*
out-standing: *ausstehend*
overcome: *Überwinden*
over-coming: *Überkommnis*
passed away: *verschieden* (ptp. of *verscheiden*)
penchant: *Vorliebe*
perfect: *vollkommen*
persuasiveness: *Überzeugungskraft*
place (v.): *setzen*
plurality: *Vielfalt, Mannigfaltigkeit*
polity: *Gemeinwesen*
posit (v.): *setzen, stellen*
positing: *Setzung, Stellen*
power of persuasion: *Überzeugungskraft*
precondition: *Vorgabe*
predilection: *Vorliebe*
predominance: *Vorherrschaft*
preference: *Vorliebe*
presage (projection): *Vordenken*
presence: *Anwesenheit, Anwesen bei*
presence for: *Anwesen für*
present: *Gegenwart*
preserving: *Wahrnis*
principle: *Prinzip, Anfang*
privation: *Versagung*
process: *Vorgang*
progressive determination: *Fortbestimmung*
projection: *Entwurf*
propinquity: *Nähe*
proportion: *Verhältnis*
proposition: *Aussage*
provenance: *Herkunft*
radical change: *Umbruch, Umwälzung*
real: *real*
reality: *Realität*
realm of justice: *Rechtsverhältnisse*
reciprocity: *Gegenwendigkeit*

recognize (v.): *erkennen*
recollection: *Besinnung*
recuperation: *Verwindung*
reflection: *Besinnung*
refusal: *Verweigerung*
refuse (v.): *verweigern*
reigning impulse: *Bestimmung*
rejection: *Abstoß*
relation(ship): *Verhältnis*
relations of communication: *Kommunikations-Verhältnisse*
relations of production: *Produktions-Verhältnisse*
relative ground: *Beziehungsgrund*
released: *gelassen*
releasement: *Gelassenheit*
remoteness: *Ferne*
renounce (v.): *verzichten auf*
represent (v.): *vorstellen, darstellen*
representation: *Vorstellung*
representative thinking: *das Vorstellen*
representiation: *Vergegenwärtigung*
res cogitans (thinking thing): *denkendes Ding*
reserve (v.): *wahren*
resonance: *Anklang*
restraint: *Verhaltenheit* (ἐποχή)
reticence: *Verhaltenheit* (ἐποχή)
reverence: *Scheu*
reversal: *Umkippung*
reversion: *Umkehr*
revert (v.): *umkehren*
role: *Bewandtnis*
salvation: *Rettung*
security: *Sicherheit*
segregation: *Absonderung*
self-actualization: *Selbst-Verwirklichung*
semblance: *Schein*
sense: *Sinn*
sense-explication: *Besinnung*
serve: *Zuspiel*
set (v.): *setzen*
set on its way (v.): *anwegen*
set-apart (v.): *auseinandersetzen*
settlement (arbitrated): *Begleichung*
shelter: *Gebirg*
shift: *Wechsel*
significance: *Bedeutung*
solidity: *Gediegenheit*
space (v.): *einräumen*
speech: *Sprache*
statement: *Aussage*
steadfastness: *Bodenständigkeit*
step back (v.): *zurücktreten*
stock(s): *Bestand*
subject: *Sache*
surrounding haze: *Dunstkreis*
sy-stem: *Gestell*
system: *System*
technicity: *Technik*
technique: *Technik*
technology: *Technologie, Technik*
the There: *das Da*
the They: *das Man*
thing: *Sache*
thinking: *Denken*
thought: *Gedanke, Denken*
thrust: *Stoß*
topic: *Sache*
topology: *Erörterung, Topologie*
turn in to: *Einkehr*
turning: *Kehre*
type: *Gestalt*
un-being: *das Unseiende*
un-ground: *Un-Grund*
unconcealedness: *Unverborgenheit*
uneventful: *geschichtslos*
uprising: *Aufbruch*
what appears: *das Erscheinende*
what has been: *das Gewesene*
what is said: *das Gesagte*
what is spoken: *das Gesprochene*
what is/has been thought: *das Gedachte*
Wherein: *Worinnen*
willfulness: *Eigenwilligkeit*
withholding: *Vorenthalt*
within itself: *in sich*
worldliness: *Weltlichkeit*

WORKS CITED AND ABBREVIATIONS

The following bibliography lists the works cited and/or mentioned in the course of the present volume. (Boeder's publications appear in a separate, subsequent list (see pp. 337-341 below)). Two conventions have been followed here.

Firstly the titles of most works have been rendered in English in the body of the foregoing, even when an English translation has yet to appear or is unavailable (exceptions have been made only in a few instances regarding Latin titles). Any difference between the rendition of titles above and those of the translations listed below is based on a difference in reading.

Secondly all works cited above in the body of the text have been keyed to abbreviations, which may be found in the left-hand margin below alongside the given work. Wherever a non-English original has been cited, an effort has been made to provide the page reference for the corresponding English translation; wherever such has proved possible, the original pagination is separated from that of the translation by a "/". In those cases in which a line number is also provided, it immediately follows the page reference and both are separated by a "." (E.g., *GW* 12, 176.21/758 is a citation of Hegel's *Science of Logic*, p. 176, line 21, which may be found on p. 758 of Miller's translation.) Further, wherever a series of citations refers to one work, its abbreviation is provided only in the first instance, i.e., the page reference pertains to the work previously cited unless a new abbreviation precedes it. Finally, names of authors are provided in in-text citations only where it might not be clear from the context which author is meant.

Although any divergence from these procedures are noted following the relevant entry below, it should be noted that the early Greek thinkers are cited by fragment number in accordance with the enumeration established by Diels; the relevant fragments may be found principally in *D-K*, vol. I. Further, Plato's dialogues are cited by their full titles, whereas Aristotle's works are abbreviated in accordance with Liddell-Scott's *A Greek-English Lexicon*, 9th ed. (Oxford: Oxford Univerity Press, 1940), xix; in both instances, the standard pagination is cited.

All translations of the Latin and the Greek are by Boeder. Translations of French works were consulted by the translator, but their final rendition was decided by Boeder's original German translation. Available translations of German works were consulted, but final versions are generally the translator's. Wherever necessary, translations relied upon more heavily have been modified without notice.

Two final points should be borne in mind by the reader regarding the works cited or mentioned in the present volume. Firstly, preference has been given to standard or critical editions; although the translations listed below are of the works in question, they are not always translations of the original-language edition cited (cf., e.g., the editions of Pseudo-Dionysius's *Divine Names* and of the New Testament). Secondly, references to English translations of Greek and Latin works (cf. Plato and Aristotle) have rarely been consulted; they have been provided here primarily in order to orient the reader unable to read those languages and who may wish to consult the relevant work.

As far as was possible the following entries have been made to correspond to the style outlined in *The Chicago Manual of Style*, 14th ed. The chief difference concerns editors: wherever the author of an essay is also the author of the volume in which it appears, the editor's name is appended to the title; in those instances in which this does not hold, the editor is listed prior to the title.

Ariès, Philippe. *L'homme devant la mort.* Paris: Éditions du Seuil, 1977. Translated by Helen Weaver under the title *The Hour of Our Death* (Oxford: Oxford University Press, 1991).

Aristotle. *Opera,* edited by Imannuel Bekker. 1831 ff. Reprint: Berlin: Walter de Gruyter, 1961 ff. Translations may be found in *The Complete Works of Aristotle,* edited by Jonathan Barnes, 2 vols. (Princeton: Princeton University Press, 1984).

Augustine, Aurelius. *Enarrationes in Psalmos CI-CL. Opera* XL, Pars X,3. *Corpus Christianorum.* Turnholt: Brepols Editores, 1956.

Aquinas, Thomas. *De potentia Dei. Opera Omnia* XIII. Paris: Vivès, 1875.

———. *In XII libros metaphysicorum, Opera Omnia* XXIV. Paris: Vivès, 1875. Translated by J. P. Rowan under the title *Commentary on the Metaphysics of Aristotle,* 2 vols. (Chicago: H. Regnery, 1961).

———. *In librum Boetii de trinitate expositio, Opera Omnia* XXVIII: 482-550. Paris: Vivès, 1875. Translated, with introduction and notes, by Armand Maurer under the title *Faith, Reason, and Theology: Questions I-IV of his Commentary on the "De Trinitate" of Boethius* (Toronto: Pontifical Institute of Medieval Studies, 1987).

———. *Summa contra gentiles. Opera Omnia* XII. Paris: Vivès, 1874. Translated, with introduction and notes, by Anton C. Pegis under the same title (Notre Dame: University of Notre Dame Press, 1975).

S. Th. ———. *Summa Theologicae. Opera Omnia* 4, ed. Leonina. Rome: Typographia Polyglotta, 1888. Translated by the Fathers of the English Dominican Province under the same title, 5 vols. (Westminister, MD: Christian Classics, 1981).

Balzac, Honoré de. *Le Chef d'oeuvre inconnu.* Geneva: Skira, 1945. Translated by Michael Heff under the title *The Unknown Masterpiece* (Berkeley: Creative Arts Books, 1984).

MP Barthes, Roland. "Le message publicitaire." In *L'aventure sémiologique,* 243-248. Paris: Éditions du Seuil, 1985. Translated by Richard Howard under the title "The Advertising Message," in *The Semiotic Challenge* (New York: Hill and Wang, 1988), 173-178.

Beckett, Samuel. *Film: A Film Script.* New York: Grove, 1969.

———. "Sans." In *Têtes-Mortes,* 66-77. Paris: Les Éditions de Minuit, 1972. Translated by the author under the title *Lessness* (London: Calder & Boyars, 1970).

Bois, Yve-Alain. "The Limit of Almost." In *Ad Reinhardt*, 11-33. New York: Rizzoli, 1991.

Derrida, Jacques. *De la grammatologie*. Paris: Les Éditions de Minuit, 1967. Translated by Gayatri Chakravorty Spivak under the title *Of Grammatology* (Baltimore: Johns Hopkins, 1976).

———. *De l'esprit: Heidegger et la question*. Paris: Éditions Galilée, 1987. Translated by Geoffrey Bennington and Rachel Bowlby under the title *Of Spirit: Heidegger and the Question* (Chicago: University of Chicago Press, 1989).

Dif ———. "Différance." In *Marges de la philosophie*, 1-29. Paris: Les Éditions de Minuit, 1972. Translated by Alan Bass under the title "Différance," in *Margins of Philosophy* (Chicago: University of Chicago Press, 1982), 1-27.

———. "Donner la mort." In J. M. Rabaté and M. Wetzel, eds., *L'Éthique du don*, 11-108. Paris: Transition, 1992. Translated by David Wills under the title *The Gift of Death* (Chicago: University of Chicago Press, 1995).

———. *Feu la cendre*. Paris: Éditions des femmes, 1987. Translated and edited by Ned Lukacher under the title *Cinders* (Lincoln: University of Nebraska Press, 1991).

FL ———. "Force de loi: le 'fondement mystique de l'authorité'; Force of Law: The 'Mystical Foundation of Authority'" (French/English). Translated by Mary Quaintance. *Cardozo Law Review* 11, no. 5-6 (July/August 1990): 919-1045.

———. "*Geschlecht:* différence sexuelle, différence ontologique." In Michel Haar, ed., *Les cahiers de l'herne*, 419-430. Paris: Éditions de l'Herne, 1983. Translated by [Ruben Berezdivin] under the title "*Geschlecht*: sexual difference, ontological difference," in *Research in Phenomenology* 13 (1983): 65-83.

———. *Glas*. Paris: Éditions Galilée, 1974. Translated by John P. Leavey, Jr. and Richard Rand under the same title (Lincoln: University of Nebraska Press, 1986).

———. *Khôra*. Paris: Éditions Galilée, 1993. Translated Ian McLeod under the same title, in *On the Name*, edited by Thomas Dutoit (Stanford: Stanford University Press, 1995), 89-127.

———. *L'autre cap*. Paris: Les Éditions de Minuit, 1991. Translated by Pascale-Anne Brault and Michael Naas under the title *The Other Heading: Reflections on Today's Europe* (Bloomington: Indiana University Press, 1992).

P ———. *Passions*. Paris: Éditions Galilée, 1993. Translated by David Wood under the title "Passions: 'An Oblique Offering'," in *On the Name*, edited by Thomas Dutoit (Stanford: Stanford University Press, 1995), 3-31.

———. *Sauf le nom*. Paris: Éditions Galilée, 1993. Translated by John P. Leavey, Jr. under the same title, in *On the Name*, edited by Thomas Dutoit (Stanford: Stanford University Press, 1995), 35-85.

D-K Diels, Hermann and Walther Kranz, *Die Fragmente der Vorsokratiker*. 3 vols. 6th ed. Zürich: Weidmann, 1952. Translated by Kathleen Freeman under the title *Ancilla to the Pre-Socratic Philosophers* (Cambridge, MA: Harvard University

Press, 1966). [In many cases, alternate English translations may be found in: G. S. Kirk, J. E. Raven, and M. Schofield. *The Presocratic Philosophers*. 2nd ed. Cambridge: Cambridge University Press, 1983. For alternate translations of Heraclitus, see also: Charles H. Kahn. *The Art and Thought of Heraclitus*. Cambridge: Cambridge University, 1979; and of Parmenides, see also: A. H. Coxon. *The Fragments of Parmenides*. Assen/Maastricht: Van Gorcum, 1986.]

GS VII — Dilthey, Wilhelm. *Der Aufbau der geschichtlichen Welt. Gesammelte Schriften* VII. 4th ed. Göttingen: Vandenhoeck & Ruprecht, 1968.

GS V — ———. *Die geistige Welt. Einleitung in die Philosophie des Lebens. Gesammelte Schriften* V. Göttingen: Vandenhoeck & Ruprecht, 1974.

GS I — ———. *Einleitung in die Geisteswissenschaften. Gesammelte Schriften* I. Göttingen: Vandenhoeck & Ruprecht, 1973. Translated by Michael Neville, and Jeffrey Barnouw and Franz Schreiner under the title *Introduction to the Human Sciences. Selected Works* I, edited, with an introduction, by Rudolf A. Makkreel and Frithjof Rodi (Princeton: Princeton University Press, 1989). [Dilthey's *Selected Works* I does not render *Gesammelte Schriften* I *in toto*.]

GS VIII — ———. *Weltanschauungslehre. Abhandlungen zur Philosophie der Philosophie. Gesammelte Schriften* VIII. 7th ed. Göttingen: Vandenhoeck & Ruprecht, 1958.

Pseudo-Dionysius Areopagita. *De divinus nominibus*, edited by Beate Regina Suchla. *Corpus Dionysiacum* I. Berlin: Walter de Gruyter, 1990. Translated by John D. Jones under the title *The Divine Names and Mystical Theology* (Milwaukee, WI: Marquette University Press, 1980).

Eliot, T. S. *Collected Poems 1909-1962*. New York: Harcourt Brace Jovanovich, 1963.

GPZ — Feuerbach, Ludwig. *Grundsätze der Philosophie der Zukunft* (1843), edited by Gerhart Schmidt. Frankfurt a. M.: Klostermann, 1967. Translated by Manfred H. Vogel under the title *The Principles of the Philosophy of the Future* (Indianapolis: Hackett, 1986).

Fichte, J. G. *Erste Einleitung in die Wissenschaftslehre* (1797). *Werke* I, 417-449. Berlin: Walter de Gruyter, 1971. Translated and edited by Daniel Breazeale under the title "First Introduction to the *Wissenschaftslehre*," in *Foundations of Transcendental Philosophy* (Ithaca: Cornell University Press, 1992), 77-86.

Foucault, Michel. *L'Archéologie du savoir*. Paris: Éditions Gallimard, 1969. Translated by A. M. Sheridan Smith under the title *The Archaeology of Knowledge* (New York: Pantheon, 1974).

LI — ———. "La langage à l'infini." *Tel Quel* 15 (1963): 44-53. Translated by Donald F. Bouchard and Sherry Simon under the title "Language to Infinity," in *Language, Counter-Memory, Practice*, edited by Donald F. Bouchard (Ithaca: Cornell University Press, 1977), 53-67.

———. *Le souci de soi*, vol. 3 of *Histoire de la sexualité*. Paris: Éditions Gallimard, 1984. Translated by Robert Hurley under the title *The Care of the Self*, vol. 3 of *The History of Sexuality* (New York: Pantheon, 1986).

———. *Les mots et les choses*. Paris: Éditions Gallimard, 1966. Translated under the title *The Order of Things* (New York: Pantheon, 1970).

———. "Technologies of the Self." In *Technologies of the Self: A Seminar with Michel Foucault*, edited by Luther H. Martin, Huck Gutman, and Patrick H. Hutton, 16-49. Amherst: University of Massachusetts Press, 1988.

BS Frege, Gottlob. *Begriffsschrift, eine der arithmetischen nachgebildete Formelsprache des reinen Denkens* (1879). In: *Begriffsschrift und andere Aufsätze*, edited by Ignacio Angelelli, i-viii, 1-88. Darmstadt: Wissenschaftliche Buchgesellschaft, 1988. Translated by S. Bauer-Mengelberg under the title "*Begriffsschrift*, a Formula Language, modeled upon that of Arithmetic, for Pure Thought," in Jean van Heijenoort, ed., *Frege to Gödel: A Source Book in Mathematical Logic, 1879-1931* (Cambridge, MA: Harvard University Press, 1967), 1-82.

Enz. Hegel, Georg Wilhelm Friedrich. *Enzykopaedie der philosophischen Wissenschaften im Grundrisse.* 1st ed. Heidelberg: August Oßwald's Universitätsbuchhandlung, 1817.

GW 20 ———. *Enzyklopädie der philosophischen Wissenschaften im Grundrisse* (1830). *Gesammelte Werke* 20, edited by the Rheinisch-Westfälischen Akademie der Wissenschaften. Hamburg: Meiner, 1992. Translated by William Wallace under the title *Hegel's Philosophy of Mind* (Oxford: Oxford University Press, 1971). [It renders only Part III of *The Encyclopaedia of the Philosophical Sciences* (1830).]

GW 9 ———. *Phänomenologie des Geistes. Gesammelte Werke* 9, edited by the Rheinisch-Westfälischen Akademie der Wissenschaften. Hamburg: Meiner, 1980. Translated A. V. Miller under the title *Hegel's Phenomenology of Spirit* (Oxford: Oxford University Press, 1977).

Werke 13 ———. *Vorlesungen über die Ästhetik* I. *Werke* 13. Frankfurt a. M.: Suhrkamp, 1986. Translated by Bernard Bosanquet under the title *Introductory Lectures on Aesthetics* (1886; reprint: New York: Penguin, 1993).

GW 11 ———. *Wissenschaft der Logik* I: *Die objektive Logik* (1812/1813). *Gesammelte Werke* 11, edited by the Rheinisch-Westfälischen Akademie der Wissenschaften. Hamburg: Meiner, 1978. Translated by A. V. Miller as the first part of *Hegel's Science of Logic* (Atlantic Highlands, NJ: Humanities Press, 1989).

GW 12 ———. *Wissenschaft der Logik* II: *Die subjektive Logik. Gesammelte Werke* 12, edited by the Rheinisch-Westfälischen Akademie der Wissenschaften. Hamburg: Meiner, 1981. Translated by A. V. Miller as the second part of *Hegel's Science of Logic* (Atlantic Highlands, NJ: Humanities Press, 1989).

GA 13 Heidegger, Martin. *Aus der Erfahrung des Denkens* [From the Experience of Thinking]. *Gesamtausgabe* 13. Frankfurt a. M.: Klostermann, 1983.

BWD ———. "Bauen Wohnen Denken." In *Vorträge und Aufsätze*, 139-156. 6th ed. Pfullingen: Neske,1990. Translated by Albert Hofstadter under the title "Building Dwelling Thinking," in *Poetry, Language, Thought* (New York: Harper & Row, 1971), 143-161.

GA 65 ———. *Beiträge zur Philosophie (Vom Ereignis)* [Contributions to Philosophy (Of Appropriation)]. *Gesamtausgabe* 65. Frankfurt a. M.: Klostermann, 1989.

BH ———. "Brief über den 'Humanismus'." In *Wegmarken*, 311-360. 2nd ed. Frankfurt a. M.: Klostermann,1978. Translated by F. A. Capuzzi and J. G. Gray under the title "Letter on Humanism," in *Basic Writings*, edited by David Farrell Krell (New York: Harper & Row, 1977), 193-242.

D ———. "Das Ding." In *Vorträge und Aufsätze*, 157-175. 6th ed. Pfullingen: Neske, 1990. Translated by Albert Hofstadter under the title "The Thing," in *Poetry, Language, Thought* (New York: Harper & Row, 1971), 165-186.

EP ———. "Das Ende der Philosophie und die Aufgabe des Denkens." In *Zur Sache des Denkens*, 61-80. Tübingen: Niemeyer, 1969. Translated by Joan Stambaugh under the title "The End of Philosophy and the Task of Thinking," in *On Time and Being* (New York: Harper & Row, 1972), 55-73.

N I ———. "Der Wille zur Macht als Kunst." In *Nietzsche* I: 11-254. Pfullingen: Neske, 1961. Translated by David Farrell Krell under the title *Nietzsche* I: *The Will to Power as Art* (London: Routledge & Kegan Paul, 1981).

———. "Die Frage nach der Technik." In *Vorträge und Aufsätze*. 6th ed. Pfullingen: Neske, 1990, 9-40. Translated by William Lovitt under the title "The Question Concerning Technology," in *Basic Writings*, edited by David Farrell Krell (New York: Harper & Row, 1977), 287-317.

ZW ———. "Die Zeit des Weltbildes." In *Holzwege*, 73-110. 6th ed. Frankfurt a. M.: Klostermann,1980. Translated by William Lovitt under tht title "The Age of the World Picture," in *The Question Concerning Technology and Other Essays* (New York: Harper & Row, 1977), 115-154.

———. *Einführung in die Metaphysik*. Tübingen: Niemeyer, 1953. Translated by Ralph Mannheim under the title *An Introduction to Metaphysics* (New Haven: Yale University Press, 1959).

———. *Feldweg* [The Country Path]. Frankfurt a. M.: Klostermann, 1953.

———. "Grundsätze des Denkens" [Principles of Thinking]. In *Bremer und Freiburger Vorträge. Gesamtausgabe* 79: 79-176. Frankfurt a. M.: Klostermann, 1994.

GA 55 ———. *Heraklit. Gesamtausgabe* 55. 2nd ed. Frankfurt a. M.: Klostermann, 1987.

ID ———. *Identität und Differenz.* Pfullingen: Neske, 1957. Translated Joan Stambaugh under the title *Identity and Difference* (New York: Harper & Row, 1969).

NW ———. "Nietzsches Wort 'Gott ist tot'." In *Holzwege*, 205-263. Frankfurt a. M.: Klostermann, 1950. Translated by William Lovitt under the title "The Word of Nietzsche: 'God is Dead'," in *The Question Concerning Technology and Other Essays* (New York: Harper & Row, 1977), 53-112.

RGM ———. "Der Rückgang in den Grund der Metaphysik" [Einleitung zu: "Was ist Metaphysik?"]. In *Wegmarken*, 361-377. 2nd ed. Frankfurt a. M.: Klostermann,1978. Translated by Walter Kauffmann under the title "The Way Back into the Ground of Metaphysics," in Walter Kaufmann, ed., *Existentialism from Dostoevsky to Sartre* (New York: New American Library, 1975), 265-279.

SZ ———. *Sein und Zeit*, 15th ed. Tübingen: Niemeyer, 1986. Translated by John Macquarrie and Edward Robinson under the title *Being and Time* (New York: Harper & Row, 1962). [All page references cited in present volume correspond to the German pagination, which is provided in the margins of the translation.]

WW ———. "Vom Wesen der Wahrheit." In *Wegmarken*, 175-199. 2nd ed. Frankfurt a. M.: Klostermann,1978. Translated by John Sallis under the title "On the Essence of Truth," in *Basic Writings*, edited by David Farrell Krell (New York: Harper & Row, 1977), 117-141.

WD ———. *Was heißt Denken?* Tübingen: Niemeyer, 1954. Translated by J. Glenn Gray under the title *What Is Called Thinking?* (New York: Harper & Row, 1968).

ZS ———. "Zeit und Sein." In *Zur Sache des Denkens*, 1-25. Tübingen: Niemeyer, 1969. Translated by Joan Stambaugh under the title "Time and Being," in *On Time and Being* (New York: Harper & Row, 1972), 1-24.

Hesiod. *Theogony*, edited, with prolegomena and commentary, by M. L. West. Oxford: Clarendon, 1966. Translated, with introduction and notes, by Apostolos N. Athanassakis under the same title in *Theogony, Works and Days, Shield* (Baltimore: Johns Hopkins, 1983).

Homer. *Iliadis. Opera* I-III, edited by David B. Munro and Thomas W. Allen. 3rd ed. Oxford: Clarendon, 1920. Translated by Robert Fitzgerald under the title *The Iliad* (Garden City, NY: Doubleday, 1974).

———. *Odysseae. Opera* III-IV, edited by Thomas W. Allen. 2nd ed. Oxford: Clarendon, 1917 and 1919. Translated by Robert Fitzgerald under the title *The Odyssey* (New York: Vintage, 1990).

LP Jakobson, Roman. "Linguistics and Poetics." In *Language in Literature*, edited by Krystyna Pomorska and Stephen Rudy, 62-94. Cambridge, MA: Harvard University Press, 1987.

———. "Linguistics in Relation to the Other Sciences." In *Selected Writings* II: *Word and Language*, 655-696. The Hague: Mouton, 1971.

Joyce, James. *Finnegans Wake*. New York: Viking, 1939.

GMS Kant, Immanuel. *Grundlegung zur Metaphysik der Sitten. Akademie-Ausgabe* IV: 385-463. Berlin: Walter de Gruyter, 1968. Translated by Lewis White Beck under the title *Foundations of the Metaphysics of Morals* (New York: Macmillan, 1990).

CPR ———. *Kritik der reinen Vernunft. Akademie-Ausgabe* III. Berlin: Walter de Gruyter, 1969. Translated by Norman Kemp Smith under the title *Critique of Pure Reason* (New York: St. Martins, 1929).

Lévi-Strauss, Claude. *La pensée sauvage*. Paris: Librairie Plon, 1962. Translated under the title *The Savage Mind* (Chicago: University of Chicago Press, 1966).

Lyotard, Jean-François. *La Condition postmoderne: rapport sur le savoir.* Paris: Les Éditions de Minuit, 1979. Translated by Geoff Bennington and Brian Massumi under the title *The Postmodern Condition: A Report on Knowledge* (Minneapolis: University of Minnesota Press, 1984).

———. *Le Différend.* Paris: Les Éditions de Minuit, 1983. Translated by Georges Van Den Abbeele under the title *The Differend: Phrases in Dispute* (Minneapolis: University of Minnesota Press, 1988).

MEW 23 Marx, Karl. *Das Kapital* I. *Marx-Engels Werke* 23. Berlin: Dietz, 1962. Translated by S. Moore and E. Aveling under the title *Capital: A Critique of Political Economy* I (New York: International Publishers, 1975).

MEW 6 ———. "Lohnarbeit und Kapital." *Marx-Engels Werke* 6: 397-423. Berlin: Dietz, 1975. Translated under the title *Wage-labor and Capital* (Chicago: Charles H. Kerr, 1948).

Marx, Werner. *Heidegger und die Tradition.* Stuttgart: Kohlhammer, 1961. Translated by T. Kisiel and M. Greene under the title *Heidegger and the Tradition* (Evanston, IL: Northwestern University Press, 1971).

———. *Vernunft und Welt. Zwischen Tradition und anderem Anfang.* The Hague: Nijhoff, 1970. Translated by T. Yates and R. Geuss under the title *Reason and World: Between Tradition and the Other Beginning* (The Hague: Nijhoff, 1971).

Masullo, Aldo. "Il gioco dei significati e solitudine del senso" [The Play of Significance and the Solitude of Sense]. In *Filosofie del soggetto e diritto del senso,* 177-214. Genoa: Marietti, 1990.

———. *Struttura soggeto prassi* [Structure, Subject, Predicate]. Naples: Edizioni Scientifiche Italiane, 1994.

PhP Merleau-Ponty, Maurice. *Phénoménologie de la perception.* Paris: Éditions Gallimard, 1992. Translated by Colin Smith under the title *Phenomenology of Perception* (London: Routledge & Kegan Paul, 1962).

PM ———. *La prose du monde,* edited by Claude Lefort. Paris: Éditions Gallimard, 1992. Translated by John O'Neill under the title *The Prose of the World* (Evanston, IL: Northwestern University Press, 1973).

VI ———. *Le visible et l'invisible,* edited by Claude Lefort. Paris: Éditions Gallimard, 1991. Translated by Alphonso Lingis under the title *The Visible and the Invisible* (Evanston, IL: Northwestern University Press, 1968).

S ———. *Signes.* Paris: Éditions Gallimard, 1960. Translated by Richard C. McCleary under the title *Signs* (Evanston, IL: Northwestern University Press, 1964).

KGW VI.1 Nietzsche, Friedrich. *Also sprach Zarathustra. Kritische Gesamtausgabe* VI.1, edited by Giorgio Colli and Mazzino Montinari. Berlin: Walter de Gruyter, 1968. Translated by Walter Kaufmann under the title *Thus Spoke Zarathustra* in *The Portable Nietzsche,* edited by Walter Kaufmann (New York: Viking, 1954).

KGW V.2 ———. *Die fröhliche Wissenschaft. Kritische Gesamtausgabe* V.2, edited by Giorgio Colli and Mazzino Montinari. Berlin: Walter de Gruyter, 1973. Translated by Walter Kaufmann under the title *The Gay Science* (New York: Vintage, 1974).

Novum Testamentum Graece, edited by Nestle-Aland. 26th ed. Stuttgart: Deutsche Bibelstiftung, 1979. The English translation of the New Testament referred to in translating certain of the texts in the present volume may be found in *The New Jerusalem Bible* (Garden City, NY: Doubleday, 1985).

Plato, *Opera*, edited by John Burnet. 5 vols. Oxford: Clarendon, 1900 ff. Translations may be found in *Collected Dialogues*, edited by Edith Hamilton and Huntington Cairns. Princeton: Princeton University Press, 1961.

Plotinus. *Enneads*. 7 vols. Translated by A. H. Armstrong. Cambridge, MA: Harvard University Press (Loeb Classical Library), 1966 ff.

Proclus. *The Elements of Theology*. Revised text, with translation, introduction, and commentary by E. R. Dodds. 2nd ed. Oxford: Clarendon, 1963.

CGP Rousseau, Jean-Jacques. "Considérations sur le gouvernement de Pologne et sur sa réformation projettée," edited and annotated by Jean Fabre. In: *Œuvres complètes* III: 953-1041. Paris: Éditions Gallimard, 1964. Translated, with introduction and notes, by W. Kendall under the title *The Government of Poland* (Indianapolis: Hackett, 1985).

CS ———. *Du Contrat sociale. Œuvres complètes* III: 347-470. Paris: Éditions Gallimard, 1964. Translated by Maurice Cranston under the title *The Social Contract* (New York: Penguin, 1968).

———. *La Nouvelle Héloïse*, edited by Henri Coulet, annotated by Bernard Guyon. *Œuvres complètes* II: 1-794. Paris: Éditions Gallimard, 1964. Translated by Judith H. McDowell under the title *La Nouvelle Heloise: Julie, or the New Eloise* (University Park, PA: Pennsylvania State University Press, 1987).

AE Schlick, Moritz. *Allgemeine Erkenntnislehre*. 2nd ed., 1925. Reprint: Frankfurt a. M.: Suhrkamp, 1979. Translated by Albert E. Blumberg under the title *General Theory of Knowledge* (New York: Springer, 1974).

WP ———. "Die Wende der Philosophie." *Erkenntnis* I (1930): 4-11. Translated by David Rynin under the title "The Turning Point in Philosophy," in A. J. Ayer, ed., *Logical Positivism* (New York: Free Press, 1959), 53-59.

Seneca, Annaeus. *Ad Lucilium epistulae morales I-LXIX/Epistulae: An Lucilius, Briefe über Ethik*, III (Latin/German), edited by Manfred Rosenbach. 3rd ed. Darmstadt: Wissenschaftliche Buchgesellschaft, 1989. Translated by E. Phillips Barker under the title *Letters to Lucilius*, 2 vols. (Oxford: Clarendon, 1932).

Sterne, Laurence. *A Sentimental Journey. Works* V. London: Strahan et al., 1780.

———. *The Life and Opinions of Tristram Shandy. Works* I. London: Strahan et al., 1780.

Suarez. *Metaphysicae Disputationes*. Salmanticae: Iohannes & Andreas Renaut, 1597.

SVF *Stoicorum Veterum Fragmenta*, edited by Johannes von Arnim. 4 vols. Stuttgart: Teubner, 1964.

Super Librum de Causis expositio, edited by H. D. Saffrey. Fribourg: Société philosophique, 1954. Translated, with introduction, by Dennis J. Brand under the title *The Book of Causes* (Milwaukee, WI: Marquette University Press, 1984).

Vergil. *Aeneidos*. In *Opera*, edited by R. A. B. Mynors, 103-422. Oxford: Clarendon, 1969. Translated by Robert Fitzgerald under the title *Aeneid* (New York: Random House, 1990).

Welsch, Wolfgang. *Postmoderne – Pluralität als ethischer und politischer Wert.* Cologne: Wirtschaftsverlag Bachem, 1988.

TLP Wittgenstein, Ludwig. *Tractatus logico-philosophicus.* London: Kegen Paul, Trench, Trubner & Co., 1922.

PUBLICATIONS BY HERIBERT BOEDER

1. "Origine et préhistoire de la question philosophique de l'*Aition.*" Translated by G. Leger. *Revue des sciences philosophiques et théologiques* 40 (1956): 421-442.

2. "La question de l'*Aition* das les premiers dialogues de Platon." Translated by G. Leger. *Revue des sciences philosophiques et théologiques* 41 (1957): 3-43.

3. "Der frühgriechische Wortgebrauch von *Logos* und *Aletheia*" [The Early Greek Usage of the Words *Logos* and *Aletheia*]. *Archiv für Begriffsgeschichte* 4 (1959): 82-112 [= *BG*, 1-30].

4. *Grund und Gegenwart als Frageziel der früh-griechischen Philosophie* [Ground and Present as the Aim of Early Greek Philosophical Inquiry]. The Hague: Nijhoff, 1962. 235 pp.

5. "Milesische Philosophie." *Archiv für Begriffsgeschichte* 9 (1964): 53-57 [= *BG*, 31-35].

6. "Das Prinzip des Widerspruchs oder der Sachverhalt als Sachverhalt" [The Principle of Non-Contradiction or the State of Affairs as State of Affairs]. In Ludwig Landgrebe, ed., *Beispiele. Festschrift für Eugen Fink zum 60. Geburtstag,* 141-160. The Hague: Nijhoff, 1965. [= *BG*, 239-256]

7. "Parmenides und der Verfall des kosmologischen Wissens" [Parmenides and the Decline of Cosmological Knowledge]. *Philosophisches Jahrbuch im Auftrag der Görres-Gesellschaft* 74 (1966): 30-77 [= *BG*, 117-187].

8. "Der Ursprung der 'Dialektik' in der Theorie des 'Seienden'. Parmenides und Zenon" [The Origin of "Dialectic" in the Theory of "Being": Parmenides and Zeno]. *Studium Generale* 21 (1968): 184-202 [= *BG*, 95-115].

9. "Zu Platons eigener Sache" [On Plato's Proper Topic]. *Philosophisches Jahrbuch im Auftrag der Görres-Gesellschaft* 76 (1968): 37-66 [= *BG*, 189-222].

10. "Causa exemplaris." In Martin Gosebruch and Lorenz Dittmann, eds., *Argo. Festschrift für Kurt Badt zum 80. Geburtstag,* 15-20. Cologne: Dumont, 1970.

11. "Die 'fünf Wege' und das Princip der thomasischen Theologie" [The "Five Paths" and the Principle of Thomasian Theology]. *Philosophisches Jahrbuch im Auftrag der Görres-Gesellschaft* 77 (1970): 66-80 [= *BG*, 345-361].

12. "Fruitio Dei." In Walter Wimmel, ed., *Forschungen zur römischen Literatur. Festschrift zum 60. Geburtstag von Karl Büchner*, 14-20. Wiesbaden: Franz Steiner, 1970. [= *BG*, 363-370]

13. "Weshalb 'Sein des Seienden'?" *Philosophisches Jahrbuch im Auftrag der Görres-Gesellschaft* 78 (1971): 111-133 [= *BG*, 279-303].

14. "Was vollbringt die Erste Philosophie?" *Mitteilungen der Technischen Universität Braunschweig* VII, no. 3 (1973): 3-10.

15. "Leibniz und das Prinzip der neueren Philosophie." *Philosophisches Jahrbuch im Auftrag der Görres-Gesellschaft* 81 (1974): 1-29.

16. "'Der Weg des Überzeugens' oder Platons Sorge" ["The Path of Persuasion" or Plato's Concern]. In Klaus Döring and Wolfgang Kullmann, eds., *Studia Platonica. Festschrift für Hermann Gundert zum 65. Geburtstag*, 125-138. Amsterdam: Grüner, 1974. [= *BG*, 223-238]

17. "Das Verschiedene im 'anderen Anfang'." In Ute Guzzoni, Bernhard Rang, and Ludwig Siep, eds., *Der Idealismus und seine Gegenwart. Festschrift für Werner Marx zum 65. Geburtstag*, 3-35. Hamburg: Meiner, 1976.

18. "Das natürliche Bewußtsein" [The Natural Consciousness]. *Hegel-Studien* 12 (1977): 157-178.

19. "Vernunft und Wissenschaft." *Sitzungsberichte und Mitteilungen der Braunschweigischen Wissenschaftlichen Gesellschaft* 1978, no. 2: 4-44.

20. *Topologie der Metaphysik* [Topology of Metaphysics]. Freiburg/Munich: Alber, 1980. 714 pp.

21. "Reason in Present Thought." *Research in Phenomenology* 11 (1981): 159-175.

22. "Was ist *Physis*?" [What is *Physis*?]. *Abhandlungen der Braunschweigischen Wissenschaftlichen Gesellschaft* 32 (Göttingen 1981): 129-151 [= *BG*, 69-94].

23. "Vom Begriff der aristotelischen *Poetik*." *Abhandlungen der Braunschweigischen Wissenschaftlichen Gesellschaft* 34 (Göttingen 1982): 47-65 [= *BG*, 257-277].

24. "An End with Distinction." *Research in Phenomenology* 13 (1983): 149-158.

25. "Von der Kunst in 'absoluter Bedeutung'." In Frank Steigerwald, ed., *Martin Gosebruch zu Ehren. Festschrift anläßlich seines 65. Geburtstag*, 9-14. Munich: Hirmer, 1984.

26. "Dilthey 'und' Heidegger. Zur Geschichtlichkeit des Menschen." *Phänomenologische Forschungen* 16 (1984): 161-176.

27. "La Considerazione Filosofica del Linguaggio" [Die Rücksicht der Philosophie auf die Sprache]. Translated by Maria Failla. *Paradigmi* 3, no. 7 (Bari 1985): 35-50.

28. "Il Distacco di Heidegger da Dilthey nella sua Questione sull' Essenza della Verità" [Heideggers Trennung von Dilthey in seiner Frage nach dem Wesen der Wahrheit]. Translated by Patricia Cipolletta. In Franco Bianco, ed., *Dilthey e il Pensiero del Novecento,* 228-234. Milan: Franc Angel, 1985.

29. "Natur und Menschenwesen." *Acta Institutionis Philosophiae et Aestheticae* 3 (Tokyo 1985): 27-39.

30. "Discussione sulla 'ratio' in Dilthey e Heidegger" [Erörterung der diltheyschen und heideggerschen ratio]. Translated by Francesco Donadio and Rossella Bonito Oliva. In Giuseppe Cacciatore and Giuseppe Cantillo, eds., *Wilhelm Dilthey. Critica della metafisica e ragione storica*, 419-429. Bologna: Società editrice il Mulino, 1985.

31. "Nichts Fremdes." In Dieter Henrich, ed., *All-Einheit. Wege eines Gedankens in Ost und West*, 87-99. Stuttgart: Klett-Cotta, 1985.

32. "Das Vernunftinteresse an der Sprache" [summary of 33]. *Braunschweigische Wissenschaftliche Gesellschaft, Jahrbuch 1985* (Göttingen 1985): 71-72.

33. "Vom Vernunftinteresse an der Sprache." *Acta Institutionis Philosophiae et Aestheticae* 4 (Tokyo 1986): 45-56.

34. "Dissensions." In Kenneth Maly and Parvas Emad, eds., *Heidegger on Heraclitus: A New Reading. Studies in the History of Philosophy* 5: 167-177. Lewiston, NY: Edwin Mellen, 1986.

35 "Sterbliche welchen Todes?" In Walter Brüstle and Ludwig Siep, eds., *Sterblichkeitserfahrung und Ethikbegründung. Ein Kolloquium für Werner Marx*, 38-48. Essen: Die blaue Eule, 1988.

36. *Das Vernunft-Gefüge der Moderne* [The Rational Architectonic of Modernity]. Freiburg/Munich: Alber, 1988. 380 pp.

37. "Einführung in die Vernünftigkeit des Neuen Testaments" [Introduction into the Rationality of the New Testament]. *Braunschweigische Wissenschaftliche Gesellschaft, Jahrbuch 1988* (Göttingen 1988): 95-109 [= *BG*, 305-321].

38. "Die Unterscheidung der Vernunft." *Osnabrücker Philosophische Schriften* (April 1989): 10-20.

39. "Vom Schein einer heraklitischen Dialektik." In Manfred Riedel, ed., *Hegel und die antike Dialektik*, 98-106. Frankfurt a. M.: Suhrkamp, 1990.

40. "Il Confine del Moderno e il 'Legato' di Heidegger" [translation of 47]. Translated by Elisabetta Ruggerini. *Paradigmi* 7, no. 22 (Bari 1990): 45-62.

41. "Rousseau oder der Aufbruch des Selbstbewußtseins" [Rousseau or the Awakening of Self-Consciousness]. In Hubertus Busche, George Heffernan, and Dieter Lohmar, eds., *Bewußtsein und Zeitlichkeit. Ein Problemschnitt durch die Philosophie der Neuzeit*, 1-21. Würzburg: Königshausen & Neumann, 1990.

42. "Laudatio Karl Heinrich Olsen." *Braunschweigische Wissenschaftliche Gesellschaft, Jahrbuch 1989* (Göttingen 1990): 21-25.

43. "Rousseau oder der Aufbruch des Selbstbewußtseins" [summary of 41]. *Braunschweigische Wissenschaftliche Gesellschaft, Jahrbuch 1989* (Göttingen 1990): 167-170.

44. "Action or/and Dwelling." Translated by Marcus Brainard and Friederike-Andrea Dorner. In Marcus Brainard et al., eds., *Heidegger and the Political. Graduate Faculty Philosophy Journal* 14, no. 2–15, no. 1 (New York 1991): 47-59.

45. "Zwielicht der Moderne." *Philosophische Rundschau* 38 (1991): 275-285.

46. "Die Grenze der Moderne und Heideggers 'Vermächtnis'." *Braunschweigische Wissenschaftliche Gesellschaft, Jahrbuch 1990* (Göttingen 1991): 75-88.

47. "Laudatio Raymond Klibansky." *Braunschweigische Wissenschaftliche Gesellschaft, Jahrbuch 1990* (Göttingen 1991): 161-165.

48) "Privilege of Presence?" *Graduate Faculty Philosophy Journal* 16, no. 1 (New York 1992): 77-86.

49. "Die conceptuale Vernunft in der Letzten Epoche der Metaphysik" [Conceptual Reason in the Final Epoch of Metaphysics]. *Abhandlungen der Braunschweigischen Wissenschaftlichen Gesellschaft* 43 (Göttingen 1992): 345-360.

50. "Is Totalizing Thinking Totalitarian?" Translated by Marcus Brainard. In Pierre Adler, Marcus Brainard, and Dirk Effertz, eds., *In memoriam David Rapport Lachterman. Graduate Faculty Philosophy Journal* 17, no. 1-2 (New York 1994): 299-312.

51. *Das Bauzeug der Geschichte* [= *BG*]. *Aufsätze und Vorträge zur griechischen und mittelalter-*

lichen Philosophie, edited by Gerald Meier. Würzburg: Königshausen & Neumann, 1994. 376 pp. [Contains essays 3, 5-9, 11-13, 16, 22, 23, 38, 52-54.]

52. "Das sogenannte 'Vergessen' im heraklitischen Gedanken." In *BG,* 51-67.

53. "Platons Verwandlung der zenonischen Dialektik." In *BG,* 171-187.

54. "Die philo-sophischen Conceptionen der Mittleren Epoche" [The Philo-Sophical Conceptions of the Middle Epoch]. In *BG,* 323-343.

55. "Die philo-sophischen Conceptionen der Mittleren Epoche" [summary of 54]. *Braunschweigische Wissenschaftliche Gesellschaft, Jahrbuch 1993* (Göttingen 1994): 123-127.

56. "Agire o/e Dimorare" [Handlen oder/und Wohnen; cf. 44 above]. Translated by Elisabetta Ruggerini. In Piero Di Giovanni, ed., *Heidegger e la Filosofia Pratica,* 125-143. Palermo: S. F. Flaccovio Editore, 1994.

57. "La trasformazione platonica della dialettica zenoniana" [translation of 53]. Translated by Elisabetta Ruggerini. In Piero Di Giovanni, ed., *Platone e la Dialettica,* 59-78. Bari: Biblioteca di Cultura Moderna Laterza, 1995.

58. "Die Dimension der Submoderne." *Abhandlungen der Braunschweigischen Wissenschaftlichen Gesellschaft* 46 (Göttingen 1995): 139-150.

59. "Die Unterscheidung des ersten Anfangs der Philosophie." *Abhandlungen der Braunschweigischen Wissenschaftlichen Gesellschaft* 47 (Göttingen 1997): 1-13.

60. "Heideggers Vermächtnis. Zur Unterschedung der 'Αλήθεια." In Ewald Richter, ed., *Die Frage nach der Wahrheit. Schriftenreihe der Martin-Heidegger-Gesellschaft* 4 (Frankfurt a. M. 1997): 105-120.

INDEX OF NAMES

INDEX OF SUBJECTS